EDUCATION
in the History
of
Western Civilization

SELECTED READINGS

FREDERICK M. BINDER

City College of New York

THE MACMILLAN COMPANY
COLLIER-MACMILLAN LIMITED, LONDON

EDUCATION
in the History
of
Western Civilization

SELECTED READINGS

To my Mother and Father,
Beatrice and Harry Binder

First Printing

Library of Congress catalog card number: 77-81549

The Macmillan Company
Collier-Macmillan Canada, Ltd., Toronto, Ontario

Printed in the United States of America

Preface

This book of readings offers the student of educational history an opportunity to share an experience that has always been among the most rewarding for scholars—contact with primary source materials. In no other way can the past be more fully brought to life; and without an understanding of the continuity of human experience, history can have little meaning for the present. This work employs a wide variety of documents in tracing the historical development of education in Western civilization. Selections are included from diaries, letters, government decrees, poems, essays, and textbooks. Among the authors are statesmen, teachers, philosophers, poets, students, political leaders, and social and religious reformers. Also included are a few excerpts from secondary sources, the works of scholars who are particularly able to capture the spirit of the times.

The concern for the training of the young displayed by men of such varied stations in life and fields of endeavor illustrates that education has never existed in a vacuum, divorced from the activities of society at large. Rather, it has tended through the centuries to mirror the conditions, values, and aspirations of those it serves. As the title implies, this work views the history of education as it is related to the total social, political, and economic development of Western civilization. Each of the ten chapters begins with a brief essay setting the educational and social scene of the historical period under discussion. Within the essays reference is made to the several documents that follow and complete the chapters. The limitations of a book of selected readings prevent the inclusion of all the facts of history. For this the reader may turn to a survey textbook. What this work can do is provide a picture of the primary developments in educational history and, more important, through its readings offer a vivid, realistic account of the human faith, creativity, successes, and failures that have marked education's progress through the centuries.

I wish gratefully to acknowledge the advice and encouragement tended by Mr. Lloyd Chilton of The Macmillan Company and Professor Joel Wiener of C.C.N.Y. A special word of deepest appreciation goes to my wife, Teris, for her invaluable editorial and typing assistance.

F. M. B.

Contents

I. EDUCATION AND THE GLORY
    THAT WAS GREECE   1

    1. Education in Homeric Times   3
    2. Lycurgus and Education for the Spartan
        State   7
    3. Athens: Education in the Archaic Age   15
    4. Athens: The New Education   24
    5. The Ephebia   34
    6. Oratory, The Crown of Classical Education   36

II. EDUCATION AND THE GRANDEUR
    THAT WAS ROME   40

    1. The Roman Father, Educator   42
    2. The Laws of the Twelve Tables   44
    3. The Advent of Greek Learning in Rome   46
    4. Cicero, Model for the Ages   50
    5. Quintilian, Greatest of Roman Teachers   52
    6. Roman Education Becomes Remote from
        Life   59
    7. Justinian's *Body of the Civil Law*   64

III. EUROPE AND ITS EDUCATION
     BECOME CHRISTIAN   67

    1. Church Fathers Proclaim the Superiority of
        the Scriptures   69
    2. St. Augustine and the Bounds of Christian
        Scholarship   71

vii

3. Catechumenal Training   76
4. St. Benedict's *Rule*   79
5. Cassiodorus, Father of Literary Monasticism   81
6. Educational Revivals Under Charlemagne
   and Alfred the Great   84

IV. EDUCATION AND THE LATER MIDDLE
    AGES   90

1. The Schools of the Cathedrals and Collegiate
   Churches   92
2. The Renaissance of the Twelfth Century   97
3. The Scholastic Movement   99
4. The Rise of the Universities   105
5. University Studies   112

V. EDUCATION AND THE RENAISSANCE   122

1. The Revolt Against Scholasticism   123
2. Petrarch, Man of Many Titles   127
3. Humanist Education for Prince, Courtier,
   and Statesman   132
4. Two Educational Theorists of the
   Renaissance   139
5. Patrons and Scholars Create Schools of the
   Renaissance   146
6. From Humanism to Ciceronianism   151

VI. EDUCATION IN AN AGE OF CHALLENGES
    TO AUTHORITY   156

1. Early Reformers Burned for Keeping Schools   158
2. The Call for Education for Faith and State   159
3. Education and the Reformation in England   166
4. The "Ratio Studiorum" of the Jesuits   168
5. Francis Bacon, Proponent of the Inductive
   Method   174
6. The Inductive Method Applied to
   Educational Theory   179

VII. EDUCATION AND THE ENLIGHTENMENT   195

1. John Locke on Education   198
2. The *Emile* of Jean Jacques Rousseau   208

3. Education in Revolutionary France   221
4. English Education for the Masses   226
5. Reform and Nationalism in German
   Education   230

VIII. THE ESTABLISHMENT OF EDUCATION IN
AMERICA, 17TH AND 18TH CENTURIES   249

1. Education in the Massachusetts Bay Colony:
   Governmental Initiative   252
2. Education in the Middle Colonies:
   Sponsorship by Religious and Cultural Groups   259
3. Education Among the Virginia Aristocracy   262
4. Benjamin Franklin: Education for Utility   268
5. Thomas Jefferson: Education for a
   Democratic Republic   279
6. George Washington and Noah Webster:
   Education and Nationalism   289

IX. EDUCATION AND THE BIRTH OF THE
MODERN ERA, 1800–1860   297

1. Johann Heinrich Pestalozzi   300
2. Friedrich Froebel   307
3. Johann Friedrich Herbart   315
4. National Control of French Education   318
5. Prussian Education, A Model for the World   323
6. Horace Mann and the American Common
   School Movement   329
7. English Education, Stronghold of Tradition   335

X. EDUCATION IN A TECHNOLOGICAL
CIVILIZATION, 1860–   342

1. Herbert Spencer,
   What Knowledge Is of Most Worth?   344
2. Daniel Coit Gilman, Spokesman for the
   University   350
3. John Dewey, Philosopher of Progressive
   Education   354
4. The Progress of Education in the United States   362
5. British Education and the March of
   Democracy   371

6. Nazi Germany: Education for a
   Totalitarian State   378
7. The U.S.S.R.: Commitment to Education   385

I

Education
and the Glory
That Was Greece

In the vicinity of 700 B.C. there emerged from the misty shadows of what might be called a "dark age" the beginnings of a society that was to reach such heights as to provide Western civilization its most clearly defined beginning and most emulated model. Never again would the Western world begin so seemingly fresh as it did in Greece nearly twenty-seven hundred years ago. After a later period of relative stagnation a new era, a Renaissance, would take the products of ancient Greece as a prime inspiration. Subsequent bursts of creative energy and declarations of freedom would time and again pay homage to the Greek spirit and Greek achievement. One need only view the early national architecture of the United States for visual evidence of this spirit. Indeed, how many of our cities, proud of their cultural attainments or determined to reach great heights, have laid claim to the title "Athens" of the East or North or South, and how many states are filled with the place names Sparta, Athens, and Corinth?

Behind the curtain of 700 B.C. is a land of warrior-kings and knights who lived to perform great deeds of courage in the eyes of their fellow men. The window through which we and the ancient Greeks have been able to best observe this era has been provided by Homer. His lyrics of gods who inspired men and men who inspired boys furnished a textbook in religion, morals, and manners for centuries of Greek youth and for those who sought to capture the Greek spirit. In The Iliad and The Odyssey we can catch glimpses of an education for the young warrior-to-be. Here we view the youth trained by a teacher-inspirer for the day when he would perform heroic deeds in the assembly and on the field of battle. (1)*

* Numbers in parentheses refer to the number of the reading selection in the chapter.

1

The first two hundred years of Greek civilization down to c. 500 B.C., often referred to as the Archaic Period, introduced most of the characteristics we associate with the greatness of that land—columned temples, figured pottery, drama, philosophy, Olympic games, the city-state. By 600 B.C., the two most famous of these city-states, Athens and Sparta, had marked the trail for which they would become famous. Sparta, skilled in conquering yet unable to rule in peace those she conquered, placed a brake on the progress of culture and, under the rule of the half-mythical Lycurgus established a militaristic state whose great objective was an educational one, the rearing of soldier-citizens. (2) Meanwhile Athens, under the reforms of Solon, was guided by its aristocratic leaders to greater heights. No less demanding of the loyalty of its citizens than Sparta, the Athenian state in return provided an environment for the freest development of creative talents. Here individualism and patriotism achieved a near-perfect harmony and balance, the same harmony and balance evident in Athenian sculpture, music, poetry, drama, and dance. The education of youth in every respect reflected the Athenian spirit. No compulsory, state-controlled system was imposed upon the citizen. He freely sent his son to the grammatist, cithera player, *and* paedotribe *for training which sought to create a fine balance of mind, morals, and body. (3)*

The fifth century B.C. marked the greatest period of Athenian glory. At Marathon and Salamis, Athens had led the Greek cities to victory over the might of the Persian Empire. The Periclean Age that followed saw Athens establish within her borders the purest form of democracy ever known, and, at the same time, lead the military and commercial empire of the Delian League. These years also saw Athens rise to the heights of artistic and intellectual creativity. This was the century of Socrates, Hippocrates, Sophocles, Euripides, Aristophanes, Aeschylus, Protagoras, and so many others who were to awe later generations.

The men who created this greatness were the products of the values and education of the Archaic Period, of the age of balance. But in the glory of this century were planted seeds of change. Not all the newly enfranchised citizens from the lower middle class shared the veneration for the old aristocratic training; the progress in all areas stimulated demands for a higher level of training; democracy and the brilliant creations of man were forces for individualism; in an age of expansion and commerce the boundaries of the city-state seemed narrow and confining to many.

To meet the intellectual demands of the day came the sophists, a group of professional teachers of the useful. Knowledge of subjects as diverse as tactics, diplomacy, gymnastics, and astronomy could be attained for a price. However, of all the arts and sciences practiced by the sophists, none were more valued than oratory and the attendant scientific study of language. For, in the environment of Athens of that day, the success of one's ideas was very much dependent on the words with which they rode to battle.

Though greeted with enthusiasm by the youth who had coins to dispense, the sophists faced the scorn of conservatives who insisted that Athens' glory was dependent on its old education for balance and civic virtue. Only on such a foundation, they argued, could the ideals of the city-state be maintained. (4)

The conflict in the educational sphere was reflected in the political arena, and the great century ended in a series of struggles between aristocratic and democratic forces and an external war with Sparta that left Athens defeated and prostrate. No longer was the grandeur of Greece to be centered within the bounds of the city-state. In the next century Alexander of Macedon, infused with the spirit of Greek culture, would conquer and Hellenize most of the Mediterranean world.

To Persia, to Syria, to Egypt, and eventually even to Rome, the Greek culture spread and prevailed—and education was a prime vehicle of conquest. The ephebic college, established in Athens with limited success in the fourth century B.C., was copied throughout the Hellenistic world and represented the ultimate training for those who would be Greek regardless of their national origins. (5) The spirit of Periclean Athens lived on to the sixth century A.D. in the gymnasiums hundreds of miles from Greece where boys played Greek games; in the elementary schools of the grammaticus where reading and basic arithmetic were taught; in the schools of the grammarian where Homer was primary among all literary works and from which grammar, rhetoric, and logic along with arithmetic, geometry, astronomy, and music were to evolve as the traditional seven liberal arts; and in the schools of the rhetor where the spoken word was equated, in the tradition of Isocrates, with virtue and wisdom. (6) To Alexandria came scholars from all over the Western world to study, organize, and synthesize Greek science. To Rhodes came Marc Antony, Pompey, Caesar, and Brutus to be trained in oratory. To Athens came Horace and Cicero to study the philosophies of Plato, Aristotle, Zeno, and Epicurus. Such Romans would help ensure the longevity of the Greek influence on the Western mind.

回 1. Education in Homeric Times

In a few brief passages of The Iliad *and* The Odyssey *Homer presents glimpses of the training of youth for the life of a knight, an education in which an older man both instructed and inspired by his own example. In* The Iliad *Achilles' old tutor Phoenix returns to urge the hero to battle and recalls his role as teacher of the arts of war and oratory, the two essential ingredients in the making of a knight.*

William Cullen Bryant (trans.), The Iliad of Homer *(Boston: Houghton, Mifflin and Company, 1898), pp. 239–243.*

... At last
Phoenix, the aged knight, with many tears
And sighs, took up the word, in grief and fear
Lest Hector should destroy the Grecian fleet:—
    "Illustrious son of Peleus, if indeed
Thou wilt return, nor carest to repel
From our swift galleys the consuming fire,
Because thou are offended, how shall I,
Dear child, remain without thee? When at first
Peleus, the aged knight, from Phthia sent
Thee, yet a boy, to Agamemnon's aid,
Unskilled as then thou wert in cruel war
And martial councils,—where men also gain
A great renown,—he sent me with thee, charged
To teach thee both, that so thou mightst become
In words an orator, in warlike deeds
An actor Therefore, my beloved child,
Not willingly shall I remain behind;
Not even though a god should promise me
That, overcoming the decays of age,
I might become a beardless youth again,
As when from Hellas and its companies
Of lovely maids I came a fugitive,
And left Amyntor, son of Ormenus,—
My father,—angry with me for the sake
Of a fair-tressèd wanton, whom he loved,
Treating my mother basely. To my knees
My mother came and prayed me ceaselessly,
First, to possess the woman, that she then
Might loathe the elder one; and I obeyed.
My father knew it, and with many a curse
Invoked the hateful furies to forbid
That any child who owed his birth to me
Should ever sit upon his knees. The gods—
The Jove of Hades and dread Proserpine—
Confirmed his curse. To slay him with the sword
Was my first thought. Some god subdued my wrath,
Reminding me of what the public voice
Would say, and infamy that would ensue,—
Lest I among the Achaians should be called
A parricide. I could not brook to dwell
Within my father's palace while he thus
Was wroth with me. My kindred and my friends
Came round me, and besought me to remain,

And stayed beside me. Many a fatling ewe
And many a slow-paced ox with curving horns
They slew, and many a fattened swine they stretched
Over the flame of Vulcan. From the casks
Of the old chief his wine was freely drawn.
Nine nights they slept surrounding me, while each
Kept watch in turn: nor ever were the fires
Put out; one blazed beneath the portico
Of the fair hall, and near the chamber-door
Another glimmered in the vestibule.
But when upon me rose the tenth dark night,
I broke my aptly-jointed chamber-doors,
And issued forth, and easily o'erleaped
The wall around the palace, quite unseen
Of watching men and of the serving maids.
I fled through spacious Hellas to the fields
Of Phthia, nurse of flocks, and to her king,
Peleus, who kindly welcomed me, and loved
Me as a father loves his only son,
Born to large wealth in his declining years.
He made me rich, and gave me sovereign rule
Over much people. My abode was fixed
In farthest Phthia, where I was the prince
Of the Dolopians. As for thee, my care,
Godlike Achilles, made thee what thou art.
I loved thee from my soul: thou wouldst not go
With any other to the feast, nor take
Thy food at home until upon my knees
I placed thee, carved thy meats, and gave them thee,
And poured thy wine. The tunic on my breast
Was often wetted by thee when the wine
Gushed in thy petulant childhood from thy lips.
Thus many things did I endure for thee,
And many toils perform; and since the gods
Vouchsafed no son to me, it was my thought
To train thee as a son, that thou mightst be,
O godlike man! the bulwark of my age.
And now subdue that mighty spirit of thine:
Ill it becomes thee to be merciless:
The gods themselves are placable, though far
Above us all in honor and in power
And virtue. We propitiate them with vows,
Incense, libations, and burnt-offerings,
And prayers for those who have offended. Prayers

Are daughters of almighty Jupiter,—
Lame, wrinkled, and squint-eyed,—that painfully
Follow Misfortune's steps; but strong of limb
And swift of foot Misfortune is, and, far
Outstripping all, comes first to every land,
And there wreaks evil on mankind, which prayers
Do afterwards redress. Whoe'er receives
Jove's daughters reverently when they approach,
Him willingly they aid, and to his suit
They listen. Whosoever puts them by
With obstinate denial, they appeal
To Jove, the son of Saturn, and entreat
That he will cause Misfortune to attend
The offender's way in life, that he in turn
May suffer evil and be punished thus.
Wherefore, Achilles! do thou also yield
The honor due Jove's daughters, freely given
By other valiant men. If Atreus' son
Brought thee no gifts, nor promised others still,
But kept his anger, I would never ask
That thou shouldst lay aside thy wrath and come
To help the Argives in their bitter need.
But he bestows large gifts, and adds a pledge
Of others yet in store, and he hath sent
The best men of the army, who to thee
Are dearest, to entreat thee. Spurn thou not
These, nor their embassy, although at first
Thine anger was not causeless. We have heard
The praise of heroes of the elder time,
Inflamed to vehement anger, yet appeased
By gifts, and yielding to persuasive words.

In The Odyssey *the goddess Minerva in the guise of Mentes inspires Telemachus to perform courageous deeds—to rid his home of his mother's suitors and search the seas for his father. Again the perfect knight is viewed as one skilled in oratory as well as warfare.*

. . . But I charge thee to take counsel how thou mayest thrust forth the wooers from the hall. Come now, mark and take heed unto my words. On the morrow call the Achaean lords to the assembly, and declare thy saying to all, and take the gods to witness. As for the wooers bid them scatter them each one to his own, and for thy mother, if her

S. H. Butcher (trans.), The Odyssey of Homer *(New York: Macmillan and Co., 1882), pp. 10–11.*

heart is moved to marriage, let her go back to the hall of that mighty man her father, and her kinsfolk will furnish a wedding feast, and array the gifts of wooing exceeding many, all that should go back with a daughter dearly beloved. And to thyself I will give a word of wise counsel, if perchance thou wilt hearken. Fit out a ship, the best thou hast, with twenty oarsmen, and go to inquire concerning thy father that is long afar, if perchance any man shall tell thee aught, or if thou mayest hear the voice from Zeus, which chiefly brings tidings to men. Get thee first to Pylos and inquire of goodly Nestor, and from thence to Sparta to Menelaus of the fair hair, for he came home the last of the mail-coated Achaeans. If thou shalt hear news of the life and the returning of thy father, then verily thou mayest endure the wasting for yet a year. But if thou shalt hear that he is dead and gone, return then to thine own dear country and pile his mound, and over it pay burial rites, full many as is due, and give thy mother to a husband. But when thou hast done this and made an end, thereafter take counsel in thy mind and heart, how thou mayest slay the wooers in thy halls, whether by guile or openly; for thou shouldest not carry childish thoughts, being no longer of years thereto. Or hast thou not heard what renown the goodly Orestes gat him among all men in that he slew the slayer of his father, guileful Aegisthus, who killed his famous sire? And thou, too, my friend, for I see that thou art very comely and tall, be valiant, that even men unborn may praise thee. But I will now go down to the swift ship and to my men, who methinks chafe much at tarrying for me; and do thou thyself take heed and give ear unto my words.

回 2. Lycurgus and Education for the Spartan State

While it is debatable whether the hero of Plutarch's Life of Lycurgus *was an historical or a legendary figure, there is little doubt that the descriptions of Spartan educational and social practices presented in this work are quite accurate. Here is an educational system that clearly reflects the authoritarian, militaristic society for which it was created.*

Nor was it in the power of the father to dispose of the child as he thought fit; he was obliged to carry it before certain triers at a place called Lesche; these were some of the elders of the tribe to which the

A. H. Clough (ed.), Plutarch's Lives (Boston: Little, Brown, and Company, 1888), I, 105–16.

child belonged; their business it was carefully to view the infant, and, if they found it stout and well made, they gave order for its rearing, and allotted to it one of the nine thousand shares of land above mentioned for its maintenance, but, if they found it puny and ill-shaped, ordered it to be taken to what was called the Apothetae, a sort of chasm under Taygetus; as thinking it neither for the good of the child itself, nor for the public interest, that it should be brought up, if it did not, from the very outset, appear made to be healthy and vigorous. Upon the same account, the women did not bathe the new-born children with water, as is the custom in all other countries, but with wine, to prove the temper and complexion of their bodies; from a notion they had that epileptic and weakly children faint and waste away upon their being thus bathed, while, on the contrary, those of a strong and vigorous habit acquire firmness and get a temper by it, like steel. There was much care and art, too, used by the nurses; they had no swaddling bands; the children grew up free and unconstrained in limb and form, and not dainty and fanciful about their food; not afraid in the dark, or of being left alone; without any peevishness or ill humor or crying. Upon this account, Spartan nurses were often bought up, or hired by people of other countries; and it is recorded that she who suckled Alcibiades was a Spartan; who, however, if fortunate in his nurse, was not so in his preceptor; his guardian, Pericles, as Plato tells us, chose a servant for that office called Zopyrus, no better than any common slave.

Lycurgus was of another mind; he would not have masters bought out of the market for his young Spartans, nor such as should sell their pains; nor was it lawful, indeed, for the father himself to breed up the children after his own fancy; but as soon as they were seven years old they were to be enrolled in certain companies and classes, where they all lived under the same order and discipline, doing their exercises and taking their play together. Of these, he who showed the most conduct and courage was made captain; they had their eyes always upon him, obeyed his orders, and underwent patiently whatsoever punishment he inflicted; so that the whole course of their education was one continued exercise of a ready and perfect obedience. The old men, too, were spectators of their performances, and often raised quarrels and disputes among them, to have a good opportunity of finding out their different characters, and of seeing which would be valiant, which a coward, when they should come to more dangerous encounters. Reading and writing they gave them, just enough to serve their turn; their chief care was to make them good subjects, and to teach them to endure pain and conquer in battle. To this end, as they grew in years, their discipline was proportionably increased; their heads were close-clipped, they were accustomed to go bare-foot, and for the most part to play naked.

After they were twelve years old, they were no longer allowed to wear any under-garment; they had one coat to serve them a year;[1] their bodies were hard and dry, with but little acquaintance of baths and unguents; these human indulgences they were allowed only on some few particular days in the year. They lodged together in little bands upon beds made of the rushes which grew by the banks of the river Eurotas, which they were to break off with their hands without a knife; if it were winter, they mingled some thistle-down with their rushes, which it was thought had the property of giving warmth. By the time they were come to this age, there was not any of the more hopeful boys who had not a lover to bear him company. The old men, too, had an eye upon them, coming often to the grounds to hear and see them contend either in wit or strength with one another, and this as seriously and with as much concern as if they were their fathers, their tutors, or their magistrates; so that there scarcely was any time or place without some one present to put them in mind of their duty, and punish them if they had neglected it.

Besides all this, there was always one of the best and honestest men in the city appointed to undertake the charge and governance of them; he again arranged them into their several bands, and set over each of them for their captain the most temperate and boldest of those they called Irens, who were usually twenty years old, two years out of the boys; and the eldest of the boys, again, were Mell-Irens, as much as to say, who would shortly be men. This young man, therefore, was their captain when they fought, and their master at home, using them for the offices of his house; sending the oldest of them to fetch wood, and the weaker and less able, to gather salads and herbs, and these they must either go without or steal; which they did by creeping into the gardens, or conveying themselves cunningly and closely into the eating-houses; if they were taken in the fact, they were whipped without mercy, for thieving so ill and awkwardly. They stole, too, all other meat they could lay their hands on, looking out and watching all opportunities, when people were asleep or more careless than usual. If they were caught, they were not only punished with whipping, but hunger, too, being reduced to their ordinary allowance, which was but very slender, and so contrived on purpose, that they might set about to help themselves, and be forced to exercise their energy and address. This was the principal design of their hard fare; there was another not inconsiderable, that they might grow taller; for the vital spirits, not being overburdened and oppressed by too great a quantity of nourishment, which necessarily discharges itself into thickness and breadth, do, by their natural lightness, rise; and the body, giving and yielding because it is pliant, grows

---

[1] *The* chitōn *and the* himation, *one inside and one out, constituted the ordinary Greek dress; corresponding in use to the Roman tunic and toga.*

in height. The same thing seems, also, to conduce to beauty of shape; a dry and lean habit is a better subject for nature's configuration, which the gross and over-fed are too heavy to submit to properly. Just as we find that women who take physic whilst they are with child, bear leaner and smaller but better-shaped and prettier children; the material they come of having been more pliable and easily moulded. The reason, however, I leave others to determine.

To return from whence we have digressed. So seriously did the Lacedæmonian children go about their stealing, that a youth, having stolen a young fox and hid it under his coat, suffered it to tear out his very bowels with its teeth and claws, and died upon the place, rather than let it be seen. What is practised to this very day in Lacedæmon is enough to gain credit to this story, for I myself have seen several of the youths endure whipping to death at the foot of the altar of Diana surnamed Orthia.

The Iren, or under-master, used to stay a little with them after supper, and one of them he bade to sing a song, to another he put a question which required an advised and deliberate answer; for example, Who was the best man in the city? What he thought of such an action of such a man? They used them thus early to pass a right judgment upon persons and things, and to inform themselves of the abilities or defects of their countrymen. If they had not an answer ready to the question Who was a good or who an ill-reputed citizen, they were looked upon as of a dull and careless disposition, and to have little or no sense of virtue and honor; besides this, they were to give a good reason for what they said, and in as few words and as comprehensive as might be; he that failed of this, or answered not to the purpose, had his thumb bit by his master. Sometimes the Iren did this in the presence of the old men and magistrates, that they might see whether he punished them justly and in due measure or not; and when he did amiss, they would not reprove him before the boys, but, when they were gone, he was called to an account and underwent correction, if he had run far into either of the extremes of indulgence or severity.

Their lovers and favorers, too, had a share in the young boy's honor or disgrace; and there goes a story that one of them was fined by the magistrates, because the lad whom he loved cried out effeminately as he was fighting. And though this sort of love was so approved among them, that the most virtuous matrons would make professions of it to young girls, yet rivalry did not exist, and if several men's fancies met in one person, it was rather the beginning of an intimate friendship, whilst they all jointly conspired to render the object of their affection as accomplished as possible.

They taught them, also, to speak with a natural and graceful raillery, and to comprehend much matter of thought in few words. For Lycurgus who ordered, as we saw, that a great piece of money should be but of an inconsiderable value, on the contrary would allow no discourse to be current which did not contain in few words a great deal of useful and curious sense; children in Sparta, by a habit of long silence, came to give just and sententious answers; for, indeed, as loose and incontinent livers are seldom fathers of many children, so loose and incontinent talkers seldom originate many sensible words. King Agis, when some Athenian laughed at their short swords, and said that the jugglers on the stage swallowed them with ease, answered him, "We find them long enough to reach our enemies with;" and as their swords were short and sharp, so, it seems to me, were their sayings. They reach the point and arrest the attention of the hearers better than any. Lycurgus himself seems to have been short and sententious, if we may trust the anecdotes of him; as appears by his answer to one who by all means would set up democracy in Lacedæmon. "Begin, friend," said he, "and set it up in your family." Another asked him why he allowed of such mean and trivial sacrifices to the gods. He replied, "That we may always have something to offer to them." Being asked what sort of martial exercises or combats he approved of, he answered, "All sorts, except that in which you stretch out your hands."[2] Similar answers, addressed to his countrymen by letter, are ascribed to him; as, being consulted how they might best oppose an invasion of their enemies, he returned this answer, "By continuing poor, and not coveting each man to be greater than his fellow." Being consulted again whether it were requisite to enclose the city with a wall, he sent them word, "The city is well fortified which hath a wall of men instead of brick." But whether these letters are counterfeit or not is not easy to determine.

Of their dislike to talkativeness, the following apophthegms are evidence. King Leonidas said to one who held him in discourse upon some useful matter, but not in due time and place, "Much to the purpose, Sir, elsewhere." King Charilaus, the nephew of Lycurgus, being asked why his uncle had made so few laws, answered, "Men of few words require but few laws." When one blamed Hecatæus the sophist because that, being invited to the public table, he had not spoken one word all supper-time, Archidamidas answered in his vindication, "He who knows how to speak, knows also when."

The sharp and yet not ungraceful retorts which I mentioned may be instanced as follows. Demaratus, being asked in a troublesome manner by an importunate fellow, Who was the best man in Lacedæmon? answered at last, "He, Sir, that is the least like you." Some, in company where Agis was, much extolled the Eleans for their just and honorable management of the Olympic games; "Indeed," said Agis, "they are

---

[2] *The form of crying quarter among the ancients.*

highly to be commended if they can do justice one day in five years."
Theopompus answered a stranger who talked much of his affection to
the Lacedæmonians, and said that his countrymen called him Philolacon
(a lover of the Lacedæmonians), that it had been more for his honor if
they had called him Philopolites (a lover of his own countrymen). And
Plistoanax, the son of Pausanias, when an orator of Athens said the
Lacedæmonians had no learning, told him, "You say true, Sir; we
alone of all the Greeks have learned none of your bad qualities." One
asked Archidamidas what number there might be of the Spartans; he
answered, "Enough, Sir, to keep out wicked men."

We may see their character, too, in their very jests. For they did not
throw them out at random, but the very wit of them was grounded upon
something or other worth thinking about. For instance, one, being
asked to go hear a man who exactly counterfeited the voice of a
nightingale, answered, "Sir, I have heard the nightingale itself."
Another, having read the following inscription upon a tomb,

> Seeking to quench a cruel tyranny,
> They, at Selinus, did in battle die,

said, it served them right; for instead of trying to quench the tyranny
they should have let it burn out. A lad, being offered some game-cocks
that would die upon the spot, said that he cared not for cocks that would
die, but for such that would live and kill others. Another, seeing people
easing themselves on seats, said, "God forbid I should sit where I could
not get up to salute my elders." In short, their answers were so sententious and pertinent, that one said well that intellectual much more
truly than athletic exercise was the Spartan characteristic.

Nor was their instruction in music and verse less carefully attended
to than their habits of grace and good breeding in conversation. And
their very songs had a life and spirit in them that inflamed and possessed
men's minds with an enthusiasm and ardor for action; the style of
them was plain and without affectation; the subject always serious and
moral; most usually, it was in praise of such men as had died in defence
of their country, or in derision of those that had been cowards; the
former they declared happy and glorified; the life of the latter they
described as most miserable and abject. There were also vaunts of
what they would do, and boasts of what they had done, varying with
the various ages, as, for example, they had three choirs in their solemn
festivals, the first of the old men, the second of the young men, and the
last of the children; the old men began thus:

> We once were young, and brave and strong;

the young men answered them, singing,

> And we're so now, come on and try;

the children came last and said,

> But we'll be strongest by and by.

Indeed, if we will take the pains to consider their compositions, some of which were still extant in our days, and the airs on the flute to which they marched when going to battle, we shall find that Terpander and Pindar had reason to say that music and valor were allied. The first says of Lacedæmon—

> The spear and song in her do meet,
> And Justice walks about her street;

and Pindar—

> Councils of wise elders here,
> And the young men's conquering spear,
> And dance, and song, and joy appear;

both describing the Spartans as no less musical than war-like; in the words of one of their own poets—

> With the iron stern and sharp
> Comes the playing on the harp.

For, indeed, before they engaged in battle, the king first did sacrifice to the Muses, in all likelihood to put them in mind of the manner of their education, and of the judgment that would be passed upon their actions, and thereby to animate them to the performance of exploits that should deserve a record. At such times, too, the Lacedæmonians abated a little the severity of their manners in favor of their young men, suffering them to curl and adorn their hair, and to have costly arms, and fine clothes; and were well pleased to see them, like proud horses, neighing and pressing to the course. And, therefore, as soon as they came to be well-grown, they took a great deal of care of their hair, to have it parted and trimmed, especially against a day of battle, pursuant to a saying recorded of their lawgiver, that a large head of hair added beauty to a good face, and terror to an ugly one.

When they were in the field, their exercises were generally more moderate, their fare not so hard, nor so strict a hand held over them by their officers, so that they were the only people in the world to whom war gave repose. When their army was drawn up in battle array and the enemy near, the king sacrificed a goat, commanded the soldiers to set their garlands upon their heads, and the pipers to play the tune of the hymn to Castor, and himself began the pæan of advance. It was at once a magnificent and a terrible sight to see them march on to the tune of their flutes, without any disorder in their ranks, any discompo- sure in their minds or change in their countenance, calmly and cheer- fully moving with the music to the deadly fight. Men, in this temper, were not likely to be possessed with fear or any transport of fury, but with the deliberate valor of hope and assurance, as if some divinity were attending and conducting them. The king had always about his person some one who had been crowned in the Olympic games; and upon this account a Lacedæmonian is said to have refused a consider- able present, which was offered to him upon condition that he would not come into the lists; and when he had with much to-do thrown his antagonist, some of the spectators saying to him, "And now, Sir Lacedæmonian, what are you the better for your victory?" he answered smiling, "I shall fight next [to] the king." After they had routed an enemy, they pursued him till they were well assured of the victory, and then they sounded a retreat, thinking it base and unworthy of a Grecian people to cut men in pieces, who had given up and abandoned all resistance. This manner of dealing with their enemies did not only show magnanimity, but was politic too; for, knowing that they killed only those who made resistance, and gave quarter to the rest, men generally thought it their best way to consult their safety by flight.

Hippias the sophist says that Lycurgus himself was a great soldier and an experienced commander. Philostephanus attributes to him the first division of the cavalry into troops of fifties in a square body; but Demetrius the Phalerian says quite the contrary, and that he made all his laws in a continued peace. And, indeed, the Olympic holy truce, or cessation of arms, that was procured by his means and management, inclines me to think him a kindnatured man, and one that loved quietness and peace. Notwithstanding all this, Hermippus tells us that he had no hand in the ordinance; that Iphitus made it, and Lycurgus came only as a spectator, and that by mere accident too. Being there, he heard as it were a man's voice behind him, blaming and wondering at him that he did not encourage his countrymen to resort to the assembly, and, turning about and seeing no man, concluded that it was a voice from heaven, and upon this immediately went to Iphitus, and assisted him in ordering the ceremonies of that feast, which by his means, were better established, and with more repute than before.

To return to the Lacedæmonians. Their discipline continued still after they were full-grown men. No one was allowed to live after his own fancy; but the city was a sort of camp, in which every man had his share of provisions and business set out, and looked upon himself not so much born to serve his own ends as the interest of his country. Therefore, if they were commanded nothing else, they went to see the boys perform their exercises, to teach them something useful, or to learn it themselves of those who knew better. And, indeed, one of the greatest and highest blessings Lycurgus procured his people was the abundance of leisure, which proceeded from his forbidding to them the exercise of any mean and mechanical trade. Of the money-making that depends on troublesome going about and seeing people and doing business, they had no need at all in a state where wealth obtained no honor or respect. The Helots tilled their ground for them, and paid them yearly in kind the appointed quantity, without any trouble of theirs. To this purpose there goes a story of a Lacedæmonian who, happening to be at Athens when the courts were sitting, was told of a citizen that had been fined for living an idle life, and was being escorted home in much distress of mind by his condoling friends; the Lacedæmonian was much surprised at it, and desired his friend to show him the man who was condemned for living like a freeman. So much beneath them did they esteem the frivolous devotion of time and attention to the mechanical arts and to money-making.

▣ 3. Athens: Education in the Archaic Age

Much of what we know of the old Athenian education is gleaned from the writings of men who lived in the fifth and early fourth centuries B.C. Thucydides and Plato were products of the old training, and in passages of their works we catch sight of an educational system that reflected the ideals of aristocratic Athens, to which these men paid homage. No better example of such homage is to be found than that of Thucydides' account of Pericles' funeral oration honoring the heroes of Marathon.

Most of those who have spoken here before me have commended the lawgiver who added this oration to our other funeral customs: it seemed to them a worthy thing that such an honour should be given at their burial to the dead who have fallen on the field of battle. But I should have preferred that, when men's deeds have been brave, they should be honoured in deed only, and with such an honour as this public funeral,

B. *Jowett (trans.),* Thucydides *(Oxford: At the Clarendon Press, 1881),* I, 116–24.

which you are now witnessing. Then the reputation of many would not
have been imperilled on the eloquence or want of eloquence of one,
and their virtues believed or not as he spoke well or ill. For it is difficult
to say neither too little nor too much; and even moderation is apt not to
give the impression of truthfulness. The friend of the dead who knows
the facts is likely to think that the words of the speaker fall short of his
knowledge and of his wishes; another who is not so well informed, when
he hears of anything which surpasses his own powers, will be envious and
will suspect exaggeration. Mankind are tolerant of the praises of others
so long as each hearer thinks that he can do as well or nearly as well
himself, but, when the speaker rises above him, jealousy is aroused and
he begins to be incredulous. However, since our ancestors have set the
seal of their approval upon the practice, I must obey, and to the utmost
of my power shall endeavour to satisfy the wishes and beliefs of all who
hear me.

I will speak first of our ancestors, for it is right and becoming that
now, when we are lamenting the dead, a tribute should be paid to their
memory. There has never been a time when they did not inhabit this
land, which by their valour they have handed down from generation
to generation, and we have received from them a free state. But if they
were worthy of praise, still more were our fathers, who added to their
inheritance, and after many a struggle transmitted to us their sons this
great empire. And we ourselves assembled here to-day, who are still
most of us in the vigour of life, have chiefly done the work of improvement, and have richly endowed our city with all things, so that she
is sufficient for herself both in peace and war. Of the military exploits by
which our various possessions were acquired, or of the energy with
which we or our fathers drove back the tide of war, Hellenic or Barbarian, I will not speak; for the tale would be long and is familiar to
you. But before I praise the dead, I should like to point out by what
principles of action we rose to power, and under what institutions and
through what manner of life our empire became great. For I conceive
that such thoughts are not unsuited to the occasion, and that this
numerous assembly of citizens and strangers may profitably listen to
them.

Our form of government does not enter into rivalry with the institutions of others. We do not copy our neighbours, but are an example to
them. It is true that we are called a democracy, for the administration is
in the hands of the many and not of the few. But while the law secures
equal justice to all alike in their private disputes, the claim of excellence
is also recognized; and when a citizen is in any way distinguished, he
is preferred to the public service, not as a matter of privilege, but as
the reward of merit. Neither is poverty a bar, but a man may benefit
his country whatever be the obscurity of his condition. There is no

exclusiveness in our public life, and in our private intercourse we are not suspicious of one another, nor angry with our neighbour if he does what he likes; we do not put on sour looks at him which, though harmless, are not pleasant. While we are thus unconstrained in our private intercourse, a spirit of reverence pervades our public acts; we are prevented from doing wrong by respect for authority and for the laws, having an especial regard to those which are ordained for the protection of the injured as well as to those unwritten laws which bring upon the transgressor of them the reprobation of the general sentiment.

And we have not forgotten to provide for our weary spirits many relaxations from toil; we have regular games and sacrifices throughout the year; at home the style of our life is refined; and the delight which we daily feel in all these things helps to banish melancholy. Because of the greatness of our city the fruits of the whole earth flow in upon us; so that we enjoy the goods of other countries as freely as of our own.

Then, again, our military training is in many respects superior to that of our adversaries. Our city is thrown open to the world, and we never expel a foreigner or prevent him from seeing or learning anything of which the secret if revealed to an enemy might profit him. We rely not upon management or trickery, but upon our own hearts and hands. And in the matter of education, whereas they from early youth are always undergoing laborious exercises which are to make them brave, we live at ease, and yet are equally ready to face the perils which they face. And here is the proof. The Lacedæmonians come into Attica not by themselves, but with their whole confederacy following; we go alone into a neighbour's country; and although our opponents are fighting for their homes and we on a foreign soil, we have seldom any difficulty in overcoming them. Our enemies have never yet felt our united strength; the care of a navy divides our attention, and on land we are obliged to send our own citizens everywhere. But they, if they meet and defeat a part of our army, are as proud as if they had routed us all, and when defeated they pretend to have been vanquisehd by us all.

If then we prefer to meet danger with a light heart but without laborious training, and with a courage which is gained by habit and not enforced by law, are we not greatly the gainers? Since we do not anticipate the pain, although, when the hour comes, we can be as brave as those who never allow themselves to rest; and thus too our city is equally admirable in pcacc and in war. For we are lovers of the beautiful, yet simple in our tastes, and we cultivate the mind without loss of manliness. Wealth we employ, not for talk and ostentation, but when there is a real use for it. To avow poverty with us is no disgrace; the true disgrace is in doing nothing to avoid it. An Athenian citizen does not neglect the state because he takes care of his own household; and even those of us who are engaged in business have a very fair idea of politics. We alone regard a man who takes no interest in public affairs, not as a harmless, but as a useless character; and if few of us are originators, we are all sound judges of a policy. The great impediment to action is, in our opinion, not discussion, but the want of that knowledge which is gained by discussion preparatory to action. For we have a peculiar power of thinking before we act and of acting too, whereas other men are courageous from ignorance but hesitate upon reflection. And they are surely to be esteemed the bravest spirits who, having the clearest sense both of the pains and pleasures of life, do not on that account shrink from danger. In doing good, again, we are unlike others; we make our friends by conferring, not by receiving favours. Now he who confers a favour is the firmer friend, because he would fain by kindness keep alive the memory of an obligation; but the recipient is colder in his feelings, because he knows that in requiting another's generosity he will not be winning gratitude but only paying a debt. We alone do good to our neighbours not upon a calculation of interest, but in the confidence of freedom and in a frank and fearless spirit. To sum up: I say that Athens is the school of Hellas, and that the individual Athenian in his own person seems to have the power of adapting himself to the most varied forms of action with the utmost versatility and grace. This is no passing and idle word, but truth and fact; and the assertion is verified by the position to which these qualities have raised the state. For in the hour of trial Athens alone among her contemporaries is superior to the report of her. No enemy who comes against her is indignant at the reverses which he sustains at the hands of such a city; no subject complains that his masters are unworthy of him. And we shall assuredly not be without witnesses; there are mighty monuments of our power which will make us the wonder of this and of succeeding ages; we shall not need the praises of Homer or of any other panegyrist whose poetry may please for the moment, although his representation of the facts will not bear the light of day. For we have compelled every land and every sea to open a path for our valour, and have everywhere planted eternal memorials of our friendship and of our enmity. Such is the city for whose sake these men nobly fought and died; they could not bear the thought that she might be taken from them; and every one of us who survive should gladly toil on her behalf.

I have dwelt upon the greatness of Athens because I want to show you that we are contending for a higher prize than those who enjoy none of these privileges, and to establish by manifest proof the merit of these men whom I am now commemorating. Their loftiest praise has been already spoken. For in magnifying the city I have magnified them, and men like them whose virtues made her glorious. And of how few Hellenes can it be said as of them, that their deeds when weighed in the balance have been found equal to their fame! Methinks that a death such as theirs has been gives the true measure of a man's worth; it may be the first revelation of his virtues, but is at any rate their final seal. For even those who come short in other ways may justly plead the valour with which they have fought for their country; they have blotted out the evil with the good, and have benefited the state more by their public services than they have injured her by their private actions. None of these men were enervated by wealth or hesitated to resign the pleasures of life; none of them put off the evil day in the hope, natural to poverty, that a man, though poor, may one day become rich. But, deeming that the punishment of their enemies was sweeter than any of these things, and that they could fall in no nobler cause, they determined at the hazard of their lives to be honourably avenged, and to leave the rest. They resigned to hope their unknown chance of happiness; but in the face of death they resolved to rely upon themselves alone. And when the moment came they were minded to resist and suffer, rather than to fly and save their lives; they ran away from the word of dishonour, but on the battle-field their feet stood fast, and in an instant, at the height of their fortune, they passed away from the scene, not of their fear, but of their glory.

Such was the end of these men; they were worthy of Athens, and the living need not desire to have a more heroic spirit, although they may pray for a less fatal issue. The value of such a spirit is not to be expressed in words. Any one can discourse to you for ever about the advantages of a brave defence which you know already. But instead of listening to him I would have you day by day fix your eyes upon the greatness of Athens, until you become filled with the love of her; and when you are impressed by the spectacle of her glory, reflect that this empire has been acquired by men who knew their duty and had the courage to do it, who in the hour of conflict had the fear of dishonour always present to them, and who, if ever they failed in an enterprize, would not allow their virtues to be lost to their country, but freely gave their lives to her as the fairest offering which they could present at her feast. The sacrifice which they collectively made was individually repaid to them; for they received again each one for himself a praise which grows not old, and the noblest of all sepulchres—I speak not of that in which their remains are laid, but of that in which their glory survives, and is proclaimed always and on every fitting occasion both in word and deed. For the whole earth is the sepulchre of famous men; not only are they commemorated by columns and inscriptions in their own country, but in foreign lands there dwells also an unwritten memorial of them, graven not on stone but in the hearts of men. Make them your examples, and, esteeming courage to be freedom and freedom to be happiness, do not weigh too nicely the perils of war. The unfortunate who has no hope of a change for the better has less reason to throw away his life than the prosperous who, if he survive, is always liable to a change for the worse, and to whom any accidental fall makes the most serious difference. To a man of spirit, cowardice and disaster coming together are far more bitter than death striking him unperceived at a time when he is full of courage and animated by the general hope.

Wherefore I do not now commiserate the parents of the dead who stand here; I would rather comfort them. You know that your life has been passed amid manifold vicissitudes; and that they may be deemed fortunate who have gained most honour, whether an honourable death like theirs, or an honourable sorrow like yours, and whose days have been so ordered that the term of their happiness is likewise the term of their life. I know how hard it is to make you feel this, when the good fortune of others will too often remind you of the gladness which once lightened your hearts. And sorrow is felt at the want of those blessings, not which a man never knew, but which were a part of his life before they were taken from him. Some of you are of an age at which they may hope to have other children, and they ought to bear their sorrow better; not only will the children who may hereafter be born make them forget their own lost ones, but the city will be doubly a gainer. She will not be left desolate, and she will be safer. For a man's counsel cannot have equal weight or worth, when he alone has no children to risk in the general danger. To those of you who have passed their prime, I say: "Congratulate yourselves that you have been happy during the greater part of your days; remember that your life of sorrow will not last long, and be comforted by the glory of those who are gone. For the love of honour alone is ever young, and not riches, as some say, but honour is the delight of men when they are old and useless."

To you who are the sons and brothers of the departed, I see that the struggle to emulate them will be an arduous one. For all men praise the dead, and, however pre-eminent your virtue may be, hardly will you be thought, I do not say to equal, but even to approach them. The living have their rivals and detractors, but when a man is out of the way, the honour and good-will which he receives is unalloyed. And, if I am to speak of womanly virtues to those of you who will henceforth be widows, let me sum them up in one short admonition: To a woman not to show more weakness than is natural to her sex is a great glory, and not to be talked about for good or for evil among men.

I have paid the required tribute, in obedience to the law, making use of such fitting words as I had. The tribute of deeds has been paid in part; for the dead have been honourably interred, and it remains only that their children should be maintained at the public charge until they are grown up: this is the solid prize with which, as with a garland, Athens crowns her sons living and dead, after a struggle like theirs. For where the rewards of virtue are greatest, there the noblest citizens are enlisted in the service of the state. And now, when you have duly lamented, every one his own dead, you may depart.

In arriving at an educational system for his Republic, Plato turned to that of old Athens and provided us with knowledge of its basic elements and its goal of creating a balance of sound mind, healthy morals, and beautiful, graceful body.

Come then, and let us pass a leisure hour in story-telling, and our story shall be the education of our heroes.

By all means.

And what shall be their education? Can we find a better than the traditional sort?—and this has two divisions, gymnastics for the body, and music for the soul.

True.

Shall we begin education with music, and go on to gymnastics afterward?

By all means.

And when you speak of music, do you include literature or not?

I do.

* * * * *

Neither are the two arts of music and gymnastics really designed, as is often supposed, the one for the training of the soul, the other for the training of the body.

What then is the real object of them?

I believe, I said, that the teachers of both have in view chiefly the improvement of the soul.

How can that be? he asked.

Did you never observe, I said, the effect on the mind itself of exclusive devotion to gymnastics, or the opposite effect of an exclusive devotion to music?

In what way shown? he said.

The one producing a temper of hardness and ferocity, the other of softness and effeminacy, I replied.

Yes, he said, I am quite aware that the mere athlete becomes too much of a savage, and the mere musician is melted and softened beyond what is good for him.

Yet surely, I said, this ferocity only comes from spirit, which if rightly educated, would give courage, but, if too much intensified, is liable to become hard and brutal.

That I quite think.

Benjamin Jowett (trans.), The Republic of Plato *(London and New York: The Colonial Press, 1901), pp. 56–57, 96–98.*

On the other hand the philosopher will have the quality of gentleness. And this also, when too much indulged, will turn to softness, but, if educated rightly, will be gentle and moderate.

True.

And in our opinion the guardians ought to have both these qualities? Assuredly.

And both should be in harmony?

Beyond question.

And the harmonious soul is both temperate and courageous?

Yes.

And the inharmonious is cowardly and boorish?

Very true.

And, when a man allows music to play upon him and to pour into his soul through the funnel of his ears those sweet and soft and melancholy airs of which we were just now speaking, and his whole life is passed in warbling and the delights of song; in the first stage of the process the passion or spirit which is in him is tempered like iron, and made useful, instead of brittle and useless. But, if he carries on the softening and soothing process, in the next stage he begins to melt and waste, until he has wasted away his spirit and cut out the sinews of his soul; and he becomes a feeble warrior.

Very true.

If the element of spirit is naturally weak in him the change is speedily accomplished, but if he have a good deal, then the power of music weakening the spirit renders him excitable; on the least provocation he flames up at once, and is speedily extinguished; instead of having spirit he grows irritable and passionate and is quite impractical.

Exactly.

And so in gymnastics, if a man takes violent exercise and is a great feeder, and the reverse of a great student of music and philosophy, at first the high condition of his body fills him with pride and spirit, and he becomes twice the man that he was.

Certainly.

And what happens? if he do nothing else, and holds no converse with the muses, does not even that intelligence which there may be in him, having no taste of any sort of learning or inquiry or thought or culture, grow feeble and dull and blind, his mind never waking up or receiving nourishment, and his senses not being purged of their mists?

True, he said.

And he ends by becoming a hater of philosophy, uncivilized, never using the weapon of persuasion—he is like a wild beast, all violence and fierceness, and knows no other way of dealing; and he lives in all ignorance and evil conditions, and has no sense of propriety and grace.

That is quite true, he said.

And as there are two principles of human nature, one the spirited and the other the philosophical, some god, as I should say, has given mankind two arts answering to them (and only indirectly to the soul and body), in order that these two principles (like the strings of an instrument) may be relaxed or drawn tighter until they are duly harmonized.

That appears to be the intention.

And he who mingles music with gymnastics in the fairest proportions, and best attempers them to the soul, may be rightly called the true musician and harmonist in a far higher sense than the tuner of the strings.

You are quite right, Socrates.

And such a presiding genius will be always required in our State if the government is to last.

Yes, he will be absolutely necessary.

In Protagoras *Plato has his subject describe the old system to illustrate that virtue can indeed be taught.*

Education and admonition commence in the first years of childhood, and last to the very end of life. Mother and nurse and father and tutor are quarrelling about the improvement of the child as soon as ever he is able to understand them: he cannot say or do anything without their setting forth to him that this is just and that is unjust; this is honorable, that is dishonorable; this is holy, that is unholy; do this and abstain from that. And if he obeys, well and good; if not, he is straightened by threats and blows, like a piece of warped wood. At a later stage they send him to teachers, and enjoin them to see to his manners even more than to his reading and music; and the teachers do as they are desired. And when the boy has learned his letters and is beginning to under-stand what is written, as before he understood only what was spoken, they put into his hands the works of great poets, which he reads at school; in these are contained many admonitions, and many tales, and praises, and *encomia* of ancient famous men, which he is required to learn by heart, in order that he may imitate or emulate them and desire to become like them. Then, again, the teachers of the lyre take similar care that their young disciple is temperate and gets into no mischief; and when they have taught him the use of the lyre, they introduce him to the poems of other excellent poets, who are the lyric poets; and these they set to music, and make their harmonies and rhythms quite familiar to the children, in order that they may learn to be more gentle, and

Benjamin Jowett (trans.), Dialogues of Plato (*New York: The Colonial Press, 1900*), *pp. 170–71.*

harmonious, and rhythmical, and so more fitted for speech and action;
for the life of man in every part has need of harmony and rhythm. Then
they send them to the master of gymnastic, in order that their bodies
may better minister to the virtuous mind, and that the weakness of
their bodies may not force them to play the coward in war or on any
other occasion. . . .

▣ 4. Athens: The New Education

*Both the excitement occasioned by the arrival of the sophists in Athens
and the reservations concerning their impact on the minds of the young citizens
are evident in this excerpt from Plato's* Protagoras. *Socrates is speaking:*

Last night, or rather very early this morning, Hippocrates, the son
of Apollodorus and the brother of Phason, gave a tremendous thump
with his staff at my door; someone opened to him, and he came rushing
in and bawled out: Socrates, are you awake or aslecp?

I knew his voice, and said: Hippocrates, is that you? and do you
bring any news?

Good news, he said; nothing but good.

Very good, I said; but what news? and why have you come here at
this unearthly hour?

He drew nearer to me and said: Protagoras is come.

Yes, I said; he came two days ago: have you only just heard of his
arrival?

Yes, indeed, he said; I heard yesterday evening.

At the same time he felt for the truckle-bed, and sat down at my feet,
and then he said: I heard yesterday quite late in the evening, on my
return from Œnœ whither I had gone in pursuit of my runaway slave
Satyrus—as I was going to have told you if some other matter had not
come in the way; on my return, when we had done supper and were
about to retire to rest, my brother said to me: Protagoras is come. And
I was going to you at once, if I had not considered that the night was
far spent. But when sleep relaxed her hold on me after my toil, I got up
and came hither direct.

I, who knew the very courageous madness of the man, said: What is
the matter? has Protagoras robbed you of anything?

He replied, laughing: Yes, indeed he has, Socrates, of the wisdom
which he keeps to himself.

Dialogues of Plato, *pp. 155–60.*

But, surely, I said, if you give him money, and make friends with him, he will make you as wise as he is himself.

Would to Heaven, he replied, that he would! He might take all that I have, and all that my friends have, if he would. And that is why I have come to you now, in order that you may speak to him on my behalf; for I am young, and also I have never seen nor heard him (when he visited Athens before I was but a child); and all men praise him, Socrates, as being the most accomplished of speakers. There is no reason why we should not go to him at once, and then we shall find him at home. He lodges, as I hear, with Callias, the son of Hipponicus. Let us start.

I replied: Not yet, my good friend; the hour is too early. But let us rise and take a turn in the court and wait there until daybreak, and when the day breaks, then we will go; for Protagoras is generally at home, and we shall be sure to find him; never fear.

Upon this we got up and walked about in the court, and I thought that I would make trial of the strength of his resolution. So I examined him and put questions to him. Tell me, Hippocrates, I said, as you are going to Protagoras, and will be paying your money to him, what is he to whom you are going? and what will he make of you? If you were going to Hippocrates, the Coan, the Asclepiad, and were about to give him money, and some one said to you: As being what, do you give money to your namesake Hippocrates, O Hippocrates? what would you answer?

I should say, he replied, that I give money to him as a physician.

And what will he make of you?

A physician, he said.

And if you went to Polycleitus the Argive, or Pheidias the Athenian, and intended to give them money, and someone were to ask you: As being what, do you give this money to Polycleitus and Pheidias? what would you answer?

I should answer, as being statuaries.

And what will they make of you?

A statuary, of course.

Well, now, I said, you and I are going to Protagoras, and we are ready to pay him money for you. If our own means are sufficient, and we can gain him with these, we shall be too glad; but if not, then we are to spend your friend's money as well. Now suppose that while we are in this intense state of excitement, someone were to say to us: Tell me, Socrates, and you, Hippocrates, as being what, are you going to pay money to Protagoras? how should we answer him? I know that Pheidias is a sculptor, and Homer is a poet; but what appellation is given to Protagoras? how is he designated?

They call him a Sophist, Socrates, he replied.

Then we are going to pay our money to him in the character of a Sophist?

Certainly.

But suppose a person were to ask this further question: And how about yourself? what will Protagoras make you, if you go to see him?

He answered, with a blush upon his face (for the day was just beginning to dawn, so that I could see him): Unless this differs in some way from the former instances, I suppose that he will make a Sophist of me.

And are you not in sober earnest ashamed, I said, at having to appear before the Hellenes in the character of a Sophist?

Indeed, Socrates, if I am to confess the truth, I am.

But why do you assume, Hippocrates, that the instruction of Protagoras is of this nature? and why may you not learn of him in the same way that you learned the arts of the grammarian or musician or trainer, not with the view of making any of them a profession, but only as a part of education, and because a private gentleman and freeman ought to know them?

Just so, he said; and that, in my opinion, is a far truer account of the teaching of Protagoras.

I said: I wonder whether you know what you are doing?

And what am I doing?

You are going to commit your soul to the care of a man whom you call a Sophist. And yet I hardly think that you know what a Sophist is; and if not, then you do not even know whether you are committing your soul to good or evil.

I certainly think that I do know, he replied.

Then tell me, what do you imagine that he is?

I take him to be one who is wise and knowing, he replied, as his name implies.

And might you not, I said, affirm this of the painter and the carpenter also; are not they, too, wise and knowing? But suppose a person were to ask us: In what are the painters wise? We should answer: In what relates to the making of likenesses, and similarly of other things. And if he were further to ask: What is the wisdom of the Sophist, and what is the manufacture over which he presides? how should we answer him?

How should we answer him, Socrates? What other answer could there be but that he presides over the art which makes men eloquent?

Yes, I replied, that is very likely a true, but not a sufficient, answer; for a further question is involved: About what does the Sophist make a man eloquent? The player on the lyre may be supposed to make a man eloquent about that which he makes him understand, that is about playing the lyre. Is not that true?

Yes.

Then about what does the Sophist make him eloquent? must not he make him eloquent in that which he understands?

Yes, that may be assumed.

And what is that which the Sophist knows and makes his disciple know?

Indeed, he said, that I cannot tell.

Then I proceeded to say: Well, but are you aware of the danger which you are incurring? If you were going to commit the body to someone, and there was a risk of your getting good or harm from him, would you not carefully consider and ask the opinion of your friends and kindred, and deliberate many days as to whether you should give him the care of your body? But when the soul is in question, which you hold to be of far more value than the body, and upon the well or ill being of which depends your all—about this you never consulted either with your father or with your brother, or with anyone of us who are your companions. But no sooner does this foreigner appear, than you instantly commit your soul to his keeping. In the evening, as you say, you hear of him, and in the morning you go to him, never deliberating, or taking the opinion of anyone as to whether you ought to intrust yourself to him or not; you have quite made up your mind that you will be a pupil of Protagoras, and are prepared to expend all the property of yourself and of your friends in carrying out at any price this determination, although, as you admit, you do not know him, and have never spoken with him: and you call him a Sophist, but are manifestly ignorant of what a Sophist is; and yet you are going to commit yourself to his keeping.

When he heard me say this he replied: That I suppose, Socrates, is the conclusion which I must draw from your words.

I proceeded: Is not a Sophist, Hippocrates, one who deals wholesale or retail in the food of the soul? To me that appears to be the sort of man.

And what, Socrates, is the food of the soul?

Surely, I said, knowledge is the food of the soul; and we must take care, my friend, that the Sophist does not deceive us when he praises what he sells, like the dealers wholesale or retail who sell the food of the body; for they praise indiscriminately all their goods, without knowing what are really beneficial or hurtful; neither do their customers know, with the exception of any trainer or physician who may happen to buy of them. In like manner those who carry about the wares of knowledge, and make the round of the cities, and sell or retail them to any customer who is in want of them, praise them all alike; and I should not wonder, O my friend, if many of them were really ignorant of their effect upon the soul; and their customers equally ignorant, unless he who buys of them happens to be a physician of the soul. If therefore you have understanding of what is good and evil, you may safely buy knowledge of Protagoras or of anyone; but if not, then, O my friend, pause, and do not hazard your dearest interests at a game of chance. For there is far greater peril in buying knowledge than in buying meat and drink: the one you purchase of the wholesale or retail dealer, and carry them away in other vessels, and before you receive them into the body as food you may deposit them at home and call in any experienced friend who knows what is good to be eaten or drunken, and what not, and how much and when; and hence the danger of purchasing them is not so great. But when you buy the wares of knowledge you cannot carry them away in another vessel; they have been sold to you, and you must take them into the soul and go your way, either greatly harmed or greatly benefited by the lesson: and therefore we should think about this and take council with our elders; for we are still young—too young to determine such a matter. And now let us go, as we were intending, and hear Protagoras; and when we have heard what he has to say, we may take council of others; for not only is Protagoras at the house of Callias, but there is Hippias of Elis, and, if I am not mistaken, Prodicus of Ceos, and several other wise men.

To this we agreed, and proceeded on our way until we reached the vestibule of the house; and there we stopped in order to finish a dispute which had arisen as we were going along; and we stood talking in the vestibule until we had finished and come to an understanding. And I think that the doorkeeper, who was a eunuch, and who was probably annoyed at the great inroad of the Sophists, must have heard us talking. At any rate, when we knocked at the door, and he opened and saw us, he grumbled: They are Sophists—he is not at home; and instantly gave the door a hearty bang with both his hands. Again we knocked, and he answered without opening: Did you not hear me say that he is not at home, fellows? But, my friend, I said, we are not Sophists, and we are not come to see Callias; fear not, for we want to see Protagoras; and I must request you to announce us. At last, after a good deal of difficulty, the man was persuaded to open the door.

No more virulent attack on the sophists and the spirit of individualism and specialization they bred can be found than in Aristophanes' biting satire The Clouds. *In this excerpt the dramatist contrasts the glories of the old ("Just") education with what he considers to be the debilitating character of the new ("Unjust").*

JUST.   Come hither! show yourself to the spectators, although being audacious.

Paul Monroe (ed.), Source Book of the History of Education for the Greek and Roman Period (New York: The Macmillan Co., 1901), pp. 80–86.

UNJUST.   Go whither you please; for I shall far rather do for you, if I speak before a crowd.

JUST.   You destroy me? Who are you?

UNJ.   A cause.

JUST.   Aye, the worse.

UNJ.   But I conquer you, who say that you are better than I.

JUST.   By doing what clever trick?

UNJ.   By discovering new contrivances.

JUST.   For these *innovations* flourish by the favour of these silly persons.

UNJ.   No; but wise persons.

JUST.   I will destroy you miserably.

UNJ.   Tell me, by doing what?

JUST.   By speaking what is just.

UNJ.   But I will overturn them by contradicting them: for I deny that justice even exists at all.

JUST.   Do you deny that it exists?

UNJ.   For come, where is it?

JUST.   With the gods.

UNJ.   Now then, if justice exists, has Jupiter not perished, who bound his own father?

JUST.   Bah! this profanity now is spreading! Give me a basin.

UNJ.   You are a dotard and absurd.

JUST.   You are debauched and shameless.

UNJ.   You have spoken roses of me.

JUST.   And a dirty lickspittle.

UNJ.   You crown me with lilies.

JUST.   And a parricide.

UNJ.   You don't know that you are sprinkling me with gold.

JUST.   Certainly not so formerly, but with lead.

UNJ.   But now this is an ornament to me.

JUST.   You are very impudent.

UNJ.   And you are antiquated.

JUST.   And through you, no one of our youths is willing to go to school; and you will be found out some time or other by the Athenians, what sort of doctrines you teach the simple-minded.

UNJ.   You are shamefully squalid.

JUST.   And you are prosperous. And yet formerly you were a beggar, saying that you were the Mysian Telephus,[1] and gnawing the maxims of Pandeletus[2] out of your little wallet.

---

[1] *Telephus, king of Mysia, wounded by Achilles during the Trojan War, sought a cure, at the direction of the Delphic oracle, from the one who had wounded him. This he did, disguised as a beggar, and through the mediation of Agamemnon was successful. In the play of Euripides he is presented as an accomplished Sophist in the guise of a beggar. Hence the reference.*

[2] *Pandeletus was one of the minor Sophists.*

Unj.   Oh, the wisdom—

Just.   Oh, the madness—

Unj.   Which you have mentioned.

Just.   And of your city, which supports you who ruin her youth.

Unj.   You shan't teach this *youth*, you old dotard.

Just.   Yes, if he is to be saved, and not merely to practise loquacity.

Unj.   [*to* Phidippides].   Come hither, and leave him to rave.

Just.   You shall howl, if you lay your hand on him.

Cho.   Cease from contention and railing. But show to us, you, what you used to teach the men of former times, and you, the new system of education; in order that, having heard you disputing, he may decide and go to the school *of one or the other*.

Just.   I am willing to do so.

Unj.   I also am willing.

Cho.   Come now, which of the two shall speak first?

Unj.   I will give him the precedence; and then, from these things which he adduces, I will shoot him dead with new words and thoughts. And at last, if he mutter, he shall be destroyed, being stung in his whole face and his two eyes by my maxims, as if by bees.

Cho.   Now the two, relying on very dexterous arguments and thoughts, and sententious maxims, will show which of them shall appear superior in argument. For now the whole crisis of wisdom is here laid before them; about which my friends have a very great contest. But do you, who adorned our elders with many virtuous manners, utter the voice in which you rejoice, and declare your nature.

Just.   I will, therefore, describe the ancient system of education, how it was ordered, when I flourished in the advocacy of justice, and temperance was the fashion. In the first place it was incumbent that no one should hear the voice of a boy uttering a syllable; and next, that those from the same quarter of the town should march in good order through the streets to the school of the Harp-master, naked, and in a body, even if it were to snow as thick as meal. Then again, *their master* would teach them, not sitting cross-legged, to learn by rote a song, either "Pallas Terrible Destroyer of Cities"[1] or "Far Reaching Shriek,"[2] raising to a higher pitch the harmony which our fathers transmitted to us. But if any of them were to play the buffoon, or turn any quavers like these difficult turns the present artists make after the manner of Phrynis,[3] he used to be thrashed, being beaten with many blows, as banishing the Muses. And it behoved the boys, while sitting in the school of the

---

[1] *First line of a song composed by Lamprocles, son of Didon, an ancient Athenian poet.*

[2] *First line of a song composed by Cydides, a harper of Hermione.*

[3] *Phrynis of Mitylene introduced a new species of modulation in music, deviating from the simplicity of the ancients.*

Gymnastic-master, to cover the thigh, so that they might exhibit nothing indecent to those outside; then again, after rising *from the ground*, to sweep *the sand* together, and to take care not to leave an impression of the person for their lovers. And no boy used in those days to anoint himself below the navel; so that their bodies wore the appearance of blooming health. Nor used he to go to his lover, having made up his voice in an effeminate tone, prostituting himself with his eyes. Nor used it to be allowed when one was dining to take the head of a radish, or to snatch from their seniors dill or parsley, or to eat fish, or to giggle, or to keep the legs crossed. [1]

UNJ.   Aye, antiquated and Dipolia-like, [2] and full of grasshoppers, and of Cecydes, [3] and of the Buphonian festival! [4]

JUST.   Yet certainly these are those principles by which my system of education nurtured the men who fought at Marathon. But you teach the men of the present day, from their earliest years, to be wrapped up in himatia; so that I am choked, when at the Panathenaia [5] a fellow, holding his shield before his person, neglects Tritogenia, [6] when they ought to dance. Wherefore, O youth, choose, with confidence, me, the better cause, and you will learn to hate the Agora, and to refrain from baths, and to be ashamed at what is disgraceful, and to be enraged if any one jeer you, and to rise up from seats before your seniors when they approach, and not to behave ill toward your parents, and to do nothing else that is base, because you are to form in your mind an image of Modesty: and not to dart into the house of a dancing woman, lest, while gaping after these things, being struck with an apple by a wanton, you should be damaged in your reputation: and not to contradict your father in anything; nor by calling him Iapetus, [7] to reproach him with the ills of age, by which you were reared in your infancy.

UNJ.   If you shall believe him in this, O youth, by Bacchus, you will be like the sons of Hippocrates, [8] and they will call you a booby.

JUST.   Yet certainly shall you spend your time in the gymnastic schools, sleek and blooming; not chattering in the market-place rude

---

[1] *"Among the remains of ancient art there is, perhaps, not one representing a man, woman, god, or dæmon sitting cross-legged."*—FELTON.

[2] *One of the most ancient festivals in Attica, in honor of Jupiter, the protector of cities. These ceremonies had become antiquated and were ridiculed.*

[3] *An ancient poet.*

[4] *Same Festival as the Dipolia, mentioned above.*

[5] *The most ancient and most important of Athenian festivals, held in honor of Athene, the patron deity of Athens. The lesser festival held every year, the greater every fifth year.*

[6] *A surname of Athene.*

[7] *Son of Uranus and Gæa; regarded by the Greeks as the father of the human race.*

[8] *A nephew of Pericles. His sons were often derided for their silliness.*

jests, like the youths, of the present day; nor dragged into court for a petty suit, greedy, petty-fogging, knavish; but you shall descend to the Academy[1] and run races beneath the sacred olives along with some modest compeer, crowned with white reeds, redolent of yew, and care- less ease, and of leaf-shedding white poplar, rejoicing in the season of spring, when the plane-tree whispers to the elm. If you do these things which I say, and apply your mind to these, you will ever have a stout chest, a clear complexion, broad shoulders, a little tongue, large hips, little lewdness. But if you practise what the youths of the present day do, you will have, in the first place, a pallid complexion, small shoulders, a narrow chest, a large tongue, little hips, great lewdness, a long psephism; and *this deceiver* will persuade you to consider every thing that is base to be honourable, and what is honourable to be base; and, in addition to this, he will fill you with the lewdness of Antimachus.[2]

CHO.   O thou that practisest most renowned high-towering wisdom! how sweetly does a modest grace attend your words! Happy, therefore, were they who lived in those days, in the times of former men! In reply, then, to these, O thou that hast a dainty-seeming muse, it behoveth thee to say something new; since the man has gained renown. And it appears you have need of powerful arguments against him, if you are to conquer the man, and not incur laughter.

UNJ.   And yet I was choking in my heart, and was longing to con- found all these with contrary maxims. For I have been called among the deep thinkers the "worse cause," on this very account, that I first contrived how to speak against both law and justice: and this *art* is worth more than ten thousand staters, that one should choose the worse cause, and nevertheless be victorious. But mark how I will confute the system of education on which he relies, who says, in the first place, that he will not permit you to be washed with warm water. And yet, on what principle do you blame the warm baths?

JUST.   Because it is most vile, and makes a man cowardly.

UNJ.   Stop! For immediately I seize and hold you by the waist without escape. Come, tell me, which of the sons of Jupiter do you deem to have been the bravest in soul, and to have undergone most labours?

JUST.   I consider no man superior to Hercules.

UNJ.   Where, pray, did you ever see cold Herculean baths?[3] And yet, who was more valiant *than he?*

---

[1] *A public grove in the suburbs of Athens, where Plato and his followers taught.*

[2] *A composer of lewd songs.*

[3] *Herculean baths were warm baths, for Athena had called the warm springs of Thermopylæ into existence in order that Hercules might refresh himself. This passage is a type of the "sophistic" reasoning.*

JUST. These are the very things which make the bath full of youths always chattering all day long, but the palæstras empty.

UNJ. You next find fault with their living in the market-place; but I commend it. For if it had been bad, Homer would never have been for representing Nestor as an orator; nor all the *other* wise men. I will return, then, from thence to the tongue, which this fellow says our youths ought not to exercise, while I maintain *they should*. And, again, he says they ought to be modest: two very great evils. For tell me to whom you have ever seen any good accrue through modesty; and confute me by your words. . . . For [*to* PHIDIPPIDES] consider, O youth, all that attaches to modesty, and of how many pleasures you are about to be deprived—of women, of games at cottabus,[1] of dainties, of drinking-bouts, of giggling. And yet, what is life worth to you, if you be deprived of these *enjoyments?* Well, I will pass from thence to the necessities of our nature. You have gone astray, you have fallen in love, you have been guilty of some adultery, and then have been caught. You are undone, for you are unable to speak. But if you associate with me, indulge your inclination, dance, laugh, and think nothing disgraceful. For if you should happen to be detected as an adulterer, you will make this reply to him, "that you have done him no injury": and then refer him to Jupiter, how even he is overcome by love. And yet, how could you, who are a mortal, have greater power than a god?

JUST. But what, if he should suffer the radish through obeying you, and be depillated with hot ashes? What argument will he be able to state, *to prove* that he is not a blackguard?

UNJ. And if he be a blackguard, what harm will he suffer?

JUST. Nay, what could he ever suffer still greater than this?

UNJ. What then will you say, if you be conquered by me in this?

JUST. I will be silent: what else *can I do?*

UNJ. Come now, tell me; from what class do the advocates come?

JUST. From the blackguards.

UNJ. I believe you. What then? from what class do the tragedians come?

JUST. From the blackguards.

UNJ. You say well. But from what class do the public orators come?

JUST. From the blackguards.

UNJ. Then have you perceived that you say nothing to the purpose? And look which class among the audience is the more numerous.

JUST. Well now, I'm looking.

UNJ. What, then, do you see?

JUST. By the gods, the blackguards *to be* far more numerous. This fellow, at any rate, I know; and him yonder; and this fellow with the long hair.

[1] *A Greek game, popular at drinking bouts.*

UNJ.   What, then, will you say?

JUST.   We are conquered. Ye blackguards, by the gods, receive my cloak,[1] for I desert to you.

▣ 5. The Ephebia

*The ephebia, which first appeared in Athens in the fourth century B.C.
as a training school for democratic citizenship and later evolved into an aristocratic
finishing school of gymnastics, was an extremely important Hellenizing force
down to the sixth century A.D. Not only did boys from all the Mediterranean
lands flock to the Athenian ephebia, but similar institutions were also established
in hundreds of locations throughout the Hellenistic world. Here fathers sent their
sons to receive the Hellenic gymnastic education so that they could thus become,
regardless of national origins, Greeks.*

*The early Athenian ephebia as described by Aristotle was obviously a training
ground for citizenship and military service. The examination to which Aristotle
referred in the following passage was administered to the Athenian young man
to determine whether he was entitled to the franchise. What was required was that
the youth prove that he was eighteen years old and the son of two citizen parents.*

. . . When the youths [Ephébi] have passed this examination, their
fathers meet by their tribes, and appoint on oath three of their fellow
tribesmen, over forty years of age, who, in their opinion, are the best
and most suitable persons to have charge of the youths; and of these
the Assembly elects one from each tribe as guardian, together with a
director, chosen from the general body of Athenians, to control the
while. Under the charge of these persons the youths first of all make the
circuit of the temples; then they proceed to Piraeus, and some of them
garrison Munichia and some the south shore. The Assembly also elects
two trainers, with subordinate instructors, who teach them to fight in
heavy armour, to use the bow and javelin, and to discharge a catapult.
The guardians receive from the state a drachma apiece for their keep,
and the youths four obols apiece. Each guardian receives the allowance
for all the members of his tribe and buys the necessary provisions for

Sir Frederic Kenyon (trans.), Atheniensium Respublica, *Ch. 42, 2–5, in W. D. Ross
(ed.)*, The Works of Aristotle *(Oxford: At the Clarendon Press, 1921), Vol. X.*

[1] *An allusion to Socrates' ceremony of stripping his disciples before they were initiated into
his school.*

the common stock (they mess together by tribes), and generally superin-
tends everything. In this way they spend the first year. The next year,
after giving a public display of their military evolutions, on the occasion
when the assembly meets in the theatre, they receive a shield and spear
from the state; after which they patrol the country and spend their
time in the forts. For these two years they are on garrison duty, and
wear the military cloak, and during this time they are exempt from all
taxes. They also can neither bring an action at law, nor have one
brought against them, in order that they may have no excuse for requiring leave of absence; though exception is made in cases of actions
concerning inheritances and wards of state, or of any sacrificial ceremony connected with the family. When the two years have elapsed they
thereupon take their position among the other citizens. Such is the
manner of the enrolment of the citizens and the training of the youths.

*Plato's description of the ephebia emphasizes the training youth received in the
laws of Athens.*

... When they have done with masters, the State again compels
them to learn the laws, and live after the pattern which they furnish,
and not after their own fancies; and just as in learning to write, the
writing-master first draws lines with a style for the use of the young
beginner, and gives him the tablet and makes him follow the lines, so
the city draws the laws, which were the invention of good lawgivers
who were of old time; these are given to the young man, in order to
guide him in his conduct whether as ruler or ruled; and he who trans-
gresses them is to be corrected, or, in other words, called to account,
which is a term used not only in your country, but also in many
others. ...

OATH OF THE ATHENIAN EPHEBES

I will never disgrace these sacred arms, nor desert my companion in
the ranks. I will fight for temples and public property, both alone and
with many. I will transmit my fatherland, not only not less, but greater
and better, than it was transmitted to me. I will obey the magistrates
who may at any time be in power. I will observe both the existing laws
and those which the people may unanimously hereafter make, and, if
any person seek to annul the laws or to set them at nought, I will do my
best to prevent him, and will defend them both alone and with many.

Plato, Protagoras, *in* Dialogues of Plato, *p. 171.*
Monroe, op. cit., *p. 23.*

I will honor the religion of my fathers. And I call to witness Agraulos,[1] Enyalios,[2] Ares,[3] Zeus, Thallo,[4] and Auxo,[5] and Hegemone.[5]

回 6. Oratory, The Crown of Classical Education

> *The educational tradition that sprang from Periclean Athens to dominate Hellenistic and Roman civilizations was predominantly one of literary training in which the student endeavored to master the knowledge and arts necessary to excel as an orator. The greatest master, exponent, and defender of this culture was Isocrates. In his oration, "On the Exchange of Estates," Isocrates defends the morality and effectualness of the teaching of the sophists and glorifies rhetorical training as Athens' great gift to the world.*

This, I well know, will not satisfy those against whose prejudices I am contending. Much more must be said before they can be converted or refuted. Their prejudice utters itself in one of two assertions:—that the system of the sophists is futile; or that it is effectual, but immoral.

Those who say that it is futile try it by a standard which they apply to none of those arts in which they believe. They demand that all its disciples shall become finished speakers in a year. The success of the sophists is, in fact, equal to that of any other class of teachers. Some of their pupils become powerful debaters; others become competent teachers; all become more accomplished members of society, better critics, more prudent advisers. And what proves the training to be scientific, is that all bear the stamp of a common method. These who despise such culture assume that practice, which develops every other faculty, is useless to the intellect; that the human mind can educate the instincts of horses and dogs, but cannot train itself; that tame lions and learned bears are possible, but not instructed men.

Monroe, op. cit., pp. 104–09.

[1] *Daughter of Cecrops and Angraulos. She threw herself from the Acropolis because an oracle had declared that the Athenians would conquer if some one would sacrifice himself for his country.*

[2] *A surname frequently given to Mars in the* Iliad, *and corresponding with the name Enyo given to Bellona.*

[3] *The Greek god of war, called Mars by the Romans.*

[4] *Daughter of Zeus and Themis. Guarded and promoted the order of nature in the springtime.*

[5] *Auxo (increase) and Hegemone (queen) were the two graces worshipped at Athens. When the Athenian youth received his weapons of war he swore by them.*

Others maintain that Philosophy has an immoral tendency, and hold it responsible for the faults of a few who pervert it. I am not going to defend all who *say* that they are sophists, but only those who say so truly. And first—What are the objects which tempt men to be dishonest? I answer that the object is always one of three things—pleasure, profit, or honour. Could it be pleasant, profitable, or honourable for a sophist that his pupils should be known as rascals? It may perhaps be replied that men do not always calculate; that a margin must be left for intemperate impulse. But, even if a sophist indulged such impulses in himself, it could be no more for his pleasure than for his interest to encourage them in his pupil. Are the strangers who come from Sicily, from the Euxine and other quarters to the rhetorical schools of Athens brought hither by the desire to become knaves? Or, if that were their wish, could they not find teachers at home? But the whole tenor of their life among us proves them honest men. Again, if power in discourse is in itself a corrupting thing, all those who have possessed it, and not some only, ought to have been tainted by it. Yet the best statesmen of our generation and of the last were those who had most studied oratory. To go back to old times, Solon, Kleisthenes, Themistocles, Perikles, were all distinguished orators: Solon was even called one of the Seven Sophists. Perikles studied under Anaxagoras[1] of Klazomenæ, and under Damon,[2] who was the ablest Athenian of his time.

But I can point out the places in which may be found those who are really liable to the charges falsely brought against the sophists. Read the tablets, giving notice of lawsuits, which are published by the Thesmothetæ,[3] by the Eleven, and by the Forty.[4] Among the names of wrongdoers and of false accusers which figure there will be found those of Lysimachos and his friends,—not mine, nor that of any member of our profession. Were we really corrupters of youth, our accusers would have been the fathers and relatives of those whom we corrupted,—not such men as Lysimachos, whose interest it is that Athens should be demoralised. Just now I spoke of the hostility which some educated men feel towards our art. That hostility, I venture to hope, will have been disarmed by these plain statements. But there is, I think, a jealousy which is even more widely spread. It is because all ambitious men wish to be able speakers, but are too indolent to work for that end, that they dislike those who are ready to go through the necessary toil. It is strange

---

[1] *A Greek philosopher of Klazomenæ in Asia Minor.*

[2] *A celebrated musician and music teacher. Plato commends him as a desirable companion for young men.*

[3] *The six junior archons at Athens, who administered justice in all cases not specifically under the jurisdiction of the three senior archons, or some other authority.*

[4] *Judges who went on circuit through the Attic demes trying minor cases.*

that, while Athenians reproach the Thebans and others with neglecting culture, they should revile their fellow-citizens for seeking it; that the goddess of Persuasion should be honoured with yearly sacrifice, while those who wish to share her power should be regarded as desiring something evil; that bodily training should be esteemed, while mental training—to which Athens owes her place in Hellas—is slighted.

If a man used his inherited wealth, his skill as a hoplite[1] or as an athlete, in doing harm to his fellow-citizens, he would be punished, though the founders of his fortune, the teachers of his skill, might be praised. The gods have given us speech—the power which has civilised human life; and shall we not strive to make the best use of it?

Lysimachos and such as he are not the only enemies of Rhetoric. It is attacked also by the professors of Eristic.[2] Instead of retorting their reproaches, I wish simply to aid you in estimating their studies relatively to ours. Eristic discussion, like Astrology or Geometry, seems to me not to deserve the name of Philosophy, since it has no practical bearing; but, rather, to be a good preparation for Philosophy. School-boys are trained to work and to think accurately by grammar and literary study; Philosophy forms a more manly discipline of the same sort for young men. But no one should allow his mind to be dried up by barren subtleties, or to drift into such speculations as those with which the Ionic physicists juggled.

Having said what Philosophy is not, I must try to explain what (as I think) it is. My view is very simple. A wise man is one who can make a good guess (knowledge being impossible) as to what he ought to say and do. A philosopher, a lover of wisdom, is one who spends his time in the pursuits by which he may best gain such perception. And what are these pursuits? My answer will probably shock you; but I should be ashamed to betray the truth for the sake of peace in the fraction of life remaining to me. Well, then, I hold that there is no communicable science of Virtue or Justice; but that a man ambitious of speaking well, of persuading others, and (in the true sense) of *gain*, will incidentally become more virtuous and more just. Desirous of speaking with applause, he will occupy himself with the noblest themes, and dwell upon the worthiest topics of these. Desirous of persuading, he will strive to be just, since nothing is so persuasive as a character which is felt to be upright. Desirous of real gain, he will seek the approval of the gods and the esteem of his fellow-citizens. It is only by a perversion of language that the "desire of gain" has been associated with knavery; as "witti-ness" with buffoonery, and "philosophy" with the mystifications of the elder sophists. This conception of philosophy as something unpractical

---

[1] *A heavy-armed soldier.*
[2] *Controversial philosophical discussion of the character of the Socratic and Platonic schools.*

—this tendency to discourage all systematic training for affairs—has its result in the lives of our youth. Their occupations are to cool wine in the Enneakrunos,—to drink in taverns,— to gamble,—to haunt the music-schools. The informers do not molest those who foster *these* pursuits. They attack us, who discourage them; and say that youths who spend on their education a tithe of what others spend on vice, are being corrupted.

Power of speaking, when simply natural, is admired; it is strange, then, that blame should be cast upon the attempt to cultivate it. When acquired by labour, the faculty is more likely to be used discreetly than when it is an accident of genius. Athenians, of all men, ought not to despise culture. It is cultivated intelligence which distinguishes men from beasts, Hellenes from barbarians, Athenians from Hellenes. Athens is regarded as the teacher of all who can speak or teach others to speak; the greatest prizes, the best schools, the most constant practice are supplied by her. For her to disown the study of eloquence would be as if Sparta laid disabilities on military education or the Thessalians on skill in horsemanship. In athletic prowess, Athens has many rivals; in culture, none. Her intellectual culture is what most commands the admiration of foreigners; as the prevalence of informers is the one blot to which they can point. You ought to punish those who bring disgrace upon you, and honour those who do you credit. Miltiades, Themistokles, Perikles, became great by the pursuits which these informers vilify. Remembering this, strive to keep the law-courts pure for the citizens generally; and honour the ablest and most cultivated among them as the truest guardians of the democracy.

The length of my defence has already passed due limits; but there are still a few words that I would say to you. It is bitter to me to see the informer's trade prospering better than the cause of education. Would our ancestors have looked for this? Solon, eldest of the Sophists, was put by them at the head of the State; against informers they appointed not one mode of procedure only but many,—indictment before the Thesmothetæ, impeachment before the Senate, plaint to the Assembly. And informers are worse now than they were then. Their audacity has grown with the licence of those demagogues to whom our fathers entrusted the protection of the Athenian empire; who, by reproaching our most distinguished citizens as oligarchs and partisans of Sparta, made them such, who harassed, and so estranged, our allies,— who brought Athens to the verge of slavery. Time is failing me; I must cease. Others conclude by committing their cause to the mercy of their judges, and the entreaties of their friends; *I* appeal to my past life. The gods, who have protected it hitherto, will protect it now. Your verdict, whatever it may be, will be for my good. Let each of you give what sentence he will.

II

Education and the Grandeur That Was Rome

IT is neither uncommon nor incorrect for the student of history to view Rome and Greece linked together as the powerful parents of Western civilization. One often thinks of Greece as the creator and Rome the transmitter of classical or Greco-Roman culture. Yet it must be remembered that long before Rome crossed paths with the Hellenes, she had a past that made and kept Rome Roman even in the presence of dazzling Greece.

While Athens was embarking on the glorious Age of Pericles in the fifth century B.C., Rome was a rather primitive city-state recently freed from Etruscan dominance and just beginning to flex its muscles at the expense of her Italian neighbors. Though Rome was governed by an oligarchical republic of patricians, its citizens had yet to develop a strong sense of state patriotism.

The Roman's basic loyalty was most clearly identified with the family, which was ruled by the father with virtually unchecked power. The Roman paterfamilias governed a family that was at the same time a social entity, a political body, an economic unit, and a religious congregation. When it was time to plant, the father was the overseer; when it was time to pray, the father was the priest; and when it was time to learn, the father was the teacher of everything the sons had to know of family occupation, manners, morals, religious duties, and military skills. (1) As life became more complex, the family was to surrender many of its duties and prerogatives to other institutions, but it remained an acknowledged force throughout the history of Rome.

The Laws of the Twelve Tables (449 B.C.) were in many respects to the Romans what Homer's epics were to the Greeks and illustrate to no small degree the differences between the two nations. Like Homer's works the Laws marked the beginning of a literary heritage, reflected the customs and practices of the people, and, when committed to memory, provided an essential ingredient in the education of boys. However, whereas The Iliad *and The* Odyssey *were lyric poems, the Laws of the Twelve Tables constituted a body of jurisprudence. Such was the Greek primer and such the Roman.* (2)

The victories of Rome—first over her neighbors and then over Carthage— moved her closer to the Hellenistic world created by Alexander, now a vacuum waiting to be filled by such a new power. When the city of Tarentum fell to Rome in 272 B.C., *the victors carried back to their city Greek captives. Among them was Livius Andronicus, who was to translate The* Odyssey *into Latin. The Greek-Latin synthesis was begun, and Roman boys had a new primer to accompany the Laws of the Twelve Tables. By the middle of the second century* B.C. *schools were established in Rome in which the whole round of Greek subjects were taught: reading and arithmetic in the school of the* litterator, *Greek grammar and literature in the school of the* grammaticus, *and finally oratory in the school of the* rhetor. *The advent of Greek culture in Rome like the appearance of sophists in Athens was greeted with scorn by conservatives or traditionalists; but like the sophists, the grammarians and rhetoricians ultimately triumphed.* (3)

The success of the Greek schools and the popularity of Greek philosophy were due to more than the attraction of the Romans to something new. The last century- and-a-half of the Republic was a time of political, social, and military upheaval. It was a time when sincere men as well as opportunists sought to find the solution to the innumerable problems besetting a republic that ruled an empire. In Greek philosophy they sought both the key to success and solace for setbacks. But it was in the Senate and in the Forum that the battles for men's minds were fought, and here oratory was the ultimate weapon. The keen competition among political leaders is made all the more obvious when one considers that such figures as Marc Antony, Pompey, Julius Caesar, Brutus, Cassius, and Cicero had all received schooling in oratory at Rhodes. It is no coincidence that Cicero, the supreme literary figure and greatest of all Roman orators, was also very much involved in the political struggles that ultimately led to the death of the Republic and the creation of the Empire. The political execution of Cicero silenced one of the chief spokesmen for the Republic and ended the career of a man whose writings were to be studied by centuries of students as the ultimate in Latin prose and who provided a model of the ideal orator to future generations of Roman teachers. (4)

The establishment of the Empire did not mean the death of the Greco-Roman schools. Indeed, during the Golden Age of Augustus, Roman literary creativity provided the content for a Latin grammar school, and oratorical education flourished. Quintilian, the greatest of all Roman teachers of rhetoric, was patron- ized by the imperial government as were a countless number of artists, architects, and physicians. (5) *However, in the bureaucratic empire the spring from which Latin eloquence drank was destined to dry up. The oratorical combat of the Republic had little place in Rome of the Emperor-gods. Schools prospered under municipal support; teachers were granted all sorts of special privileges. But, the subjects of student oratorical exercises became more and more divorced from real life. The curriculum of the Classical Era was viewed as containing subjects to be memorized, memorization being an end unto itself. Like the Empire, Roman education became interested only in maintaining its boundaries. The dynamism that marked the writings of Cicero and Quintilian gave way to encyclopedic compilations of the creations of past generations. (6)*

It was fitting that in the sixth century, as the forces of barbarian armies and Christian missionaries were gaining control in the West, one of the last imperial acts to leave a permanent mark on Western education was the issuance of Justinian's Body of the Civil Law. *This compilation was designed to standardize and reform the teaching of law, Rome's most significant contribution to classical culture. (7)*

In Roman hands Greek culture was adapted, formalized and systematized. Outside the field of law it is difficult to describe the Romans as creators. Yet, although it is true that Greece provided the true spirit and greatest achievements of the Classical Era, it was in Roman vessels that Europe, centuries later, would rediscover many of the glories of the Hellenistic period. Roman textbooks, Roman scholars and poets, and Roman schools for centuries provided the content and form for the secondary schools and universities of the Western world.

回 1. The Roman Father, Educator

The almost unlimited power of the Roman father over his family carried with it equally awesome responsibilities for safeguarding its welfare. Certainly the duty to ensure that his sons received a proper education was a serious concern for the paterfamilias. *Though the following reading reflects a period long after Rome had evolved from a simple city-state, it is quite clear that the father's role as an educator was still of primary importance. Here Plutarch commends Cato the Censor (234–149 B.C.) for his conduct as husband and father.*

He was also a good father, an excellent husband to his wife, and an extraordinary economist; and as he did not manage his affairs of this kind carelessly, and as things of little moment, I think I ought to record a little further whatever was commendable in him in these points. He married a wife more noble than rich; being of opinion, that the rich and the high-born are equally haughty and proud; but that those of

A. H. Clough (trans.), Plutarch's Lives (Boston: Little, Brown, and Company, 1888), II, 341–43.

noble blood, would be more ashamed of base things, and consequently more obedient to their husbands in all that was fit and right. A man who beat his wife or child, laid violent hands, he said, on what was most sacred; and a good husband he reckoned worthy of more praise than a great senator; and he admired the ancient Socrates for nothing so much, as for having lived a temperate and contented life with a wife who was a scold, and children who were half-witted.

As soon as he had a son born, though he had never such urgent business upon his hands, unless it were some public matter, he would be by when his wife washed it, and dressed it in its swaddling clothes. For she herself suckled it, nay, she often too gave her breast to her servants' children, to produce, by sucking the same milk, a kind of natural love in them to her son. When he began to come to years of discretion, Cato himself would teach him to read, although he had a servant, a very good grammarian, called Chilo, who taught many others; but he thought not fit, as he himself said, to have his son reprimanded by a slave, or pulled, it may be, by the ears when found tardy in his lesson: nor would he have him owe to a servant the obligation of so great a thing as his learning; he himself, therefore, (as we were saying,) taught him his grammar, law, and his gymnastic exercises. Nor did he only show him, too, how to throw a dart, to fight in armor, and to ride, but to box also and to endure both heat and cold, and to swim over the most rapid and rough rivers. He says, likewise, that he wrote histories, in large characters, with his own hand, that so his son, without stirring out of the house, might learn to know about his country-men and forefathers: nor did he less abstain from speaking any thing obscene before his son, than if it had been in the presence of the sacred virgins, called vestals. Nor would he ever go into the bath with him; which seems indeed to have been the common custom of the Romans. Sons-in-law used to avoid bathing with fathers-in-law, disliking to see one another naked: but having, in time, learned of the Greeks to strip before men, they have since taught the Greeks to do it even with the women themselves.

Thus, like an excellent work, Cato formed and fashioned his son to virtue; nor had he any occasion to find fault with his readiness and docility; but as he proved to be of too weak a constitution for hardships, he did not insist on requiring of him any very austere way of living. However, though delicate in health, he proved a stout man in the field, and behaved himself valiantly when Paulus Æmilius fought against Perseus; where when his sword was struck from him by a blow, or rather slipped out of his hand by reason of its moistness, he so keenly resented it, that he turned to some of his friends about him, and taking them along with him again, fell upon the enemy; and having by a long fight and much force cleared the place, at length found it among great heaps of arms, and the dead bodies of friends as well as enemies piled one upon another. Upon which Paulus, his general, much commended the youth; and there is a letter of Cato's to his son, which highly praises his honorable eagerness for the recovery of his sword. Afterwards he married Tertia, Æmilius Paulus's daughter, and sister to Scipio; nor was he admitted into this family less for his own worth than his father's. So that Cato's care in his son's education came to a very fitting result.

▣ 2. The Laws of the Twelve Tables

It is not surprising that the Twelve Tables should have played an important role in the curriculum of the early Roman youth, for they consisted of a summary of social, political, and economic practices of the society in which he lived. By studying and memorizing this codification of Roman law the boy was indeed engaging in education for life.

The publication of the Twelve Tables was the culmination of plebian agitation for access to laws that up to that time (449 B.C.) had been held in secret by the patricians. This strong reliance upon written law resulted in the most significant Roman contribution to the storehouse of classical creativity.

The following are selections that illustrate the wide variety of concerns touched upon in the Twelve Tables.

TABLE IV

The Rights of the Father.
   I. Provision as to the immediate destruction of monstrous or deformed offspring.
  II. Provision relating to the control of the father over his children, the right existing during their whole life to imprison, scourge, keep to rustic labour in chains, to sell or slay, even though they may be in the enjoyment of high state offices.
 III. "Three consecutive sales of the son by the father releases the former from the *patria potestas*."
  IV. Provision relating to the duration of gestation: no child born more than ten months after the decease of his reputed father to be held legitimate.

Paul Monroe (ed.), Source Book of the History of Education for the Greek and Roman Period (New York: The Macmillan Co., 1901), pp. 337, 340, 343–44.

TABLE VIII

On Torts.
  I. Capital punishment is decreed against libellers and public defamers.
  II. "Retaliation against him who breaks the limb of another and does not offer compensation."
  III. For the fracture of the bone (of the tooth) of a freeman, the penalty is 300 asses;[1] in the case of a slave, 150.
  IV. "For any injury whatsoever committed upon another the penalty shall be 25 asses."
  V. "... For damage unjustly caused ... (but if by accident) reparation."

TABLE X

Sacred Law.
  I. "The dead must not be buried nor burned within the city."
  II. "Do no more than this ... The wood of the funeral pile shall not be smoothed."
  III. Restrictions against sumptuous funerals; the dead are not to be buried nor burned in more than three robes; nor in more than three fillets of purple; nor shall the funeral be attended by more than ten flute players.
  IV. "Women shall not be allowed to tear their hair nor make immoderate wailings."
  V. "The bones of the deceased shall not be collected for the purpose of giving him a subsequent funeral (except in the case of death in battle, or in a foreign country)."
  VI. Provision prohibiting the embalming the bodies of slaves, funeral banquets, expensive libations, coronal garlands, and the erection of incense altars.
  VII. "But if the deceased has either personally or by his slaves or horses obtained any public trophy, he shall be entitled to the honour it confers."
  VIII. Prohibition against more than one funeral, or more than one funeral ceremony, for the same deceased.
  IX. "Gold must not be buried with the dead; but if the teeth are fastened with gold, this may be either buried or burned."
  X. No funeral pile or sepulchre shall be erected within sixty feet of another man's house, except with his consent.
  XI. Neither a sepulchre nor its vestibule can be acquired by *usucapio.*

[1] *A small copper coin, worth in the earlier period about 16⅔ cents; depreciated until by the time of the Second Punic War it was worth about two-thirds of a cent.*

▣ 3. The Advent of Greek Learning in Rome

In the selection that follows the reader is given the opportunity to view through the eyes of Plutarch the explosive impact of the initial contact of Rome with Greek learning and culture. Plutarch, himself a student and proponent of Greek learning, enthusiastically describes the delight with which Roman youth received Greek philosophy, oratorical studies, and medicine. However, in relating the life of Cato the Censor, he makes it quite clear that there were those who saw this phenomenon as a parasite threatening to sap the vigor from Roman life.

He was now grown old, when Carneades the Academic, and Diogenes the Stoic, came as deputies from Athens to Rome, praying for release from a penalty of five hundred talents laid on the Athenians, in a suit, to which they did not appear, in which the Oropians were plaintiffs, and Sicyonians judges. All the most studious youth immediately waited on these philosophers, and frequently, with admiration, heard them speak. But the gracefulness of Carneades's oratory, whose ability was really greatest, and his reputation equal to it, gathered large and favorable audiences, and erelong filled, like a wind, all the city with the sound of it. So that it soon began to be told, that a Greek, famous even to admiration, winning and carrying all before him, had impressed so strange a love upon the young men, that quitting all their pleasures and pastimes, they ran mad, as it were, after philosophy; which indeed much pleased the Romans in general; nor could they but with much pleasure see the youth receive so welcomly the Greek literature, and frequent the company of learned men. But Cato, on the other side, seeing this passion for words flowing into the city, from the beginning, took it ill, fearing lest the youth should be diverted that way, and so should prefer the glory of speaking well before that of arms, and doing well. And when the fame of the philosophers increased in the city, and Caius Acilius, a person of distinction, at his own request, became their interpreter to the senate at their first audience, Cato resolved, under some specious pretence, to have all philosophers cleared out of the city; and, coming into the senate, blamed the magistrates for letting these deputies stay so long a time without being despatched, though they were persons that could easily persuade the people to what they pleased; that therefore in all haste something should be determined

Plutarch's Lives, *pp. 345–46.*

about their petition, that so they might go home again to their own schools, and declaim to the Greek children, and leave the Roman youth, to be obedient, as hitherto, to their own laws and governors.

Yet he did this not out of any anger, as some think, to Carneades; but because he wholly despised philosophy, and out of a kind of pride, scoffed at the Greek studies and literature; as, for example, he would say, that Socrates was a prating seditious fellow, who did his best to tyrannize over his country, to undermine the ancient customs, and to entice and withdraw the citizens to opinions contrary to the laws. Ridiculing the school of Isocrates, he would add, that his scholars grew old men before they had done learning with him, as if they were to use their art and plead causes in the court of Minos in the next world. And to frighten his son from any thing that was Greek, in a more vehement tone than became one of his age, he pronounced, as it were with the voice of an oracle, that the Romans would certainly be destroyed when they began once to be infected with Greek literature; . . .

The essays of Suetonius, "On Grammarians" and "On Rhetoricians," in addition to relating events concerned with the advent of Greek studies in Rome, provide valuable information regarding the content and methods employed in the schools of the grammaticus and rhetor.

ON GRAMMARIANS

I. The study of Grammar was not even pursued at Rome in early days, still less held in any esteem; and naturally enough, since the state was then still uncultivated and given to war, and had as yet little leisure for liberal pursuits. The beginnings of the subject, too, were humble, for the earliest teachers, who were also both poets and Italian Greeks (I refer to Livius and Ennius, who gave instruction in both tongues at home and abroad, as is well known), did no more than interpret the Greeks or give readings from whatever they themselves had composed in the Latin language. For while some tell us that this same Ennius published a book "On Letters and Syllables" and another "On Metres," Lucius Cotta is right in maintaining that these were not the work of the poet, but of a later Ennius, who is also the author of the volumes "On the Science of Augury."

II. In my opinion then, the first to introduce the study of grammar into our city was Crates of Mallos, a contemporary of Aristarchus. He was sent to the senate by King Attalus between the second and third

J. C. Rolfe (trans.), Suetonius *(Cambridge, Mass.: Loeb Classical Library, Harvard University Press, 1959)*, II, 397, 399, 435, 437, 439, 441. Reprinted by permission of the publishers and THE LOEB CLASSICAL LIBRARY from J. C. Rolfe, translator, Suetonius, *Grammarians & Rhetoricians* (Vol. II), Cambridge, Mass.: Harvard University Press.

Punic wars, at about the time when Ennius died; and having fallen into the opening of a sewer in the Palatine quarter and broken his leg, he held numerous and frequent conferences during the whole time both of his embassy and of his convalescence, at which he constantly gave instruction, and thus set an example for our countrymen to imitate. Their imitation, however, was confined to a careful criticism of poems which had as yet but little circulation, either those of deceased friends or others that met with their approval, and to making them known to the public by reading and commenting on them. For example, Gaius Octavius Lampadio thus treated the "Punic War" of Naevius, which was originally written in a single volume without a break, but was divided by Lampadio into seven books. At a later time Quintus Vargunteius took up the "Annals" of Ennius, which he expounded on set days to large audiences; and Laelius Archelaus and Vettius Philocomus the satires of their friend Lucilius, which Lenaeus Pompeius prides himself on having read with Archelaus, and Valerius Cato with Philocomus.

ON RHETORICIANS

I. The study of rhetoric was introduced into our country in about the same way as that of grammar, but with somewhat greater difficulty, since, as is well known, its practice was at times actually prohibited. To remove any doubt on this point, I shall append an ancient decree of the senate, as well as an edict of the censors:

"In the consulship of Gaius Fannius Strabo and Marcus Valerius Messala the praetor Marcus Pomponius laid a proposition before the senate. As the result of a discussion about philosophers and rhetoricians, the senate decreed that Marcus Pomponius, the praetor, should take heed and provide, in whatever way seemed in accord with the interests of the State and his oath of office, that they be not allowed to live in Rome." Some time afterward the censors Gnaeus Domitius Ahenobarbus and Lucius Licinius Crassus issued the following edict about the same class of men: "It has been reported to us that there be men who have introduced a new kind of training, and that our young men frequent their schools; that these men have assumed the title of Latin rhetoricians, and that young men spend whole days with them in idleness. Our forefathers determined what they wished their children to learn and what schools they desired them to attend. These innovations in the customs and principles of our forefathers do not please us nor seem proper. Therefore it appears necessary to make our opinion known, both to those who have such schools and to those who are in the habit of attending them, that they are displeasing to us."

By degrees rhetoric itself came to seem useful and honourable, and

many devoted themselves to it as a defence and for glory. Cicero continued to declaim in Greek as well as Latin up to the time of his
praetorship, and in Latin even when he was getting on in years; and
that too in company with the future consuls Hirtius and Pansa, whom
he calls "his pupils and his big boys." Some historians assert that
Gnaeus Pompeius resumed the practice of declaiming just before the
civil war, that he might be the better able to argue against Gaius Curio,
a young man of very ready tongue, who was espousing Caesar's cause;
and that Marcus Antonius, and Augustus as well, did not give it up
even during the war at Mutina. The emperor Nero declaimed in the
first year of his reign, and had also done so in public twice before.
Furthermore, many even of the orators published declamations. In
this way general enthusiasm was aroused, and a great number of
masters and teachers flocked to Rome, where they were so well received
that some advanced from the lowest estate to senatorial dignity and to
the highest magistracies.

But they did not all follow the same method of teaching, and the
individual teachers also varied in their practice, since each one trained
his pupils in various ways. For they would explain fine speeches with
regard to their figures, incidents and illustrations, now in one way and
now in another, and compose narratives sometimes in a condensed
and brief form, again with greater detail and flow of words. Sometimes
they would translate Greek works, and praise or censure distinguished
men. They would show that some practices in everyday life were
expedient and essential, others harmful and superfluous. Frequently
they defended or assailed the credibility of myths, an exercise which
the Greeks call "destructive" and "constructive" criticism. But finally
all these exercises went out of vogue and were succeeded by the debate.

The earlier debates were based either upon historical narrative, as
indeed is sometimes the case at present, or upon some event of recent
occurrence in real life. Accordingly they were usually presented with
even the names of the localities included. At any rate that is the case
with the published collections, from which it may be enlightening to
give one or two specimens word for word.

"Some young men from the city went to Ostia in the summer season,
and arriving at the shore, found some fishermen drawing their nets.
They made a bargain to give a certain sum for the haul. The money was
paid and they waited for some time until the nets were drawn ashore.
When they were at last hauled out, no fish was found in them, but a
closed basket of gold. Then the purchasers said that the catch belonged
to them, the fishermen that it was theirs."

"When some dealers were landing a cargo of slaves from a ship at
Brundisium, they dressed a handsome and high-priced young slave in
the amulet and fringed toga for fear of the collectors of customs, and

their fraud easily escaped detection. When they reached Rome, the case was taken to court and a claim was made for the slave's liberty, on the ground that his master had voluntarily freed him."

Such discussions they formerly called by their Greek name of "syntheses," but afterwards "debates"; but they might be either fictitious or legal.

▣ 4. Cicero, Model for the Ages

To generations of students Cicero has been synonymous with Latin III. After two years of wrestling with the rudiments of this difficult tongue, the student is finally prepared to gain some appreciation of the nobler writings of the Romans, among which Cicero's prose has no equal. In ancient Rome he was also hailed as the greatest master of the art of oratory. It is interesting to note that, while Cicero strongly advocated study of the liberal arts for the prospective orator, he insisted that practical experience was superior to the technical training of the schools of the rhetor *in developing the skills of effective speech. Unlike many in his own day as well as ours, Cicero's definition of education was not narrowly confined to formal schooling.*

In the selections that follow from Cicero's De Oratore *the reader perceives not only a great orator's call for broad training but also the obvious conviction that he who has mastered the skills of his honored profession has truly accomplished a magnificent feat. In insisting that the orator required "a wide knowledge of very many subjects," Cicero helped to establish a principle in Western education long held dear: that professional training must be preceded by education in the liberal arts.*

For when we consider the very large number of learners, the rich supply of teachers, the exceptional abilities of the persons engaged, the infinite variety of causes, the splendour of the prizes which eloquence may win, where else can we look for the explanation of the fact, except in the really incredible greatness and difficulty of the subject? Eloquence, in fact, requires many things: a wide knowledge of very many subjects (verbal fluency, without this, being worthless and even ridiculous), a style, too, carefully formed not merely by selection, but by arrangement of words, and a thorough familiarity with all the feelings which nature has given to man, because the whole force and art of the orator must be put forth in allaying or exciting the emotions of his audience. Further than this it requires a certain play of humour and

E. N. P. Moor (trans.), Cicero: De Oratore, Book I, I, 7–10; II, 48–49. Copyright, 1904, by Methuen & Co. Reprinted by permisison of Methuen & Company, Ltd.

wit, a liberal culture, a readiness and brevity in reply and attack, combined with a nice delicacy and refinement of manner. It requires also an acquaintance with all history, and a store of instances, nor can it dispense with a knowledge of the statute-books and all civil law. I need hardly add, I presume, any remarks on mere delivery. This must be combined with appropriate movement of the body, gestures, looks, and modulation and variety of tone. How important this is in itself may be seen from the insignificant art of the actor and the procedure of the stage; for though all actors pay great attention to the due management of their features, voice, and gestures, it is a matter of common notoriety how few there are, or have been, whom we can watch without discomfort. One word I must add on memory, the treasure-house of all knowledge. Unless the orator calls in the aid of memory to retain the matter and the words with which thought and study have furnished him, all his other merits, however brilliant, we know will lose their effect. We may therefore well cease to wonder why it is that real orators are so few, seeing that eloquence depends on a combination of accomplishments, in each one of which it is no slight matter to achieve success; let us rather urge our children, and all others whose fame and reputation is dear to us, to realise the greatness of the task, and to believe that though they cannot attain to the goal of their ambition by the help of those rules, or teachers, or exercises which are in general use, there are certain others which will enable them to do so.

My own private opinion is, that no one can be a real orator in the full sense of the word unless he first acquires a knowledge of all the great subjects of human study; for a wide knowledge is needed to give a luxuriance and richness to language which, unless the speaker has thoroughly mastered his subject, suffers from what I may perhaps call a puerile vapidity of expression. Still I would not lay so great a burden on the orator, especially in our own country amid the urgent calls of the city-life of to-day, as to think that there is nothing of which they may enjoy the privilege of ignorance; although the very meaning of the word "orator," and the mere profession of eloquence, seems to imply a promise and undertaking to speak in good style, and with full know-ledge, on any subject which may be proposed. This I am very sure most men would consider a task of incalculable and infinite difficulty. The Greeks also, I know, rich as they were not only in native wit and acquired learning, but also in leisure and enthusiasm for study, made a certain division of the arts, and did not devote their efforts individually to even one department as a whole, but separated from the other provinces of speech that particular subdivision which is concerned with the public discussions of the law-courts and deliberative assemblies, and assigned this only to the orator. For these reasons I shall not in this present treatise include more than what has been, after careful inquiry and much discussion, allotted to this division of the art by the all but unanimous judgment of the highest authorities; and I shall not go back to the beggarly elements of the old-fashioned teaching which we received in our boyhood for any definite system of rules, . . .

*   *   *   *   *

. . . In the orator, however, we require the subtlety of the logician, the thoughts of the philosopher, the language almost of the poet, the memory of the lawyer, the voice of the tragedian, the gestures I may add of the consummate actor. This is the reason why nothing in the world is so rare as a perfect orator; for merits, which win applause if found singly, even in a moderate degree, in the professors of the several arts, cannot command approval for the orator, unless they are all present in the highest perfection.

▣ 5. Quintilian, Greatest of Roman Teachers

Adopting Cicero as the model of an orator and Cato's definition of an orator as "a good man skilled in speaking." Marcus Fabius Quintilian (c. 35 A.D.–c. 95) trained orators and compiled his educational ideas in the twelve-volume Institutes of Oratory. *As a practitioner Quintilian gained fame in his own day; as a theorist he has dazzled readers from the Renaissance to the present.*

In the following selections one can recognize the influence of Cicero in Quintilian's emphasis upon moral character, in his insistence that education be related to life, and in his stress on the need for a wellrounded education for the orator. But there is much more. Here is truly a perceptive teacher who, in his attention to readiness, motivation, individual differences, and his condemnation of corporal punishment, appears strikingly modern. As might be expected, without the benefits of modern psychology and scientific testing, Quintilian also advocated practices that we cannot today accept. Among them were his stress on the importance of memory as the first sign of ability and his urging the study of a foreign language before one's native tongue because the latter will be learned anyway. Unfortunately, in the centuries following, it was the more positive suggestions that were ignored.

The rediscovery of the Institutes *during the Renaissance was instrumental in providing the form of Latin-grammar secondary schooling for generations and in offering inspiration to countless reformers who to modern times continue to protest the isolation of the school from society and the failure of teachers to recognize the needs, interests, and abilities of their students.*

Rev. John Selby Watson (trans.), Quintilian's Institutes of Oratory *(London: George Bell and Sons, 1905), II, 402–05; I, 77–79, 13–14, 15, 25–28, 91–93.*

Since an orator, then, is a good man, and a good man cannot be conceived to exist without virtuous inclinations, and virtue, though it receives certain impulses from nature, requires notwithstanding to be brought to maturity by instruction, the orator must above all things study *morality*, and must obtain a thorough knowledge of all that is just and honourable, without which no one can either be a good man or an able speaker. 2. Unless, indeed, we feel inclined to adopt the opinion of those who think that the moral character is formed by nature, and is not at all influenced by discipline; and who forsooth, acknowledge that manual operations, and even the meanest of them, cannot be acquired without the aid of teachers, but say that we possess virtue, (than which nothing has been given to man that raises him nearer to the immortal gods,) unsought and without labour, simply because we are born what we are. 3. But will that man be temperate, who does not know even what temperance is? Or will that man be possessed of fortitude, who has used no means to free his mind from the terrors of pain, death, and superstition? Or will that man be just, who has entered into no examination of what is equitable and good, and who has never ascertained from any dissertation of the least learning, the principles either of the laws which are by nature prescribed to all men, or of those which are instituted among particular people and nations? Of how little consequence do they think all this, to whom it appears so easy! 4. But I shall say no more on this point, on which I think that no man, who *has tasted of learning*, as they say, *with but the slightest touch of his lips*, will entertain the least doubt.

I pass on to my second proposition, that no man will ever be thoroughly accomplished in eloquence, who has not gained a deep insight into the impulses of human nature, and formed his moral character on the precepts of others and on his own reflection. 5. It is not without reason that Lucius Crassus, in the third book *De Oratore*, asserts that everything that can come under discussion respecting equity, justice, truth, goodness, and whatever is of an opposite nature, are the proper concerns of the orator; and that the philosophers, when they inculcate those virtues with the force of eloquence, use the arms of the orator and not their own. Yet he admits that the knowledge of these subjects must now be sought from philosophy, because philosophy, apparently, seems to him to be more fully in possession of them. 6. Hence also it is that Cicero remarks, in many passages both of his books and of his letters, that the power of eloquence is to be derived from the deepest sources of wisdom, and that accordingly the same persons were for a considerable time the teachers at once of eloquence and of morality.

This exhortation of mine, however, is not designed to intimate that I should wish the orator to be a philosopher, since no other mode of life has withdrawn itself further from the duties of civil society, and all that

concerns the orator. 7. Which of the philosophers, indeed, ever frequented courts of justice, or distinguished himself in public assemblies?
Which of them ever engaged even in the management of political
affairs, on which most of them have given such earnest precepts? But
I should desire the orator, whom I am trying to form, to be a kind of
Roman wise man, who may prove himself a true statesman, not by
discussions in retirement, but by personal experience and exertions in
public life. 8. But because the pursuits of philosophy have been deserted
by those who have devoted their minds to eloquence, and because they
no longer display themselves in their proper field of action and in the
open light of the forum, but have retreated, at first into the porticoes
and gymnasia, and since into the assemblies of the schools, the orator
must seek that which is necessary for him, and which is not taught by
the masters of eloquence, among those with whom it has remained, by
perusing with the most diligent application the authors that give
instruction in virtue, that his life may be in conformity with a thorough
knowledge of divine and human things; and how much more important
and noble would these things appear, if those were to teach them who
could discourse on them with the highest eloquence? 9. Would that
there may some day come a time, when some orator, perfect as we wish
him to be, may vindicate to himself the study of philosophy, (which has
been rendered odious as well by the arrogant assumptions, as by the
vices, of those who have disgraced its excellent nature,) and, by a
reconquest as it were, annex it again to the domain of eloquence!

*   *   *   *   *

1. These remarks I have made, as briefly as I could, upon grammar,
not so as to examine and speak of every thing, which would be an
infinite task, but merely of the most essential points. I shall now add
some concise observations on the other departments of study, in which I
think that boys should be initiated before they are committed to the
teacher of rhetoric, in order that that circle of instruction, which the
Greeks call ἐγκύκλιος παιδεία, may be completed.

2. For about the same age the study of other accomplishments must
be commenced; concerning which, as they are themselves arts, and
cannot be complete without the art of oratory, but are nevertheless
insufficient of themselves to form an orator, it is made a question
whether they are necessary to this art. 3. Of what service is it, say some
people, for pleading a cause, or pronouncing a legal opinion, to know
how equilateral triangles may be erected upon a given line? Or how
will he, who has marked the sounds of the lyre by their names and
intervals, defend an accused person, or direct consultations, the
better on that account? 4. They may perhaps reckon, also, many
speakers, effective in every way in the forum, who have never attended a

geometrician, and who know nothing of musicians except by the common pleasure of listening to them. To these observers I answer in the first place (what Cicero also frequently remarks in his book addressed to Brutus), that it is not such an orator as is or has been, that is to be formed by us, but that we have conceived in our mind an idea of *the perfect orator,* an orator deficient in no point whatever. 5. For when the philosophers would form their *wise man,* who is to be perfect in every respect, and, as they say, a kind of mortal god, they not only believe that he should be instructed, in a general knowledge of divine and human things, but conduct him through a course of questions which are certainly little, if you consider them merely in themselves, (as, sometimes, through studied subtleties of argument,) not because questions about *horns* or *crocodiles* can form a wise man, but because a wise man ought never to be in error even in the least matters. 6. In like manner, it is not the geometrician, or the musician, or the other studies which I shall add to theirs, that will make the perfect orator (who ought to be a wise man), yet these accomplishments will contribute to his perfection. We see an antidote, for example, and other medicines to heal diseases and wounds, compounded of many and sometimes opposite ingredients, from the various qualities of which results that single compound, which resembles none of them, yet takes its peculiar virtues from them all; 7. mute insects, too, compose the exquisite flavour of honey, inimitable by human reason, of various sorts of flowers and juices; and shall we wonder that eloquence, than which the providence of the gods has given nothing more excellent to men, requires the aid of many arts, which, even though they may not appear, or put themselves forward, in the course of a speech, yet contribute to it a secret power, and are silently felt? 8. "People have been eloquent," some one may say, "without these arts;" but I want a perfect orator. "They contribute little assistance," another may observe; but that, to which even little shall be wanting, will not be a whole; and it will be agreed that perfection is a whole, of which though the hope may be on a distant height as it were, yet it is for us to suggest every means of attaining it, that something more, at least, may thus be done. But why should our courage fail us? Nature does not forbid the formation of a perfect orator; and it is disgraceful to despair of what is possible.

* * * * *

20. Yet I am not so unacquainted with differences of age, as to think that we should urge those of tender years severely, or exact a full complement of work from them: for it will be necessary, above all things, to take care lest the child should conceive a dislike to the application which he cannot yet love and continue to dread the bitterness which he has once tasted even beyond the years of infancy. Let his

instruction be an amusement to him; let him be questioned, and praised; and let him never feel pleased that he does not know a thing; and sometimes, if he is unwilling to learn, let another be taught before him, of whom he may be envious. Let him strive for victory now and then, and generally suppose that he gains it and let his powers be called forth by rewards . . . .

* * * * *

For that at least, which I see practised in regard to most children, by no means pleases me, namely they learn the names and order of the letters before they learn their shapes. 25. This method hinders their recognition of them, as, while they follow their memory that takes the lead, they do not fix their attention on the forms of the letters. This is the reason why teachers, even when they appear to have fixed them sufficiently in the minds of children, in the straight order in which they are usually first written, make them go over them again the contrary way, and confuse them by variously changing the arrangement, until their pupils know them by their shape, not by their place. It will be best for children, therefore, to be taught the appearances and names of the letters at once, as they are taught those of men. 26. But that which is hurtful with regard to letters, will be no impediment with regard to syllables. I do not disapprove, however, the practice, which is well known, of giving children, for the sake of stimulating them to learn, ivory figures of letters to play with or whatever else can be invented, in which that infantine age may take delight, and which may be pleasing to handle, look at, or name.

* * * * *

1. Let him that is skilled in teaching, ascertain first of all, when a boy is entrusted to him, his ability and disposition. The chief symptom of ability in children is memory, of which the excellence is twofold, to receive with ease and retain with fidelity. The next symptom is imitation; for that is an indication of a teachable disposition, but with this provision, that it express merely what it is taught, and not a person's manner or walk, for instance, or whatever may be remarkable for deformity. 2. The boy who shall make it his aim to raise a laugh by his love of mimicry, will afford me no hope of good capacity; for he who is possessed of great talent will be well disposed; else I should think it not at all worse to be of a dull, than of a bad, disposition; but he who is honourably inclined will be very different from the stupid or idle. 3. Such a pupil as I would have, will easily learn what is taught him, and will ask questions about some things, but will still rather follow than run on before. That precocious sort of talent scarcely ever comes to good fruit. 4. Such are those who do little things easily, and, impelled by impudence, show at once all that they can accomplish in such

matters. But they succeed only in what is ready to their hand; they string words together, uttering them with an intrepid countenance, not in the least discouraged by bashfulness; and do little, but do it readily. 5. There is no real power behind, or any that rests on deeply fixed roots; but they are like seeds which have been scattered on the surface of the ground and shoot up prematurely, and like grass that resembles corn, and grows yellow, with empty ears, before the time of harvest. Their efforts give pleasure, as compared with their years; but their progress comes to a stand, and our wonder diminishes.

6. When a tutor has observed these indications, let him next consider how the mind of his pupil is to be managed. Some boys are indolent, unless you stimulate them; some are indignant at being commanded; fear restrains some, and unnerves others; continued labour forms some; with others, hasty efforts succeed better. 7. Let the boy be given to me whom praise stimulates, whom honour delights, who weeps when he is unsuccessful. His powers must be cultivated under the influence of ambition; reproach will sting him to the quick; honour will incite him; and in such a boy I shall never be apprehensive of indifference.

8. Yet some relaxation is to be allowed to all; not only because there is nothing that can bear perpetual labour, (and even those things that are without sense and life are unbent by alternate rest, as it were, in order that they may preserve their vigour,) but because application to learning depends on the will, which cannot be forced. 9. Boys, accordingly, when reinvigorated and refreshed, bring more sprightliness to their learning, and a more determined spirit, which for the most part spurns compulsion. 10. Nor will play in boys displease me; it is also a sign of vivacity; and I cannot expect that he who is always dull and spiritless will be of an eager disposition in his studies when he is indifferent even to that excitement which is natural to his age. 11. There must however be bounds set to relaxation, lest the refusal of it beget an aversion to study, or too much indulgence in it a habit of idleness. There are some kinds of amusement, too, not unserviceable for sharpening the wits of boys, as when they contend with each other by proposing all sorts of questions in turn. 12. In their plays, also, their moral dispositions show themselves more plainly, supposing that there is no age so tender that it may not readily learn what is right and wrong; and the tender age may best be formed at a time when it is ignorant of dissimulation, and most willingly submits to instructors; for you may break, sooner than mend, that which has hardened into deformity. 13. A child is as early as possible, therefore, to be admonished that he must do nothing too eagerly, nothing dishonestly, nothing without self-control; and we must always keep in mind the maxim of Virgil, *Adeo in teneris consuescere multum est,* "of so much importance is the acquirement of habit in the young."

14. But that boys should suffer corporal punishment, though it be a received custom, and Chrysippus makes no objection to it, I by no means approve; first, because it is a disgrace, and a punishment for slaves, and in reality (as will be evident if you imagine the age changed) an affront; secondly, because, if a boy's disposition be so abject as not to be amended by reproof, he will be hardened, like the worst of slaves, even to stripes; and lastly, because, if one who regularly exacts his tasks be with him, there will not be the least need of any such chastisement. 15. At present, the negligence of *paedagogi* seems to be made amends for in such a way that boys are not obliged to do what is right, but are punished whenever they have not done it. Besides, after you have coerced a boy with stripes, how will you treat him when he becomes a young man, to whom such terror cannot be held out, and by whom more difficult studies must be pursued? 16. Add to these considerations, that many things unpleasant to be mentioned, and likely afterwards to cause shame, often happen to boys while being whipped, under the influence of pain or fear; and such shame enervates and depresses the mind, and makes them shun people's sight and feel a constant uneasiness. 17. If, moreover, there has been too little care in choosing governors and tutors of reputable character, I am ashamed to say how scandalously unworthy men may abuse their privilege of punishing, and what opportunity also the terror of the unhappy children may sometimes afford to others. I will not dwell upon this point; what is already understood is more than enough. It will be sufficient therefore to intimate, that no man should be allowed too much authority over an age so weak and so unable to resist ill-treatment.

*   *   *   *   *

1. It is a common question whether, supposing all these things are to be learned, they can all be taught and acquired at the same time; for some deny that this is possible, as the mind must be confused and wearied by so many studies of different tendency for which neither the understanding, nor the body, nor time itself, can suffice; and even though mature age may endure such labour, yet that of childhood ought not to be thus burdened.

2. But these reasoners do not understand how great the power of the human mind is; that mind which is so busy and active, and which directs its attention, so to speak, to every quarter, so that it cannot even confine itself to do only one thing, but bestows its force upon several, not merely in the same day, but at the same moment. 3. Do not players on the harp, for example, exert their memory, and attend to the sound of their voice, and the various inflexions of it, while, at the same time, they strike part of the strings with their right hand, and pull, stop, or let loose others with their left, while not even their foot is idle, but beats time to their playing, all these acts being done simultaneously?

4. Do not we advocates, when surprised by a sudden necessity to plead, say one thing while we are thinking of what is to follow, and while, at the very same moment, the invention of arguments, the choice of words, the arrangement of matter, gesture, delivery, look, and attitude, are necessarily objects of our attention? If all these considerations, of so varied a nature, are forced, as by a single effort, before our mental vision, why may we not divide the hours of the day among different kinds of study, especially as variety itself refreshes and recruits the mind, while, on the contrary, nothing is more annoying than to continue at one uniform labour? Accordingly writing is relieved by reading, and the tedium of reading itself is relieved by changes of subject. 5. However many things we may have done, we are yet to a certain degree fresh for that which we are going to begin. Who, on the contrary, would not be stupified, if he were to listen to the same teacher of any art, whatever it might be, through the whole day? But by change a person will be recruited; as is the case with respect to food, by varieties of which the stomach is re-invigorated, and is fed with several sorts less unsatisfactorily than with one. Or let those objectors tell me what other mode there is of learning. Ought we to attend to the teacher of grammar only, and then to the teacher of geometry only, and cease to think, during the second course, of what we learned in the first? Should we then transfer ourselves to the musician, our previous studies being still allowed to escape us? Or while we are studying Latin, ought we to pay no attention to Greek? Or, to make an end of my questions at once, ought we to do nothing but what comes last before us? 7. Why, then, do we not give similar counsel to husbandmen, that they should not cultivate at the same time their fields and their vineyards, their olives and other trees, and that they should not bestow attention at once on their meadows, their cattle, their gardens, and their bee-hives? Why do we ourselves devote some portion of our time to our public business, some to the wants of our friends, some to our domestic accounts, some to the care of our persons, and some to our pleasures, any one of which occupations would weary us, if we pursued it without intermission? So much more easy is it to do many things one after the other, than to do one thing for a long time.

6. Roman Education Becomes Remote from Life

In a selection from "A Dialogue on Oratory" Tacitus provides a revealing comparison between the standards of oratorical training honored

during the Republic and the changes wrought by the schools of the rhetoricians,
which by 75 A.D. the author already found "remote from all reality." It is
apparent that, even at this early date, Quintilian's insistence that institutionalized
oratorical training must provide a broad curriculum and be related to life
was not mirrored in the schools of Rome. In a sense, the schools of Imperial
Rome, like its citizens, were turning from involvement in the activities of the
Forum and Senate to "a liking for actors and a passion for gladiators and horses."

. . . Who does not know that eloquence and all other arts have declined from their ancient glory, not from dearth of men, but from the indolence of the young, the carelessness of parents, the ignorance of teachers, and neglect of the old discipline? The evils which first began in Rome soon spread through Italy, and are now diffusing themselves into the provinces. But your provincial affairs are best known to yourselves. I shall speak of Rome, and of those native and home-bred vices which take hold of us as soon as we are born, and multiply with every stage of life, when I have first said a few words on the strict discipline of our ancestors in the education and training of children. Every citizen's son, the child of a chaste mother, was from the beginning reared, not in the chamber of a purchased nurse, but in that mother's bosom and embrace, and it was her special glory to study her home and devote herself to her children. It was usual to select an elderly kinswoman of approved and esteemed character to have the entire charge of all the children of the household. In her presence it was the last offence to utter an unseemly word or to do a disgraceful act. With scrupulous piety and modesty she regulated not only the boy's studies and occupations, but even his recreations and games. Thus it was, as tradition says, that the mothers of the Gracchi, of Cæsar, of Augustus, Cornelia, Aurelia, Atia, directed their children's education and reared the greatest of sons. The strictness of the discipline tended to form in each case a pure and virtuous nature which no vices could warp, and which would at once with the whole heart seize on every noble lesson. Whatever its bias, whether to the soldier's or the lawyer's art, or to the study of eloquence, it would make that its sole aim, and imbibe it in its fullness.

But in our day we entrust the infant to a little Greek servant-girl who is attended by one or two, commonly the worst of all the slaves, creatures utterly unfit for any important work. Their stories and their prejudices from the very first fill the child's tender and uninstructed mind. No one in the whole house cares what he says or does before his infant master. Even parents themselves familiarise their little ones, not

John Alfred Church and William Jackson Brodribb (trans.), The Agricola and Germany of Tacitus *(London and New York: Macmillan and Co., 1893), pp. 179–80, 182–89.*

with virtue and modesty, but with jesting and glib talk, which lead on by degrees to shamelessness and to contempt for themselves as well as for others. Really I think that the characteristic and peculiar vices of this city, a liking for actors and a passion for gladiators and horses, are all but conceived in the mother's womb. When these occupy and possess the mind, how little room has it left for worthy attainments! Few indeed are to be found who talk of any other subjects in their homes, and whenever we enter a class-room, what else is the conversation of the youths. Even with the teachers, these are the more frequent topics of talk with their scholars. In fact, they draw pupils, not by strictness of discipline or by giving proof of ability, but by assiduous court and cunning tricks of flattery.

*   *   *   *   *

. . . The strength and power of oratory, unlike all other arts, is not confined within narrow and straitened limits, but the orator is he who can speak on every question with grace, elegance, and persuasiveness, suitably to the dignity of his subject, the requirements of the occasion, and the taste of his audience.

Such was the conviction of the ancients, and to produce this result they were aware that it was necessary not only to declaim in the schools of rhetoricians, or to exercise the tongue and the voice in fictitious controversies quite remote from reality, but also to imbue the mind with those studies which treat of good and evil, of honour and dishonour of right and wrong. All this, indeed, is the subject-matter of the orator's speeches. Equity in the lawcourt, honour in the council-chamber, are our usual topics of discussion. Still, these often pass into each other, and no one can speak on them with fulness, variety, and elegance but he who has studied human nature, the power of virtue, the depravity of vice, and the conception of those things which can be classed neither among virtues nor vices. These are the sources whence flows the greater ease with which he who knows what anger is, rouses or soothes the anger of a judge, the readier power with which he moves to pity who knows what pity is, and what emotions of the soul excite it. An orator practised in such arts and exercises, whether he has to address the angry, the biassed, the envious, the sorrowful, or the trembling, will understand different mental conditions, apply his skill, adapt his style, and have every instrument of his craft in readiness, or in reserve for every occasion. Some there are whose assent is more secured by an incisive and terse style, in which each inference is rapidly drawn. With such, it will be an advantage to have studied logic. Others are more attracted by a diffuse and smoothly flowing speech, appealing to the common sentiments of humanity. To impress such we must borrow from the Peripatetics commonplaces suited and ready prepared for every discussion.

The Academy will give us combativeness, Plato, sublimity, Xenophon, sweetness. Nor will it be unseemly in an orator to adopt even certain exclamations of honest emotion, from Epicurus and Metrodorus, and to use them as occasion requires. It is not a philosopher after the Stoic school whom we are forming, but one who ought to imbibe thoroughly some studies, and to have a taste of all. Accordingly, knowledge of the civil law was included in the training of the ancient orators, and they also imbued their minds with grammar, music, and geometry. In truth, in very many, I may say in all cases, acquaintance with law is desirable, and in several this last-mentioned knowledge is a necessity.

Let no one reply that it is enough for us to learn, as occasion requires, some single and detached subject. In the first place we use our own property in one way, a loan in another, and there is evidently a wide difference between possessing what one exhibits and borrowing it. Next, the very knowledge of many subjects sits gracefully on us, even when we are otherwise engaged, and makes itself visible and conspicuous where you would least expect it. Even the average citizen, and not only the learned and critical hearer, perceives it, and forthwith showers his praises in the acknowledgment that the man has been a genuine student, has gone through every branch of eloquence, and is, in short, an orator. And I maintain that the only orator is, and ever has been, one who, like a soldier equipped at all points going to the battle-field, enters the forum armed with every learned accomplishment.

All this is so neglected by the speakers of our time that we detect in their pleadings the style of every-day conversation, and unseemly and shameful deficiencies. They are ignorant of the laws, they do not understand the senate's decrees, they actually scoff at the civil law, while they quite dread the study of philosophy, and the opinions of the learned; and eloquence, banished, so to say, from her proper realm, is dragged down by them into utter poverty of thought and constrained periods. Thus she who, once mistress of all the arts, held sway with a glorious retinue over our souls, now clipped and shorn, without state, without honour, I had almost said without her freedom, is studied as one of the meanest handicrafts. This then I believe to be the first and chief cause of so marked a falling off among us from the eloquence of the old orators. If witnesses are wanted, whom shall I name in preference to Demosthenes among the Greeks, who is said by tradition to have been a most attentive hearer of Plato? Cicero too tells us, I think, in these very words, that whatever he had achieved in eloquence he had gained, not from rhetoricians, but in the walks of the Academy. There are other causes, some of them great and important, which it is for you in fairness to explain, as I have now done my part, and, after my usual way, have offended pretty many persons who, if they happen to hear all this, will, I am sure, say that, in praising an acquaintance with law and philosophy as a necessity for an orator, I have been applauding my own follies.

It was accordingly usual with our ancestors, when a lad was being prepared for public speaking, as soon as he was fully trained by home discipline, and his mind was stored with culture, to have him taken by his father, or his relatives to the orator who held the highest rank in the state. The boy used to accompany and attend him, and be present at all his speeches, alike in the law-court and the assembly, and thus he picked up the art of repartee, and became habituated to the strife of words, and indeed, I may almost say, learnt how to fight in battle. Thereby young men acquired from the first great experience and confidence, and a very large stock of discrimination, for they were studying in broad daylight, in the very thick of the conflict, where no one can say anything foolish or self-contradictory without its being refuted by the judge, or ridiculed by the opponent, or, last of all, repudiated by the very counsel with him. Thus from the beginning they were imbued with true and genuine eloquence, and, although they attached themselves to one pleader, still they became acquainted with all advocates of their own standing in a multitude of cases before the courts. They had too abundant experience of the popular ear in all its greatest varieties, and with this they could easily ascertain what was liked or disapproved in each speaker. Thus they were not in want of a teacher of the very best and choicest kind, who could show them eloquence in her true features, not in a mere resemblance; nor did they lack opponents and rivals, who fought with actual steel, not with a wooden sword, and the audience too was always crowded, always changing, made up of unfriendly as well as of admiring critics, so that neither success nor failure could be disguised. You know, of course, that eloquence wins its great and enduring fame quite as much from the benches of our opponents as from those of our friends; nay, more, its rise from that quarter is steadier, and its growth surer. Undoubtedly it was under such teachers that the youth of whom I am speaking, the disciple of orators, the listener in the forum, the student in the law-courts, was trained and practised by the experiences of others. The laws he learnt by daily hearing; the faces of the judges were familiar to him; the ways of popular assemblies were continually before his eyes; he had frequent experience of the ear of the people, and whether he undertook a prosecution or a defence, he was at once singly and alone equal to any case. We still read with admiration the speeches in which Lucius Crassus in his nineteenth, Cæsar and Asinius Pollio in their twenty-first year, Calvus, when very little older, denounced, respectively, Carbo, Dolabella, Cato, and Vatinius.

But in these days we have our youths taken to the professors' theatre, the rhetoricians, as we call them. The class made its appearance a little

before Cicero's time, and was not liked by our ancestors, as is evident
from the fact that, when Crassus and Domitius were censors, they were
ordered, as Cicero says, to close "the school of impudence." However,
as I was just saying, the boys are taken to schools in which it is hard to
tell whether the place itself, or their fellow-scholars, or the character of
their studies, do their minds most harm. As for the place, there is no
such thing as reverence, for no one enters it who is not as ignorant as
the rest. As for the scholars, there can be no improvement, when boys
and striplings with equal assurance address, and are addressed by,
other boys and striplings. As for the mental exercises themselves, they
are the reverse of beneficial. Two kinds of subject-matter are dealt with
before the rhetoricians, the persuasive and the controversial. The persuasive, as being comparatively easy and requiring less skill, is given to
boys. The controversial is assigned to riper scholars, and, good heavens!
what strange and astonishing productions are the result! It comes to
pass that subjects remote from all reality are actually used for declamation. Thus the reward of a tyrannicide, or the choice of an outraged
maiden, or a remedy for a pestilence, or a mother's incest, anything,
in short, daily discussed in our schools, never, or but very rarely in the
courts, is dwelt on in grand language.

▣ 7. Justinian's *Body of the Civil Law*

*Two acts of the Eastern emperor Justianian (c. 527–565) were of
great significance in the history of Western culture. In 529 the Christian emperor
closed forever the pagan University of Athens. With this decree the doom of the
thousand-year Hellenistic Era was finally sealed in the city of its birth and
greatest glory. When this same emperor issued the* Body of the Civil Law, *he
presented Europe with one of Rome's most enduring gifts. Justianian's short-lived
reconquest of Rome established the* Body of the Civil Law *in Italy, where it
continued to be taught, particularly in the north, and where it furnished the basis
for the intellectual activity that led to the establishment of the University of
Bologna late in the eleventh century.*

The Body of the Civil Law *reflects the passion so predominant among the
later Romans for organizing and synthesizing bodies of knowledge. It also
illustrates the dominant role in education played by the imperial government, for
it was designed to reform legal education and provide the basis for the curriculum
at the three public schools of law at Constantinople, Beirut, and Rome. The
four parts of the* Body of the Civil Law *include the* Institutes, *a basic legal
textbook; the* Code, *a collection of imperial ordinances; the* Digest, *a collection*

of legal opinions of famous Roman jurists; and the Novels, *imperial ordinances issued after the publication of the* Code. *The following selection is the introduction to the* Institutes.

IN THE NAME OF OUR LORD JESUS CHRIST.

THE EMPEROR CÆSAR FLAVIUS JUSTINIANUS, VANQUISHER OF THE ALAMANI, GOTHS, FRANCS, GERMANS, ANTES, ALANI, VANDALS, AFRICANS, PIOUS, HAPPY, GLORIOUS, TRIUMPHANT CONQUEROR, EVER AUGUST, TO THE YOUTH DESIROUS OF STUDYING THE LAW, GREETING.

The imperial majesty should be not only made glorious by arms, but also strengthened by laws, that, alike in time of peace and in time of war, the state may be well governed, and that the emperor may not only be victorious in the field of battle, but also may by every legal means repel the iniquities of men who abuse the laws, and may at once religiously uphold justice and triumph over his conquered enemies.

1. By our incessant labours and great care, with the blessing of God, we have attained this double end. The barbarian nations reduced under our yoke know our efforts in war; to which also Africa and very many other provinces bear witness, which, after so long an interval, have been restored to the dominion of Rome and our empire, by our victories gained through the favour of heaven. All nations moreover are governed by laws which we have either promulgated or arranged.

2. When we had arranged and brought into perfect harmony the hitherto confused mass of imperial constitutions, we then extended our care to the endless volumes of ancient law; and, sailing as it were across the mid ocean, have now completed, through the favour of heaven, a work we once despaired of.

3. When by the blessing of God this task was accomplished, we summoned the most eminent Tribonian, master and ex-quæstor of our palace, together with the illustrious Theophilus and Dorotheus, professors of law, all of whom have on many occasions proved to us their ability, legal knowledge, and obedience to our orders; and we specially charged them to compose, under our authority and advice, Institutes, so that you may no more learn the first elements of law from old and erroneous sources, but apprehend them by the clear light of imperial wisdom; and that your minds and ears may receive nothing that is useless or misplaced, but only what obtains in actual practice. So that, whereas, formerly, the foremost among you could scarcely, after four years' study, read the imperial constitutions, you may now commence your studies by reading them, you who have been thought worthy of

Thomas Collett Sanders (trans.), The Institutes of Justinian *(London: Longmans, Green and Co., 1869),* I, 73–75.

an honour and a happiness so great as that the first and last lessons in the knowledge of the law should issue for you from the mouth of the emperor.

4. When therefore, by the assistance of the same eminent person Tribonian and that of other illustrious and learned men, we had compiled the fifty books, called Digests or Pandects, in which is collected the whole ancient law, we directed that these Institutes should be divided into four books, which might serve as the first elements of the whole science of law.

5. In these books a brief exposition is given of the ancient laws, and of those also, which, overshadowed by disuse, have been again brought to light by our imperial authority.

6. These four books of Institutes thus compiled, from all the Institutes left us by the ancients, and chiefly from the commentaries of our Gaius, both from his Institutes and his Journal, and also from many other commentaries, were presented to us by the three learned men we have above named. We read and examined them, and have accorded to them all the force of our constitutions.

7. Receive, therefore, with eagerness, and study with cheerful diligence, these our laws, and show yourselves persons of such learning that you may conceive the flattering hope of yourselves being able, when your course of legal study is completed, to govern our empire in the different portions that may be entrusted to your care.

Given at Constantinople on the eleventh day of the calends of December, in the third consulate of the Emperor Justinian, ever August.

III

Europe and Its Education Become Christian

A popular view of the fall of the Roman Empire depicts the barbarian invaders and Christianity as mutually responsible for the destruction of the thousand-year classical civilization. Of course, this is a gross oversimplification. In the late years of the Empire, Rome was decaying from within while she faced destruction from without. The success of the Christian missionaries was due in no small part to their offer of new loyalties and a new purpose in life to fill the vacuum created by the demise of Roman institutions, Roman patriotism, and Roman gods. Often in a conversion experience, the acceptance of the new is accomplished by a rejection of much of the old. Some of the Church fathers, including St. Jerome and St. Augustine, were themselves students of classical literature and philosophy who later were convinced that the true purpose of life was to be found in the realm of faith in God rather than the mind and works of man. (1)

Those who sought to construct a Christian society were no less aware of the importance of education than were the earlier pagan Greeks and Romans. Elements of the old education that could help foster faith in God and loyalty to the Church were welcomed in the new schema. However, Church leaders disagreed about just which elements were to be accepted. The Eastern fathers tended to be more receptive to the blending of the Hellenistic ideal of the well-balanced individual with the moral teachings of Christianity. But in the West much of Greco-Roman learning was suspect for its emphasis upon the desires of the body at the expense of the salvation of the soul. Aristotelian science, Greek medicine, architecture, materialistic philosophy, and other studies that laid stress on glorifying man's life on earth and the power of human intellect were rejected by the Western Church, seeking through faith to save man's soul for life after death. On the other hand, history, foreign languages, shorthand and the subjects of the trivium (grammar, rhetoric, logic) and quadrivium (arithmetic, geometry, astronomy, music) could be of service to the Church and eventually were accepted into the Christian curriculum. Aspects of Plato's idealistic philosophy found a welcome home in the Church and were incorporated into its doctrine. (2)

It is interesting that the Church's first significant educational endeavor was directed toward adults. During the early years of the Empire it was found necessary to prepare converts for baptism by presenting them with a two- to three-year catechumenal education. This school was to play an important role in Christian education for several centuries, reaching its height in the fifth century and then gradually disappearing as infant baptism became predominant in Europe. (3) Beginning in the fourth century various Church councils expressed concern for the education of Christian youth and decreed that local church authorities assume responsibility for the task. The response to these decrees varied. During the Early Middle Ages (sixth to eleventh centuries), parish schools and municipal schools continued as educational agencies in the Italian towns. However, throughout most of Western Europe the cities, which had been the vital links of the Roman Empire, crumbled before the Germanic invasions. With the demise of the urban centers, the schools they supported fell into decay. Europe in these centuries is often described as rural, feudal, and chaotic. The years were marked by constant warfare among petty feudal lords and an almost continuous stream of invaders and plunderers—Germanic tribes, Northmen, Arabs. Only the Church knew unity; only the Church was capable of establishing a degree of order. It was inevitable that the Church would provide the great stimulus for what little formal education continued to exist. It is not surprising that the most significant educational institution of this period was the monastery, ecclesiastical and rural.

Under St. Benedict of Nursia (c. 480–c. 543) monasticism lost its extreme emphasis on solitary contemplation and mortification of the body for the sake of the soul's salvation. At Monte Cassino Benedict established an order that employed asceticism in a manner that stressed moderation and utilized industry as well as prayer, humility, and obedience as means of religious devotion and service. (4) Spread throughout Europe by the ninth century, the Benedictine monasteries extended the varieties of labor practiced by the monks beyond the original agrarian and mechanical arts. The monk Cassiodorus (c. 490–c. 585) added the Scriptorium, a factory for the copying of books, to the monastery and thus enabled the Benedictines and other orders to preserve many of the great classical and theological works for future generations. The monasteries also established schools in which the seven liberal arts (trivium and quadrivium) and theological subjects were taught, initially to boys who were to become monks and later also to those whose futures lay in the secular (nonmonastic) clergy and outside the priesthood. (5)

With the Popes and the Church they governed representing the most powerful *force in Western Europe, education continued to be sponsored and directed for the most part by religious authority. When, for brief periods, strong secular leaders like Charlemagne and Alfred the Great arose to exert influence over large areas, they joined the Church in championing the extension and improvement of education. (6) Though education in the lands of these kings never sank to the low levels that existed before their ascendancy, the reappearance of warfare and the growth of feudalism, which followed their deaths, resulted in serious setbacks for the advancement of learning. Until the revival of commerce led to the rebirth of towns and cities and until strong rulers united and brought a measure of stability to large areas of Western Europe, the monasteries continued to offer the best oases for scholarly endeavor.*

1. Church Fathers Proclaim the Superiority of the Scriptures

St. Jerome (c. 345–420), one of the Latin Fathers of the Church, provides an excellent example of a dramatic religious experience with accompanying renunciation of classical studies in favor of the Holy Scriptures. During his early years among the splendors of Rome and later in the austere environment of the monastery he founded at Bethlehem, Jerome's labors included translations of the Bible, Biblical commentaries, books on scriptural subjects, works on Church history and controversy, and brilliant letters.

Many years ago for the sake of the kingdom of heaven I cut myself off from home, parents, sister, relations, and, what was harder, from the dainty food to which I had been used. But even when I was on my way to Jerusalem to fight the good fight there, I could not bring myself to forgo the library which with great care and labour I had got together at Rome. And so, miserable man that I was, I would fast, only to read Cicero afterwards. I would spend many nights in vigil, I would shed bitter tears called from my inmost heart by the remembrance of my past sins; and then I would take up Plautus again. Whenever I returned to my right senses and began to read the prophets, their language seemed harsh and barbarous. With my blind eyes I could not see the light: but I attributed the fault not to my eyes but to the sun.

While the old serpent was thus mocking me, about the middle of Lent a fever attacked my weakened body and spread through my inmost veins. It may sound incredible, but the ravages it wrought on my unhappy frame were so persistent that at last my bones scarcely held together.

Meantime preparations were made for my funeral: my whole body grew gradually cold, and life's vital warmth only lingered faintly in my poor throbbing breast. Suddenly I was caught up in the spirit and dragged before the Judge's judgment seat: and here the light was so dazzling, and the brightness shining from those who stood around so radiant, that I flung myself upon the ground and did not dare to look up. I was asked to state my condition and replied that I was a Christian. But He who presided said: "Thou liest; thou art a Ciceronian, not a Christian. 'For where thy treasure is there will thy heart be also.' " Straightway I became dumb, and amid the strokes of the whip—for He had ordered me to be scourged—I was even more bitterly tortured by the fire of conscience, considering with myself the verse: "In the grave who shall give thee thanks?" Yet for all that I began to cry out and to bewail myself, saying: "Have mercy upon me, O Lord, have mercy upon me": and even amid the noise of the lash my voice made itself heard. At last the bystanders fell at the knees of Him who presided, and prayed Him to pardon my youth and give me opportunity to repent of my error, on the understanding that the extreme of torture should be inflicted on me if ever I read again the works of Gentile authors. In the stress of that dread hour I should have been willing to make even larger promises, and taking oath I called upon His name: "O Lord, if ever again I possess worldly books or read them, I have denied thee."

After swearing this oath I was dismissed, and returned to the upper world. There to the surprise of all I opened my eyes again, and they were so drenched with tears, that my distress convinced even the incredulous. That this experience was no sleep nor idle dream, such as often mocks us, I call to witness the judgment seat before which I fell and the terrible verdict which I feared. May it never be my lot again to come before such a court as that! I profess that my shoulders were black and blue, and that I felt the bruises long after I awoke from my sleep. And I acknowledge that henceforth I read the books of God with a greater zeal than I had ever given before to the books of men.

St. Augustine's life (354–430) contains all the drama one could wish for in the story of the pagan-Christian struggle. Raised a Christian by his mother, he abandoned the religion to embrace the doctrines of Manichaeanism and the literature and philosophies of the classical world. Later, influenced by the teachings of St. Ambrose, Augustine returned to Christianity, renounced his past, rose to the position of Bishop of Hippo, and, like Jerome, turned his brilliant intellect to the cause of the Church. In the brief selection from On Christian Doctrine, *Augustine glorifies Holy Scripture as supreme among all writings.*

. . . But just as poor as the store of gold and silver and garments which the people of Israel brought with them out of Egypt was in comparison with the riches which they afterwards attained at Jerusalem, and which reached their height in the reign of King Solomon, so poor is all the useful knowledge which is gathered from the books of the heathen when compared with the knowledge of Holy Scripture. For whatever man may have learnt from other sources, if it is hurtful, it is there condemned; if it is useful, it is therein contained. And while every man may find there all that he has learnt of useful elsewhere, he will find there in much greater abundance things that are to be found nowhere else, but can be learnt only in the wonderful sublimity and wonderful simplicity of the Scriptures.

回 2. St. Augustine and the Bounds of Christian Scholarship

Throughout his writing St. Augustine insisted on the superiority of the Scriptures as the source of the highest knowledge and the authority of the Church to proscribe the character and extent of studies. However, he did acknowledge that, within certain bounds and under Church guidance, studies developed by pagans could be of value to the Christian. He accepted subjects of practical, day-to-day utility and studies that help the faithful understand Scripture and perceive Christian truths. In Augustine's discussion of the uses of philosophy and history, one can readily perceive his influence on the retardation of free inquiry and scholarship during the Middle Ages.

58. Accordingly, I think that it is well to warn studious and able young men, who fear God and are seeking for happiness of life, not to venture heedlessly upon the pursuit of the branches of learning that are in vogue beyond the pale of the Church of Christ, as if these could secure for them the happiness they seek; but soberly and carefully to discriminate among them. And if they find any of those which have been instituted by men varying by reason of the varying pleasure of their

J. F. Shaw (trans.), On Christian Doctrine *(Vol. IX of* The Works of Aurelius Augustine, Bishop of Hippo, *Marcus Dods, ed., 14 vols.; Edinburgh: T. and T. Clark, 1873), pp. 78–79.*

Shaw (trans.), On Christian Doctrine, *pp. 74–77, 63–65.*

founders, and unknown by reason of erroneous conjectures, especially if they involve entering into fellowship with devils by means of leagues and covenants about signs, let these be utterly rejected and held in detestation. Let the young men also withdraw their attention from such institutions of men as are unnecessary and luxurious. But for the sake of the necessities of this life we must not neglect the arrangements of men that enable us to carry on intercourse with those around us. I think, however, there is nothing useful in the other branches of learning that are found among the heathen, except information about objects, either past or present, that relate to the bodily senses, in which are included also the experiments and conclusions of the useful mechanical arts, except also the sciences of reasoning and of number. And in regard to all these we must hold by the maxim, "Not too much of anything;" especially in the case of those which, pertaining as they do to the senses, are subject to the relations of space and time.

59. What, then, some men have done in regard to all words and names found in Scripture, in the Hebrew, and Syriac, and Egyptian, and other tongues, taking up and interpreting separately such as were left in Scripture without interpretation; and what Eusebius has done in regard to the history of the past with a view to the questions arising in Scripture that require a knowledge of history for their solution;— what, I say, these men have done in regard to matters of this kind, making it unnecessary for the Christian to spend his strength on many subjects for the sake of a few items of knowledge, the same, I think, might be done in regard to other matters, if any competent man were willing in a spirit of benevolence to undertake the labour for the advantage of his brethren. In this way he might arrange in their several classes, and give an account of the unknown places, and animals, and plants, and trees, and stones, and metals, and other species of things that are mentioned in Scripture, taking up these only, and committing his account to writing. This might also be done in relation to numbers, so that the theory of those numbers, and those only, which are mentioned in Holy Scripture, might be explained and written down. And it may happen that some or all of these things have been done already (as I have found that many things I had no notion of have been worked out and committed to writing by good and learned Christians), but are either lost amid the crowds of the careless, or are kept out of sight by the envious. And I am not sure whether the same thing can be done in regard to the theory of reasoning; but it seems to me it cannot, because this runs like a system of nerves through the whole structure of Scripture, and on that account is of more service to the reader in disentangling and explaining ambiguous passages, of which I shall speak hereafter, than in ascertaining the meaning of unknown signs, the topic I am now discussing.

Chap. XL.—Whatever has been rightly said by the heathen, we must
appropriate to our uses.

60. Moreover, if those who are called philosophers, and especially
the Platonists, have said aught that is true and in harmony with our
faith, we are not only not to shrink from it, but to claim it for our own
use from those who have unlawful possession of it. For, as the Egyptians
had not only the idols and heavy burdens which the people of Israel
hated and fled from, but also vessels and ornaments of gold and silver,
and garments, which the same people when going out of Egypt appropriated to themselves, designing them for a better use, not doing this
on their own authority, but by the command of God, the Egyptians
themselves, in their ignorance, providing them with things which they
themselves were not making a good use of; in the same way all branches
of heathen learning have not only false and superstitious fancies and
heavy burdens of unnecessary toil, which every one of us, when going
out under the leadership of Christ from the fellowship of the heathen,
ought to abhor and avoid; but they contain also liberal instruction
which is better adapted to the use of the truth, and some most excellent
precepts of morality; and some truths in regard even to the worship of
the One God are found among them. Now these are, so to speak, their
gold and silver, which they did not create themselves, but dug out of
the mines of God's providence which are everywhere scattered abroad,
and are perversely and unlawfully prostituting to the worship of devils.
These, therefore, the Christian, when he separates himself in spirit from
the miserable fellowship of these men, ought to take away from them,
and to devote to their proper use in preaching the gospel. Their garments, also,—that is, human institutions such as are adapted to that
intercourse with men which is indispensable in this life,—we must take
and turn to a Christian use.

61. And what else have many good and faithful men among our
brethren done? Do we not see with what a quantity of gold and silver
and garments Cyprian, that most persuasive teacher and most blessed
martyr, was loaded when he came out of Egypt? How much Lactantius
brought with him! And Victorinus, and Optatus, and Hilary, not to
speak of living men! How much Greeks out of number have borrowed!
And prior to all these, that most faithful servant of God, Moses, had
done the same thing; for of him it is written that he was learned in all
the wisdom of the Egyptians. And to none of all these would heathen
superstition (especially in those times when, kicking against the yoke
of Christ, it was persecuting the Christians) have ever furnished
branches of knowledge it held useful, if it had suspected they were about
to turn them to the use of worshipping the One God, and thereby over-
turning the vain worship of idols. But they gave their gold and their

silver and their garments to the people of God, as they were going out of Egypt, not knowing how the things they gave would be turned to the service of Christ. For what was done at the time of the exodus was no doubt a type prefiguring what happens now. And this I say without prejudice to any other interpretation that may be as good, or better.

*   *   *   *   *

Chap. XXVI.—What human contrivances we are to adopt, and what we are to avoid.

For certain institutions of men are in a sort of way representations and likenesses of natural objects. And of these, such as have relation to fellowship with devils must, as has been said, be utterly rejected and held in detestation; those, on the other hand, which relate to the mutual intercourse of men, are, so far as they are not matters of luxury and superfluity, to be adopted, especially the forms of the letters which are necessary for reading, and the various languages as far as is required —a matter I have spoken of above. To this class also belong shorthand characters, those who are acquainted with which are called shorthand writers. All these are useful, and there is nothing unlawful in learning them, nor do they involve us in superstition, or enervate us by luxury, if they only occupy our minds so far as not to stand in the way of more important objects to which they ought to be subservient.

Chap. XXVII.—Some departments of knowledge, not of mere human invention, aid us in interpreting Scripture.

41. But, coming to the next point, we are not to reckon among human institutions those things which men have handed down to us, not as arrangements of their own, but as the result of investigation into the occurrences of the past, and into the arrangements of God's providence. And of these, some pertain to the bodily senses, some to the intellect. Those which are reached by the bodily senses we either believe on testimony, or perceive when they are pointed out to us, or infer from experience.

Chap. XXVIII.—To what extent history is an aid.

42. Anything, then, that we learn from history about the chronology of past times assists us very much in understanding the Scriptures, even if it be learnt without the pale of the Church as a matter of childish instruction. For we frequently seek information about a variety of matters by use of the Olympiads, and the names of the consuls; and ignorance of the consulship in which our Lord was born, and that in

which He suffered, has led some into the error of supposing that He was forty-six years of age when He suffered, that being the number of years He was told by the Jews the temple (which He took as a symbol of His body) was in building. Now we know on the authority of the evangelist that He was about thirty years of age when He was baptized; but the number of years He lived afterwards, although by putting His actions together we can make it out, yet that no shadow of doubt might arise from another source, can be ascertained more clearly and more certainly from a comparison of profane history with the gospel. It will still be evident, however, that it was not without a purpose it was said that the temple was forty and six years in building; so that, as this cannot be referred to our Lord's age, it may be referred to the more secret formation of the body which, for our sakes, the only-begotten Son of God, by whom all things were made, condescended to put on.

43. As to the utility of history, moreover, passing over the Greeks, what a great question our own Ambrose has set at rest! For, when the readers and admirers of Plato dared calumniously to assert that our Lord Jesus Christ learnt all those sayings of His, which they are compelled to admire and praise, from the books of Plato—because (they urged) it cannot be denied that Plato lived long before the coming of our Lord!—did not the illustrious bishop, when by his investigations into profane history he had discovered that Plato made a journey into Egypt at the time when Jeremiah the prophet was there, show that it is much more likely that Plato was through Jeremiah's means initiated into our literature, so as to be able to teach and write those views of his which are so justly praised? For not even Pythagoras himself, from whose successors these men assert Plato learnt theology, lived at a date prior to the books of that Hebrew race, among whom the worship of one God sprang up, and of whom as concerning the flesh our Lord came. And thus, when we reflect upon the dates, it becomes much more probable that those philosophers learnt whatever they said that was good and true from our literature, than that the Lord Jesus Christ learnt from the writings of Plato,—a thing which it is the height of folly to believe.

44. And even when in the course of an historical narrative former institutions of men are described, the history itself is not to be reckoned among human institutions; because things that are past and gone and cannot be undone are to be reckoned as belonging to the course of time, of which God is the author and governor. For it is one thing to tell what has been done, another to show what ought to be done. History narrates what has been done, faithfully and with advantage; but the books of the haruspices, and all writings of the same kind, aim at teaching what ought to be done or observed, using the boldness of an adviser, not the fidelity of a narrator.

▣ 3. Catechumenal Training

*The two-to-three-year period between the time the Christian con-
vert presented himself for membership in the Church and his baptism was spent
in schooling in the faith. The following excerpt from Joseph Bingham's* The
Antiquities of the Christian Church, *first published in 1845, describes the
purpose and character of catechumenal education. Note that the author also
managed to employ history for a bit of propagandizing for the Protestant position
of encouraging Bible reading in the vernacular.*

. . . a longer time was generally thought necessary to discipline and
train men up gradually for baptism; partly for the reason already
mentioned, that some just experiment might be made of their conversation during that time; and partly to instruct them by degrees,
first in the more common principles of religion, to wean them from their
former errors, and then in the more recondite and mysterious articles
of the Christian faith: upon which account they usually began their
discourses with the doctrine of repentance and remission of sins, and
the necessity of good works, and the nature and use of baptism, by
which the catechumens were taught, how they were to renounce the
devil and his works, and enter into a new covenant with God. Then
followed the explication of the several articles of the Creed, to which
some added the nature and immortality of the soul, and an account of
the canonical books of Scripture; which is the substance and method
of St. Cyril's eighteen famous discourses to the catechumens. The
author of the Apostolical Constitutions prescribes these several heads
of instruction: Let the catechumen be taught before baptism the
knowledge of the Father unbegotten, the knowledge of his only begotten Son, and Holy Spirit; let him learn the order of the world's
creation, and series of Divine providence, and the different sorts of
legislation; let him be taught, why the world, and man, the citizen of
the world, were made; let him be instructed about his own nature, to
understand for what end he himself was made; let him be informed
how God punished the wicked with water and fire, and crowned his
saints with glory in every generation, viz. Seth, Enos, Enoch, Noah,
Abraham and his posterity, Melchisedeck, Job, Moses, Joshua, Caleb,
and Phineas the priest, and the saints of every age; let him also be

Joseph Bingham, The Antiquities of the Christian Church *(London: Henry G. Bohn,
1856), I, 432–33.*

taught, how the providence of God never forsook mankind, but called them at sundry times, from error and vanity to the knowledge of the truth, reducing them from slavery and impiety to liberty and godliness, from iniquity to righteousness, and from everlasting death to eternal life. After these, he must learn the doctrine of Christ's incarnation, his passion, his resurrection, and assumption; and what it is to renounce the devil, and enter into covenant with Christ. These were the chief heads of the ancient catechisms before baptism: in which it is observable, there is no mention made of the doctrine of the eucharist, or confirmation, because these were not allowed to catechumens till after baptism; and the instruction upon the former points was not given all at once, but by certain degrees, as the discipline of the church then required, which divided the catechumens into several distinct orders or classes, and exercised them gradually, according to the difference of their stations. . . .

Here I shall only remark further, that they allowed them to read some portions of the Scripture; for the moral and historical books were thought most proper at first for their instruction; and the chief use of those which are now called apocryphal books, was then to instil moral precepts into the catechumens. Upon this account Athanasius says, Though they were not canonical books, as the rest of the books of the Old and New Testament; yet they were such as were appointed to be read by those who were new proselytes, and desirous to be instructed in the ways of godliness: such were The Wisdom of Solomon, The Wisdom of Sirach, Esther, Judith, Tobit: to which he also adds, the book called, The Doctrine of the Apostles, and the Shepherd, that is, Hermes pastor. The author of the Synopsis of the Holy Scripture also, under the name of Athanasius, has much the same observation, That besides the canonical books, there were other books of the Old Testament, which were not in the canon, but only read to or by the catechumens. But this was not allowed in all churches; for it seems to have been otherwise in the church of Jerusalem, at the time when Cyril wrote his Catechetical Discourse; for he forbids his catechumens to read all apocryphal books whatsoever, and charges them to read those books only which were securely read in the church, viz. those books which the apostles and ancient bishops (who were wiser than the catechumens) had handed down to them. Then he specifies particularly the canonical books of the Old and New Testament, all the same as are now in our Bibles, except the Revelation, because I presume it was not then read in the church: and at last concludes with this charge to the catechumens, that they should not read any other books privately by themselves, which were not read publicly in the church. From whence I conclude, that as the books which we now call apocryphal, were not then read in the church of Jerusalem, so neither were they allowed to be read by the catechumens, though they were read both publicly and privately in many other churches. I know some learned persons are of a different opinion, and think that Cyril, by apocryphal books, means not those which we now call apocryphal, viz. Wisdom, Ecclesiasticus, but other pernicious and heretical books, which were absolutely re-probated and forbidden to all Christians. But if that had been his meaning, he would not have said, that the canonical books were the only books that were read in the church of Jerusalem, but would have distinguished, as other writers in other churches do, between canonical, ecclesiastical, and apocryphal books, and have intimated that the ecclesiastical books were such as were allowed to be read in the church, as well as the canonical, for moral instruction, though not to confirm articles of faith. Whereas he says nothing of this, but the express contrary, that none but the canonical books were read publicly in the church, nor were any other to be read privately by the catechumens. Which, at least, must mean thus much, that in the church of Jerusalem there was a different custom from some other churches; and that though in some churches the catechumens were allowed to read both the canonical books and the apocryphal, or, as others call them, the ecclesiastical; yet in the church of Jerusalem they were allowed to read only the canonical Scriptures, and no other. However, it is observable, that no church anciently denied any order of Christians the use of the Holy Scriptures in the vulgar tongue, since even the catechumens themselves, who were but an imperfect sort of Christians, were exhorted and commanded to read the canonical books in all churches, and the apocryphal books in some churches for moral instruction. Nay, if we may believe Bede, they were obliged to get some of the Holy Scriptures by heart, as a part of their exercise and discipline, before they were baptized. For he commends it as a laudable custom in the ancient church, that such as were to be catechised and baptized, were taught the beginnings of the four Gospels, and the intent and order of them, at the time when the ceremony of opening their ears was solemnly used; that they might know and remember, what, and how many, those books were, from whence they were to be instructed in the true faith. So far were they from locking up the Scriptures from any order of men in an unknown tongue, that they thought them useful and instructive to the meanest capacities; according to that of the psalmist, "Thy word giveth light and understanding to the simple." And therefore they allowed them to be vulgarly read, not only by the more perfect and complete Christians, but even by the very catechumens; among whom, as St. Austin and others have observed, those were commonly the most tractable and the best proficients, who were the most conversant in the Holy Scriptures. For which reason they made it one part of the catechumens' care, to exercise themselves in the knowledge of them, and did not then fear that men should turn heretics by being acquainted with the word of truth.

回 4. St. Benedict's *Rule*

In the prologue of his Rule, *St. Benedict (c. 480–c. 543) set forth his intent to found "a school for the Lord's service." The emphasis upon moderation, service, obedience, and religious learning, rather than upon the isolation and self-mortification characteristic of earlier orders, attracted thousands from throughout Western Europe to the Benedictine monasteries. Not only did the environment of these monasteries offer a striking contrast to earlier orders, but they afforded a welcome retreat from the upheavals of early medieval Europe. The* Rule's *emphasis upon periods of work and reading helped lay the foundation for the introduction of schools and the practice of book copying, which were to occupy the attention of monks in the years to come and make the monasteries the primary centers of learning in Western Europe for five centuries.*

FROM THE RULE OF ST. BENEDICT

Prologue. . . . . we are about to found, therefore, a school for the Lord's service; in the organization of which we trust that we shall ordain nothing severe and nothing burdensome. But even if, the demands of justice dictating it, something a little irksome shall be the result, for the purpose of amending vices or preserving charity;—thou shalt not therefore, struck by fear, flee the way of salvation, which can not be entered upon except through a narrow entrance. But as one's way of life and one's faith progresses, the heart becomes broadened, and, with the unutterable sweetness of love, the way of the mandates of the Lord is traversed. Thus, never departing from His guidance, continuing in the monastery in His teaching until death, through patience we are made partakers in Christ's passion, in order that we may merit to be companions in His kingdom.

*   *   *   *   *

Concerning the daily manual labour. Idleness is the enemy of the soul. And therefore, at fixed times, the brothers ought to be occupied in

Ernest F. Henderson (ed. and trans.), Select Documents of the Middle Ages, *pp. 274, 297–98. Copyright, 1910, by George Bell and Sons. Reprinted by permission of G. Bell & Sons, Ltd.*

manual labour; and again, at fixed times, in sacred reading. Therefore we believe that, according to this disposition, both seasons ought to be arranged; so that, from Easter until the Calends of October, going out early, from the first until the fourth hour they shall do what labour may be necessary. Moreover, from the fourth hour until about the sixth, they shall be free for reading. After the meal of the sixth hour, moreover, rising from table, they shall rest in their beds with all silence; or, perchance, he that wishes to read may so read to himself that he do not disturb another. And the nona (the second meal) shall be gone through with more moderately about the middle of the eighth hour; and again they shall work at what is to be done until Vespers. But, if the exigency or poverty of the place demands that they be occupied by themselves in picking fruits, they shall not be dismayed: for then they are truly monks if they live by the labours of their hands; as did also our fathers and the apostles. Let all things be done with moderation, however, on account of the fainthearted. From the Calends of October, moreover, until the beginning of Lent they shall be free for reading until the second full hour. At the second hour the tertia (morning service) shall be held, and all shall labour at the task which is enjoined upon them until the ninth. The first signal, moreover, of the ninth hour having been given, they shall each one leave off his work; and be ready when the second signal strikes. Moreover after the refection they shall be free for their readings or for psalms. But in the days of Lent, from dawn until the third full hour, they shall be free for their readings; and, until the tenth full hour, they shall do the labour that is enjoined on them. In which days of Lent they shall all receive separate books from the library; which they shall read entirely through in order. These books are to be given out on the first day of Lent. Above all there shall certainly be appointed one or two elders, who shall go round the monastery at the hours in which the brothers are engaged in reading, and see to it that no troublesome brother chance to be found who is open to idleness and trifling, and is not intent on his reading; being not only of no use to himself, but also stirring up others. If such a one— may it not happen—be found, he shall be admonished once and a second time. If he do not amend, he shall be subject under the Rule to such punishment that the others may have fear. Nor shall brother join brother at unsuitable hours. Moreover on Sunday all shall engage in reading: expecting those who are deputed to various duties. But if anyone be so negligent and lazy that he will not or can not read, some task shall be imposed upon him which he can do; so that he be not idle. On feeble or delicate brothers such a labour or art is to be imposed, that they shall neither be idle, nor shall they be so oppressed by the violence of labour as to be driven to take flight. Their weakness is to be taken into consideration by the abbot.

▣ 5. Cassiodorus, Father of Literary Monasticism

Flavius Magnus Cassiodorus (c. 490–c. 585) was in the fullest sense a Roman Christian. Devoted both to Latin learning and to the Church, he spent his life promoting his thesis that scholarship was an effective means of developing Christian character. Cassiodorus is believed to have been the first Christian writer to employ the phrase "the seven liberal arts," finding Scriptural sanction for their study by the analogy of the seven pillars of wisdom found in the book of Proverbs: "Wisdom builded her house; she has hewn out her seven pillars." (Proverbs 9:1).

Cassiodorus' efforts to save Latin scholarship as an essential ingredient of civilization were first directed toward Athalaric, king of the Ostrogoths. As a trusted and intimate advisor to the young ruler, Cassiodorus attempted to use his influence to save the schools of grammar and rhetoric and to educate his sovereign as a Roman. After palace intrigues forced him to abandon these plans, Cassiodorus turned to the Church. However, his attempts to convince the Pope to establish Christian schools of higher learning such as existed in the East also came to naught. It was at this juncture that Cassiodorus turned to monasticism. On his ancestral lands he founded two monasteries in which literary endeavors were the principal forms of work. It was here that Cassiodorus introduced the Scriptorium for the copying and binding of books. The story of Cassiodorus reveals the movement of the last vestiges of classical learning from the schools of Rome, no longer supported by imperial patronage, to the Scriptoriums of the monasteries.

The letter that follows, written by Cassiodorus in the name of Athalaric, reflects his devotion to Latin studies and his attempts to preserve Roman institutions even in the midst of barbarian rule.

KING ATHALARIC TO THE SENATE OF THE CITY OF ROME

You who are called Fathers should be interested in all that concerns the education of your sons. We hear by certain whisperings that the teachers of eloquence at Rome are not receiving their proper reward, and that the sums appointed to be paid to the masters of schools are lessened by the haggling of some persons.

Thomas Hodgkin (trans.), The Letters of Cassiodorus *(London: Henry Froude, 1886), pp. 406–07.*

Grammar is the noble foundation of all literature, the glorious mother of eloquence. As a virtuous man is offended by any act of vice, as a musician is pained by a discordant note, so does the grammarian in a moment perceive a false concord.

The grammatical art is not used by barbarous kings: it abides peculiarly with legitimate sovereigns. Other nations have arms: the lords of the Romans alone have eloquence. Hence sounds the trumpet for the legal fray in the Forum. Hence comes the eloquence of so many chiefs of the State. Hence, to say nothing more, even this discourse which is now addressed to you.

Wherefore let the teacher of grammar and of rhetoric, if he be found suitable for his work and obey the decrees of the Praefect of the City, be supported by your authority, and suffer no diminution of his salary.

To prevent his being dependent in any way on the caprice of his employer, let him receive half his salary at the end of half a year, and his *annonae* at the customary times. If the person whose business it is to pay him neglects this order, he shall be charged interest on the arrears.

The Grammarian is a man to whom every hour unemployed is misery, and it is a shame that such a man should have to wait the caprice of a public functionary before he gets his pay. We provide for the salaries of the play-actors, who minister only to the amusement of the public; and how much more for these men, the moulders of the style and character of our youth! Therefore let them henceforward not have to try the philosophical problem of thinking about two things at once, but, with their minds at ease about their subsistence, devote themselves with all their vigour to the teaching of liberal arts.

The following excerpt from "The Life of Cassiodorus," written by Thomas Hodgkin as an introduction to his collection of Cassiodorus' letters, provides an insight into that scholar's efforts and notable achievements within monasticism.

In the earliest days of Monasticism men like the hermits of the Thebaid had thought of little else but mortifying the flesh by vigils and fastings, and withdrawing from all human voices to enjoy an ecstatic communion with their Maker. The life in common of monks like those of Nitria and Lerinum had chastened some of the extravagances of these lonely enthusiasts while still keeping their main ends in view. St. Jerome, in his cell at Bethlehem, had shown what great results might be obtained for the Church of all ages from the patient literary toil of one religious recluse. And finally St. Benedict, in that Rule of his which was to be the code of monastic Christendom for centuries, had sanctified Work as one of the most effectual preservatives of the bodily

Hodgkin, op. cit., *pp. 56–59.*

and spiritual health of the ascetic, bringing together *Laborare* and *Orare* in friendly union, and proclaiming anew for the monk as for the untonsured citizen the primal ordinance, "In the sweat of thy brow thou shalt eat bread."

The great merit of Cassiodorus, that which shows his deep insight into the needs of his age and entitles him to the eternal gratitude of Europe, was his determination to utilise the vast leisure of the convent for the preservation of Divine and human learning and for its transmission to after ages. In the miserable circumstances of the times Theology was in danger of becoming brutified and ignorant; the great treasures of Pagan literature were no longer being perpetuated by the slaves who had once acted as *librarii* to the Greek or Roman noble; and with every movement of the Ostrogothic armies, or of the yet more savage hordes who served under the Imperial standard, with every sacked city and with every ravaged villa, some Codex, it may be such as we should now deem priceless and irreplaceable, was perishing. This being the state of Italy, Cassiodorus resolved to make of his monastery not merely a place for pious meditation, but a theological school and a manufactory for the multiplication of copies, not only of the Scriptures, not only of the Fathers and the commentators on Scripture, but also of the great writers of pagan antiquity. In the chapter which he devotes to the description of the *scriptorium* of his monastery he describes, with an enthusiasm which must have been contagious, the noble work done there by the *antiquarius:* "He may fill his mind with the Scriptures while copying the sayings of the Lord. With his fingers he gives life to men and arms them against the wiles of the devil. So many wounds does Satan receive as the *antiquarius* copies words of Christ. What he writes in his cell will be scattered far and wide over distant Provinces. Man multiplies the heavenly words, and by a striking figure—if I may dare so to speak—the three fingers of his hand express the utterances of the Holy Trinity. The fast-travelling reed writes down the holy words, and thus avenges the malice of the Wicked One, who caused a reed to be used to smite the head of the Saviour."

It is true that the passage here quoted refers only to the work of the copyist of the Christian Scriptures, but it could easily be shown from other passages that the literary activity of the monastery was not confined to these, but was also employed on secular literature.

Cassiodorus then goes on to describe the care which he has taken for the binding of the sacred Codices in covers worthy of the beauty of their contents, following the example of the householder in the parable, who provided wedding garments for all who came to the supper of his son. One pattern volume had been prepared, containing samples of various sorts of binding, that the amanuensis might choose that which pleased him best. He had moreover provided, to help the nightly toil of the *scriptorium*, mechanical lamps of some wonderful construction, which appears to have made them self-trimming, and to have ensured their having always a sufficient supply of oil. Sun-dials also for bright days, and water-clocks for cloudy days and the night-season, regulated their labour, and admonished them when it was time to unclose the three fingers, to lay down the reed, and to assemble with their brethren in the chapel of the convent for psalmody and prayer.

Upon the whole, though the idea of using the convent as a place of literary toil and theological training was not absolutely new, Cassiodorus seems certainly entitled to the praise of having first realised it systematically and on an extensive scale. It was entirely in harmony with the spirit of the Rule of St. Benedict, if it was not formally ordained in that document. At a very early date in the history of their order, the Benedictines, influenced probably by the example of the monastery of Vivaria, commenced that long series of services to the cause of literature which they have never wholly intermitted. Thus, instead of accepting the obsolete formula for which some scholars in the last age contended, "Cassiodorus was a Benedictine," we should perhaps be rather justified in maintaining that Benedict, or at least his immediate followers, were Cassiodorians.

🔲 6. Educational Revivals Under Charlemagne and Alfred the Great

Charlemagne (742–814) on the Continent and Alfred the Great (849–899) in England were exceptions to the rules of the early Middle Ages. Both were able to consolidate and govern from the throne large areas of land; and both, recognizing the importance of education to their kingdoms' welfare, attempted with some success to improve the levels of learning among their subjects. In the capitulary that follows, Charlemagne entrusts the Church with the tasks of improving and extending education in his empire. However, he makes it quite clear that the Church itself is not immune to ignorance and error and must attend to the education of its clergy.

Charles, by the grace of God, king of the Franks and Lombards and Patrician of the Romans. To Abbot Baugulf, and to all the congregation

Frederick Austin Ogg (ed.), A Source Book of Medieval History (*New York: American Book Co., 1907*), *pp. 146–48. By permission of American Book Company.*

—also to the faithful placed under your care—we have sent loving greetings by our ambassadors in the name of all-powerful God.

Be it known, therefore, to you, devoted and acceptable to God, that we, together with our faithful, have deemed it expedient that the bishoprics and monasteries intrusted by the favor of Christ to our control, in addition to the order of monastic life and the relationships of holy religion, should be zealous also in the cherishing of letters, and in teaching those who by the gift of God are able to learn, according as each has capacity. So that, just as the observance of the rule adds order and grace to the integrity of morals, so also zeal in teaching and learning may do the same for sentences, to the end that those who wish to please God by living rightly should not fail to please Him also by speaking correctly. For it is written, "Either from thy words thou shall be justified or from thy words thou shalt be condemned" [Matt, xii, 37]. Although right conduct may be better than knowledge, nevertheless knowledge goes before conduct. Therefore each one ought to study what he desires to accomplish, in order that so much the more fully the mind may know what ought to be done, as the tongue speeds in the praises of all-powerful God without the hindrances of mistakes. For while errors should be shunned by all men, so much the more ought they to be avoided, as far as possible, by those who are chosen for this very purpose alone. They ought to be the specially devoted servants of truth. For often in recent years when letters have been written to us from monasteries, in which it was stated that the brethren who dwelt there offered up in our behalf sacred and pious prayers, we have recognized, in most cases, both correct thoughts and uncouth expressions; because what pious devotion dictated faithfully to the mind, the tongue, uneducated on account of the neglect of study, was not able to express in the letter without error. Whence it happened that we began to fear lest perchance, as the skill in writing was less, so also the wisdom for understanding the Holy Scriptures might be much less than it rightly ought to be. And we all know well that, although errors of speech are dangerous, far more dangerous are errors of the understanding.

Therefore, we exhort you not only not to neglect the study of letters, but also with most humble mind, pleasing to God, to study earnestly in order that you may be able more easily and more correctly to penetrate the mysteries of the divine Scriptures. Since, moreover, images [similes], tropes and like figures are found in the sacred pages, nobody doubts that each one in reading these will understand the spiritual sense more quickly if previously he shall have been fully instructed in the mastery of letters. Such men truly are to be chosen for this work as have both the will and the ability to learn and a desire to instruct others. And may this be done with a zeal as great as the earnestness with which we command it. For we desire you to be, as the soldiers of the Church ought to be, devout in mind, learned in discourse, chaste in conduct, and eloquent in speech, so that when any one shall seek to see you, whether out of reverence for God or on account of your reputation for holy conduct, just as he is edified by your appearance, he may also be instructed by the wisdom which he has learned from your reading or singing, and may go away gladly, giving thanks to Almighty God.

In addition to stimulating the Church to establish village schools and to improve monastic education, Charlemagne enlarged and improved the palace school for the benefit of his family and nobility, adults as well as children. To his school were summoned scholars from throughout Europe who were placed under the direction of the learned Alcuin of York (Albinus). From Charlemagne's biographer Einhard we learn that the king's zeal for education was not restricted to the improvement of others.

Charles had the gift of ready and fluent speech, and could express whatever he had to say with the utmost clearness. He was not satisfied with ability to use his native language merely, but gave attention to the study of foreign ones, and in particular was such a master of Latin that he could speak it as well as his native tongue; but he could understand Greek better than he could speak it. He was so eloquent, indeed, that he might have been taken for a teacher of oratory. He most zealously cherished the liberal arts, held those who taught them in great esteem, and conferred great honors upon them. He took lessons in grammar of the deacon Peter of Pisa, at that time an aged man. Another deacon, Albin of Britain, surnamed Alcuin, a man of Saxon birth, who was the greatest scholar of the day, was his teacher in other branches of learning. The king spent much time and labor with him studying rhetoric, dialectic, and especially astronomy. He learned to make calculations, and used to investigate with much curiosity and intelligence the motions of the heavenly bodies. He also tried to write, and used to keep tablets and blanks in bed under his pillow, that at leisure hours he might accustom his hand to form the letters; however, as he began his efforts late in life, and not at the proper time, they met with little success.

An interesting specimen of Alcuin's teaching is provided in his The Disputation of Pepin, the Most Noble and Royal Youth, with Albinus the Scholastic, *part of which follows:*

"*Pepin.*   What is writing?
Albinus.   The guardian of history.

Ogg, op. cit., *pp. 112–13, citing Einhard,* Life of Charles the Great.
Andrew F. West, Alcuin and the Rise of Christian Schools *(New York; Charles Scribner's Sons, 1892), pp. 106–07.*

Pepin. What is language?
Albinus. The betrayer of the soul.
Pepin. What generates language?
Albinus. The tongue.
Pepin. What is the tongue?
Albinus. The whip of the air.
Pepin. What is air?
Albinus. The guardian of life.
Pepin. What is life?
Albinus. The joy of the happy; the expectation of death.
Pepin. What is death?
Albinus. An inevitable event; an uncertain journey; tears for the living; the probation of wills; the stealer of men.
Pepin. What is man?
Albinus. The slave of death; a passing traveler; a stranger in his place.
Pepin. What is man like?
Albinus. An apple."

Let us understand this short and sudden definition. Alcuin means that man hangs like an apple on a tree without being able to know when he is to fall.

The questions on natural phenomena are not less instructive:—
"*Pepin.* What is water?
Albinus. A supporter of life; a cleanser of filth.
Pepin. What is fire?
Albinus. Excessive heat; the nurse of growing things; the ripener of crops.
Pepin. What is cold?
Albinus. The febricity of our members.[1]
Pepin. What is frost?
Albinus. The persecutor of plants; the destruction of leaves; the bond of the earth; the source of waters.
Pepin. What is snow?
Albinus. Dry water.
Pepin. What is the winter?
Albinus. The exile of summer.
Pepin. What is the spring?
Albinus. The painter of the earth.
Pepin. What is the autumn?
Albinus. The barn of the year."

In England King Alfred followed very much the same educational pattern established by Charlemagne. He too encouraged the Church to improve educational

[1] *This "cold" is apparently a chill.*

facilities and standards, established a palace school with scholars gathered from near and far, and sought to extend his own learning. In the following passages Alfred tells of some of his educational achievements and ambitions. Of particular interest was his desire to utilize the English language in extending learning. This at a time when Latin was generally considered to be the exclusive language of schooling.

King Alfred greets Bishop Werfrith with loving words and with friendship.

I let it be known to thee that it has very often come into my mind what wise men there formerly were throughout England, both within the Church and without it; also what happy times there were then and how the kings who had power over the nation in those days obeyed God and His ministers; how they cherished peace, morality, and order at home, and at the same time enlarged their territory abroad; and how they prospered both in war and in wisdom. Often have I thought, also, of the sacred orders, how zealous they were both in teaching and learning, and in all the services they owed to God; and how foreigners came to this land in search of wisdom and instruction, which things we should now have to get from abroad if we were to have them at all.

So general became the decay of learning in England that there were very few on this side of the Humber who could understand the rituals in English, or translate a letter from Latin into English; and I believe that there were not many beyond the Humber who could do these things. There were so few, in fact, that I cannot remember a single person south of the Thames when I came to the throne. Thanks be to Almighty God that we now have some teachers among us. And therefore I enjoin thee to free thyself, as I believe thou art ready to do, from worldly matters, that thou mayst apply the wisdom which God has given thee wherever thou canst. Consider what punishments would come upon us if we neither loved wisdom ourselves nor allowed other men to obtain it. We should then care for the name only of Christian, and have regard for very few of the Christian virtues.

When I thought of all this I remembered also how I saw the country before it had been all ravaged and burned; how the churches throughout the whole of England stood filled with treasures and books. There was also a great multitude of God's servants, but they had very little knowledge of books, for they could not understand anything in them because they were not written in their own language. When I remembered all this I wondered extremely that the good and wise men who were formerly all over England and had learned perfectly all the books,

Ogg, op. cit., *pp. 191–94, citing the preface of King Alfred's West-Saxon Version of Pope Gregory's* Pastoral Rule.

did not wish to translate them into their own language. But again I soon answered myself and said: "Their own desire for learning was so great that they did not suppose that men would ever become so indifferent and that learning would ever so decay; and they wished, moreover, that wisdom in this land might increase with our knowledge of languages." Then I remembered how the law was first known in Hebrew and when the Greeks had learned it how they translated the whole of it into their own tongue, and all other books besides. And again the Romans, when they had learned it, translated the whole of it into their own language. And also all other Christian nations translated a part of it into their languages.

Therefore it seems better to me, if you agree, for us also to translate some of the books which are most needful for all men to know into the language which we can all understand. It shall be your duty to see to it, as can easily be done if we have tranquility enough, that all the freeborn youth now in England, who are rich enough to be able to devote themselves to it, be set to learn as long as they are not fit for any other occupation, until they are well able to read English writing. And let those afterwards be taught more in the Latin language who are to continue learning and be promoted to a higher rank.

When I remembered how the knowledge of Latin had decayed through England, and yet that many could read English writing, I began, among other various and manifold troubles of this kingdom, to translate into English the book which is called in Latin *Pastoralis*, and in English *The Shepherd's Book*, sometimes word for word, and sometimes according to the sense, as I had learned it from Plegmund, my archbishop, and Asser, my bishop, and Grimbald, my mass-priest, and John, my mass-priest. And when I had learned it, as I could best understand it and most clearly interpret it, I translated it into English.

I will send a copy of this book to every bishopric in my kingdom, and on each copy there shall be a clasp worth fifty mancuses. And I command in God's name that no man take the clasp from the book, or the book from the minster. It is uncertain how long there may be such learned bishops as, thanks be to God, there now are almost everywhere; therefore, I wish these copies always to remain in their places, unless the bishop desires to take them with him, or they be loaned out anywhere, or any one wishes to make a copy of them.

IV

Education and the Later Middle Ages

THE school is the servant of society, at times embraced and appreciated, at other times virtually ignored. For a thousand years after Rome's decline, the rise and fall of interest in classical studies provides a rather accurate barometer of conditions in Western Europe. Each wave of invasion, rebellion, or similar calamity struck damaging blows against the schools. When the peace and good order of Charlemagne's rule came to an end, so too, in most of the empire, did the progress in education that he had encouraged. The tenth century brought feudalism, anarchy, Saracens, Magyars, and Northmen to much of Europe. In the bloody wake of warfare monasteries were plundered, cathedrals destroyed, and scholars murdered. In such periods, the great educational task was one of preservation—protecting the books, saving the manuscripts.

By the middle of the eleventh century, the tide of events turned. The armies of the continent moved outward from their barricades. The Norman conquest of England brought to that land an order and progress rare in its history. Later in the century Norman conquerers wrested Sicily from the Byzantine Empire and thus re-established a direct tie with Greek language and culture. Christian advances into southern Spain and, through the Crusades, into the Middle East brought scholars into contact with Arabic studies and Greek learning, which the Arabs had adopted so readily.

The scholarly discoveries of the Christian offensive were of immense importance in stimulating the so-called "twelfth century Renaissance." However, other significant changes were wrought by these events, which contributed mightily to fostering the revival of learning: trade brought wealth to revitalize urban centers and called forth conditions that stimulated the study of Roman law; travel to foreign and exotic lands stirred the poetic imagination; educational patronage and employment for scholars were by-products of the increased stability, wealth, and

90

more complex governmental structures brought about by the strengthening of the Papacy, the Emperor, and monarchs at the expense of the feudal barons. This concentration of power in the hands of Church and secular princes along with the growing significance of towns in European life tended to place the schools of the cathedrals, collegiate churches, and palaces in the center of educational activity. Meanwhile, the monasteries, which had been the pre-eminent educational institutions for centuries, lost much of their attraction for scholars. Their rural locations, which had once meant security in the midst of chaos, now made them appear remote. Also, various monastic reforms had resulted in a de-emphasis of scholarly activities in favor of a return to simpler, manual tasks. *(1)*

The revival of the twelfth century was, in large measure, humanistic, devoted both to the study of the Latin classics and the creation of literature in Latin and the vernacular. In the cathedral and collegiate church schools, students had their curriculum of Latin grammar, the trivium and quadrivium, and theology enriched by the study of literature. Needless to say, Latin was the primary language of all studies. *(2)*

By the middle of the twelfth century, the humanistic revival had been successfully challenged by the fascination of scholars with logic and Aristotelian science. Logic had always been studied as part of the trivium, but the recovery of Aristotle's Posterior Analytics, translated from the Greek in Sicily and from the Arabic at Toledo, caused a sensation. The deductive logic of Aristotle was ideally suited to the primary interests of scholars in theology and law, both dialectic disciplines. It was a system of thought that sought to attain truth through the application of human reason after an analysis and synthesis of authoritative writings such as the Scriptures and Church Fathers in religious matters, Justinian and Gratian in law, and, with the appearance in the twelfth century of translations of vast quantities of his works, Aristotle in science, ethics, politics and metaphysics. It was the logic of the syllogism employed by scholarly debaters that led to the Scholastic movement.

To many theologians the application of reason to religious matters and the appearance of Aristotelian philosophy boded evil for the Church. In the cathedrals, disputes over theological questions were often stated in terms of universals. Is the universal proposition most real (realist position), or is the individual object most real (nominalist position)? Is revealed truth supported by faith superior to the conclusions obtained by reason (realists) or is the reverse more valid (nominalists)? Scholasticism was brought to its highest point when Saint Thomas Aquinas (1225–75) reconciled Aristotelian philosophy with Christian faith by distinguishing between the realm of the natural world, whose secrets may be revealed through reason, and the realm of the supernatural world, where reason must eventually give way to faith in the search for truth. *(3)*

The Scholastics stirred the minds of Europe with their application of logical argumentation to all fields of knowledge. To the cathedral and collegiate church schools, where they debated, came students by the hundreds from throughout the continent. Organizing into guilds, the students and masters eventually cut their

*ties with their parent cathedral and collegiate schools and formed the nucleus
of a new institution—the university. From the twelfth century to the fourteenth,
the university movement spread throughout Europe.*

*The growth of the university was due to many factors. The fervor of the scholas-
tic movement was certainly important as was the desire to enter one of the three
great prestigious professions: theology, law, and medicine. However, of great
significance was the climate of relative peace and stability in Europe at the time.
Prosperous cities could welcome a university and the attendant prestige despite the
cost of the riots and destruction often promoted by students. Princes and Popes
were powerful enough to guarantee the safety and security of the students and
masters. (4)*

*By the mid-fourteenth century, the universities had become the treasure
houses in which the works of all the great masters were stored, studied, memorized,
and used as the basis for lectures, debates, and declamations. Galen and Hippocrates were the authorities in medicine, Justinian in civil law, Gratian in canon law,
Peter Lombard and St. Thomas in theology. In the arts faculty, Aristotle ruled
supreme. His writings in the mental, moral, and natural philosophies absorbed
most of the attention of the students of the liberal arts. At the height of the Middle
Ages the time had finally come when a scholar might study both Augustine and
Aristotle and, in so doing, glorify God's work. (5)*

1. The Schools of the Cathedrals and Collegiate Churches

*The eleventh and twelfth centuries saw the construction of a great
number of cathedrals throughout Western Europe. In addition to being a house of
worship, the cathedral was the seat of government of a bishop, head of a diocese
that included a number of churches within a given area. Large staffs of cathedral
priests, called canons, engaged in various activities, including charitable and
medical work, keeping records, collecting and disbursing church funds, composing
liturgical music, and designing church structures. It is not surprising that such an
institution, requiring so large a body of educated clerics, would establish schools.
Indeed, every cathedral had its canon, whose primary responsibility was to direct
the educational program. In England he was called chancellor; on the continent
the term "scholasticus" was common. Another canon, the precentor, was placed
in charge of cathedral musical activities, including the maintenance of a song
school for the training of choir boys who were expected to be as adept in the
liberal arts as they were in vocalizing. The collegiate churches, usually located
in important towns, shared a similar organizational pattern with the cathedrals
and engaged in similar educational endeavors. They were not, however, residences*

of bishops. In the following reading, Osmund, Bishop of Salisbury during the reign of William the Conquerer, provides a description of the administrative organization of Salisbury Cathedral.

These are the dignities and customs of the church of Salisbury, which I, Osmund, bishop of that church, in the name of the Holy Trinity, in the year of our Lord 1091, established and granted to the persons and canons of the same church, with the advice of the lords, the archbishop and other my co-bishops whose names are subscribed, and with the assent of the lord King William; namely, that Dean and Chanter, Chancellor and Treasurer shall be continually resident in the church at Salisbury, without any kind of excuse. . . . Nothing can excuse the canons from being personally resident in the church of Salisbury, except attendance at the schools and the service of the lord King, who can have one in his chapel, and the archbishop one, and the bishop three.

The dean presides over all canons and vicars [choral] as regards the cure of souls and correction of conduct.

The precentor ought to rule the choir as to chanting and can raise or lower the chant.

The treasurer is pre-eminent in keeping the treasures and ornaments and managing the lights. In like manner the chancellor in ruling the school and correcting the books.

The archdeacons excel in the superintendence of parishes and the cure of souls.

Dean and precentor, treasurer and chancellor, receive double, the rest of the canons single commons.

The sub-dean holds from the dean the archdeaconry of the city and suburbs, the succentor from the precentor all that pertains to the singing. If the dean is away from the church the sub-dean fills his place, and the succentor in like manner the precentor's.

In the reading that follows, a canon of the Waltham Holy Cross Collegiate Church relates some of his boyhood experiences as a student in the church school during the twelfth century.

I from a boy of five years old to the present time have seen many things, being made a canon in the Holy Cross Church by Dean Ernulf of good memory, with the assent and on the presentation of the lady Adaliza the Queen, in whose gift the prebends were, and for the first rudiments of learning sent to Master Peter, son of Master Athelard,

Arthur Leach (ed.), Educational Charters and Documents, 598 to 1909 *(Cambridge: The University Press, 1911), p. 73. By permission of Cambridge University Press.*

Leach, op. cit., pp. 57, 59.

the organizer and founder of the present church. A most copious spring of learning and instruction flowed from that Peter, after the Dutch fashion, for besides reading and the composition of letters and verses, singing was no less learnt and practised in the church; and a well ordered difference from the usual habit of boys was that they walked, stood, read and chanted, like brethren in religion, and whatever had to be sung at the steps of the choir or in the choir itself they sang and chanted by heart, one or two or more together, without the help of a book. One boy never looked at another, when they were in their places in choir, except sideways and that very seldom, and they never spoke a word to one another; they never walked about the choir to carry copes or books or for any other reason, unless sent on an errand by the master, remaining in the choir. As if walking in procession from school they go to choir, and on leaving the choir go to school, like canons getting up in the night [for service].

This blood struck from the flint . . . and placed in a silver shrine, I by the mercy of God gained a sight of, for I was brought up from tender years in Waltham church for 53 years, and in its bosom instructed in grammar learning. Unhappy me! to whom it has happened to see myself in this life torn from the breasts which gave me life.

Throughout the Middle Ages and for centuries afterwards, Latin was the language of learning. In the early stages of a boy's education, whether in a monastic school or the song school of a cathedral or collegiate church, he was introduced to a Latin grammar and a Latin reader. Mastery of these works, which included memorization of its contents, was a necessary first step to the study of the liberal arts. The most commonly used elementary grammar between 400 A.D. and 1500 was the Ars Minor of Donatus, *written by a Roman teacher of rhetoric around 350 A.D. The* Distichs of Cato, *a Latin reader created by an unknown Roman about 200 A.D., has had an even longer history of use in the schools. As recently as 1735, Benjamin Franklin published an English translation of the work. The basic style of the* Distichs, *with its little moral verses, can be found in school readers well into the nineteenth century.*

Here is an excerpt from the Ars Minor of Donatus *(translated into English):*

CONCERNING THE ADVERB

What is an adverb? A part of speech which, added to a verb, explains the meaning of it and completes it. What attributes has an adverb? Three. Meaning, comparison, form. In what does the

Wayland Johnson Chase (trans.), The Ars Minor of Donatus *(Madison: University of Wisconsin Studies in the Social Sciences and History, No. 11, 1926), p. 47.*

meaning of adverbs consist? Because they are adverbs of place, or of time, or of number, or of denying, or of affirming, or of showing, or of desiring, or of encouraging, or of order, or of enquiry, or of likeness, or of quality, or of quantity, or of doubting, or personal, or of calling, or of replying, or of separating, or of swearing, or of choosing, or of grouping, or of preventing, or of result, or of comparing. Give the adverbs of place. As hic or ibi, intus or foris, illic or inde. Give those of time. As hodie, nuper, aliquando; those of number, as semel, bis; of negation, as non; of affirmation, as etiam quinni; of demonstration, as eu, ecce; of desire, as utinam; of urging, as eia; of order, as deinde; of interrogation, as cur, quare, quamobrem; of likeness, as quasi, ceu; of quality, as docte, pulchre; of quantity as multum, parum; of doubt, as forsitan, fortasse; personal, as mecum, tecum, secum, nobiscum, vobiscum; of calling, as heus; of replying, as heu; of separating, as seorsum; of swearing, as edepol, ecastor, hercle, medius fidius; of selecting, as potius, immo; of grouping, as simul, una; of preventing, as ne; of result, as forte, fortuitu; of comparing, as magis or tam. Comparison of adverbs consists in what? In three degrees of comparison: positive, comparative, superlative. Give an adverb of the positive degree. As docte: of the comparative, as doctius; of the superlative, as doctissime. We do not say, "magis doctius" and "tam doctissime" because magis and tam are joined only to the positive degree, although our ancestors said "tam magis" and "quam magis." How many forms of adverbs are there? Two. What? Simple and compound; simple, as docte, prudenter; compound as indocte, imprudenter. Adverbs of location are concerned with in the place, or from the place, or to the place. But in loco and de loco have the same meaning, as intus sum, intus exeo, foris sum, foris venio. Ad locum has another meaning, as intro eo, foras eo. But we do not say thus, "de intus and de foris," though we say, "in foras" or "ad foras."

The following is an excerpt from the Distichs of Cato *(translated into English):*

THE COMMON COLLECTION OF DISTICHS

When I noticed how very many go seriously wrong in their manner of living I concluded that I must apply a corrective to their belief and take counsel of the experience of mankind in order that they may live most gloriously and attain honor. Now I will teach thee, dearest son, in

Wayland Johnson Chase (trans.), The Distichs of Cato: A Famous Medieval Textbook *(Madison: University of Wisconsin Studies in the Social Sciences and History, No. 7, 1922), pp. 13, 17.*

what way thou mayest fashion a rule for thy life. Therefore, so read
my precepts that thou mayest understand them, for to read and not to
understand is equivalent to not reading.

Pray to God.
Love thy parents.
Cherish those of kin to thee.
Guard that entrusted to thee.
Shun the market place.
Walk with the upright.
Attack not until you have challenged.
Be neat.
Salute freely.
Yield to him who is older than thou.
Respect the magistrate.
Preserve thy sense of shame.
Guard well thine own interests.
Practice diligence.
Care for thy family.
Return like for like.
Consider well to whom to make presents.
Indulge rarely in banquets.
Sleep enough.

Love thy wife.
Keep thy word.
Be moderate with wine.
Fight for thy country.
Be not easily imposed upon.

BOOK I

1. If God a spirit is as poets sing,
   With mind kept pure make thou thy offering.

2. Be oft awake: from too much sleep abstain,
   For vice from sloth doth ever nurture gain.

3. Who rules his tongue doth highest praises reap:
   Godlike is he who silence well doth keep.

4. Ne'er with thyself perversely disagree;
   Who's out with self in peace with none will be.

5. If on men's lives and deeds thou look'st, thou'lt see
   That from those faults they blame, not one is free.

6. Shun that which harms, e'en tho thy love is caught;
   Before mere wealth should safety first be sought.

7. Be ever kind or stern to suit the time:
   The wise may change his practice without crime.

8. Heed not when of thy slave thy wife complains,
   For whom her husband loves, she aye disdains.

9. When thou giv'st counsel, cease not till the end,
   Though it unwelcome be, e'en to thy friend.

10. Try not with words the talker to outdo;
    On all is speech bestowed: good sense on few.

11. Love others so that thou'rt to self a friend;
    Prefer the good and thus dire harm forfend.

囻 2. The Renaissance of the Twelfth Century

The foremost figure of the twelfth-century revival of classical studies was the Englishman, John of Salisbury (c. 1120–1180). His wanderings in pursuit of knowledge led him to the great center of the humanistic movement—the cathedral school of Chartres. In the excerpt that follows from his "Metalogicus," John describes the curriculum and teaching methods of his master, Bernard of Chartres.

Bernard of Chartres, the most copious source of letters in Gaul in modern times, followed this method, and in the reading of authors showed what was simple, and fell under the ordinary rules; the figures of grammar, the adornments of rhetoric, the quibbles of sophistries; and where the subject of his own lesson suggested reading related to other arts, these matters he brought into full view, yet in such wise that he did not teach everything about each topic but, in proportion to the capacity of his audience, dispensed to them in due time the full scope of the subject. And because the brilliancy of any speech depends either on *Propriety* (that is, the correct agreement of adjective or verb with the

Arthur O. Norton (ed.), Readings in the History of Education, Medieval Universities *(Cambridge: Harvard University Press, 1909), pp. 31–33. Reprinted by permission of the publishers from Arthur O. Norton,* Readings in the History of Education: Medieval Universities. *Cambridge, Mass.: Harvard University Press.*

substantive) or on *Metathesis* (that is, the transfer of the meaning of an expression for a worthy reason to another signification), these were the things which he took every opportunity to inculcate in the minds of his hearers.

And since the memory is strengthened by exercise and the wits are sharpened by imitating what is heard, he urged some by warnings, and some by floggings and punishments [to the constant practice of memorizing and imitation]. They were individually required on the following day to reproduce some part of what they had heard the day before, some more, some less, for with them the following day was the pupil of the day preceding.

Evening drill, which was called *declension*, was packed with so much grammar that if one gave a whole year to it he would have at his command, if he were not unusually dull, a method of speaking and writing, and he could not be ignorant of expressions which are in common use. . . . For those of the boys for whom preliminary exercises in imitating prose or poetry were prescribed, he announced the poets or orators and bade them imitate their example, pointing out the way they joined their words and the elegance of their perorations.

But if any one to make his own work brilliant had borrowed the cloak of another he detected the theft and convicted him, though he did not very often inflict a punishment; but he directed the culprit thus convicted, if the poorness of his work had so merited, to condescend with modest favor to express the exact meaning of the author; and he made the one who imitated his predecessors worthy of imitation by his successors.

The following matters, too, he taught among the first rudiments and fixed them in their minds:—the value of order; what is praiseworthy in embellishment and in [choice of] words; where there is tenuity and, as it were, emaciation of speech; where, a pleasing abundance; where, excess; and where, a due limit in all things. . . .

And since in the entire preliminary training of those who are to be taught there is nothing more useful than to grow accustomed to that which must needs be done with skill, they repeatedly wrote prose and poetry every day, and trained themselves by mutal comparisons,—a training than which nothing is more effective for eloquence, nothing more expeditious for learning; and it confers the greatest benefit upon life, at least, if affection [rather than envy] rules these comparisons, if humility is not lost in literary proficiency.

One significant aspect of the Renaissance of the twelfth century was the appearance of literature in the vernacular. This by no means sounded the death of Latin as the language of scholarship, nor did it even mean that the vernacular was accepted as an equal to Latin by churchmen and scholars. Nevertheless, the publication in the eleventh century of the first English-Latin grammar, although its intent was to accommodate the study of Latin, provides a clue to the emergence of local languages throughout Europe. The preface of this work follows; note the author's realization that he would likely be criticized for producing such a book.

I Aelfric, as not being very learned, have taken pains to translate these extracts from the larger and smaller Priscian for you tender children into your own language, so that when you have gone through Donatus on the Parts of Speech, you may be able to instil both languages, Latin and English, into your youthful minds, by this little book, until you reach more advanced studies. I am aware that many will blame me, for being willing to devote my mind to such a pursuit as to turn "The Art of Grammar" into English. But I destine this lesson-book for little boys who know nothing, not for their elders. I know that words can be construed in many different ways, but to avoid raising difficulties I follow the simplest meaning. If anyone is offended at it he can call it my construction, if he pleases. I am content to do it, as I learnt it in the school of the venerable prelate Ethelwold, who taught many the elements to good purpose. It must be remembered however that in many places "The Art of Grammar" cannot easily be turned into English, as in the part about metres and feet, of which I say nothing here. But I think that for a beginning this translation may help little boys, as I have already said. I often wonder indeed why many people pronounce syllables short in prose which are short in verse, seeing that prose is not governed by the laws of metre. Thus they pronounce pater păter like the Britons, and malus mallus and the like. But in my opinion it is better to invoke God the Father "Deus pāter," giving Him honour by making the syllable long than by making it short like the Britons, for God ought not to be subject to the rules of grammar. Farewell, little boys, in the Lord.

回 3. The Scholastic Movement

The issues dividing the advocates of the Scholastic method and their detractors did not concern struggles between religion and science or authority in religious matters versus complete freedom of inquiry. What was primarily involved was a dispute over method, over how the authority of the Scriptures and Church Fathers was to be utilized in arriving at and supporting religious dogma.

Leach, op. cit., p. 49.

The realists insisted that the religious doctrines of the Church must be accepted first on faith. Only then might the authoritative writings be gleaned for passages that would support the dogma and strengthen faith. The nominalists, on the other hand, argued that the search for religious truth must begin with the various authorities and be attained deductively by applying reason in dialectical exercises.

Peter Abelard (1079–1142) scored a major point for the Scholastic proponents of Aristotelian logic when in his Sic et non *(Yes and No) he illustrated that the Scriptures and Church Fathers could be employed to support both sides of a theological question. Only through reason, he argued, could truth be attained. His position is stated in the prologue of* Sic et non, *which follows. Also included is an example of his treatment of one of the 156 religious questions he raised in this work. Abelard did not state his position on these questions but left the reader to reason the answers for himself.*

In truth, constant or frequent questioning is the first key to wisdom; and it is, indeed, to the acquiring of this [habit of] questioning with absorbing eagerness that the famous philosopher, Aristotle, the most clear sighted of all, urges the studious when he says: "It is perhaps difficult to speak confidently in matters of this sort unless they have often been investigated. Indeed, to doubt in special cases will not be without advantage." For through doubting we come to inquiry and through inquiry we perceive the truth. As the Truth Himself says: "Seek and ye shall find, knock and it shall be opened unto you." And He also, instructing us by His own example, about the twelfth year of His life wished to be found sitting in the midst of the doctors, asking them questions, exhibiting to us by His asking of questions the appearance of a pupil, rather than, by preaching, that of a teacher, although there is in Him, nevertheless, the full and perfect wisdom of God.

Now when a number of quotations from [various] writings are introduced they spur on the reader and allure him into seeking the truth in proportion as the authority of the writing itself is commended....

In accordance, then, with these forecasts it is our pleasure to collect different sayings of the holy Fathers as we planned, just as they have come to mind, suggesting (as they do) some questioning from their apparent disagreement, in order that they may stimulate tender readers to the utmost effort in seeking the truth and may make them keener as the result of their seeking.

* * * * *

THAT IT IS LAWFUL TO KILL A MAN, AND THE OPPOSITE THESIS

Jerome on Isaiah, Bk. V. He who cuts the throat of a man of blood, is not a man of blood.

Norton, op. cit., pp. 19–23.

Idem, On the Epistle to the Galatians: He who smites the wicked because they are wicked and whose reason for the murder is that he may slay the base, is a servant of the Lord.

Idem, on Jeremiah: For the punishment of homicides, impious persons and poisoners is not bloodshed, but serving the law.

Cyprian, in the Ninth Kind of Abuse: The King ought to restrain theft, punish deeds of adultery, cause the wicked to perish from off the face of the earth, refuse to allow parricides and perjurers to live.

Augustine: Although it is manslaughter to slaughter a man, a person may sometimes be slain without sin. For both a soldier in the case of an enemy and a judge or his official in the case of a criminal, and the man from whose hand, perhaps without his will or knowledge, a weapon has flown, do not seem to me to sin, but merely to kill a man.

Likewise: The soldier is ordered by law to kill the enemy, and if he shall prove to have refrained from such slaughter, he pays the penalty at the hands of his commander. Shall we not go so far as to call these laws unjust or rather no laws at all? For that which was not just does not seem to me to be a law.

Idem, on Exodus ch. xxvii: The Israelites committed no theft in spoiling the Egyptians, but rendered a service to God at his bidding, just as when the servant of a judge kills a man whom the law hath ordered to be killed; certainly if he does it of his own volition he is a homicide, even though he knows that the man whom he executed ought to be executed by the judge.

Idem, on Leviticus ch. lxxv: When a man is justly put to death, the law puts him to death, not thou.

Idem, Bk. I of the "City of God": Thou shalt not kill, except in the case of those whose death God orders, or else when a law hath been passed to suit the needs of the time and express command hath been laid upon a person. But he does not kill who owes service to the person who gives him his orders, for he is as it were a mere sword to the person who employs his assistance.

Likewise: When a soldier, in obedience to the power under which he is legitimately placed, kills a man, by no law of the state is he accused of murder; nay if he has not done it, he is accused of desertion and insubordination. But if he had acted under his own initiative and of his own will, he would have incurred the charge of shedding human blood. And so he is punished if he does not do when ordered that for which he would receive punishment if he did it without orders.

Idem, to Publicola: Counsel concerning the slaying of men pleaseth me not, that none may be slain by them, unless perhaps a man is a soldier or in a public office, so that he does the deed not in his own behalf, but for others and for the state, accepting power legitimately conferred, if it is consonant with the task imposed on him.

Likewise: It has been said: let us not resist the evil man, let not the vengeance delight us which feeds the mind on others' ill, let us not neglect the reproofs of men.

Idem, to Marcella: If that earthly commonwealth of thine keep to the teachings of Christ, even wars will not be waged without goodwill, for with pitying heart even wars if possible will be waged by the good, so that the lusts of desire may be subdued and those faults destroyed which ought under just rule to be either rooted out or chastised. For if Christian training condemned all wars, this should rather be the advice given in the gospel for their safety to the soldiers who ask for it, namely to throw aside their arms and retire altogether from the field. But this is the word spoken to them: Do violence to no man, neither accuse any falsely; and be content with your wages.

He warns them that the wages that belong to them should satisfy them, but he by no means forbids them to take the field.

Abelard's successors were not content to merely state the views of various authorities on a given question. They also introduced their own reasonings. An excert from Dante's "Quaestro de Aqua et Terra" provides an excellent example of the medieval method of disputation. It also makes one quite aware of the weakness of the Scholastic method as a technique for attaining scientific knowledge.

Introduction: Author's reasons for undertaking the discussion.

Let it be known to you all that, whilst I was in Mantua, a certain Question arose, which, often argued according to appearance rather than to truth remained undetermined. Wherefore, since from boyhood I have ever been nurtured in love of truth, I could not bear to leave the Question I have spoken of undiscussed: rather I wished to demonstrate the truth concerning it, and likewise, hating untruth as well as loving truth, to refute contrary arguments. And lest the spleen of many, who, when the objects of their envy are absent, are wont to fabricate lies, should behind my back transform well-spoken words, I further wished in these pages, traced by my own fingers, to set down the conclusion I had reached and to sketch out, with my pen, the form of the whole controversy.

THE QUESTION: IS WATER, OR THE SURFACE OF THE SEA, ANYWHERE HIGHER THAN THE EARTH, OR HABITABLE DRY LAND?

AFFIRMATIVE ARGUMENT: Five affirmative arguments generally accepted.

Reason 1. Geometrical Proof: Earth and Water are spheres with different centers; the center of the Earth's sphere is the center of the universe; consequently the surface of the Water is above that of the Earth.

Reason 2. Ethical Proof: Water is a nobler element than Earth; hence it deserves a nobler, or higher, place in the scheme of the universe.

Reason 3. Experimental Proof: based on sailors seeing the land disappear under their horizon when at sea.

Reason 4. Economical Proof: The supply of Water, namely, the sea, must be higher than the Earth; otherwise, as Water flows downwards, it could not reach, as it does, the fountains, lakes, etc.

Reason 5. Astronomical Proof: Since Water follows the moon's course, its sphere must be excentric, like the moon's excentric orbit; and consequently in places be higher than the sphere of Earth.

NEGATIVE ARGUMENT: These reasons unfounded.

I. REFUTATION BY OBSERVATION.

Water flows down to the sea from the land; hence the sea cannot be higher than the land.

II. REFUTATION BY REASONING:

    A. *Water cannot be higher than the dry land.*
        Proof: Water could only be higher than the Earth,
            1. If it were excentric, or
            2. If it were concentric, but had some excrescence.
            But since
                x. Water naturally moves downwards,
                and
                y. Water is naturally a fluid body:
            1. Cannot be true, for three impossibilities would follow:
                a. Water would move upwards as well as downwards;
                b. Water and Earth would move downwards in different directions;
                c. Gravity would be taught ambiguously of the two bodies.
            Proof of these impossibilities by a diagram.
            2. Cannot be true, for
                a. The Water of the excrescence would be diffused, and consequently the excrescence could not exist:
                b. It is unnecessary, and what is unnecessary is contrary to the will of God and Nature.

B. *All land is higher than the sea.*

   Proof: It has been shown that Water is of one level, and con-concentric with the Earth:

     Therefore, since the shores are higher than the edges of the sea, and since the shores are the lowest portions of the land,

     It follows that all the land is higher than the sea.

C. *Objections to the foregoing reasoning, and their refutation.*

   1. *Possible affirmative argument:* Earth is the heaviest body; hence it is drawn down to its own center, and lies beneath the lighter body, Water.

   2. *Objection to this argument:* Earth is the heaviest body only by comparison with others; for Earth is itself of different weights.

   3. *Refutation of this objection:* On the contrary, Earth is a simple body, and as such subject to be drawn equally in every part.

   4. *Answer to the refutation, with minor objections and their refutation.* Since the objection is in itself sound, and Earth by its own Particular Nature, due to the stubborness of matter, would be lower than the sea; and since Universal Nature requires that the Earth project somewhere, in order that its object, the mixture of the elements, may be fulfilled:

  It follows that there must be some final and efficient cause, whereby this projection may be accomplished.

     a. The final cause has been seen to be the purpose of Universal Nature.

     b. The efficient cause cannot be (i) the Earth, (ii) the Water, (iii) the Air or Fire, (iv) the heaven of the Moon, (v) the Planets, nor (vi) the Primum Mobile:

  Therefore it must be ascribed to the heaven of the Fixed Stars (for this has variety in efficiency, as is seen in the various constellations), and in particular to those Stars of the Northern Hemisphere which overhang the dry land.

      (*x*) *First objection:* Why is the projecting continent then, not circular, since the motion of these stars is circular?

      Answer: Because the material did not suffice for so great an elevation.

      (*y*) *Second objection:* Why is this elevation in this particular place?

      Answer: Because God whose ways are inscrutable, willed it so.

We should therefore desist from examining too closely the reasons, which we can never hope to fathom.

D. *Refutation of the original arguments:*

Reason 1. Invalid because Earth and Water are spheres with the same center.

Reason 2. Invalid because of the external influence of Universal Nature, counteracting the internal influence of Particular Nature.

Reason 3. Invalid because it is sphericity of the sea and not the lowness of the land which interferes with one's view at sea.

Reason 4. Invalid because Water does not flow to the tops of mountains, but ascends thither in the form of vapors.

Reason 5. Invalid because Water imitating the moon in one respect, need not imitate it in all.

▣ 4. The Rise of the Universities

It is impossible to fix a specific date for the founding of a medieval university. These institutions were the products of an evolutionary process involving several steps. Generally the pattern was as follows: outstanding teachers at cathedral and collegiate churches attracted students from vast distances and thus acquired for their schools the title studium generale; *the Pope granted the chancellors of these better schools the right to issue to their graduates a license to teach anywhere in Christendom* (licentia docendi unique); *as a means of protecting their interests against interference by the scholasticus (chancellor) or secular rulers, the teachers formed a guild* (universitas); *also feeling the necessity for protection, students organized their own guilds. The appearance of the teachers' guild or* universitas *best marks the dividing line between cathedral school and university. When through Papal charter de facto control over the issuance of the teaching license was passed into the hands of the masters, the independence of the university was secured.*

The charter cited here provides an interesting account of the student examination and the granting of the teaching license.

PAPAL CHARTER FOR THE ESTABLISHMENT OF THE UNIVERSITY OF AVIGNON, 1303

The city of Avignon for many reasons is eminently suited and fitted to become the seat of a university. Believing that it would be for the

Oliver J. Thatcher and Edgar Holmes McNeal (eds.), A Source Book for Medieval History (New York: Charles Scribner's Sons, 1905), pp. 334–36.

public good if those who cultivate wisdom were introduced into the city, and that they would in time bear rich fruit, by this document we grant that a university may be established there, in which Masters [*magistri*] may teach, and scholars freely study and hear lectures, in all faculties. And when those who study in the university attain a high degree of knowledge, and ask for the permission to teach others, we grant that they may be examined in the canon and civil law, and in medicine, and in the liberal arts, and that they may be decorated with the title of Master in those faculties. All who are to be promoted to this honor shall be presented to the bishop of Avignon. He shall call together all the Masters in the faculty concerned, and without any charge he shall examine the candidates to discover their learning, eloquence, manner of reading [lecturing], and the other things which are required in those who are to be made Doctors or Masters. He shall then consult the Masters about the examination and they shall vote on the question of granting the degree [that is, decide whether the candidate passed the examination or not]. But their vote shall be kept secret, and the bishop shall never tell how they voted on the question. Those whom he finds fit, he shall approve, and grant them the permission to teach others. But those whom he finds are not fit, he shall refuse without fear or favor. If the bishopric of Avignon is vacant, the candidates shall present themselves to the *præpositus* of the church, who shall examine them and approve them in the way prescribed for the bishop.

Those who are examined and approved in Avignon and receive the license to teach, shall thereafter have the full and free right to read and teach everywhere, in that faculty in which they have been approved, without further examination or approval by anyone else.

In order that such examinations may be properly held, we command that all Masters who wish to read in the University of Avignon shall, before beginning their work there as teachers, take a public oath that they will come in person to all the examinations whenever called, and that they will, *gratis* and without fear or favor, faithfully give the bishop their judgement about the examination, in order that those who are worthy may be approved, and those who are unworthy may be rejected. Those who refuse to take this oath shall not be permitted to read in the university, or to be present at the examinations, or to share in any of the advantages or benefits of the university.

In order that the Doctors [teachers] and scholars of the university may be able to devote themselves freely to their studies, and to make good progress in them, we grant that all who are in the university, whether teachers or scholars, shall have all the privileges, liberties, and immunities which are generally granted to teachers and scholars of other universities.

The prestige of the university was such that both princes and Popes were concerned for its well-being. The response of King Philip Augustus to a serious "town-gown" riot in Paris in 1200 reflects upon the stature of the university and the recognition by the king that dissatisfied masters and students could easily pack up and leave the city.

THE GRANTING OF PRIVILEGES TO THE UNIVERSITY OF PARIS BY PHILIP AUGUSTUS, KING OF FRANCE

Concerning the safety of the students at Paris in the future, by the advice of our subjects we have ordained as follows:

We will cause all the citizens of Paris to swear that if any one sees an injury done to any student by any layman, he will testify truthfully to this, nor will any one withdraw in order not to see [the act]. And if it shall happen that any one strikes a student, except in self-defense, especially if he strikes the student with a weapon, a club, or a stone, all laymen who see [the act] shall in good faith seize the malefactor, or malefactors, and deliver them to our judge; nor shall they run away in order not to see the act, or seize the malefactor, or testify to the truth. Also, whether the malefactor is seized in open crime or not, we will make a legal and full examination through clerks, or laymen, or certain lawful persons; and our count and our judges shall do the same. And if by a full examination we, or our judges, are able to learn that he who is accused, is guilty of the crime, then we, or our judges, shall immediately inflict a penalty, according to the quality and nature of the crime; notwithstanding the fact that the criminal may deny the deed and say that he is ready to defend himself in single combat, or to purge himself by the ordeal by water.

Also, neither our provost nor our judges shall lay hands on a student for any offense whatever; nor shall they place him in our prison, unless such a crime has been committed by the student, that he ought to be arrested. And in that case, our judge shall arrest him on the spot, without striking him at all, unless he resists, and shall hand him over to the ecclesiastical judge, who ought to guard him in order to satisfy us and the one suffering the injury. And if a serious crime has been committed, our judge shall go or shall send to see what is done with the student. If, indeed, the student does not resist arrest and yet suffers any injury, we will exact satisfaction for it, according to the aforesaid examination and the aforesaid oath. Also our judges shall not lay hands on the chattels of the students of Paris for any crime whatever. But if it

Frederick A. Ogg (ed.), A Source Book of Medieval History (*New York: American Book Co., 1907*), *pp. 343–45.*

shall seem that these ought to be sequestrated, they shall be sequestrated and guarded after sequestration by the ecclesiastical judge, in order that whatever is judged legal by the Church may be done with the chattels. But if students are arrested by our count at such an hour that the ecclesiastical judge cannot be found and be present at once, our provost shall cause the culprits to be guarded in some student's house without any ill-treatment, as is said above, until they are delivered to the ecclesiastical judge. *[Note: All students at Paris held clerical status.]*

In order, moreover, that these [decrees] may be kept more carefully and may be established forever by a fixed law, we have decided that our present provost and the people of Paris shall affirm by an oath, in the presence of the scholars, that they will carry out in good faith all the above-mentioned [regulations]. And always in the future, whosoever receives from us the office of provost in Paris, among the inaugural acts of his office, namely, on the first or second Sunday, in one of the churches of Paris—after he has been summoned for the purpose—shall affirm by an oath, publicly in the presence of the scholars, that he will keep in good faith all the above-mentioned [regulations]. And that these decrees may be valid forever, we have ordered this document to be confirmed by the authority of our seal and by the characters of the royal name signed below.

That the citizens of a university town often had to bear much at the hands of the privileged students is illustrated by a fourteenth-century petition from the Senators of Rome to the Pope.

To the most holy Father, etc.

The detestable infamy of crimes which are continually committed by certain sons of iniquity, who claim only in word the distinction of the clerical character, being themselves utter strangers to all honesty of morals and knowledge of letters, hath moved us to write to the feet of your Holiness. Know indeed, most Holy Father, that many in the city, furnished only with the shield and privilege conferred by the first tonsure, strive not in honesty of manners, but rather are ordinarily guided by the rule of horrible misdeeds; wandering armed from tavern to tavern and other unhonest places; sometimes going on to quarrel or fight in arms with laymen; committing manslaughter, thefts, robberies and very many other things that are far from honesty. For which things no safeguard or remedy is applied by the ecclesiastical judges holding the place of your most Holy See; but rather, when [these evildoers] are accused of the aforesaid misdeeds in our courts, they compel us

G. G. Coulton (ed.), A Medieval Garner, *pp. 488–89. Copyright, 1911, by Constable &
Co. Ltd. Reprinted by permission of Constable & Co. Ltd.*

to release them from our examination, saying that they themselves will see to the infliction of a fine upon them; and thus, under the cloke of such assertions, these so nefarious and most criminal men, hateful both to God and to man, pass unpunished; which is known to redound no little to the dishonour of the Holy See and to the damage of the Romans. Moreover, this is imputed to our official negligence, when misdeeds so enormous are not quelled by the rigour of our justice; and a most horrible and detestable belief haunts the minds of the Romans, who will say at times, in our presence or elsewhere: "Alas! these miscreants who call themselves clerics and yet comport themselves as layfolk, wherefore are they not punished out of their evil courses? In this the Senators do ill; for in the past, when our lord Boniface of blessed memory sat on the papal chair, the Senate made complaint to him concerning like matters, and he not only commanded their punishment but was as it were troubled in mind against them, for those who had gone scot-free; so likewise, if our present Lord learned the truth, he also would be displeased at their impunity." Wherefore we most piously beseech your Holiness, with all humility and devotion, that if it should so befall that our rigour should go so far as to punish them in virtue of our office as judges, then you would vouchsafe (if it so please you) to permit this unto us and to support us in future with the authority of your Holiness. For let not your clemency believe that we are on this account minded to go so far as to touch clerics in possession of church benefices, whom we are purposed and ready to treat with all due reverence, since we are unwilling to do anything derogatory to ecclesiastical liberties. For, most Holy Father, we fear lest, if the aforesaid impious fellows are not controlled to some extent by the secular arm, then the people of Rome will grow to such horror of these their misdeeds as to rise up in wrath and fury not only against these, but even against the aforesaid clerics who are zealous for the orthodox faith. Meanwhile we are ready from the bottom of our heart to carry out cheerfully whatsoever may conduce to the honour of the Papal See.

If the reader still possesses the impression that the medieval student was, like the cloistered monk, interested only in his prayers and books, these lyrics of student songs should provide second thoughts.

The first is a tenth century piece, marked by an element of tenderness in sentiment which is essentially modern. It is the invitation of a young man to his mistress, bidding her to a little supper at his home.

Ogg, op. cit., *pp. 353–57.*

"Come therefore now, my gentle fere,
Whom as my heart I hold full dear;
Enter my little room, which is
Adorned with quaintest rarities:
There are the seats with cushions spread,
The roof with curtains overhead:
The house with flowers of sweetest scent
And scattered herbs is redolent:
A table there is deftly dight
With meats and drinks of rare delight;
There too the wine flows, sparkling, free;
And all, my love, to pleasure thee.
There sound enchanting symphonies;
The clear high notes of flutes arise;
A singing girl and artful boy
Are chanting for thee strains of joy;
He touches with his quill the wire,
She tunes her note unto the lyre:
The servants carry to and fro
Dishes and cups of ruddy glow;
But these delights, I will confess,
Than pleasant converse charm me less;
Nor is the feast so sweet to me
As dear familiarity.

Then come now, sister of my heart,
That dearer than all others art,
Unto mine eyes thou shining sun,
Soul of my soul, thou only one!
I dwelt alone in the wild woods,
And loved all secret solitudes;
Oft would I fly from tumults far,
And shunned where crowds of people are.
O dearest, do not longer stay!
Seek we to live and love to-day!
I cannot live without thee, sweet!
Time bids us now our love complete."

The next is a begging petition, addressed by a student on the road to some resident of the place where he was temporarily staying. The supplication for alms, in the name of learning, is cast in the form of a sing-song doggerel.

I, a wandering scholar lad,
    Born for toil and sadness,
Oftentimes am driven by
    Poverty to madness.

Literature and knowledge I
　　Fain would still be earning,
Were it not that want of pelf
　　Makes me cease from learning.

These torn clothes that cover me
　　Are too thin and rotten;
Oft I have to suffer cold,
　　By the warmth forgotten.

Scarce I can attend at church,
　　Sing God's praises duly;
Mass and vespers both I miss,
　　Though I love them truly.

Oh, thou pride of N——,
　　By thy worth I pray thee
Give the suppliant help in need,
　　Heaven will sure repay thee.

Take a mind unto thee now
　　Like unto St. Martin;
Clothe the pilgrim's nakedness
　　Wish him well at parting.

So may God translate your soul
　　Into peace eternal,
And the bliss of saints be yours
　　In His realm supernal.

The following jovial *Song of the Open Road* throbs with exhilaration and even impudence. Two vagabond students are drinking together before they part. One of them undertakes to expound the laws of the brotherhood which bind them together. The refrain is intended apparently to imitate a bugle call.

We in our wandering,
Blithesome and squandering,
　　Tara, tantara, teino!

Eat to satiety,
Drink to propriety;
　　Tara, tantara, teino!

Laugh till our sides we split,
Rags on our hides we fit;
　　Tara, tantara, teino!

Jesting eternally,
Quaffing infernally;
　　Tara, tantara, teino!

Craft's in the bone of us,
Fear 'tis unknown of us;
   Tara, tantara, teino!

When we're in neediness,
Thieve we with greediness:
   Tara, tantara, teino!

Brother catholical,
Man apostolical,
   Tara, tantara, teino!

Say what you will have done,
What you ask 'twill be done!
   Tara, tantara, teino!

Folk, fear the toss of the
Horns of philosophy!
   Tara, tantara, teino!

Here comes a quadruple [quadrivium]
Spoiler and prodigal!
   Tara, tantara, teino!

License and vanity
Pamper insanity:
   Tara, tantara, teino!

As the Pope bade us do,
Brother to brother's true:
   Tara, tantara, teino!

Brother, best friend, adieu!
Now, I must part from you!
   Tara, tantara, teino!

When will our meeting be?
Glad shall our greeting be!
   Tara, tantara, teino!

Vows valedictory
Now have the victory:
   Tara, tantara, teino!

Clasped on each other's breast,
Brother to brother pressed,
   Tara, tantara, teino!

回 5. University Studies

Whether the medieval university student found himself in the faculty of Arts, Medicine, Law, or Theology, the regimen leading to the degree and teaching license involved listening to his masters read and lecture on required books and engage in scholarly debate. For his part he was expected to repeat the content of the master's lecture by answering prescribed questions, to engage in formal disputations, and, with the exceptions of Cambridge and Oxford, to submit to oral examinations as part of the graduation ceremony. The list of books cited below provides striking evidence of the predominant role of the works of Aristotle in the Arts curriculum.

LIST OF BOOKS PRESCRIBED FOR THE DEGREES OF A.B. AND A.M. AT PARIS, 1254

The following list from the Statutes of 1254 does not separate the books into the groups required for each degree, but indicates the total requirement for both.

(1) The "Old" Logic
- Introduction to the Categories of Aristotle (Isagoge), Porphyry.
- Categories, and On Interpretation, Aristotle.
- Divisions, and Topics except Bk. IV, Boethius.

(2) The "New" Logic
- Prior and Posterior Analytics, Aristotle.
- Sophistical Refutations, "
- Topics, "

(4) Natural Philosophy
- Physics, Aristotle.
- On the Heavens and the Earth, "
- Meteorics, "
- On Animals, "
- " the Soul, "
- " Generation, "
- " Sense and Sensible Things, "
- " Sleep and Waking, "
- " Memory and Recollection, "
- Life and Death, "
- Plants, " (?)

(5) Metaphysics: Metaphysics, "

(6) Other Books
- On the Six Principles, Gilbert de la Porrée.
- Barbarismus (Bk. 3, Larger Grammar), Donatus.
- Grammar (Major and Minor), Priscian.
- On Causes, Costa ben Luca.
- On the Differences of Spirit and Soul (another translation of On Causes).

Norton, op. cit., pp. 136–37.

The following compilation of medical books used at Montpellier attests both to the predominant influence of Galen and Hippocrates and the enormous debt owed to the Arabs as transmittors of ancient learning.

Books read at Montpellier	When Translated
1. *De Complexionibus* = De Temperamentis—Galeni.	From Arabic, by Gerard, of Cremona, at Toledo in twelfth century. Afterwards direct from Greek (by Linacre in sixteenth century).
2. *De Malicia complexionis diversæ* =De Inæquali intemperie —Galeni.	From Arabic by the same. Also by Linacre as above.
3. *De Simplici Medicina* = De Simplicium medicamen torum temperamentis et facultatibus—Galeni. Translated into Arabic by Honain (Joannitius).	From Arabic by the same. (Many Arabic expressions in the Paris MSS.—Leclerc.) The short title is significant.
4. *De Morbo et Accidenti*—doubtful, probably = De Morborum causis, De Morborum differentiis, De Symptomat. causis (lib. iii.), De Sympt. differentiis, or an abridgement of all these books— Galen. In some printed editions they are called *De Morbis et Symptomatibus*.	This is not in any list of translations made at Toledo, or by Gerard or Constantine. For other reasons also I think it does not belong to the oldest group of translations, and was made probably in the thirteenth century, not in the twelfth; but from the *Arabic*, as shown by the title.
5. *De Crisi et Criticis Diebus*= De Crisibus (lib. iii.), and De diebus criticis—Galeni.	From Arabic, by Gerard, in the twelfth century.
6. *De Ingenio Sanitatis* = Methodus Medendi, sometimes called Megatechne or Megategni (lib. xii) — Galeni. Not the work *De Sanitate tuenda*.	From Arabic, among the earliest group of translations, being referred to by the translator of No. 7; and probably, but not certainly, by Gerard (perhaps Constantine?).

Hastings Rashdall, The Universities of Europe in the Middle Ages, *eds. F. M. Powicke and A. B. Emden, II, pt. 2, 780–83. Copyright 1895 by the Clarendon Press, new edition 1936 (material reprinted here not contained in new edition). Reprinted by permission of the Clarendon Press, Oxford.*

7. *Tegni* of Galen=τέχνη ἰατρική =Ars parva, often with the comment of Haly ben Rodoan.

Translated from Arabic by Constantine; and with the comment of Haly by Gerard.

8. *Prognostics* of Aratus=Διοσημεῖα, a meteorological poem said to be founded on Meteorologica of Artistotle.

No record of any Arabic translation. It is said there were Latin translations made from the Greek.

9. *Aphorisms* of Hippocrates (with commentary of Galen, —the first work of Galen translated into Latin, according to Constantinus Africanus).

From Arabic by Constantine at Monte Cassino—eleventh century.

10. *Johannicius* = 'Regimenti,' This must mean the Ysagoge in Medicinam, the only work of Joann. translated; prefixed to numerous MSS.

Early translation from Arabic; name of translator not given.

11. *Liber Febrium* of Isaac= Isaac Judæus, written in Arabic.

From Arabic by Constantine— eleventh century.

12. *Antidotarium,* probably of Nicolaus, Præpositus of Salerno, twelfth century.

Latin original.

* * * * *

BOOKS LECTURED ON IN 1340	WHEN AND WHERE TRANSLATED
1. *Primus Canonis*—Avicennæ.	From Arabic by Gerard of Cremona at Toledo; twelfth century.
2. *De Morbo et Accid.*—Galeni.	A 'versio antiqua,' probably from Arabic, of this treatise is referred to more than once. (Kühn's Galen, I. c. i.)
Dedifferentiis Febrium—Galeni.	See above.
3. *De crisi,* &c.; De Malicia, &c. —Galeni. (See in other list).	See other list.
4. *De Simplicibus Medicinis*= probably No. 3 in other list —Galeni.	See other list.
De Complexionibus — Galeni. (See other list).	See other list.

5. *De Juvamentis Membrorum* = Galeni de Usu Partium. — From Arabic—anonymous. Probably not in earliest group.

   De Interioribus = Galeni de Locis Affectis. — From Arabic, by Constantine.

6. *Liber Amphorism.* Hippocratis. — See other list

   De Regimine Acutorum. Hippocratis.

   De Prognosticis = Prognosticon Hippocratis.

        Both from Arabic by Gerard, at Toledo. (Some MSS. attribute to Constantine.)

These three works were all commented by Galen, and occur together with the comment in MSS.

7. *Liber de Ingenio* = De Ingenio Sanitatis Galeni. (See No 6 in other list.) — See other list.

   Ad Glauconem = Therapeutica vel de Methodo Medendi ad Glauconem, Galeni (not the same as the great Methodus Medendi). — I cannot trace translation; but is known to have existed in Arabic

8. *Quartus Canonis* — Avicennæ quoad duas primas (Fen.). — Translated from the Arabic, at Toledo, by Gerard of Cremona.

   Johannicius *de Pulsibus.* There is no known work of J. thus entitled; probably = Philareti de Pulsibus.

   De Urinis = Theophili Protospatharii de Urinis (Greek Christian writer of the seventh century A. D.; *Philaretus* is believed to be the same man).

        Old translations: traditional; not known to have passed through Arabic.

These two works are constantly found in MSS. immediately following the Isagoge of Johannitius; hence the confusion. These *three* works form the beginning of the printed collection called Articella, which, in early editions, also includes Hipp. Aphorism, Regim. Acutorum and Prognostics all with comments by Galen; and Tegni Galeni (as in other list).

9. *Tegni* Galeni, &c. (See No. 6 in this list and No. 7 in other list.)
10. *De Regimine Sanit.* =*possibly* the Regimen of the Schola Salernitana; but on the other hand Galen's *De Sanitate tuenda* bears this title in the old MSS., and it may refer to this. The old rhyming poem was meant for popular use and perhaps would hardly be used as a text book.
11. *De Virtutibus Naturalibus* = Galeni de Alimentorum Facultatibus. This was translated at Bologna by Accursius Pistoriensis in 1200 A.D. (from Arabic—Leclerc). (Merton College MSS. 218, Coxe's Catalogue.)

The teacher Odofredus (c. 1200–65) provides a description of the mode of lecturing on Roman Law at the University of Bologna.

First, I shall give you summaries of each title before I proceed to the text; secondly, I shall give you as clear and explicit a statement as I can of the purport of each Law (included in the title); thirdly, I shall read the text with a view to correcting it; fourthly, I shall briefly repeat the contents of the Law; fifthly, I shall solve apparent contradictions, adding any general principles of Law (to be extracted from the passage), commonly called "Brocardica", and any distinctions or subtle and useful problems (*quaestiones*) arising out of the Law with their solutions, as far as the Divine Providence shall enable me. And if any Law shall seem deserving, by reason of its celebrity or difficulty, of a Repetition, I shall reserve it for an evening Repetition.

Hastings Rashdall, The Universities of Europe in the Middle Ages, *eds. F. M. Powicke and A. B. Emden, I, 218. Copyright 1895 by the Clarendon Press, new edition 1936. Reprinted by permission of The Clarendon Press.*

The following statute illustrates that the masters at Bologna shared at least one difficulty with their modern counterparts: the problem of completing a prescribed course in the allotted time. The students, who governed the university, were obviously determined that the masters fulfill their responsibilities. The term "glosses" refers to the commentaries and explanations of scholars, which the masters presented after their reading of the day's portion of the text.

We have decreed also that all Doctors actually lecturing must read the glosses immediately after reading the chapter or the law, unless the continuity of the chapters or of the laws requires otherwise, taking the burden in this matter on their own consciences in accordance with the oath they have taken. Nor, with regard to those things that are not to be read, must they yield to the clamor of the scholars. Furthermore we decree that Doctors, lecturing ordinarily or extraordinarily, must come to the sections assigned *de novo*, according to the regulations below. And we decree, as to the close observance by them of the passages, that any Doctor, in his ordinary lecturing in Canon or Civil Law, must deposit, fifteen days before the Feast of Saint Michael, twenty-five Bologna pounds with one of the treasurers whom the rectors have appointed; which treasurer shall promise to give said money to the rectors, or the general beadle in their name, all at once or in separate amounts, as he shall be required by them or by him.

The form, moreover, to be observed by the Doctors as to the sections is this: Let the division of the book into sections (*puncta*) be determined, and then let him be notified. [And if any Doctor fails to reach any section on the specified date he shall be fined three Bologna pounds, while for a second offense he shall be fined five pounds, and for a third and each succeeding violation of the rule, ten pounds.] And if the twenty-five pounds are exhausted, he must deposit in said place a second twenty-five pounds; and the second deposit must be made within eight days from the time when the first was exhausted. . . .

We decree also that no Doctor shall hereafter exceed one section in one lecture. And if the contrary be done by any one he shall be charged with perjury and punished to the extent of three pounds, to be taken from the money deposited for the purpose; and as often as the violation occurs, so often shall the penalty be inflicted, so long as the statute is in force; and the Rector also must exact it.

We add that at the end of a section the Doctors must announce to the scholars at what section they are to begin afterwards, and they shall be obliged to follow that section which they have begun, even to the end of the section. But if by chance, after due weight is given to the glosses or text, it seems useful to transfer a part of the lecture to another

Norton, op. cit., *pp. 112–13.*

section, he shall be obliged in his preceding lecture to announce that to the scholars, so that those who wish may make provision beforehand; under penalty of five Bologna shillings for each occasion for the Doctor who does to the contrary.

We order this statute to be published in each school at the beginning of the term. . . .

An excellent description of the graduation ceremonies at Bologna is furnished by Hastings Rashdall, leading authority in the study of medieval universities.

The account which must now be given of the graduation ceremony at Bologna relates to the period in which it was presided over by the archdeacon. Of the earlier procedure we know nothing; but in all probability the main outlines of the ceremony were already established before the introduction of the archidiaconal presidency. The process of graduation consisted of two parts: (1) the private examination, (2) the public examination or *conventus*.

The private examination was the real test of competence, the so-called public examination being in practice a mere ceremony. Before admission to each of these tests the candidate was presented by the *consiliarius* of his nation to the rector for permission to enter it, and swore that he had complied with all the statutable conditions, that he would give no more than the statutable fees or entertainments to the rector himself, the doctor or his fellow-students, and that he would obey the rector. Within a period of eight days before the examination the candidate was presented by 'his own' doctor or by some other doctor or by two doctors to the archdeacon, the presenting doctor being required to have satisfied himself by private examination of his presentee's fitness. Early on the morning of the examination, after attending a Mass of the Holy Ghost, the candidate appeared before the assembled college and was assigned by one of the doctors present two passages (*puncta*) in the civil or canon law as the case might be. He then retired to his house to study the passages, in doing which it would appear that he had the assistance of the presenting doctor. Later in the day the doctors were summoned to the cathedral or some other public building by the archdeacon, who presided over but took no active part in the ensuing examination. The candidate was then introduced to the archdeacon and doctors by the presenting doctor or *promotor* as he was styled. The prior of the college then administered a number of oaths in which the candidate promised respect to that body and solemnly renounced all the rights of which the college had succeeded in robbing all doctors not included in its ranks. The candidate then gave a lecture

Rashdall, op. cit., I, 224–29. Reprinted by permission of The Clarendon Press.

or exposition of the two prepared passages: after which he was examined upon them by two of the doctors appointed by the college. Other doctors might ask supplementary questions of law (which they were required to swear that they had not previously communicated to the candidate) arising more indirectly out of the passages selected, or might suggest objections to the answers. With a tender regard for the feelings of their comrades at this 'rigorous and tremendous examination' (as they style it) the students by their statutes required the examiner to treat the examinee 'as his own son'. The examination concluded, the votes of the doctors present were taken by ballot and the candidate's fate determined by the majority, the decision being announced by the archdeacon.

A candidate who had passed the private, and had been admitted to the public examination, became a licentiate. Normally and naturally the licentiate proceeded to the ceremony which made him a full doctor after a very short interval; but the expense of this step sometimes compelled candidates to postpone it, while others (in spite of statutory prohibition) went off and took it at a cheaper university. On the day of the *conventus,* or public examination, the love of pageantry characteristic of the medieval and especially of the Italian mind was allowed the amplest gratification. Shortly before the day appointed the candidate had ridden round the city to invite public officials or private friends to the ceremony or to the ensuing banquet, preceded by the bedels of the archdeacon and of the promotor or promotors. The statutes, indeed, forbade on this occasion the blowing of trumpets or other instruments, but on the actual day of the *conventus* no such sumptuary limitation was imposed. On that day the candidate was accompanied to the cathedral by the presenting doctor, and by his 'socii' or fellow-students lodging in the same house with him. The idea of the 'conventus' or 'public examination', was essentially the same as that of the ceremony known as the 'principium' or 'inceptio' in the northern universities. That idea was derived from the principle of the Roman law according to which a man was invested with the *de facto* possession of his office by an actual and solemn performance of its functions. At the same time and by the same act the new doctor was recognized by his colleagues and received into the teaching guild or brotherhood, though at Bologna (as has been explained), by the period with which we are dealing, that admission had ceased to carry with it a practical right to the full exercise of the doctor's teaching functions.

Arrived at the cathedral, the licentiate delivered a speech and read a thesis on some point of law, which he defended against opponents who were selected from among the students, the candidates thus playing for the first time the part of a doctor in a university disputation. He was then presented by his promotor to the archdeacon, who made a complimentary oration, and concluded by solemnly conferring the licence to teach the civil, canon, or both laws as the case might be, by the authority of the Pope and in the name of the Holy Trinity. In pursuance of the licence thus conferred, he was then invested by the promotor with the *insignia* of the teaching office, each no doubt with some appropriate formula. He was seated in the magisterial chair or *cathedra*. He was handed the open book—one of the law texts which it was his function to expound. A gold ring was placed upon his finger, whether in token of his espousal to science, or in indication of the doctor's claim to be the equal of knights, and the magisterial *biretta* placed upon his head: after which the promotor left him with a paternal embrace, a kiss, and a benediction. The ceremony concluded, both universities were required to escort him in triumph through the town, surrounded no doubt by a mounted cavalcade of personal friends or wealthier students, and preceded by the three university pipers and the four university trumpeters.

V

Education and the Renaissance

MOST *students of history are well aware that "renaissance" means "rebirth" and that the term has been applied to an era embracing the fourteenth, fifteenth, and early sixteenth centuries, which witnessed a dramatic revival of interest in and a desire to emulate the art, literature, and spirit of classical Greece and Rome. However, the Renaissance was more than worship of the past and represents a more radical change than the term implies. It was a period of revolt against many things: the ascetic view of man, the restrictions of medieval church authority, the restraints that fear and superstition placed on man's knowledge of the world in which he lived. Scholars were directly involved in this period of change. In their interests, their creations, and in the developments in education, one can clearly grasp the spirit of the age.*

No period in history exists in isolation from the one that precedes it. During the decades of the late Middle Ages man's eyes began to open to the possibilities of human creativity and power. The Crusades, the rise of commerce and towns, the consolidation of political power, and the decline of feudalism played important roles. In the world of scholarship the discovery of Aristotle's works, the scholastic movement, and the rise of universities set the stage for the Renaissance. Indeed, it was not total ignorance against which Renaissance scholars revolted but the narrow confines into which learning had been squeezed, the petty squabbles of scholastic debaters, the professionalism of the universities. (1) In contrast to the theologic diatribes of the scholastics, the literature of classical poets, historians, dramatists, and essayists was truly dazzling to men like Petrarch, Vives, Erasmus, and Thomas More. In fact, so enamored was Petrarch with the classical authors that he denigrated his own brilliant creations. (2)

The relics of classical antiquity were broad in scope and provided stimulation for a variety of interests. Art and architecture were enriched, literary men were inspired, and men of nobility and wealth were provided with new models on which to pattern their lives. The days of constant feudal warfare, of moated castles, were passing. Home was becoming more a place of rest and comfort and less an armed fortress, and, like the Greeks and Romans of old, knights and gentlemen yearned to savor and sponsor the cultural life. For those who sought to be princes of the Renaissance there were scholars aplenty with advice concerning the proper path to follow. (3)

It was inevitable that education would be caught up in the Renaissance movement. Informal conversations in court and guidebooks regarding the correct interests of a Renaissance prince might suffice for the fathers, but for the sons the proper sphere of training was the school. Among the rediscoveries of the Renaissance the educational writings of Quintilian, Plutarch, Cicero, and others caused their share of excitement and furnished fuel for a revival of interest in investigating and theorizing on the nature of teaching and learning. (4) When the wealth of princes was utilized to support schools, humanist scholars were afforded an opportunity to translate theory into practice. When the Marchese Gian Francesco Gonzaga provided the scholar Vittorino Da Feltre with the facilities to establish a school, the results proved a model for the age, a magnificent blending of education for Christian character, the knightly arts and graces, and exposure to the great literary achievements of the classical age. In Vittorino's school and others like it, the ideal of the well-rounded classical education for mind, body and spirit was reborn. (5)

However, as so often happens, with the passage of time the noble purpose of this education was lost, and only the skeleton remained. The result was the classical secondary school of Europe, where young students were introduced to a curriculum almost totally devoted to the study of Latin and Greek grammar and literature and where the ability to translate, memorize, and imitate the works of the classical authors took precedence over understanding and appreciation. Here were born the Latin grammar school of the English, the collège of the French, and the gymnasium of the Germans. These schools endured for centuries in Europe and were later established in America. Ultimately they were to be criticized for excessive looking backwards, for failing to meet the needs of contemporary society, and for tending to ignore or deprecate the values of more recent contributions in the arts, sciences, and literature. (6)

回 1. The Revolt Against Scholasticism

When the excitement occasioned by the rediscovery of Aristotle's writings had turned to worship of his views as the final authority in philosophy and science, and when the scholastic debaters adopted ever more petty topics as vehicles for displaying their oratorical talents, serious scholars rose in opposition. In the selection that follows, the Spanish scholar Juan Luis Vives (1462–1540) describes the low state to which scholastic disputation and teaching had fallen.

Disputations, also, to no slight degree have blinded judgement. They were instituted originally (but only among young men) to stimulate mental vigor, often torpid, and to make young men keener in their studies, so that they might either conquer or not be conquered, and also that the instruction received from their teachers might be more deeply impressed upon them.

Among men, or older persons, there was a kind of comparison of opinions and reasons, not aimed at victory but at unravelling the truth. The very name testifies that they are called disputations because by their means the truth is, as it were, pruned or purged [dis=apart; puto=to prune, or to cleanse]. But after praise and reward came from listeners to the one who seemed to have the best ideas, and out of the praise often came wealth and resources, a base greed of distinction or money took possession of the minds of the disputants, and, just as in a battle, victory only was the consideration, and not the elucidation of truth. So that they defended strenuously whatever they once had said, and overthrew and trampled upon their adversary.

Low and sordid minds such as with drooping heads look solely at such trivial and ephemeral results, regarded as of small consequence the great benefit that results from study:—namely probity or knowledge of truth; and these two things they did not regard with sufficient acuteness nor did they comprehend their great value, but they sought the immediate reward of money or popular favor.

And so, in order to get a greater return for their labor, they admitted the populace to their contests like the spectators of a play brought out at the theatre. Then, as one might expect when the standard is lowered, the philosopher laid aside his dignified, venerable character, and put on his stage dress that he might dance more easily: the populace was made spectator, umpire, and judge, and the philosopher did that which the flute player does not do on the stage,—he suited his music, not to his own ideas and to the Muses, as his old teacher advises, but wholly to the circle of onlookers and the crowd whence distinction and gain was likely to come back to the actors.

There was no need of real, solid teaching (at least, not in the opinion

Arthur O. Norton (ed.), Readings in the History of Education, Medieval Universities *(Cambridge: Harvard University Press, 1909), pp. 121–24. Reprinted by permission of the publishers from Arthur O. Norton*, Readings in the History of Education: Medieval Universities. *Cambridge Mass.: Harvard University Press.*

of those who are going to learn); but pretence and dust were thrown in the eyes of the crowd. So the one plain road of obtaining the truth was abandoned; six hundred ways of pretending were made, by which each strove for what suited himself, especially since there is nothing made so ugly as to lack a sponsor.

Not only did the populace flock to this opinion—that the object of learning is to dispute, just as it is the object of military life to fight—but the public unanimity swept away the veterans, the *triarii* [the more experienced soldiers who were placed in the third line] as it were, of the scholastic campaign (but these have no more ability and judgement than the dregs of the people), so that they regard him as superflous and foolish who would call them back to mental activity and character and that quiet method of investigation, philosophy. [They think that] there is no other fruit of studies save to keep your wits about you and not give way to your adversary, either to attack him boldly or to bear up against him, and shrewdly to contrive by what vigor, by what skill, by what method of supplanting, he may be overturned. Therefore under this beautiful scheme, surpassing all others, it was the plan to break in the boy immediately and train him constantly; they began disputing as soon as they were born and ceased only at death. The boy brought to school, is bidden to dispute forthwith on the first day and is already taught to quarrel, before he can yet speak at all. So also in Grammar, in the Poets, in the Historians, in Logic, in Rhetoric, in absolutely every branch. Would any one wonder what they can find to do in matters that are perfectly open, very simple and elementary? There is nothing so transparent, so limpid that they do not cloud it over with some petty question as if ruffled by a breeze. It is [thought] characteristic of the most helpless stupidity, not to find something which you may make obscure by most intricate measures and involve in very hard and rigid conditions, which you may twist and twist again. For you may simply say: "Write to me,"—here comes a question, if not from Grammar then from Logic, if not from Logic then from Physics,—"What motions are made in writing?" Or, from Metaphysics, "Is it substance or quality?"

And these boys are hearing the first rudiments of Logic who were only yesterday, or the day before, admitted to the school. So they are to be trained never to be silent, but vigorously to assert whatever comes uppermost lest they may seem at any time to have given in. Nor is one dispute a day enough, nor two, like a meal. At lunch they dispute, after lunch they dispute, at dinner they dispute, after dinner they dispute. Do they do these things to learn, or to cook a new dish? They dispute at home, they dispute away from home. At a banquet, in the bath, in the tepidarium, at church, in the city, in the fields, in public, in private, in all places and at all times they dispute.

Courtesans in charge of a panderer do not wrangle so many times, or gladiators in charge of a trainer do not fight so many times for a prize as these do under their teacher of philosophy. The populace, not self-restrained and serious, but fickle, barbarous, pugnacious, is wonderfully tickled with all this as with a mock battle. So there are very many exceedingly ignorant men, utterly without knowledge of literature in any form, who take more pleasure in this form of show than in all else; and the more easily to win the fight, they employ a quick and prompt mode of fighting and deliver a blow every second, as it were, in order the more speedily to use up their foe. They neither assail their adversary with uninterrupted argument nor can they endure prolonged talk from him. If by way of explaining himself he should begin to enlarge, they raise the cry: "To the point! To the point! Answer categorically!" Showing how restless and flippant *their* minds are who cannot stand a few words. . . .

To such a degree did they go that instead of a settlement based on the strongest arguments, such as drove them into their absurdities, they considered it sufficient to say: "I admit it, for it follows from my own conclusion," and the next step is: "I deny it. Prove it. I will defend it appropriately." For he who "defends appropriately" (in their own words), no matter by what incongruous admissions and concessions, is held to be a learned man and best adapted to disputation, that is, to the apex of all knowledge.

It took no small amount of courage to attack the educational establishment. As may be seen in the following document, there were those in authority who would permit no interference with the traditional curriculum, particularly when that interference involved the introduction of poetry at the expense of religious instruction.

EPISCOPAL ATTACK ON THE CLASSICS IN THE DIOCESE OF EXETER, 1357

Mandate as to teaching boys.

John etc. to his beloved sons in Christ, all the archdeacons in our cathedral church of Exeter and their Officials, health etc.

Not without frequent wonder and a feeling of pity have we personally experienced, and daily experience, among the masters or teachers of boys and of the unlearned of our diocese, that they, while instructing them in grammar, observe a form and order of teaching which are preposterous and useless, indeed superstitious and more like heathens

Arthur Leach (ed.), Educational Charters and Documents, 598–1909 *(Cambridge: The University Press, 1911), pp. 315, 317. By permission of Cambridge University Press.*

than Christians, in that as soon as their scholars have learnt to read or say even very imperfectly the Lord's Prayer, with the Hail Mary and the Creed, also Matins and the Hours of the Blessed Virgin, and the like, which are necessary for faith and the safety of their souls, though they do not know how to construe or understand any of the things before-mentioned, or to decline or parse any of the words in them, they make them pass on prematurely to learn other school books of poetry or in metre. And so it happens that when they are grown up they do not understand what they say or read every day; moreover, which is even more damnable, through want of understanding they do not know the catholic faith.

Desiring, therefore, by all the ways and means possible, to root out so dreadful and stupid an abuse which has become too usual in our diocese, we commission and command you and each of you to order and enjoin on all masters or teachers of boys, presiding over Grammar Schools within the boundaries of your archdeaconry, by our authority, as by virtue of these presents we strictly order and enjoin, that they shall not make the boys whom they receive to learn grammar only to read or learn Latin, as hitherto, but leaving everything else make them construe and understand the Lord's Prayer and Ave Maria, the Creed, Matins and Hours of the Blessed Virgin, and decline the words there and parse them before they let them go on to other books. Informing them that we do not intend to mark any boys with the clerical character unless they have by this means been found to have become proficient.

Dated at our manor of Chudleigh 13 Feb. 1356–7, and the 30th year of our consecration.

2. Petrarch, Man of Many Titles

"Arbiter of the fourteenth century," "mainspring of the Revival," "initiator of the Renaissance," "the first modern man"—all these accolades have been showered on Francesco Petrarca, better known at his desire by the Latin name Petrarch (1304–74). As an initiator of the new, he had the courage to attack the old. Monasticism, scholasticism, legalism, and even Aristotle were subjected to his scorn. After first writing some of the grandest poetry in the Italian language, Petrarch turned his back on creativity in the vernacular to immerse himself completely in the literature of classical antiquity. As a collector and scholar of the works of ancient Greece and Rome—particularly those of Cicero, Virgil, and Ovid—Petrarch was instrumental in ushering in the Revival of Learning that captured the imagination of Europe for two centuries.

In his "Letter to Posterity," Petrarch reveals not only his love for literature but also the Renaissance man's yearning for fame, the same desire that had characterized the classical hero and that the teachings of the Medieval Church had sought to discourage.

FRANCIS PETRARCH, TO POSTERITY, GREETING:

It is possible that some word of me may have come to you, though even this is doubtful, since an insignificant and obscure name will scarcely penetrate far in either time or space. If, however, you should have heard of me, you may desire to know what manner of man I was, or what was the outcome of my labors, especially those of which some description or, at any rate, the bare titles may have reached you.

To begin, then, with myself. The utterances of men concerning me will differ widely, since in passing judgment almost every one is influenced not so much by truth as by preference, and good and evil report alike know no bounds. I was, in truth, a poor mortal like yourself, neither very exalted in my origin, nor, on the other hand, of the most humble birth, but belonging, as Augustus Cæsar says of himself, to an ancient family. As to my disposition, I was not naturally perverse or wanting in modesty, however the contagion of evil associations may have corrupted me.

My youth was gone before I realized it; I was carried away by the strength of manhood. But a riper age brought me to my senses and taught me by experience the truth I had long before read in books, that youth and pleasure are vanity—nay, that the Author of all ages and times permits us miserable mortals, puffed up with emptiness, thus to wander about, until finally, coming to a tardy consciousness of our sins, we shall learn to know ourselves.

In my prime I was blessed with a quick and active body, although not exceptionally strong; and while I do not lay claim to remarkable personal beauty, I was comely enough in my best days. I was possessed of a clear complexion, between light and dark, lively eyes, and for long years a keen vision, which, however, deserted me, contrary to my hopes, after I reached my sixtieth birthday, and forced me, to my great annoyance, to resort to glasses. Although I had previously enjoyed perfect health, old age brought with it the usual array of discomforts.

My parents were honorable folk, Florentine in their origin, of medium fortune, or, I may as well admit it, in a condition verging upon poverty. They had been expelled from their native city, and

Frederick Austin Ogg (ed.), A Source Book of Medieval History *(New York: American Book Co., 1907). pp. 470–73.*

consequently I was born in exile, at Arezzo, in the year 1304 of this latter age, which begins with Christ's birth, July the 20th, on a Monday, at dawn. I have always possessed an extreme contempt for wealth; not that riches are not desirable in themselves, but because I hate the anxiety and care which are invariably associated with them. I certainly do not long to be able to give gorgeous banquets. I have, on the contrary, led a happier existence with plain living and ordinary fare than all the followers of Apicius, with their elaborate dainties. So-called convivia, which are but vulgar bouts, sinning against sobriety and good manners, have always been repugnant to me. I have ever felt that it was irksome and profitless to invite others to such affairs, and not less so to be bidden to them myself. On the other hand, the pleasure of dining with one's friends is so great that nothing has ever given me more delight than their unexpected arrival, nor have I ever willingly sat down to table without a companion. Nothing displeases me more than display, for not only is it bad in itself and opposed to humility, but it is troublesome and distracting.

In my familiar associations with kings and princes, and in my friendship with noble personages, my good fortune has been such as to excite envy. But it is the cruel fate of those who are growing old that they can commonly only weep for friends who have passed away. The greatest kings of this age have loved and courted me. They may know why; I certainly do not. With some of them I was on such terms that they seemed in a certain sense my guests rather than I theirs; their lofty position in no way embarrassing me, but, on the contrary, bringing with it many advantages. I fled, however, from many of those to whom I was greatly attached; [and such was my innate longing for liberty that I studiously avoided those whose very name seemed incompatible with the freedom that I loved.]

I possessed a well-balanced rather than a keen intellect—one prone to all kinds of good and wholesome study, but especially inclined to moral philosophy and the art of poetry. The latter, indeed, I neglected as time went on, and took delight in sacred literature. Finding in that a hidden sweetness which I had once esteemed but lightly, I came to regard the works of the poets as only amenities.

Among the many subjects that interested me, I dwelt especially upon antiquity, for our own age has always repelled me, so that, had it not been for the love of those dear to me, I should have preferred to have been born in any other period than our own. In order to forget my own time, I have constantly striven to place myself in spirit in other ages, and consequently I delighted in history. The conflicting statements troubled me, but when in doubt I accepted what appeared most probable, or yielded to the authority of the writer.

My style, as many claimed, was clear and forcible; but to me it seemed weak and obscure. In ordinary conversation with friends, or with those about me, I never gave thought to my language, and I have always wondered that Augustus Cæsar should have taken such pains in this respect. When, however, the subject itself, or the place or the listener, seemed to demand it, I gave some attention to style, with what success I cannot pretend to say; let them judge in whose presence I spoke. If only I have lived well, it matters little to me how I talked. Mere elegance of language can produce at best but an empty renown....

Petrarch was so enamored of the classical authors that he often spoke of them as if they were still alive and dwelled in close proximity. Indeed, he wrote numerous letters addressed to Cicero, Virgil, Livy, and other ancients. In a portion of one of the letters written to contemporary "flesh and blood" scholars, his devotion to literature is apparent. Note the reference to his unfortunate inability to read Greek. Also of interest is the fact that the injury caused by the volume of Cicero falling on his leg, to which he humorously alludes, eventually led to his death. The heavy book fell on him several times, its silver clasps delivering mortal wounds.

In the succeeding paragraph of your letter you jest with much elegance , saying that I have been wounded by Cicero without having deserved it, on account of our too great intimacy. "Because," you say, "those who are nearest to us most often injure us, and it is extremely rare that an Indian does an injury to a Spaniard." True it is. It is on this account that in reading of the wars of the Athenians and Lacedaemonians, and in contemplating the troubles of our own people with our neighbors, we are never struck with astonishment; still less so at the sight of the civil wars and domestic troubles which habit has made of so little account that concord itself would more easily cause surprise. But when we read that the King of Scythia has come to blows with the king of Egypt, and that Alexander of Macedonia has penetrated to the ends of India, we experience a sensation of astonishment which the reading of our histories, filled as they are with the deeds of Roman bravery in their distant expeditions, does not afford. You bring me consolation, in representing me as having been wounded by Cicero, to whom I am fondly attached, a thing that would probably never happen to me, at the hands of either Hippocrates or Albumazar. . . .

You asked me to lend you the copy of Homer that was on sale at Padua, if, as you suppose, I have purchased it (since, you say, I have for a long time possessed another copy) so that our friend Leo may translate it from Greek into Latin for your benefit and for the benefit of our other studious compatriots. I saw this book, but neglected the

Ogg, op. cit., *pp. 466–69.*

opportunity of acquiring it, because it seemed inferior to my own. It can easily be had with the aid of the person to whom I owe my friendship with Leo; a letter from that source would be all-powerful in the matter, and I will myself write him.

If by chance the book escape us, which seems to be very unlikely, I will let you have mine. I have been always fond of this particular translation and of Greek literature in general, and if fortune had not frowned upon my beginnings, in the sad death of my excellent master, I should be perhaps to-day something more than a Greek still at his alphabet. I approve with all my heart and strength your enterprise, for I regret and am indignant that an ancient translation, presumably the work of Cicero, the commencement of which Horace inserted in his *Ars Poetica*, should have been lost to the Latin world, together with many other works. It angers me to see so much solicitude for the bad and so much neglect of the good. But what is to be done? We must be resigned. . . .

I wish to take this opportunity of warning you of one thing, lest later on I should regret having passed it over in silence. If, as you say, the translation is to be made literally in prose, listen for a moment to the opinion of St. Jerome as expressed in his preface to the book, *De Temporibus*, by Eusebius of Cæsarea, which he translated into Latin. Here are the very words of this great man, well acquainted with these two languages, and indeed with many others, and of special fame for his art of translating: *If any one*, he says, *refuses to believe that translation lessens the peculiar charm of the original, let him render Homer into Latin, word for word; I will say further, let him translate it into prose in his own tongue, and he will see a ridiculous array and the most eloquent of poets transformed into a stammerer.* I tell you this for your own good, while it is yet time, in order that so important a work may not prove useless. As for me, I wish the work to be done, whether well or ill. I am so famished for literature that just as he who is ravenously hungry is not inclined to quarrel with the cook's art, so I await with a lively impatience whatever dishes are to be set before my soul. And in truth, the morsel in which the same Leo, translating into Latin prose the beginning of Homer, has given me a foretaste of the whole work, although it confirms the sentiment of St. Jerome, does not displease me. It possesses, in fact, a secret charm, as certain viands, which have failed to take a moulded shape, although they are lacking in form, preserve nevertheless their taste and odor. May he continue with the aid of Heaven, and may he give us Homer, who has been lost to us!

In asking of me the volume of Plato which I have with me, and which escaped the fire at my transalpine country house, you give me proof of your ardor, and I shall hold this book at your disposal, whenever the time shall come. I wish to aid with all my power such noble enterprises. But beware lest it should be unbecoming to unite in one bundle these two great princes of Greece, lest the weight of these two spirits should overwhelm mortal shoulders. Let your messenger undertake, with God's aid, one of the two, and first him who has written many centuries before the other. Farewell.

▣ 3. Humanist Education for Prince, Courtier, and Statesman

The Humanist ideal of the well-rounded man, trained in mind, body, and spirit attracted the attention of powerful and influential men throughout Western Europe. In the several nations were to be found propagandists of the ideal who were ready and willing to employ the vernacular to express their belief in an education for leadership in which a knowledge of classical languages and literature was as essential as dexterity on the dance floor, skillful use of weapons, appreciation of art and music, and proper employment of the social graces. In England there was Sir Thomas Elyot, author of Boke Named the Governour *and the future Queen Elizabeth's tutor; in France, Guillaume Budé outlined a Humanistic educational plan designed for Francis I. The most famous member of this group was the Italian Baldassare Castiglione (1478–1529), who, in his* Book of the Courtier, *described the proper training for the courtly gentleman and his lady.*

In the excerpt that follows from the Book of the Courtier, *we observe Castiglione setting forth one of the principal arguments of the Humanist movement—that accomplishments in the arts and letters are worthy handmaidens for the man of action. Of course, in the spirit of the times, he draws heavily upon examples of classical heroes to illustrate his points.*

42.—"Yet besides goodness, I think that letters are for everyone the true and principal ornament of the mind: although the French recognize only the nobility of arms and esteem all else as naught. Thus they not only fail to prize but they abhor letters, and hold all men of letters most base, and think they speak very basely of any man when they call him a clerk."

Then the Magnifico Giuliano replied:

"You say truly, that this fault has long been prevalent among the French. But if kind fate decrees that Monseigneur d'Angoulême shall

Count Baldassare Castiglione, The Book of the Courtier, *trans. Leonard Eckstein Opdycke (New York: Horace Liveright, 1902), pp. 56–64.*

succeed to the crown, as is hoped, I think that just as the glory of arms flourishes and shines in France, so too ought that of letters to flourish in highest state; for it is not long since I, being at the court, saw this prince, and it seemed to me that besides the grace of his person and the beauty of his face, he had in his aspect such loftiness, joined however with a certain gracious humanity, that the realm of France must always seem small for him. I heard afterwards from many gentlemen, both French and Italian, of his very noble manner of life, of his loftiness of mind, of his valour and liberality. And among other things I was told that he loved and esteemed letters especially and held all men of letters in greatest honour; and he condemned the French themselves for being so hostile to this profession, especially as they have within their borders such a noble school as that of Paris, frequented by all the world."

Then the Count said:

"It is a great marvel that in such tender youth, solely by natural instinct and against the usage of his country, he has of himself chosen so worthy a path. And as subjects always copy the customs of their superiors, it may be that, as you say, the French will yet come to esteem letters at their true worth: whereto they may easily be persuaded, if they will but listen to reason; since nothing is by nature more desirable for men, or more proper to them, than knowledge, which it is great folly to say or believe is not always a good thing.

43.—"And If I were speaking with them, or with others who had an opinion contrary to mine, I should strive to show them how useful and necessary letters are to our life and dignity, having indeed been granted by God to men as a crowning gift. Nor should I lack instances of many excellent commanders of antiquity, who all added the ornament of letters to the valour of their arms.

"Thus you know Alexander held Homer in such veneration that he always kept the Iliad by his bedside; and he devoted the greatest attention not only to these studies but to philosophical speculation under Aristotle's guidance. Alcibiades enlarged his natural aptitudes and made them greater by means of letters and the teachings of Socrates. The care that Cæsar gave to study is also attested by the surviving works that he divinely wrote. It is said that Scipio Africanus always kept in his hand the works of Xenophon, wherein the perfect king is portrayed under the name of Cyrus. I could tell you of Lucullus, Sulla, Pompey, Brutus, and many other Romans and Greeks; but I will merely remind you that Hannibal, the illustrious commander,— although fierce by nature and a stranger to all humanity, faithless and a despiser of both men and gods,—yet had knowledge of letters and was conversant with the Greek language; and if I mistake not, I once read that he even left a book composed by him in Greek.

"However it is superfluous to tell you this, for I well know that you all see how wrong the French are in thinking that letters are injurious to arms. You know that glory is the true stimulus to great and hazardous deeds of war, and whoso is moved thereto by gain or other motive, besides doing nothing good, deserves not to be called a gentleman, but a base trafficker. And true glory is that which is preserved in the sacred treasure-house of letters, as everyone may understand except those unfortunates who have never enjoyed them.

"What soul is there so abject, timid and humble, that when he reads of the deeds of Cæsar, Alexander, Scipio, Hannibal, and many others, is not inflamed by an ardent desire to be like them, and does not make small account of this frail two days' life, in order to win the almost eternal life of fame, which in spite of death makes him live in far greater glory than before? But he who does not feel the delight of letters, cannot either know how great is the glory they so long preserve, and measures it by the life of one man or two, because his memory runs no further. Hence he cannot esteem this short-lived glory so much as he would that almost eternal glory if knowledge of it were unhappily not denied him, and as he does not esteem it so much, we may reasonably believe that he will not run such danger to pursue it as one who knew it would.

"I should be far from willing to have an antagonist cite instances to the contrary in refutation of my view, and urge upon me that with all their knowledge of letters the Italians have for some time since shown little martial valour,—which is alas, only too true. But it very certainly might be said that the fault of a few has brought not only grievous harm but eternal obloquy upon all the rest; and from them was derived the true cause of our ruin and of the decadence if not the death of valour in our souls: yet it would be far more shameful in us to publish it, than for the French to be ignorant of letters. Therefore it is better to pass over in silence that which cannot be recalled without pain: and avoiding this subject (upon which I entered against my will) to return to our Courtier.

44.—"I would have him more than passably accomplished in letters, at least in those studies that are called the humanities, and conversant not only with the Latin language but with the Greek, for the sake of the many different things that have been admirably written therein. Let him be well versed in the poets, and not less in the orators and historians, and also proficient in writing verse and prose, especially in this vulgar tongue of ours; for besides the enjoyment he will find in it, he will by this means never lack agreeable entertainment with ladies, who are usually fond of such things. And if other occupations or want of study prevent his reaching such perfection as to render his writings worthy of great praise, let him be careful to suppress them so that others may not laugh at him, and let him show them only to a friend whom he can trust: because they will at least be of this service to him, that the exercise will enable him to judge the work of others. For it very rarely happens that a man who is not accustomed to write, however learned he may be, can ever quite appreciate the toil and industry of writers, or taste the sweetness and excellence of style, and those latent niceties that are often found in the ancients.

"Moreover these studies will also make him fluent, and as Aristippus said to the tyrant, confident and assured in speaking with everyone. Hence I would have our Courtier keep one precept fixed in mind; which is that in this and everything else he should be always on his guard, and diffident rather than forward, and that he should keep from falsely persuading himself that he knows that which he does not know. For by nature we are all fonder of praise then we ought to be, and our ears love the melody of words that praise us more than any other sweet song or sound; and thus, like sirens' voices, they are often the cause of shipwreck to him who does not close his ears to such deceptive harmony. Among the ancient sages this danger was recognized, and books were written showing in what way the true friend may be distinguished from the flatterer. But what does this avail, if there be many, nay a host, of those who clearly perceive that they are flattered, yet love him who flatters them, and hold him in hatred who tells them the truth? And often when they find him who praises them too sparing in his words, they even help him and say such things of themselves, that the flatterer is put to shame, most impudent though he be.

"Let us leave these blind ones to their error, and have our Courtier of such good judgment that he will not take black for white, or have more self-confidence than he clearly knows to be well founded; and especially in those peculiarities which (if you remember) messer Cesare in his game said we had often used as an instrument to bring men's folly to light. On the contrary, even if he well knows the praises bestowed upon him to be true, let him not err by accepting them too openly or confirming them without some protest; but rather let him as it were disclaim them modestly, always showing and really esteeming arms as his chief profession, and all other good accomplishments as an ornament thereto. And particularly among soldiers let him not act like those who insist on seeming soldiers in learning, and learned men among soldiers. In this way, for the reasons we have alleged, he will avoid affectation, and even the middling things that he does, shall seem very great."

45.—Messer Pietro Bembo here replied:

"Count, I do not see why you insist that this Courtier, being lettered and endowed with so many other admirable accomplishments, should hold everything as an ornament of arms, and not arms and the rest as an ornament of letters; which without other accompaniment are as superior in dignity to arms, as the mind is to the body, for the practice of them properly pertains to the mind, as that of arms does to the body."

Then the Count replied:

"Nay, the practice of arms pertains to both mind and body. But I would not have you judge in such a cause, messer Pietro, for you would be too much suspected of bias by one of the two sides: and as the controversy has already been long waged by very wise men, there is no need to renew it; but I regard it as settled in favour of arms, and would have our Courtier so regard it too, since I may form him as I wish. And if you are of contrary mind, wait till you hear of a contest wherein he who defends the cause of arms is allowed to use arms, just as those who defend letters make use of letters in their defence; for if everyone avails himself of his proper weapons, you shall see that men of letters will be worsted."

"Ah," said messer Pietro, "a while ago you blamed the French for prizing letters little, and told what glorious lustre is shed on man by letters and how they make him immortal; and now it seems you have changed your mind. Do you not remember that

> Before the famous tomb of brave Achilles
> Thus spake the mighty Alexander, sighing:
> 'O happy youth, who found so clear a trumpet,
> And lofty bard to make thy deeds undying!'

And if Alexander envied Achilles not for his deeds, but for the fortune that had granted him the happiness of having his exploits celebrated by Homer, we may conclude that Alexander esteemed Homer's poems above Achilles's arms. For what other judge do you wait then, or for what other sentence upon the dignity of arms and letters, than that pronounced by one of the greatest commanders that have ever been?"

46.—Then the Count replied:

"I blame the French for thinking that letters are a hindrance to the profession of arms, and I hold that learning is more proper to no one than to a warrior; and in our Courtier I would have these two accomplishments joined and each aided by the other, as is most proper: nor do I think I have changed my mind in this. But as I said, I do not wish to discuss which of the two is more worthy of praise. It is enough that men of letters almost never select for praise any but great men and glorious deeds, which in themselves merit praise for the mere essential quality from which they spring; besides this they are very noble material for writers: which is a great ornament, and in part the cause of perpetuating writings, which perhaps would not be so much read and appreciated if they lacked their noble theme, but vain and of little moment.

"And if Alexander was envious that Achilles should be praised by Homer, it does not therefore follow that he esteemed letters above arms; wherein if he had felt himself as far behind Achilles as he deemed all those who wrote of him were behind Homer, I am sure he would far rather have desired fine acts on his part than fine speeches on the part of others. Hence I believe that saying of his to have been a tacit eulogy of himself, and that he was expressing a desire for what he thought he did not possess (that is, the supreme excellence of a writer), and not for what he believed he already had attained (that is, prowess in arms, wherein he did not deem Achilles at all his superior). Thus he called Achilles happy, as if hinting that although his own fame had hitherto not been so celebrated in the world as Achilles's, which was made bright and illustrious by that poem so divine,—it was not because his valour and merits were less or deserving of less praise, but because fortune bestowed upon Achilles that miracle of nature as a glorious trumpet for his achievements. Perhaps also he wished to incite some noble genius to write about him, by showing that this must be as pleasing to him as were his love and veneration for the sacred monuments of letters: whereof we have spoken long enough for the present."

"Nay, too long," replied my lord Ludovico Pio; "for I believe that in the whole world it would be impossible to find a receptacle large enough to hold all the things you would have in our Courtier."

Then the Count said:

"Wait a little, for there are many more that he must have."

"It that case," replied Pietro da Napoli, "Grasso de' Medici would have a great advantage over messer Pietro Bembo."

47.—Here everyone laughed, and the Count began anew and said:

"My lords, you must know that I am not content with the Courtier unless he be also a musician and unless, besides understanding and being able to read notes, he can play upon divers instruments. For if we consider rightly, there is to be found no rest from toil or medicine for the troubled spirit more becoming and praiseworthy in time of leisure, than this; and especially in courts, where besides the relief from tedium that music affords us all, many things are done to please the ladies, whose tender and gentle spirit is easily penetrated by harmony and filled with sweetness. Thus it is no marvel that in both ancient and modern times they have always been inclined to favour musicians, and have found refreshing spiritual food in music."

Then my lord Gaspar said:

"I admit that music as well as many other vanities may be proper to women and perhaps to some that have the semblance of men, but not to those who really are men; for these ought not to enervate their mind with delights and thus induce therein a fear of death."

"Say not so," replied the Count; "for I shall enter upon a vast sea in praise of music. And I shall call to mind how it was always celebrated and held sacred among the ancients, and how very sage philosophers were of opinion that the world is composed of music, that the heavens make harmony in their moving, and that the soul, being ordered in like fashion, awakes and as it were revives its powers through music.

"Thus it is written that Alexander was sometimes excited by it so passionately, that he was forced almost against his will to leave the banquet table and rush to arms; and when the musician changed the temper of the tune, he grew calm again, lay aside his arms, and returned to the banquet table. Moreover I will tell you that grave Socrates learned to play the cithern at a very advanced age. And I remember having once heard that Plato and Aristotle would have the man of culture a musician also; and they show by a host of arguments that the power of music over us is very great, and (for many reasons which would be too long to tell now) that it must needs be taught from childhood, not so much for the mere melody that we hear, but for the power it has to induce in us a fresh and good habit of mind and an habitual tendency to virtue, which renders the soul more capable of happiness, just as bodily exercise renders the body more robust; and that music is not only no hindrance in the pursuits of peace and war, but is very helpful therein.

"Again, Lycurgus approved of music in his harsh laws. And we read that in their battles the very warlike Lacedemonians and Cretans used the cithern and other dulcet instruments; that many very excellent commanders of antiquity, like Epaminondas, practised music; and that those who were ignorant of it, like Themistocles, were far less esteemed. Have you not read that music was among the first accomplishments which the worthy old Chiron taught Achilles in tender youth, whom he reared from the age of nurse and cradle? and that the sage preceptor insisted that the hands which were to shed so much Trojan blood, should be often busied with the cithern? Where is the soldier who would be ashamed to imitate Achilles,— to say nothing of many other famous commanders whom I could cite?

"Therefore seek not to deprive our Courtier of music, which not only soothes men's minds, but often tames wild beasts; and he who enjoys it not, may be sure that his spirit is ill attuned. See what power it has, to make (as once it did) a fish submit to be ridden by a man upon the boisterous sea. We find it used in holy temples to render praise and thanks to God; and we must believe that it is pleasing to Him and that He has given it to us as most sweet alleviation of our fatigues and troubles. Wherefore rough toilers of the field under a burning sun often cheat their weariness with crude and rustic song. With music the rude peasant lass, who is up before the day to spin or weave, wards off her drowsiness and makes her toil a pleasure; music is very cheering pastime for poor sailors after rain, wind and tempest: a solace to tired pilgrims on their long and weary journeys, and often to sorrowing captives in their chains and fetters. Thus, as stronger proof that melody even if rude is very great relief from every human toil and care, nature seems to have taught it to the nurse as chief remedy for the continual wailing of frail children, who by the sound of her voice are brought restful and placid sleep, forgetful of the tears so proper to them and given us in that age by nature as a presage of our after life."

🏮 4. Two Educational Theorists of the Renaissance

Desiderius Erasmus of Rotterdam (1469?–1536) was perhaps the greatest exponent and practitioner of the Humanist revival. He edited many of the works of classical authors and the Church Fathers, translated the New Testament into scholarly Greek, and authored Latin textbooks, satires (The Praise of Folly), and treatises concerning educational theory and practice. In his writings on education, Erasmus revealed his admiration of Quintilian and his devotion to classical literature as the foundation of knowledge. The following selection is from his argument "That Children Should Straightway from Their Earliest Years Be Trained in Virtue and Sound Learning," addressed to William, Duke of Cleves in 1529.

I desire to urge upon you, Illustrious Duke, to take into your early and serious consideration the future nurture and training of the son lately born to you. For, with Chrysippus, I contend that the young child must be led to sound learning whilst his wit is yet unwarped, his age tender, his mind flexible and tenacious. In manhood we remember nothing so well as the truths which we imbibed in our youth. Wherefore I beg you to put aside all idle chatter which would persuade you that this early childhood is unmeet for the discipline and the effort of studies.

The arguments which I shall enlarge upon are the following. First, the beginnings of learning are the work of memory, which in young children is most tenacious. Next, as nature has implanted in us the instinct to seek for knowledge, can we be too early in obeying her behest? Thirdly, there are not a few things which it imports greatly that

William Harrison Woodward (trans.), Desiderius Erasmus, Concerning the Aim and Method of Education, *pp. 180–81. Copyright, 1904, by Cambridge University Press. Reprinted by permission of Cambridge University Press.*

we should know well, and which we can learn far more readily in our tender years. I speak of the elements of Letters, Grammar, and the fables and stories found in the ancient Poets. Fourthly, since children, as all agree, are fit to acquire manners, why may they not acquire the rudiments of learning? And seeing that they must needs be busy about something, what else can be better approved? For how much wiser to amuse their hours with Letters, than to see them frittered away in aimless trifling!

It is, however, objected, first, that such knowledge as can be thus early got is of slight value. But even so, why despise it, if so be it serve as the foundation for much greater things? For if in early childhood a boy acquire such useful elements he will be free to apply his youth to higher knowledge, to the saving of his time. Moreover, whilst he is thus occupied in sound learning he will perforce be kept from some of the temptations which befall youth, seeing that nothing engages the whole mind more than studies. And this I count a high gain in such times as ours.

Next, it is urged that by such application health may be somewhat endangered. Supposing this to be true, still the compensation is great, for by discipline the mind gains far more in alertness and in vigour than the body is ever likely to lose. Watchfulness, however, will prevent any such risk as is imagined. Also, for this tender age you will employ a teacher who will win and not drive, just as you will choose such subjects as are pleasant and attractive, in which the young mind will find recreation rather than toil.

Furthermore, I bid you remember that a man ignorant of Letters is no man at all, that human life is a fleeting thing, that youth is easily enticed into sin, that early manhood is absorbed by clashing interests, that old age is unproductive, and that few reach it. How then can you allow your child, in whom you yourself live again, to lose even one of those precious years in which he may begin to acquire those means whereby he may elevate his whole life and keep at arm's length temptation and evil?

In the treatise De Ratione Studii (Upon the Right Method of Instruction), *Erasmus expressed not only his love of the classics and concern for proper instruction, but also his distaste for many of the teaching practices of his day. The reader is struck by the timeless validity of his urging that grammar is best learned through usage rather than the memorization of rules, that the classics be studied for their content as well as for the purpose of developing vocabulary and style, and that "ocular impressions" be employed as aids to learning. In the passages that follow, Erasmus also repeats his rather unfortunate agreement with Quintilian's emphasis upon training the memory.*

§ 1. THOUGHT AND EXPRESSION FORM THE TWO-FOLD MATERIAL OF INSTRUCTION. 521 A–B.

All knowledge falls into one of two divisions: the knowledge of "truths" and the knowledge of "words": and if the former is first in importance the latter is acquired first in order of time. They are not to be commended who, in their anxiety to increase their store of truths, neglect the necessary art of expressing them. For ideas are only intelligible to us by means of the words which describe them; wherefore defective knowledge of language reacts upon our apprehension of the truths expressed. We often find that no one is so apt to lose himself in verbal arguments as the man who boasts that facts, not words, are the only things that interest him. This goes to prove that true education includes what is *best* in both kinds of knowledge, taught, I must add, under the *best* guidance. For, remembering how difficult it is to eradicate early impressions, we should aim from the first at learning what need never be unlearnt, and that only.

§ 2. EXPRESSION CLAIMS THE FIRST PLACE IN POINT OF TIME. BOTH THE GREEK AND LATIN LANGUAGES NEEDFUL TO THE EDUCATED MAN, 521 B–C.

Language thus claims the first place in the order of studies and from the outset should include both Greek and Latin. The argument for this is two-fold. First, that within these two literatures are contained all the knowledge which we recognise as of vital importance to mankind. Secondly, that the natural affinity of the two tongues renders it more profitable to study them side by side than apart. Latin particularly gains by this method. Quintilian advised that a beginning should be made with Greek before systematic work in Latin is taken in hand. Of course he regarded proficiency in both as essential. The elements, therefore, of Greek and Latin should be acquired early, and should a thoroughly skilled master not be available, then—but only then—let the learner fall back upon self-teaching by means of the study of classical masterpieces.

§ 3. THE RIGHT METHOD OF ACQUIRING GRAMMAR RESTS UPON READING AND NOT UPON DEFINITIONS AND RULES. 521 C–522 A.

Amongst Greek Grammars that of Theodore Gaza stands admittedly first, next to it I rank that of Constantine Lascaris. Of the old Latin Grammarians Diomedes is the soundest; whilst the *Rudimenta* of Nicholas Perotti strikes me as the most thorough and most comprehensive of modern works. But I must make my conviction clear that, whilst a knowledge of the rules of accidence and syntax is most necessary to every student, still they should be as few, as simple, and as carefully

Woodward, op. cit., *pp. 162–66.*

framed as possible. I have no patience with the stupidity of the average teacher of grammar who wastes precious years in hammering rules into children's heads. For it is not by learning rules that we acquire the power of speaking a language, but by daily intercourse with those accustomed to express themselves with exactness and refinement, and by the copious reading of the best authors.

Upon this later point we do well to choose such works as are not only sound models of style but are instructive by reason of their subject matter. The Greek prose-writers whom I advise are, in order, Lucian, Demosthenes, Herodotus: the poets, Aristophanes, Homer, Euripides; Menander, if we possessed his works, would take precedence of all three. Amongst Roman writers, in prose and verse, Terence, for pure, terse Latinity has no rival, and his plays are never dull. I see no objection to adding carefully chosen comedies of Plautus. Next, I place Vergil, then Horace; Cicero and Caesar follow closely; and Sallust after these. These authors provide, in my judgement, sufficient reading to enable the young student to acquire a working knowledge of the two great classical tongues. It is not necessary for this purpose to cover the whole range of ancient literature; we are not to be dubbed "beginners" because we have not yet mastered the whole of the *Fragmenta*.

Some proficiency in expression being thus attained the student devotes his attention to the *content* of the ancient literatures. It is true, of course, that in reading an author for purposes of vocabulary and style the student cannot fail to gather something besides. But I have in my mind much more than this when I speak of studying "contents." For I affirm that with slight qualification the whole of attainable knowledge lies enclosed within the literary monuments of ancient Greece. This great inheritance I will compare to a limpid spring of whose undefiled waters it behoves all who truly thirst to drink and be restored.

§ 4. THE SUBJECT-MATTER AND THE METHODS WHICH ARE MOST SUITABLE TO BEGINNERS. 522 A–E.

Before touching upon the order in which the various disciplines should be acquired, and the choice of Masters, I will say something on the instruction of beginners. In reading the authors above mentioned for the purposes of vocabulary, ornament and style, you can have no better guide than Lorenzo Valla. His *Elegantiae* will show you what to look for and note down in your Latin reading. But do not merely echo his rules; make headings for yourself as well. Refer also to Donatus and Diomedes for syntax. Rules of prosody, and the rudiments of rhetoric, such as the method of direct statement, of proof, of ornament of expansion, of transition, are important both for the intelligent study of authors and for composition. Such grounding in grammar and in style will enable you to note with precision such matters as these: an unusual word, archaisms, and innovations, ingenuity in handling material, distinction of style, historical or moral instances, proverbial expressions: the notebook being ready to hand to record them. Notes of this kind should not be jotted down at hap-hazard, but carefully devised so as to recall to the mind the pith of what is read.

If it is claimed that Logic should find a place in the course proposed I do not seriously demur; but I refuse to go beyond Aristotle and I prohibit the verbiage of the schools. Do not let us forget that Dialectic is an elusive maiden, a Siren, indeed, in quest of whom a man may easily suffer intellectual shipwreck. Not here is the secret of style to be discovered. That lies in the use of the pen; whatever the form, whether prose or verse, or whatever the theme, write, write, and again write. Supplement writing by learning by heart. Upon this latter question, memory depends at bottom upon three conditions: thorough understanding of the subject, logical ordering of the contents, repetition to ourselves. Without these we can neither retain securely nor reproduce promptly. Read, then, attentively, read over and over again, test your memory vigorously and minutely. Verbal memory may with advantage be aided by ocular impressions; thus, for instance, we can have charts of geographical facts, genealogical trees, large-typed tables of rules of syntax and prosody, which we can hang on the walls. Or again, the scholar may take a practice of copying striking quotations at the top of his exercise books. I have known a proverb inscribed upon a ring, or a cup, sentences worth remembering painted on a door or a window. These are all devices for adding to our intellectual stores, which, trivial as they may seem individually, have a distinct cumulative value.

Lastly, I urge, as undeniably the surest method of acquisition, the practice of teaching what we know: in no other way can we so certainly learn the difference between what we *know*, and what we *think we know*; whilst that which we actually know we come to know better.

Juan Luis Vives, the Spanish Humanist and teacher of Catherine of Aragon, further illustrates the impact of Quintilian on Renaissance educational theory. Like the Roman master, Vives, overemphasized the training of the child's memory, but he also stressed such positive concepts as the value of play, the recognition of individual differences and interests among children, and the need for a student-teacher relationship based upon love and respect.

TEACHERS AND TAUGHT

By what means and how far the mind and nature of the boy may be clearly perceived. For there is scarcely anyone of such a stupid disposition

Foster Watson (trans.), Vives: On Education, pp. 81–83, 86–87. Copyright, 1913, by Cambridge University Press. Reprinted by permission of Cambridge University Press.

that he will not profit by some teaching, if there be sufficient care
given. How teachers should bear themselves towards their pupils and
what they should first teach. Trial of wits. Strong points of weak boys.
The relation of teachers to scholars. What should be first taught?

Subject-matter is to be presented to the boy so that his mind may
elevate itself by movement and action. For nothing of this nature can
How the be judged of when it is quiescent. Pythagoras introduced
mind reveals Arithmetic, which his shrewdness discovered. Nothing
itself. displays the sharpness of the mind so much as a ready
method of reckoning, and slowness of mind is proved by
slowness in reckoning, as we have seen in the case of the feeble-
minded and Aristotle is our authority that the very stupid race of
Arithmetic Scythians cannot count beyond the number four, while we
is, as it were, name the numerals beyond ten. Therefore, there were
the Lydian followers of wisdom among the Greeks who considered
stone of wits. that a man, simply because he knew how to reckon,
might for that reason be called λογικόν ζῷον. As in Latin, *ratio* means
both "reason" and "computation," so with the Greek word λόγος.

Quintilian considers memory to be an indication of natural ability;
he says it consists of two parts—viz. ready comprehension and faithful
retention. The former is undoubtedly a proof of keenness,
Memory the latter of capacity. Judgment follows gradually after-
a sign of wards. Therefore the child is ordered to learn by heart,
ability. then to imitate, according to what I have said above.
Children should be exercised in play, for that reveals their sharpness
and their characters, especially among those of their own age and who
are like them, where nothing is feigned but everything natural. All
emulation brings out and discloses the state of the mind, scarcely
otherwise than the heating of the plants or the roots or the fruits brings
out their special fragrance or the force of nature. The boy should be
taught, through play, both to rule and to command. As says Bias, "the
office proclaims the man." The Spaniards rather wisely say in a proverb
that "office and play are the touchstones of minds." Every two or three
months let the masters meet together, and deliberate and judge with
paternal affection and grave discretion concerning the minds of their
pupils, and send each boy to that work for which he seems most fit.
If that is done, incredible advantage will ensue to the whole human
race. Nothing would then be done badly and perversely by those who
now do it under compulsion and against their desires, concerning
whom is the advice of the wise poet, "say and do nothing against your
natural bent" ("Invita Minerva"). All things indeed will be performed
in the best manner and with wonderful happiness by those who are
naturally fitted to do them. When unwilling minds are driven to

uncongenial work, we see that almost all things turn out wrong and distorted. It is not right to think too much about having a great number of scholars; how much better it is to have a little salt of good savour than a great deal that is insipid? How many philosophers have been content with a small audience? and with this audience they used to discuss most acutely and wisely, great and weighty subjects. Our Lord, when He brought to the world the wisdom and salvation of God, contented Himself with a company of twelve men. In truth an audience of any size whatsoever will suffice to bring glory and profit to a teacher. I do not deny that in speaking a crowd is a stimulus to the mind, but speaking is a different thing from teaching. In speaking, I observe that orators are stirred by I know not what goads, from the desire of glory. With regard to doubtful natural dispositions, I think we should not despair about the evil in them nor yet trust too much in the good. Both in the state and in the school there are many examples of change of disposition and character; still, when the will is defective, more frequently changes are for the worse. Because a boy's mind is not sufficiently apt, it is not therefore a matter for despair. For there are

Wits should be tested as to their future ability. some minds which have been despised and yet they have brought forth fruit, sometime later. When a father has many sons, let him not at the beginning destine for study any one he likes, just as he would take an egg from a heap to boil or to fry, but the one who in his own opinion, and in that of his friends, is best suited for study and erudition. Some parents (and there is nothing more ridiculous) send to school those boys who are unfit for commerce or war, or other civil duties, and order them to be taught; and, what is a most impious deed, they devote to God the most contemptible and useless of their offspring, and think that he who has not judgment and intellect for the smallest and most trifling matters has quite enough for such great duties. When the boy is destined for study, as the father ought to conceive the highest hopes of his son, so should the teacher of his pupil. But there will be a difference, because a father's love is generally dim-sighted and even blind, while it is fitting that the kindness of the teacher should be combined with the keenest eyes. . . .

* * * * *

The affection of the master for his pupil will be that of a father; he will love him truly and from his heart, as if he were his own off-

Affection of the master for his pupil. spring. Does he indeed who gives birth to the body do more for the child than he who stirs the mind to action? In truth, in so far as the mind is more truly the essential part of the man than the body the teacher may be said to be more truly the parent. For we are not men because of our bodies which we have in common with the brutes, but in consequence of the likeness of our mind to God and the angels. For this reason Alexander of Macedon acknowledged that he owed more to Aristotle than to Philip; from the latter he derived his body, but from the former his mind. The Apostle Paul says that he "had begotten in the Lord" those whom he led to virtue. But this paternal love will not be blind, but observant and even keen, so that it may detect all tendencies in the pupil which ought to be strengthened, or changed and amended.

⌘ 5. Patrons and Scholars Create Schools of the Renaissance

At Mantua in 1425, a blending of the resources of a Renaissance despot and the knowledge and enthusiasm of a scholar produced the noblest school of the age. The following description of Vitorino Da Feltre's school is contained in John Symonds' erudite study of the Renaissance in Italy.

The Marchese Gian Francesco Gonzaga was looking out for a master for his children, and his choice fell on Vittorino. The admiration of antiquity was no mere matter of fashion with this prince. He loved history for its own sake, and professed a special reverence for the Roman Camillus. His practical good sense made him understand that, if he wished his sons and daughters to become thoroughly educated, not only in the humanities and mathematics, but also in the republican virtues of the ancients, which then formed the ideal of life in Italy, he must be willing to commit them wholly to the charge of their appointed governor. Vittorino, who would have undertaken the duty on no other condition, obtained full control of the young princes and their servants. An appointment of twenty sequins per month was assigned to him, together with a general order on the treasury of Mantua. A villa, called Casa Zojosa, which we may translate Joyous Gard, was allotted to the new household, and there Vittorino established himself as master in 1425. He had much to do before this dwelling could be converted from the pleasure house of a mediæval sovereign into the semimonastic resort of earnest students. Through its open galleries and painted banquet chambers the young Gonzaghi lounged with favourite friends selected from the Mantuan nobility. The tables groaned under gold and silver plate, while perfumed lacqueys handed round rich wines and highly seasoned dishes, and the garden alleys echoed to the sound of lute and viol. Without making any brusque or sudden reformation,

John Addington Symonds, Renaissance in Italy: The Revival of Learning *(London: Smith, Elder and Co.; New York: Charles Scribner's Sons, 1900), pp. 211–16.*

Vittorino managed, by degrees, and on various pretexts, to dismiss the more dangerous friends and servants of his pupils. A strict house-porter was engaged, with orders to exclude suspicious visitors. Plain clothes, simple habits, and frugal meals became the rule of the household, Vittorino contriving to render these changes no less agreeable than salutary to his pupils. When complaints arose from the former companions of the princes and their parents, he laid his plan of training clearly before the Marquis, who had the good sense to approve of all that he had done.

The eldest of Gian Francesco's children, Lodovico, was a youth of lazy habits, inclined to gluttony, and already too fat for his age. The next, Carlo, had outgrown his strength, and needed more substantial food. Vittorino devised systems of diet and physical training suited to their several temperaments, making it his one object to increase their vigour, and by multiplying sources of rational enjoyment to dispose them to the energetic exercise of their faculties. He by no means neglected what we call athletics. Indeed, it was a fundamental axiom of his method that a robust body could alone harbour a healthy mind. Boys who sat poring over books, or haunted solitary places, lost in dreaming, found no favour in his eyes. To exercises in the gymnasium or the riding-school he preferred games in the open air; hunting and fishing, wrestling and fencing, running and jumping, were practised by his pupils in the park outside their palace. To harden them against severities of heat and cold, to render them temperate in food and drink, to train their voices, and to improve their carriage was his first care. Since he could not himself superintend their education in all its branches he engaged a subordinate staff of tutors; grammarians, logicians, mathematicians, painters, and masters of riding, dancing, singing, swimming, fencing, began to crowd the halls of Joyous Gard. Each had his own allotted task to perform, while Vittorino surveyed the whole scheme. 'Perhaps,' says Rosmini, 'the only sciences that were not taught in this academy were civil and canon law and natural physics.'

It must not be imagined that so extensive an apparatus existed solely for the young Gonzaghi. Noble youths from all the Courts of Italy, and students from remote parts of Europe, sought admittance to Vittorino's school. The more promising of these pupils, who were fitted by their rank and disposition to associate with his princely charges, the master housed under his own roof; while for the rest he provided suitable lodgings near at hand. Many were the poor students who thus owed to his generosity participation in the most refined and scientific culture their century afforded. While paying this tribute to Vittorino da Feltre, we must remember the honour that is also due to Gian Francesco Gonzaga. Had this prince not been endowed with true liberality of soul and freedom from petty prejudice, Vittorino could never have developed a system based upon pure democratic principles, which even now may rank as an unrivalled educational ideal. If the master, again, was able to provide for sixty poor scholars at a time—teaching, feeding, clothing, and furnishing them with costly books, his friend the Marquis must, we feel sure, have supplied his purse with extra funds for charitable purposes.

The numerous biographers of Vittorino have transmitted many details in illustration of his method of teaching. He used to read the classic authors aloud, prefixing biographical notices by way of introduction, and explaining the matter, as well as the language of his text, as he proceeded. Sometimes he made his pupils read, correcting their pronunciation, and obliging them to mark the meaning by emphasis. He relied much on learning by heart and repetition, as the surest means of forming a good style. Gifted with a finer instinct for language than the majority of his contemporaries, he was careful that his pupils should distinguish between different types of literary excellence, not confounding Cicero with Seneca or Virgil with Lucan, but striving to appreciate the special qualities of each. With a view to the acquisition of pure principles of taste, he confined them at first to Virgil and Homer, Cicero and Demosthenes. These four authors he regarded as the supreme masters of expression. Ovid was too luxuriant, Juvenal too coarse, to serve as guides for tiros. Horace and Persius among the satirists, Terence among the comic poets, might be safely studied. In spite of Seneca's weight as a philosophic essayist, Vittorino censured the affectations of his rhetoric; and while he praised the beauty of the Latin elegists, he judged them ill-suited for the training of the young. Criticism of this kind, though it may sound to us obvious and superficial, was extremely rare in the fifteenth century, when scholars were too apt to neglect differences of style in ancient authors, and to ignore the ethics of their works. The refinement which distinguished Vittorino, made him prefer the graces of a chastened manner to the sounding phrases of emphatic declamation. His pupils were taught to see that they had something to say first, and then to say it with simplicity and elegance.

This purity of taste was no mere matter of æsthetic sensibility with Vittorino. Habits which brutalise the mind or debase the body, however sanctioned by the usage of the times, met with little toleration in his presence. Swearing, obscene language, vulgar joking, and angry altercation were severely punished. Personal morality and the observance of religious exercises he exacted from his pupils. Lying was a heinous offence. Those who proved intractable upon these points were excluded from his school. Of the rest Vespasiano writes with emphasis that 'his house was a sanctuary of manners, deeds, and words.'

Concerning the noble Italian youths who were educated with the Gonzaga family at Mantua, enough has been said in another place. Appended to Rosmini's copious biography will be found, by those who are curious to read such details, the notices of forty more or less distinguished pupils. Beside the two sons of Gian Francesco Gonzaga already mentioned, Vittorino educated three other children of his master— Gianlucido, Alessandro, and Cecilia. Wholly dedicated to the cares of teaching, and more anxious to survive in the good fame of his scholars than to secure the immortality of literature, Vittorino bequeathed no writings to posterity. He lived to a hale and hearty old age; and when he died, in 1446, it was found that the illustrious scholar, after enjoying for so many years the liberality of his princely patron, had not accumulated enough money to pay for his own funeral. Whatever he possessed, he spent in charity during his lifetime, trusting to the kindness of his friends to bury him when dead. Few lives of which there is any record in history, are so perfectly praiseworthy as Vittorino's; few men have more nobly realised the idea of living for the highest objects of their age; few have succeeded in keeping themselves so wholly unspotted by the vices of the world around them.

In England, men of wealth, individually or organized in corporate groups, played a significant role in the establishment of schools during the Renaissance. From medieval times, foundations called "chantries" had been organized by men of means to provide funds for charitable and religious purposes. The beneficiaries of such endowments were expected to sing masses and pray for the souls of their benefactors, thus the term "chantry." During the Renaissance several new chantries were founded for the expressed purpose of furnishing support for schools.

FOUNDATION OF FARTHINGHOE
FREE SCHOOL, NORTHANTS, 19 JUNE, 1443

John Abbot, citizen and mercer of the city of London, declared his last will of all his lands and tenements, with their appurtenances, as well in the city of London as in Farthinghoe and Astrop[?], in the county of Northampton, namely, that the masters or wardens of the Mystery of Mercers of London and the commonalty of the same mystery should have and hold to them and their successors for ever all those his lands and tenements in Cat Lane, on condition that such masters or wardens and commonalty and their successors should find yearly a chaplin fit and honest to celebrate divine service in the church of Farthinghoe, in the county of Northampton, for his soul and the

Leach, op. cit., pp. 415, 417, 435.

souls of his parents, friends and benefactors and all the faithful departed for ever, and to teach and instruct the little ones of the parish of the church of Farthinghoe aforesaid freely and gratis without taking any pay or profit therefor;

Provided always that the said masters or wardens and commonalty and their successors shall pay yearly from the issues, rents and profits arising out of the same lands and tenements and their appurtenances in Cat Lane to such chaplain celebrating and teaching in the place and manner aforesaid, by way of his salary and stipend for the said divine service and labour, ten marks sterling [£6. 13s. 4d.] at the four principal terms of the year by equal portions . . .

The will was proved 5 March 1443–4.

FOUNDATION OF A SPELLING AND READING SCHOOL, 8 NOV., 1489

Foundation of Aldwincle Chantry.

To all sons of holy mother church . . . William Chamber, of Aldwincle, in the county of Northampton, health. . . .

. . . I make known to you all by these presents that I . . . have given . . . to Sir John Seliman, chaplain, for his maintenance and that of his successors . . . celebrating divine service every day at the altar of St Mary the Virgin, in the parish church of All Saints . . . for all the souls aforesaid for ever my manor of Armeston [and other property].

That this ordinance may endure for ever I will and ordain that the chantry aforesaid shall be for ever called "The chantry of William Chamber, William Aldwincle and Elizabeth their wife," and that the chaplain for the time being shall every day . . . celebrate mass at the altar aforesaid. . . .

Moreover I will and ordain that the said chaplain for the time being shall teach and instruct, in spelling and reading, six of the poorest boys of the town of Aldwincle aforesaid, to be named by me and my wife Elizabeth while we are alive, and after our death three named by the rector of St Peter's church in Aldwincle aforesaid, and the other three by the chaplain for the time being, freely, without demanding or taking any remuneration from their parents or friends; and the boys, when they have been so instructed and taught, shall say every night in All Saints' church in Aldwincle aforesaid, at the direction of the chaplain aforesaid, for our souls and the souls of all the faithful departed, the psalm "Out of the deep," with the prayers "Incline thine ear" and "God of the faithful."

回 6. From Humanism to Ciceronianism

Vitorino, Erasmus, Vives, and other Humanists had advocated a rounded, general education, which would prepare a youth to assume a role of responsible leadership in society. They esteemed study of the classics as an essential ingredient in this program, not as an end unto itself. However, in the fifteenth and sixteenth centuries, despite the protestations of Erasmus and others, teachers in the secondary schools insisted that their students strive to imitate the style of writing and speech of the classical authors. Under the leadership of the Ciceronians, the schools became almost exclusively Latin, and the works of Cicero, Virgil, Tacitus, and the rest were appreciated no longer primarily for the richness of their content but rather as absolute standards in grammar and style. The Latin-grammar schools of England and their counterparts on the continent assumed the rigid curriculum and harsh environment for which they were to become infamous.

In the selection that follows, one is impressed by the contrast between the atmosphere of England's Eton of the sixteenth century and Vitorino's school in fifteenth-century Italy. At Eton, we find no mention of mathematics, physics, or music, and, although the author states that time was allowed for recreation, there is no evidence that the training of the body was considered an essential ingredient in a boy's total education.

. . . the Eton Scholars rose early, being awakened at five by one of the præpostors, who thundered forth *"Surgite."* While dressing they chanted prayers, probably consisting of Latin psalms, in alternate verses. Each boy had to make his own bed, and to sweep the dust from under it into the middle of the Long Chamber, whence it was removed by four juniors selected for the purpose by the præpostors. All then went downstairs two and two to wash—doubtless at the "children's pump" mentioned in the Audit Books. There was no morning service for the boys in the Church, as there was at Winchester; so, their ablutions ended, they proceeded at once to their respective places in the schoolroom. The Usher came in at six, and, kneeling at the upper end of the room, read prayers. While he was engaged in teaching the lower forms, one of the præpostors made a list of those who were late for prayers, while the *Præpostor Immundanorum* had to examine the

H. C. Maxwell-Lyte, A History of Eton College, *pp. 144–47. Copyright, 1875, by Macmillan & Co. Ltd. Reprinted by permission of Macmillan & Co. Ltd.*

faces and hands of his schoolfellows in order to report any who appeared dirty, to the Head-Master on his entry at seven o'clock. Work of various kinds was carried on until after nine, when there was a short interval, possibly for breakfast, as at Winchester, though Malim makes no allusion to any such meal. At ten o'clock one of the præpostors shouted "*Ad preces consurgite,*" to recall the boys to school, where, standing in order on either side of the room, they had to recite further prayers.

Dinner was served at eleven o'clock, and the boys marched to the hall and back in double file. The work in school began again at mid-day, and lasted continuously till three. The afternoon play-time ended at four, and was followed by another hour of lessons. At five the boys again left the school in procession, apparently for supper.

The duties of the Master and Usher were now ended for the day, as the work between six and eight was carried on under the superintendence of monitors chosen from among the members of the seventh form. There was a slight break at seven o'clock for another meal, which probably consisted only of a draught of beer and a slice of bread. At eight the boys went to bed chanting prayers.

Such was the ordinary routine of the first four working days of the week, but, as we shall see, more time was allowed for recreation in the summer months. Friday was at this time observed as a fast-day throughout England. At Eton, as at Winchester, it must have been doubly unpleasant, for all the offences committed during the past week were then enumerated, and the culprits were punished. On Friday and Saturday the boys were examined in what they had learned during the week, and on the latter day speeches were occasionally delivered. No mention whatever is made of Sunday.

From Malim's account of the work done in the school, it is clear that Latin was almost the only subject of study, and that no means of inculcating a sound knowledge of it was neglected. The lower boys had to decline and conjugate words, and their seniors had to repeat rules of grammar, for the illustration of which short phrases called "*Vulgaria*" were composed and committed to memory. Some sort of Latin composition, however brief, was a necessary portion of the daily work of every Eton scholar. In the lower forms it was confined to the literal translation of an English sentence or passage, while in the fifth form it consisted of a theme on a subject set by the Master. The boys in the sixth and seventh forms used to write verses. No "*Gradus ad Parnassum*" then existed, to assist the would-be poets in finding suitable words for their compositions, so they had to rely on the contents of their own MS. note-books for "flowers, phrases, or idioms of speech, antitheses, epithets, synonyms, proverbs, similes, comparisons, anecdotes, descriptions of times, places, and persons, fables, *bon-mots,* figures, and apothegms." The Master and Usher used to read aloud and explain to the boys the passages which were to be learnt by heart. The books studied in the School were:—

In the first form, Cato, and Vives.

In the second, Terence, Lucian's Dialogues (in Latin), and Æsop's Fables (in Latin).

In the third, Terence, Æsop's Fables (in Latin), and Selections by Sturmius from Cicero's Epistles.

In the fourth, Terence, Ovid's *Tristia,* and the Epigrams of Martial, Catullus, and Sir Thomas More.

In the fifth, Ovid's *Metamorphoses,* Horace, Cicero's Epistles, Valerius Maximus, Lucious Florus, Justin, and "Sysembrotus."

In the sixth and seventh, Cæsar's Commentaries, Cicero *de Officiis,* and *de Amicitia,* Virgil, Lucan and the Greek Grammar.

In the following documents and statutes the rigidity of the Latin-grammar school with its stress upon imitation of Latin authors, rote memorization of endless vocabulary lists, countless drill sessions and firmly defined standards of conduct and morality is clearly observable.

THE COUNTRY GRAMMAR SCHOOL

The course of a country Grammar School, c. 1635, and the place of verses in it, is shown by Adam Martindale who supplies us with a full account of his schoolwork as a boy at the Free School of St. Helens:

"As for the proficience I made under my master 'twas this: He received me when I was learning in *As in præsenti* and Cato, and instructed me for prose in Corderius, Æsop's Fables, Tullie's Offices, epistles, and orations, together with Aphthonius for Latin in prose, and the Greek Grammars of Camden first, and Clenard afterwards, together with a Greek Catechism, and lastly the Greek Testament (for I proceeded no further with him); and for poetry in Mantuan, Terence, Ovid's Epistles and Metamorphoses, Virgil, and Horace. The rhetorics he read to us were Susenbrotus first and Talaeus afterwards. Mine exercises were usually a piece of Latin (of which he himself dictated the English) every day of the week, save Thursdays and Saturdays; and besides somewhat weekly as I rose in ability, first a dialogue in imitation of Corderius, or Pueriles Confabulatinuculæ, then an epistle wherein I was to follow Cicero, though (alas!) at a great distance. Then themes (as we called them) in the way of Aphthonius, consisting of many parts and taking up one side of half a sheet pretty thick written, and

Foster Watson, The English Grammar Schools to 1660: Their Curriculum and Practice *(Cambridge: The University Press, 1908), pp. 486, 384–85, 134. By permission of Cambridge University Press.*

(towards the latter end) good store of verses on the back side, most hexameters and pentameters, but some sapphics and adonics. All that were presumed by their standing able to discourse in Latin were under a penalty if they either spoke English or broke Priscian's head; but barbarous language, if not incongruous for grammar, had no punishing but derision. These were the orders we were subject to at teaching hours; yea, though we had liberty by twos to go forth of the school upon the our necessary occasions, real or pretended, and sometimes (when the humour took him) he would tie us to them at our times for play."

*   *   *   *   *

Rivington Grammar School Statutes, 1566.

As the young scholar is thus learning to decline a noun and a verb, the Usher shall daily exercise him with diversity of words in every comparison, declension, gender, tense, and conjugation, teaching him the English of every such Latin word; and examine him oft what is Latin for every such thing, that by this means he and others that hear may learn what everything is called in Latin, and so be more ready to understand every word, what it signifieth in English, when they shall come to construction. As first to begin with Latin words for every part of a man and his apparel; of a house and household stuff, as bedding, kitching, buttery, meats, beasts, herbs, trees, flowers, birds, fishes, with all parts of them; virtues, vices, merchandise, and all occupations; as weavers, tanners, carpenters, ploughers, wheelwrights, tailors, tilers, and shoemakers; and cause them to write every word that belongs to one thing, together in order. And if this be done often and loud, that every one may hear and give ear, they will strive who shall learn and remember most Latin words, and will rejoice in it, one opposing another who can do the best.

Duties of boys. Heath Grammar School Statutes, c. 1600.

That they rise early in the morning, reverence their parents, love and obey both father and mother, and give good example to the whole family.

That they come early to the School without lingering, play or noise by the way, saluting those they meet bareheaded.

When the Master or Usher or any stranger entereth into the School, that they salute them, rising up dutifully, and presently sit down again with silence and apply their books.

That they wander not up and down in the School, but rest orderly in their appointed place, labour their morning task and appointed lectures with great diligence, striving rather for high commendations of their Master and strangers than for rebuke and blame.

Swearing. Heath Grammar School Statutes.

That they take not God's Name in vain by swearing in their ordinary communication, by forswearing, cursing themselves or others, lying, laughing, and vain shouting, idle and light use of God's titles, works and Word.

Boys' Conduct. Heath Grammar School Statutes.

If any scholar use railing, wrangling, fighting, giving by-names, or offer any the like abuse to his fellows, or any stranger in the ways, he shall be severely punished, and if he continue thus to molest and harm others, he shall be expelled the school.

VI

Education in an Age of Challenges to Authority

THE Renaissance contained the seeds of revolution. Its leading figures in politics, the arts, literature, and education clearly indicated dissatisfaction with the standards of the Middle Ages. Whether they reminisced on the grandeur of the classical age or embarked on new paths of creativity, the directions they took led away from the manners and institutions of their own time. Many were the dreamers like Petrarch who found refuge from present reality in their intellectual and artistic pursuits. But there were others who could not remain quiet while what was contrasted so markedly with what had been and what might be. In much of the Western world, the latter half of the sixteenth and the seventeenth and eighteenth centuries would hear the cries for change, and institutions and ideas that had dominated for over a thousand years would face challenges to their very existence.

The most powerful of all institutions, the Roman Catholic Church, was among the first to hear the rumblings of discontent. From within its own walls, scholars rediscovered the Scriptures and the writings of the early Church fathers. When men like Luther, Zwingli, and Calvin examined the original Latin, Greek, and Hebrew documents, their resultant dissatisfaction with the Church of their day burst into the flames of the Protestant Reformation. The Catholic Church had been challenged in the past. There had been heresies in isolated areas of Europe, which had been crushed rather easily. (1) But the challengers of the sixteenth century had certain advantages their predecessors lacked. Roads, towns, and maritime and river trade routes had made Europe considerably smaller. Men and ideas found the restrictions of distance far less challenging than they had been.

And consider the printing press, which was to be a potent weapon in the armory of the reformers. When Martin Luther nailed his 95 theses on the door of the cathedral of Wittenberg, he was following a time-honored tradition. This document, written in Latin, was a challenge to fellow clerics to a theological debate in the true scholastic fashion. However, translated into German and re-produced in many copies by the press, it was transformed into the revolutionary declaration of the Lutheran movement.

The theologies of Calvin and Luther placed great emphasis on the reading of Scripture. Though early pronouncements declaring the ability of each man to be his own priest were later moderated when it became apparent that there could be as many interpretations as interpretors, the central position of the Bible in home and church remained. For the sake of salvation and for the sake of the faith, religious reformers translated the Bible into the vernacular tongues. In the ensuing battle for men's minds and souls, education was to play a significant role. Not only was it important to employ the grammar schools and universities as their allies, but Calvinists and Lutherans alike called for vernacular elementary education to strengthen the allegiance of the lower classes to church and state. (2)

The power of education was not ignored in Protestant lands outside the Lutheran and Calvinist orbits. In England under Henry VIII, Edward VI, and Elizabeth I, the Catholics were stripped of their monastic schools and their chantry schools were dispossessed. Several acts during the sixteenth and seventeenth centuries limited the teaching capacities of non-Anglican sects and placed the control of education, from apprenticeship through the university, in the hands of the Church of England. (3)

The importance of the written word and its ally the school was also recognized by the Catholics, who by the second quarter of the sixteenth century were responding to attack with counterattack. To ensure reading habits conducive to the strengthening of the faith, the Index was established in 1559. To bolster Catholic education, new teaching orders such as the institute of the Brothers of the Christian Schools and the Fathers of the Oratory joined with the older Franciscan and Dominican orders. By all means the most significant army to enlist in the Catholic Counter-Reformation was the Society of Jesus, organized by Ignatius Loyola. The Jesuits became a world-wide legion of priests dedicated to converting the heathens and inducing recalcitrant Catholics to return to the fold. Their militancy led them to the field of education where they devoted themselves to the task of establishing classical secondary schools and universities capable of training a devoted and effective Catholic leadership. (4)

Although revolts against religious authority dominated the history of sixteenth-and seventeenth-century Europe, there was yet another movement occurring which, to leaders of Protestantism as well as Catholicism, often appeared threatening. Fed, like the Reformation, by dissatisfaction with the status quo, this movement concentrated its attack not on the established explanation of things spiritual but on the long-entrenched authoritarian doctrines that claimed to define the limits and scope of the material world. Accepting neither the conclusions of Aristotle and

Ptolemy nor the road of deductive logic, men of courage turned to the inductive approach to knowledge. The scientist, by employing this method, was capable of probing the unknown and arriving at answers that could weaken the hold of ignorance and superstition, but there was also the very real possibility that his findings might conflict with certain religious teachings. Protestants and Catholics might fight bloody wars against each other in the name of faith, but they stood on common ground in their hostility toward men like Francis Bacon, who envisioned a Utopia created by scientists rather than priests, and Galileo, Kepler, and Bruno, whose scientific investigations supported the heliocentric conception of the universe in which the earth, contrary to the teachings of all Christian faiths, was a satellite of the sun rather than the center of all creation. (5)

Ironically, the methods of science, which appeared so threatening to theologians when used for the purpose of explaining the nature of the universe, offered a means of improving the effectiveness of their own schools. The doctrine of sense realism, which emphasized learning through the senses and through contact with things rather than words, was an obvious utilization of scientific empiricism in education. The two most significant exponents of sense realism during the Reformation were dedicated religionists, the Lutheran Wolfgang Ratke and the Moravian bishop John Amos Comenius. (6) The teaching methods proposed by the sense realists captured the interest of many throughout Europe, but their role in the history of education was destined to be that of prophets. The authoritarian methods and rigid curricula of the schools were still too well entrenched to be effectively challenged. Science and the inductive method applied to education were still in their infancy in an era dominated by ignorance, superstition, and religious intolerance.

回 1. Early Reformers Burned for Keeping Schools

This brief excerpt from the English Statutes of the Realm *for 1400 is included to illustrate the early stirrings for Church reform and the early recognition by friend and foe that the written word and schools were essential weapons in the battle for the minds and souls of men. The Lollards were the followers of John Wycliffe. Among their beliefs were the necessity that priests be rigidly poor, that the sacraments were false, that celibacy was unnatural, and that the key to true religious belief was to be found in the Bible, which every Christian should be capable of reading and interpreting for himself.*

...None of such sect and wicked doctrines and opinions shall make any conventicles, or in any wise hold or exercise schools; and also that

Arthur Leach (ed.), Educational Charters and Documents, 598–1909 *(Cambridge: The University Press, 1911), pp. 375, 377. By permission of Cambridge University Press.*

none from henceforth in any wise favour such preacher, or maker of any such or like conventicles, or [person] holding or exercising schools, or making or writing such books, or so teaching, informing, or exciting the people, nor any of them maintain or any wise sustain. . . . . . And if any person within the said realm and dominions, upon the said wicked preachings, doctrines, opinions, schools, and heretical and erroneous informations, or any of them, be before the Diocesan of the same place or his Commissaries [sententially convict] convict by sentence, and the same wicked sect, preachings, doctrines and opinions, schools and informations, do refuse duly to abjure, or by the Diocesan of the same place or his Commissaries after abjuration made by the same person be [pronounced fall into relapse] . . . . . . then the Sheriff of the county of the same place, and Mayor and Sheriffs or Sheriff, or Mayor and Bailiffs of the city, town and borough of the same county next to the same Diocesan or the said Commissaries, shall be personally present in preferring of such sentences [by the same Diocesan or his Commissaries against such persons and every of them], when they by the same Diocesan or his Commissaries shall be required; and they the same persons and every of them, after such sentence promulgate, shall receive, and them before the people in an high place do to be burnt.

2. The Call for Education for Faith and State

The revolt against Roman authority, which Martin Luther unleashed in Germany, was both nationalistic and religious in character. In placing his Church in the protecting arms of the state, Luther demonstrated his fervid patriotism as well as his political astuteness. Reformers in Switzerland and Germany shared a recognition of the necessity for Church and state to work together to promote mutual interests. Both Calvin and Luther called upon the civil governments to extend educational opportunity.

In the selections that follow from Luther's "Letter to the Mayors and Aldermen of All the Cities of Germany in Behalf of Christian Schools," we observe the reformer during the early years of the Protestant movement. Here is Luther crying out for a defense of Church and state against its mortal enemies, Rome and Satan. Here also is Luther the educational reformer with a striking grasp of the follies of contemporary educational practices and with a prophet's vision of what could be done to improve them. Like most reformers, much of what he advocated was not appreciated in his lifetime. But one extremely important point did make an impression. Luther's call for a rudimentary education for the masses in the vernacular marks one of the great movements in the history of education in Western

Civilization. In the next centuries, the lower orders were to benefit from the crusading vigor to establish education for religious orthodoxy.

LETTER TO THE MAYORS AND ALDERMEN
OF ALL THE CITIES OF GERMANY IN BEHALF
OF CHRISTIAN SCHOOLS

First of all, we see how the schools are deteriorating throughout Germany. The universities are becoming weak, the monasteries are declining, and, as Isaiah says, "The grass withereth, the flower fadeth, because the spirit of the Lord bloweth upon it," through the Gospel. For through the word of God the unchristian and sensual character of these institutions is becoming known. And because selfish parents see that they can no longer place their children upon the bounty of monasteries and cathedrals, they refuse to educate them. "Why should we educate our children," they say, "it they are not to become priests, monks, and nuns, and thus earn a support?"

The hollow piety and selfish aims of such persons are sufficiently evident from their own confession. For if they sought anything more than the temporal welfare of their children in monasteries and the priesthood, if they were deeply in earnest to secure the salvation and blessedness of their children, they would not lose interest in education and say, "if the priestly office is abolished, we will not send our children to school." But they would speak after this manner: "If it is true, as the Gospel teaches, that such a calling is dangerous to our children, teach us another way in which they may be pleasing to God and become truly blessed; for we wish to provide not alone for the bodies of our children, but also for their souls." Such would be the language of faithful Christian parents.

It is no wonder that the devil meddles in the matter, and influences groveling hearts to neglect the children and the youth of the country. Who can blame him for it? He is the prince and god of this world, and with extreme displeasure sees the Gospel destroy his nurseries of vice, the monasteries and priesthood, in which he corrupts the young beyond measure, a work upon which his mind is especially bent. How could he consent to a proper training of the young? Truly he would be a fool if he permitted such a thing in his kingdom, and thus consented to its overthrow; which indeed would happen, if the young should escape him, and be brought up to the service of God.

*   *   *   *   *

Therefore I beg you all, in the name of God and of our neglected youth, not to think of this subject lightly, as many do who do not see

F. V. N. Painter, Great Pedagogical Essays, Plato to Spencer *(New York: American Book Co., 1905), pp. 171–72, 173–77, 180–82, 183, 184–85.*

what the prince of this world intends. For the right instruction of youth is a matter in which Christ and all the world are concerned. Thereby are we all aided. And consider that great Christian zeal is needed to overcome the silent, secret, and artful machinations of the devil. If we must annually expend large sums on muskets, roads, bridges, dams, and the like, in order that the city may have temporal peace and comfort, why should we not apply as much to our poor, neglected youth, in order that we may have a skilful schoolmaster or two?

*   *   *   *   *

It is indeed a sin and shame that we must be aroused and incited to the duty of educating our children and of considering their highest interests, whereas nature itself should move us thereto, and the example of the heathen affords us varied instruction. There is no irrational animal that does not care for and instruct its young in what they should know, except the ostrich, of which God says, "She leaveth her eggs in the earth, and warmeth them in the dust; and is hardened against her young ones, as though they were not hers." And what would it avail if we possessed and performed all else, and became perfect saints; if we neglect that for which we chiefly live, namely, to care for the young? In my judgment there is no other outward offense that in the sight of God so heavily burdens the world, and deserves such heavy chastisement as the neglect to educate children.

Parents neglect this duty from various causes. In the first place, there are some who are so lacking in piety and uprightness that they would not do it if they could, but, like the ostrich, harden themselves against their own offspring, and do nothing for them. In the second place, the great majority of parents are unqualified for it, and do not understand how children should be brought up and taught. In the third place, even if parents were qualified and willing to do it themselves, yet on account of other employments and household duties, they have no time for it, so that necessity requires us to have teachers for public schools, unless each parent employ a private instructor.

Therefore it will be the duty of the mayors and councils to exercise the greatest care over the young. For since the happiness, honor, and life of the city are committed to their hands, they would be held recreant before God and the world, if they did not day and night, with all their power, seek its welfare and improvement. Now the welfare of a city does not consist alone in great treasures, firm walls, beautiful houses, and munitions of war; indeed, where all these are found, and reckless fools come into power, the city sustains the greater injury. But the highest welfare, safety, and power of a city consist in able, learned, wise, upright, cultivated citizens, who can secure, preserve, and utilize every treasure and advantage.

Since, then, a city must have well-trained people, and since the greatest need, lack, and lament is that such are not to be found, we must not wait till they grow up of themselves; neither can they be hewed out of stones nor cut out of wood; nor will God work miracles, so long as men can attain their object through means within their reach. Therefore we must see to it, and spare no trouble or expense to educate and form them ourselves. For whose fault is it that in all the cities there are at present so few skilful people except the rulers, who have allowed the young to grow up like trees in the forest, and have not cared how they were reared and taught? The growth, consequently, has been so irregular that the forest furnishes no timber for building purposes, but like a useless hedge is good only for fuel.

Yet there must be civil government. For us, then, to permit ignoramuses and blockheads to rule when we can prevent it, is irrational and barbarous. Let us rather make rulers out of swine and wolves, and set them over peoples who are indifferent to the manner in which they are governed. It is barbarous for men to think thus: "We will now rule; and what does it concern us how those fare who shall come after us?" Not over human beings, but over swine and dogs should such people rule, who think only of their own interests and honor in governing. Even if we exercise the greatest care to educate able, learned, and skilled rulers, yet much care and effort are necessary in order to secure prosperity. How can a city prosper, when no effort is made?

But you say again, if we shall and must have schools, what is the use to teach Latin, Greek, Hebrew, and other liberal arts? It it not enough to teach the Scriptures, which are necessary to salvation, in the mother tongue? To which I answer: I know, alas! that we Germans must always remain irrational brutes, as we are deservedly called by surrounding nations. But I wonder why we do not also say: of what use to us are silk, wine, spices, and other foreign articles, since we ourselves have an abundance of wine, corn, wool, flax, wood, and stone in the German states, not only for our necessities, but also for embellishment and ornament? The languages and other liberal arts, which are not only harmless, but even a greater ornament, benefit, and honor than these things, both for understanding the Holy Scriptures and carrying on the civil government, we are disposed to despise; and the foreign articles which are neither necessary nor useful, and which besides greatly impoverish us, we are unwilling to dispense with. Are we not rightly called German dunces and brutes?

Indeed, if the languages were of no practical benefit, we ought still to feel an interest in them as a wonderful gift of God, with which he has now blessed Germany almost beyond all other lands. We do not find many instances in which Satan has fostered them through the universities and cloisters; on the contrary, these institutions have fiercely inveighed and continue to inveigh against them. For the devil scented the danger that would threaten his kingdom, if the languages should be generally studied. But since he could not wholly prevent their cultivation, he aims at least to confine them within such narrow limits that they will of themselves decline and fall into disuse. They are to him no welcome guest, and consequently he shows them scant courtesy in order that they may not remain long. This malicious trick of Satan is perceived by very few.

Therefore, my beloved countrymen, let us open our eyes, thank God for his precious treasure, and take pains to preserve it and to frustrate the design of Satan. For we can not deny that, although the Gospel has come and daily comes through the Holy Spirit, it has come by means of the languages, and through them must increase and be preserved. For when God wished through the apostles to spread the Gospel abroad in all the world, he gave the languages for that purpose; and by means of the Roman empire he made Latin and Greek the language of many lands, that his Gospel might speedily bear fruit far and wide. He has done the same now. For a time no one understood why God had revived the study of the languages; but now we see that it was for the sake of the Gospel, which he wished to bring to light and thereby expose and destroy the reign of Antichrist. For the same reason he gave Greece a prey to the Turks, in order that Greek scholars, driven from home and scattered abroad, might bear the Greek tongue to other countries, and thereby excite an interest in the study of languages.

And let this be kept in mind, that we shall not preserve the Gospel without the languages. The languages are the scabbard in which the word of God is sheathed. They are the casket in which this jewel is enshrined; the cask in which this wine is kept; the chamber in which this food is stored. And, to borrow a figure from the Gospel itself, they are the baskets in which this bread and fish and fragments are preserved. If through neglect we lose the languages (which may God forbid), we shall not only lose the Gospel, but it will finally come to pass that we shall lose also the ability to speak and write either Latin or German.

*   *   *   *   *

As for myself, if I had children and were able, I would have them learn not only the languages and history, but also singing, instrumental music, and the whole course of mathematics. For what is all this but mere child's play, in which the Greeks in former ages trained their children, and by this means became wonderfully skilful people, capable for every undertaking? How I regret that I did not read more poetry and history, and that no one taught me in these branches!

But you say, who can do without his children and bring them up, in this manner, to be young gentlemen? I reply: it is not my idea that we should establish schools as they have been heretofore, where a boy has studied Donatus and Alexander twenty or thirty years, and yet has learned nothing. The world has changed, and things go differently. My idea is that boys should spend an hour or two a day in school, and the rest of the time work at home, learn some trade and do whatever is desired, so that study and work may go on together, while the children are young and can attend to both. They now spend twofold as much time in shooting with crossbows, playing ball, running, and tumbling about.

In like manner, a girl has time to go to school an hour a day, and yet attend to her work at home; for she sleeps, dances, and plays away more than that. The real difficulty is found alone in the absence of an earnest desire to educate the young, and to aid and benefit mankind with accomplished citizens. The devil much prefers blockheads and drones, that men may have more abundant trials and sorrows in the world.

But the brightest pupils, who give promise of becoming accomplished teachers, preachers, and workers, should be kept longer at school, or set apart wholly for study, as we read of the holy martyrs, who brought up St. Agnes, St. Agatha, St. Lucian, and others. For this purpose also the cloisters and cathedral schools were founded, but they have been perverted into another and accursed one. There is great need for such instruction; for the tonsured crowd is rapidly decreasing, and besides, for the most part, the monks are unskilled to teach and rule, since they know nothing but to care for their stomachs, the only thing they have been taught. Hence we must have persons qualified to dispense the word of God and the Sacraments, and to be pastors of the people. But where shall we obtain them, if schools are not established on a more Christian basis, since those hitherto maintained, even if they do not go down, can produce nothing but depraved and dangerous corrupters of youth?

*   *   *   *   *

Finally, this must be taken into consideration by all who earnestly desire to see such schools established and the languages preserved in the German states; that no cost nor pains should be spared to procure good libraries in suitable buildings, especially in the large cities that are able to afford it. For if a knowledge of the Gospel and of every kind of learning is to be preserved, it must be embodied in books, as the prophets and apostles did, as I have already shown. This should be done, not only that our spiritual and civil leaders may have something to read and study, but also that good books may not be lost, and that the arts and languages may be preserved, with which God has graciously favored us.

* * * * *

But my advice is, not to collect all sorts of books indiscriminately, thinking only of getting a vast number together. I would have discrimination used, because it is not necessary to collect the commentaries of all the jurists, the production of all the theologians, the discussions of all the philosophers, and the sermons of all the monks.

In the first place, a library should contain the Holy Scriptures in Latin, Greek, Hebrew, German, and other languages. Then the best and most ancient commentators in Greek, Hebrew, and Latin.

Secondly, such books as are useful in acquiring the languages, as the poets and orators, without considering whether they are heathen or Christian, Greek or Latin. For it is from such works that grammar must be learned.

Thirdly, books treating of all the arts and sciences.

Lastly, books on jurisprudence and medicine, though here discrimination is necessary.

A prominent place should be given to chronicles and histories, in whatever languages they may be obtained; for they are wonderfully useful in understanding and regulating the course of the world, and in disclosing the marvelous works of God. O how many noble deeds and wise maxims produced on German soil have been forgotten and lost, because no one at the time wrote them down; or if they were written no one preserved the books: hence we Germans are unknown in other lands, and are called brutes that know only how to fight, eat, and drink. But the Greeks and Romans, and even the Hebrews, have recorded their history with such particularity, that even if a woman or child did anything noteworthy, all the world was obliged to read and know it; but we Germans are always Germans, and will remain Germans.

Since God has so graciously and abundantly provided us with art, scholars, and books, it is time for us to reap the harvest and gather for future use the treasures of these golden years. For it is to be feared (and even now it is beginning to take place), that new and different books will be produced, until at last, through the agency of the devil, the good books which are being printed, will be crowded out by the multitude of ill-considered, senseless, and noxious works.

Therefore, my dear Sirs, I beg you to let my labor bear fruit with you. And though there be some who think me too insignificant to follow my advice, or who look down on me as one condemned by tyrants: still let them consider that I am not seeking my own interest, but that of all Germany. And even if I were a fool, and should hit upon something good, no wise man should think it a disgrace to follow me. And even if I were a Turk and heathen, and it should yet appear that my advice was advantageous, not for myself, but for Christianity, no reasonable person would despise my counsel. Sometimes a fool has given better advice than a whole company of wise men. Moses received instruction from Jethro.

▣ 3. Education and the Reformation in England

The selections that follow help illustrate the course of the Reformation's impact on English education. Henry VIII, as head of church as well as state, first lashed out at the Catholic monastic schools and chantry foundations, closed them, appropriated their funds, and then "re-founded" many of them under the auspices of the Church of England. Henry, and Edward and Elizabeth after him, took special care to ensure that the schools would promote the "true religion." Henry prescribed Lily's Grammar *for all grammar schools and required that children learn the rudimentary lessons of reading from church primers. Under Elizabeth, teachers were required to swear their loyalty to the throne and to the Anglican faith.*

THE RE-FOUNDATION OF CANTERBURY CATHEDRAL AND GRAMMAR SCHOOL, 1541

The Incorporation, Statutes and Injunctions of the Cathedral Church of Canterbury.

Henry VIII by the grace of God, king of England, France and Ireland, Defender of the Faith, and on earth supreme head of the Church of England and Ireland, to all the sons of holy mother church to whose notice this present writing shall come, greeting.

Whereas it seemed good to us and the great men of our realm and to all the senate whom we call Parliament, God thereunto as we believe moving us, to suppress and abolish and to convert to far better uses, for the true worship of Almighty God and the far greater benefit of the Commonwealth, the monasteries which existed everywhere in our realm, both because the sincere and most ancient religion, the most admired uprightness of life, and the most profound knowledge of languages and learning, the praise of which virtues it appears flourished in the earliest monasteries, now in the progress of time have become

Leach, op. cit., pp. 453, 494–95.

corrupt and deficient, and changed to the foulest superstition and the most disgraceful idleness and lust and the grossest ignorance of Holy Scripture, and because of their grave and manifold enormities, as for other just and reasonable causes; Wherefore we, thinking it more in conformity with the divine will and a more Christian thing that where ignorance and superstition reigned there the true worship of God should flourish and the holy gospel of Christ be assiduously and in purity preached; and further that for the increase of Christian faith and piety the youth of my realm may be instructed in good literature and the poor for ever maintained, we have in place of the same monasteries erected and established churches, some of which we will shall be called cathedrals and others collegiate churches; . . .

ROYAL INJUNCTIONS, 1559

Injunctions given by the Queen's Majesty, concerning both the clergy and laity of this realm, published A.D. 1559, being the first year of the reign of our Sovereign lady Queen Elizabeth.

The queen's most royal majesty, by the advice of her most honourable council, intending the advancement of the true honour of Almighty God, the suppression of superstition throughout all her highness's realms and dominions, and to plant true religion to the extirpation of all hypocrisie, enormities, and abuses (as to her duty appertaineth) doth minister unto her loving subjects these godly injunctions hereafter following.

XII. And, to the intent, that learned men may hereafter spring the more, for the execution of the premises, every parson, vicar, clerk, or beneficed man within this deanry having yearly to dispend in benefices and other promotions of the church £100, shall give £3. 6s. 8d. in exhibition to one scholar in either of the universities; and for as many £100 more as he may dispend, to so many scholars more shall give like exhibition in the University of Oxford or Cambridge, or some grammar-school, which, after they have profited in good learning, may be partners of their patrons cure and charge, as well in preaching, as otherwise in executing of their offices, or may, when time shall be, otherwise profit the commonweal with their counsel and wisdom.

XXXIX. Item, that every schoolmaster and teacher shall teach the Grammar set forth by King Henry VIII of noble memory, and continued in the time of king Edward VI and none other.

XL. Item, that no man shall take upon him to teach, but such as shall be allowed by the ordinary, and found meet as well for his learning and dexterity in teaching, as for sober and honest conversation, and also for right understanding of God's true religion.

XLI. Item, that all teachers of children shall stir and move them to love and do reverence to God's true religion now truly set forth by public authority.

XLII. Item, that they shall accustom their scholars reverently to learn such sentences of scripture, as shall be most expedient to induce them to all godliness.

XLIII. Item, forasmuch as in these latter days many have been made priests, being children, and otherwise utterly unlearned, so that they could read ne say mattens or mass; the ordinaries shall not admit any such to any cure or spiritual function.

In Protestant England as well as on the Continent, there was response to the call for elementary vernacular education for the "poorer sort." The charity school movement, which began in the seventeenth century and flourished by the eighteenth, had as its primary goal the development of sober, industrious, God-fearing citizens who knew and accepted their place in society (see Chapter VII, Selection 4).

回 4. The "Ratio Studiorum" of the Jesuits

The "Ratio Studiorum," the fourth section of the Constitutions of the Jesuit order, provided guidelines for the curriculum and methods of Jesuit secondary and higher education. It represented the results of a prolonged study of the best educational practices of the period; and after being issued in 1599, it stood without alteration for almost 250 years. In 1832, more emphasis was placed on mathematics and science; and in 1906, local provinces were permitted a greater flexibility in relating curriculum to local needs. The selections that follow illustrate the Jesuit's educational utilization of theology, philosophy, and the classical languages and literature to serve "for God's greater glory."

SELECTIONS FROM THE "RATIO STUDIORUM"

SYSTEM AND PLAN OF STUDIES OF THE SOCIETY OF JESUS

Since it is one of the weightiest duties of our society to teach men all the branches of knowledge in keeping with our organization in such a manner, that they may be moved thereby to a knowledge and love of our Creator and Redeemer, let the Provincial hold it as his duty, to

Painter, op. cit., pp. 188, 190, 191, 193, 195, 196, 197, 198, 199, 201.

provide with all zeal, that the results, which the grace of our vocation demands, abundantly answer to our manifold labors in education.

*   *   *   *   *

In order to preserve a knowledge of classical literature and to establish a sort of nursery for gymnasium teachers, let him [the Provincial] endeavor to have in his province at least two or three men distinguished in these services and in eloquence. To this end, from the number of those who are capable and inclined to these studies, he shall set apart for that work alone a few who are sufficiently instructed in the other departments, in order that through their efforts and activity a body of good teachers may be maintained and provided for the future.

Schools for lower studies must not exceed five in number, namely, one for rhetoric, the second for humanity, and three for grammar. For these are five grades so intimately connected that they must not be confused or increased in number.

Furthermore, care must be exercised that where there are too few schools, always the higher classes, so far as possible, must be retained, and the lower classes given up.

*   *   *   *   *

With all diligence let him watch and esteem it a matter of the highest importance that all books of the poets and other writings, which might prove injurious to character and good manners, be kept from our schools, until they have been purged of impure passages and words; and should this expurgation not be possible, the books shall rather not be read, in order that their contents may not contaminate the purity of the soul.

*   *   *   *   *

The subject-matter of tragedies and comedies, which however shall be only in Latin and seldom acted, shall be of a sacred and pious character; the interludes also shall be in Latin and of due decorum; female roles and costumes are prohibited.

*   *   *   *   *

The special aim of the teacher, in his lectures on suitable occasion and elsewhere, should be to inspire his pupils to the service and love of God and to the exercise of the virtues through which we may please him, and to lead them to recognize this as the sole end of their studies.

*   *   *   *   *

Let him [the professor of Holy Scripture] recognize it as his principal duty, piously, learnedly, and thoroughly to explain the books given of God, according to their genuine and liberal sense, which confirms the right faith in God and the principles of good morals. Among other ends which he is to pursue, let this stand as chief, that he is to defend the translation (Vulgate) approved by the Church.

* * * * *

When the canons of the popes or councils, especially the general councils, indicate the literal sense of a passage of Scripture as the true one, let him also by all means defend it and adduce no other literal sense, except where special reasons exist. When they employ a text expressly as proof of an article of faith, let him teach likewise that this is the indubitable sense, whether literal or mystical.

* * * * *

When he comes upon a text, over which we are in controversy with heretics, or which is quoted on both sides in theological discussions, let him expound it simply, yet thoroughly and vigorously, especially against heretics, and point out what weight is in the passage for deciding the question at issue; all the rest let him lay aside, in order that he, mindful of his vocation, may be simply an expounder of the Holy Scriptures.

* * * * *

In teaching, confirmation of faith and growth in piety must above all be considered. Therefore in questions, which St. Thomas has not expressly handled, no one shall teach anything that does not well harmonize with the views of the Church and the generally received traditions, and that in any way disturbs the foundation of genuine piety.

* * * * *

Let him [the professor of Church history] treat the history of the Church with the view and with such skill, that he may render the study of theology more easy for his students, and more deeply impress upon their minds the dogmas of faith and the canons.

Let him clearly demonstrate that the rights of the Church and of its head rest upon antiquity, and let him show that the statements of innovators about the late origin of such rights are pure inventions.

* * * * *

In all important questions he must not deviate from the teaching everywhere accepted in the academies. Let him defend the orthodox faith with his might, and seek thoroughly to refute the philosophical systems and arguments directed against it. Finally let him not forget in the choice of different opinions that theology must light the way.

* * * * *

From the beginning of logic on, the students shall be so instructed that in their disputations they may be ashamed of nothing more than of a departure from syllogistic form. The teacher shall insist on nothing more than on an observance of the laws of disputation and the proper alternation between attack and defense. Therefore, let the defendant first repeat the whole argumentation without any reply to the separate propositions; then let him repeat again the propositions, and add to each one "I grant it," or "I deny the major or minor premise or the conclusion." Let him also sometimes draw distinctions, but not urge upon any one against his will the explanation or reasons which one is accustomed to introduce.

*   *   *   *   *

Finally he [the professor of physics] shall not forget that he is to pursue the secular sciences in a religious manner, in order that "the invisible things of God may be made known through those things which are made" [Rom. 1:20]; therefore let him seek, as occasion presents itself, to confirm the truths of faith also through physical science, yet without going aside to theological, metaphysical, or Scriptural exposition.

*   *   *   *   *

There shall be three examiners [in the lower gymnasium studies]: one of them must ordinarily be the Prefect; the other two must be learned in the humanities, and be appointed by the rector together with the Prefect. A majority of the three shall decide. But where the number of students is large, two or more such triumvirates may be appointed.

The order of the examination is as follows: first each student, when he is called on, shall read a part of his composition; then let him correct his mistakes and explain them, with a citation of the rule which he has failed to observe. Afterwards the grammar students shall immediately translate into Latin an exercise assigned them in the vernacular; all shall be interrogated about the rules and subjects of their class. Finally, when it is necessary, a brief interpretation of any passage from those books, which have been read in class, may be required of them.

When three students have been examined, and while the recollection of the examiners is still clear, the vote shall be taken, in which the composition, the notes of the teacher, and the oral examination shall all be considered.

*   *   *   *   *

Christian doctrine must be learned by heart in all the classes; and in the three grammar classes, and if necessary, in the other classes, it must be repeated Fridays or Saturdays. According to the grade of each class more ample explanations shall be given and required.

*   *   *   *   *

On Friday or Saturday let him [the Professor of the lower classes] deliver for half an hour a pious exhortation or explanation of the catechism; but especially let him exhort to daily prayer to God, to a daily reciting of the rosary or office of the Blessed Virgin, to an examination of the conscience every evening, to a frequent and worthy reception of the sacraments of penance and the altar, to an avoidance of evil habits, to a detestation of vice, and finally to a practice of all the virtues becoming a Christian.

*   *   *   *   *

Especial care must be exercised that the students acquire the habit of speaking Latin. Therefore the teacher, at least from the upper grammar grade, must speak in Latin, and require also that the students speak Latin, especially in the explanation of rules, the correction of Latin exercises, in disputations, and in their daily intercourse. In the translation of authors he must himself have great regard for the purity and correct pronunciation of the mother tongue, and strictly require the same from the students.

CURRICULUM OF THE JESUITS: "RATIO STUDIORUM," 1599

CLASS	SUBJECTS OF INSTRUCTION, AND TIME ALLOWANCE		AUTHORS AND REMARKS
	Morning	Afternoon	
Sixth	Recitation on the Latin author, and on Latin and Greek grammar .... ¾ h. Correction of task ½ h. Latin translation, review and advance ¾ h. Mother tongue and accessory exercises .. ½ h.	Recitation on the Latin author, and on the grammar .... 1 h. Translation of Latin author. Greek reading, a quarter-hour twice a week. Dictation of the composition work...... 1 h. Discussion. Mother tongue and accessory exercises .... ½ h.	Cicero, Extracts; Phædrus, *Fables;* Nepos, *Lives.* —— Greek, Exercises in reading and writing.
Fifth	Recitation on the Latin author, and on Latin and Greek grammar .... ¾ h. Correction of task . ½ h. Translation, review and advance .... ¾ h. Mother tongue and accessory exercises .. ½ h.	Recitation on the Latin author, and on the grammar .... 1 h. Translation of Latin and Greek authors alternately every two days. Dictation of the composition work ..... 1 h. Discussion. Mother tongue and accessory exercises .... ½ h.	Cicero, Selected letters; Cæsar; Ovid, Selections; Æsop, *Fables;* Cebes; Lucian, Selected dialogues.

Frederich E. Farrington, French Secondary Schools *(New York: Longmans, Green and Co., 1910), pp. 394–95.*

CLASS	SUBJECTS OF INSTRUCTION, AND TIME ALLOWANCE		AUTHORS AND REMARKS
	Morning	Afternoon	
Fourth	Recitation on the Latin author, and on the Latin and Greek grammar .... ¾ h. Correction of task . ½ h. Translation, review and advance .... ¾ h. Mother tongue and accessory exercises .. ½ h.	Recitation on Latin grammar, versification, and the author, on successive days .... 1 h. Translation of a Latin poet and a Greek author, alternately every other day. Dictation of the composition work .. 1 h. Discussion. Mother tongue and accessory exercises .... ½ h.	Cicero, Letters, *De amicitia*, *De senectute*; Easy speeches of Cicero; Sallust: Quintus Curtius: Extracts from Livy, Ovid, Catullus, Tibullus, Propertius and Virgil: *Eclogues: Georgics*, 4th bk.; *Æneid*, 5th and 7th bks. —— Greek: St. Chrysostom, Xenophon, and other similar authors.
Third	Recitation on the Latin author, and on the grammar. General principles of elocution and style .... ¾ h. Correction of task . ½ h. Translation, review and advance .... ¾ h. Mother tongue and accessory exercises .. ½ h.	Recitation on the Latin author, and on the grammar .... 1 h. Translation, every other day, of a Latin poet, and a Greek (or interpretation of a French) author. Dictation of the composition work .... 1 h. Discussion and accessory exercises .... ½ h.	Cicero, Speeches; Cæsar; Sallust; Livy; Quintus Curtius: *Æneid* (save the fourth book); Horace, *Odes* (selected). —— Greek: Isocrates; St. Chrysostom; St. Basil; Plato; Plutarch, Phocylides; Theognis; St. Gregory of Nazianzus; Synesius.
Second	No special program	No special program	No special program.
Rhetoric	Memory work. Translation, review and advance .... 1 h. Reading from an orator, review and advance. Dictation of a text from an oration. Discussion and accessory exercises .... 1 h.	Translation of passages from the rhetoric. Translation of a Greek, or interpretation of a French, author .... 1 h. Reading from one of the poets. Correction of the task of the morning. Dictation of the subject of an oration ... 1 h.	For the principle of rhetoric, Cicero and Quintilian. No special directions as to the Latin authors to be translated. Greek: Demosthenes, Plato, Thucydides, Homer, Hesiod, Pindar, St. Gregory of Nazianzus, St. Basil, St. Chrysostom. On holidays one of the historians or some passage of historical significance is explained.

▣ 5. Francis Bacon, Proponent of the Inductive Method

As courtier, essayist, and propagandist for the cause and methods of science, Francis Bacon (1561–1626) stands as one of the noblest representatives of Elizabethan England. Author of the New Atlantis, *he combined his literary skill and evangelical faith in the inductive method to portray a Utopia created by the implementation of the findings of scientists. In his* Dignity and Advancement of Learning *and the* Novum Organum, *he described and defended the use of the senses in the scientific method and derided the claims of the scholastics with their syllogisms and allegiance to authorities of the past in interpreting nature.*

In the excerpt that follows from Novum Organum, *one can readily observe that the advocate of the new method of science was of necessity a critic of the techniques and superstitions that had for centuries provided man with erroneous notions of the "Nature and Empire of Man."*

APHORISMS

BOOK I

On the Interpretation of Nature and the Empire of Man

Man, as the minister and interpreter of nature, does and understands as much as his observations on the order of nature, either with regard to things or the mind, permit him, and neither knows nor is capable of more.

2. The unassisted hand and the understanding left to itself possess but little power. Effects are produced by the means of instruments and helps, which the understanding requires no less than the hand; and as instruments either promote or regulate the motion of the hand, so those that are applied to the mind prompt or protect the understanding.

3. Knowledge and human power are synonymous, since the ignorance of the cause frustrates the effect; for nature is only subdued by submission, and that which in contemplative philosophy corresponds with the cause in practical science becomes the rule.

4. Man whilst operating can only apply or withdraw natural bodies; nature internally performs the rest.

5. Those who become practically versed in nature are, the mechanic,

Francis Bacon, Advancement of Learning and Novum Organum *(New York and London: The Colonial Press, 1900), pp. 315–20.*

the mathematician, the physician, the alchemist, and the magician, but all (as matters now stand) with faint efforts and meagre success.

6. It would be madness and inconsistency to suppose that things which have never yet been performed can be performed without employing some hitherto untried means.

7. The creations of the mind and hand appear very numerous, if we judge by books and manufactures; but all that variety consists of an excessive refinement, and of deductions from a few well-known matters —not of a number of axioms.

8. Even the effects already discovered are due to chance and experiment, rather than to the sciences; for our present sciences are nothing more than peculiar arrangements of matters already discovered, and not methods for discovery or plans for new operations.

9. The sole cause and root of almost every defect in the sciences is this, that while we falsely admire and extol the powers of the human mind, we do not search for its real helps.

10. The subtility of nature is far beyond that of sense or of the understanding; so that the specious meditations, speculations, and theories of mankind are but a kind of insanity, only there is no one to stand by and observe it.

11. As the present sciences are useless for the discovery of effects, so the present system of logic is useless for the discovery of the sciences.

12. The present system of logic rather assists in confirming and rendering inveterate the errors founded on vulgar notions than in searching after truth, and is therefore more hurtful than useful.

13. The syllogism is not applied to the principles of the sciences, and is of no avail in intermediate axioms, as being very unequal to the subtilty of nature. It forces assent, therefore, and not things.

14. The syllogism consists of propositions, propositions of words; words are the signs of notions. If, therefore, the notions (which form the basis of the whole) be confused and carelessly abstracted from things, there is no solidity in the superstructure. Our only hope, then, is in genuine induction.

15. We have no sound notions either in logic or physics; substance, quality, action, passion, and existence are not clear notions; much less weight, levity, density, tenuity, moisture, dryness, generation, corruption, attraction, repulsion, element, matter, form, and the like. They are all fantastical and ill-defined.

16. The notions of less abstract natures, as man, dog, dove, and the immediate perceptions of sense, as heat, cold, white, black, do not deceive us materially, yet even these are sometimes confused by the mutability of matter and the intermixture of things. All the rest which men have hitherto employed are errors, and improperly abstracted and deduced from things.

17. There is the same degree of licentiousness and error in forming axioms as in abstracting notions, and that in the first principles, which depend on common induction; still more is this the case in axioms and inferior propositions derived from syllogisms.

18. The present discoveries in science are such as lie immediately beneath the surface of common notions. It is necessary, however, to penetrate the more secret and remote parts of nature, in order to abstract both notions and axioms from things by a more certain and guarded method.

19. There are and can exist but two ways of investigating and discovering truth. The one hurries on rapidly from the senses and particulars to the most general axioms, and from them, as principles and their supposed indisputable truth, derives and discovers the intermediate axioms. This is the way now in use. The other constructs its axioms from the senses and particulars, by ascending continually and gradually, till it finally arrives at the most general axioms, which is the true but unattempted way.

20. The understanding when left to itself proceeds by the same way as that which it would have adopted under the guidance of logic, namely, the first; for the mind is fond of starting off to generalities, that it may avoid labor, and after dwelling a little on a subject is fatigued by experiment. But those evils are augmented by logic, for the sake of the ostentation of dispute.

21. The understanding, when left to itself in a man of a steady, patient, and reflecting disposition (especially when unimpeded by received doctrines), makes some attempt in the right way, but with little effect, since the understanding, undirected and unassisted, is unequal to and unfit for the task of vanquishing the obscurity of things.

22. Each of these two ways begins from the senses and particulars, and ends in the greatest generalities. But they are immeasurably different; for the one merely touches cursorily the limits of experiment and particulars, whilst the other runs duly and regularly through them —the one from the very outset lays down some abstract and useless generalities, the other gradually rises to those principles which are really the most common in nature.

23. There is no small difference between the idols of the human mind and the ideas of the Divine mind—that is to say, between certain idle dogmas and the real stamp and impression of created objects, as they are found in nature.

24. Axioms determined upon in argument can never assist in the discovery of new effects; for the subtility of nature is vastly superior to that of argument. But axioms properly and regularly abstracted from particulars easily point out and define new particulars, and therefore impart activity to the sciences.

25. The axioms now in use are derived from a scanty handful, as it were, of experience, and a few particulars of frequent occurrence, whence they are of much the same dimensions or extent as their origin. And if any neglected or unknown instance occurs, the axiom is saved by some frivolous distinction, when it would be more consistent with truth to amend it.

26. We are wont, for the sake of distinction, to call that human reasoning which we apply to nature the anticipation of nature (as being rash and premature), and that which is properly deduced from things the interpretation of nature.

27. Anticipations are sufficiently powerful in producing unanimity, for if men were all to become even uniformly mad, they might agree tolerably well with each other.

28. Anticipations, again, will be assented to much more readily than interpretations, because being deduced from a few instances, and these principally of familiar occurrence, they immediately hit the understanding and satisfy the imagination; whilst on the contrary interpretations, being deduced from various subjects, and these widely dispersed, cannot suddenly strike the understanding, so that in common estimation they must appear difficult and discordant, and almost like the mysteries of faith.

29. In sciences founded on opinions and dogmas, it is right to make use of anticipations and logic if you wish to force assent rather than things.

30. If all the capacities of all ages should unite and combine and transmit their labors, no great progress will be made in learning by anticipations, because the radical errors, and those which occur in the first process of the mind, are not cured by the excellence of subsequent means and remedies.

31. It is in vain to expect any great progress in the sciences by the superinducing or engrafting new matters upon old. An instauration must be made from the very foundations, if we do not wish to revolve forever in a circle, making only some slight and contemptible progress.

32. The ancient authors and all others are left in undisputed possession of their honors; for we enter into no comparison of capacity or talent, but of method, and assume the part of a guide rather than of a critic.

33. To speak plainly, no correct judgment can be formed either of our method or its discoveries by those anticipations which are now in common use; for it is not to be required of us to submit ourselves to the judgment of the very method we ourselves arraign.

34. Nor is it an easy matter to deliver and explain our sentiments; for those things which are in themselves new can yet be only understood from some analogy to what is old.

35. Alexander Borgia said of the expedition of the French into Italy

that they came with chalk in their hands to mark up their lodgings, and not with weapons to force their passage. Even so do we wish our philosophy to make its way quietly into those minds that are fit for it, and of good capacity; for we have no need of contention where we differ in first principles, and in our very notions, and even in our forms of demonstration.

36. We have but one simple method of delivering our sentiments, namely, we must bring men to particulars and their regular series and order, and they must for a while renounce their notions, and begin to form an acquaintance with things.

37. Our method and that of the sceptics agree in some respects at first setting out, but differ most widely, and are completely opposed to each other in their conclusion; for they roundly assert that nothing can be known; we, that but a small part of nature can be known, by the present method; their next step, however, is to destroy the authority of the senses and understanding, whilst we invent and supply them with assistance.

38. The idols and false notions which have already preoccupied the human understanding, and are deeply rooted in it, not only so beset men's minds that they become difficult of access, but even when access is obtained will again meet and trouble us in the instauration of the sciences, unless mankind when forewarned guard themselves with all possible care against them.

39. Four species of idols beset the human mind, to which (for distinction's sake) we have assigned names, calling the first Idols of the Tribe, the second Idols of the Den, the third Idols of the Market, the fourth Idols of the Theatre.

40. The formation of notions and axioms on the foundation of true induction is the only fitting remedy by which we can ward off and expel these idols. It is, however, of great service to point them out; for the doctrine of idols bears the same relation to the interpretation of nature as that of the confutation of sophisms does to common logic.

41. The idols of the tribe are inherent in human nature and the very tribe or race of man; for man's sense is falsely asserted to be the standard of things; on the contrary, all the perceptions both of the senses and the mind bear reference to man and not to the universe, and the human mind resembles those uneven mirrors which impart their own properties to different objects, from which rays are emitted and distort and disfigure them.

42. The idols of the den are those of each individual; for everybody (in addition to the errors common to the race of man) has his own individual den or cavern, which intercepts and corrupts the light of nature, either from his own peculiar and singular disposition, or from his education and intercourse with others, or from his reading, and the authority acquired by those whom he reveres and admires, or from

the different impressions produced on the mind, as it happens to be pre-occupied and predisposed, or equable and tranquil, and the like; so that the spirit of man (according to its several dispositions), is variable, confused, and, as it were, actuated by chance; and Heraclitus said well that men search for knowledge in lesser worlds, and not in the greater or common world.

43. There are also idols formed by the reciprocal intercourse and society of man with man, which we call idols of the market, from the commerce and association of men with each other; for men converse by means of language, but words are formed at the will of the generality, and there arises from a bad and unapt formation of words a wonderful obstruction to the mind. Nor can the definitions and explanations with which learned men are wont to guard and protect themselves in some instances afford a complete remedy—words still manifestly force the understanding, throw everything into confusion, and lead mankind into vain and innumerable controversies and fallacies.

44. Lastly, there are idols which have crept into men's minds from the various dogmas of peculiar systems of philosophy, and also from the perverted rules of demonstration, and these we denominate idols of the theatre: for we regard all the systems of philosophy hitherto received or imagined, as so many plays brought out and performed, creating fictitious and theatrical worlds. Nor do we speak only of the present systems, or of the philosophy and sects of the ancients, since numerous other plays of a similar nature can be still composed and made to agree with each other, the causes of the most opposite errors being generally the same. Nor, again, do we allude merely to general systems, but also to many elements and axioms of sciences which have become inveterate by tradition, implicit credence, and neglect. . . .

回 6. The Inductive Method Applied to Educational Theory

It is obvious that science has been responsible for a great share of what constitutes our modern world, including modern education. A most significant prophet of the new era in education was the Moravian bishop John Amos Comenius (1592–1670). His application of the inductive method to the education of children resulted in an advocacy of procedures that appear remarkably modern to today's reader: appeal to the child's sense experience; recognize the stages of child development; in teaching, proceed from the known to the unknown, from the simple to the complex. His most successful attempt to translate theory into practice

*was through textbooks in which he appealed to the child's senses and experiences
by introducing pictures. Following are illustrations from an English edition of
his most popular text,* Orbis Pictus, *designed to improve language teaching by
utilizing pictures accompanied by explanatory sentences in Latin and in the
vernacular.*

ORBIS SENSUALIUM PICTUS,

A World of Things Obvious to the Senses drawn in Pictures.

Invitation   I.   Invitatio.

The Master and the Boy.	*Magister & Puer.*
M. Come, Boy, learn to be wise.	M. Veni, Puer, disce sapere.
P. What doth this mean, *to be wise?*	P. Quid hoc est, *Sapere?*
M. To understand rightly to do rightly, and to speak out rightly all that are necessary.	M. Intelligere recte, agere recte, et eloqui recte omnia necessaria.
P. Who will teach me this?	P. Quis docebit me hoc?
M. I, by God's help.	M. Ego, cum DEO.
P. How?	P. Quomodo?
M. I will guide thee thorow all.	M. Ducam te per omnia.
I will shew thee all.	Ostendam tibi omnia.
I will name thee all.	Nominabo tibi omnia.
P. See, here I am; lead me in the name of God.	P. En, adsum; duc me in nomine DEI.

Charles Hoole (trans.), The Orbis Pictus of John Amos Comenius *(Syracuse, N.Y.:
C. W. Bardeen, Publisher, 1887), pp. 1–3, 52–53.*

M. Before all things, thou oughtest to learn the plain *sounds,* of which man's *speech* consisteth; which *living creatures* know how *to make,* and thy *Tongue* knoweth how *to imitate,* and thy *hand* can *picture out.*

Afterwards we will go into the *World,* and we will view all things.

Here thou hast a lively and Vocal Alphabet.

M. Ante omnia, debes discere simplices *Sonos* ex quibus *Sermo* humanus constat; quos *Animalia* sciunt *formare,* & tua *Lingua* scit *imitari,* & tua *Manus* potest *pingere.*

Postea ibimus *Mundum,* & spectabimus omnia.

Hic habes vivum et vocale Alphabetum.

	Cornix cornicatur, The *Crow* crieth.	à à	A a
	Agnus balat, The *Lamb* blaiteth.	b è è è	B b
	Cicàda stridet, The *Grasshopper* chirpeth.	cì cì	C c
	Upupa dicit, The *Whooppoo* saith	du du	D d
	Infans ejulat, The *Infant* crieth.	è è è	E e
	Ventus flat, The *Wind* bloweth	fi fi	F f
	Anser gingrit, The *Goose* gagleth.	ga ga	G g
	Os halat, The *Mouth* breatheth out.	hà'h hà'h	H h
	Mus mintrit, The *Mouse* chirpeth.	ì ì ì	I i
	Anas tetrinnit, The *Duck* quaketh	kha, kha	K k
	Lupus ululat, The *Wolf* howleth.	lu ulu	L
	Ursus murmurat, The *Bear* grumbleth.	[mum mum-	M

XLII.

The Outward and Inward Senses.

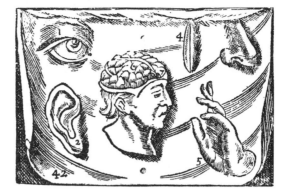

Sensus externi & interni.

There are five outward *Senses;*

The *Eye,* 1. seeth Colours, what is white or black, green or blew, red or yellow.

The *Ear,* 2. heareth *Sounds,* both natural, Voices and Words; and artificial,

Musical Tunes.

The *Nose,* 3. scenteth smells and stinks.

The *Tongue,* 4. with the roof of the Mouth tastes *Savours,* what is sweet or bitter, keen or biting, sower or harsh.

The *Hand,* 5. by touching discerneth the quantity and quality of things;
the hot and cold,
the moist and dry,
the hard and soft,
the smooth and rough,
the heavy and light.

The inward *Senses* are three.

The *Common Sense,* 7. under the *forepart of the head,* apprehendeth things taken from the outward Senses.

Sunt quinque externi *Sensus;*

Oculus, 1. videt *Colores,* quid album vel atrum, viride vel cœruleum, rubrum aut luteum, sit.

Auris, 2. audit *Sonos,* tum naturales, Voces & Verba; tum artificiales,

Tonos Musicos.

Nasus, 3, *olfacit* odores & fœtores.

Lingua, 4. cum Palato gustat *Sapores,* quid dulce aut amarum, acre aut acidum, acerbum aut austerum.

Manus, 5. tangendo dignoscit quantitatem, & qualitatem rerum;
calidum & frigidum,
humidum & siccum,
durum & molle,
læve & asperum,
grave & leve.

Sensus interni sunt tres.

Sensus Communis, 7. sub *sincipite* apprehendit res perceptas a Sensibus externis.

The *Phantasie*, 6. under the *crown of the head* judgeth of those things, thinketh and dreameth,	*Phantasia*, 6. sub *vertice*, dijudicat res istas, cogitat, somniat.
The *Memory*, 8. under the *hinder part of the head*, layeth up every thing and fetcheth them out: it loseth some, and this is *forgetfulness*.	*Memoria*, 8. sub *occipitio*, recondit singula & depromit: deperdit quædam, & hoc est *oblivio*.
Sleep, is the rest of the Senses.	*Somnus*, est requies Sensuum.

In his Great Didactic *(Didactica magna), Comenius showed himself a modern not only in his advocacy of sense realism in education but also in his faith that education could be a tool for social reform. Specifically, he was a proponent of pansophism, teaching "all things to all men." In the* Great Didactic *he described an educational ladder beginning with the School of the Mother's Knee for infants up to six followed by the vernacular school, grammar school, and finally the university. He offered an education in which the children's experiences and senses would be utilized, in which study of the familiar vernacular language would precede the classical tongues, in which students would be graded according to their stage of development and ability, and in which the child's moral, religious, and physical development as well as his intellectual growth were to be stressed.*

In the excerpt that follows, Comenius explains the goals of pansophism. Here surely was a man who saw the senses as allies rather than enemies of the soul.

THE INSTRUCTION GIVEN IN SCHOOLS SHOULD BE UNIVERSAL

1. We have already shown that every one ought to receive a universal education, and this at school. But do not, therefore, imagine that we demand from all men a knowledge (that is to say, an exact or deep knowledge) of all the arts and sciences. This would neither be useful of itself, nor, on account of the shortness of life, can it be attained by any man. For we see that each science is so vast and so complicated (as are physics, arithmetic, geometry, astronomy, or even agriculture and arboriculture) that it would occupy the lifetime of even the strongest intellects if they wished to master it thoroughly by investigation and experiment. Thus did Pythagoras devote himself to arithmetic, Archimedes to mechanics, Agricola to metallurgy, and Longolius (who spent his whole life in endeavouring to acquire a perfect Ciceronian style) to rhetoric. It is the principles, the causes, and the uses of all the

most important things in existence that we wish all men to learn; all, that is to say, who are sent into the world to be actors as well as spectators. For we must take strong and vigorous measures that no man, in his journey through life, may encounter anything so unknown to him that he cannot pass sound judgment upon it and turn it to its proper use without serious error.

2. We must, therefore, concentrate our energies on obtaining that, throughout our whole lives, in schools and by the aid of schools: (i) our talents may be cultivated by study of the sciences and of the arts; (ii) languages may be learned; (iii) honest morals may be formed; (iv) God may be sincerely worshipped.

3. He spoke wisely who said that schools were the workshops of humanity, since it is undoubtedly through their agency that man really becomes man, that is to say (to refer to our previous analysis): (i) a rational creature; (ii) a creature which is lord over all creatures and also over himself; (iii) a creature which is the delight of his Creator. This will be the case if schools are able to produce men who are wise in mind, prudent in action, and pious in spirit.

4. These three principles, then, must be implanted in all the young in all schools, and this I shall prove, starting from the following fundamental points:—

(i)   From the circumstances by which we are surrounded;

(ii)   From ourselves;

(iii) From Christ the God-man, the most perfect example of our perfection.

5. Things themselves, as far as they concern us, can be divided into three classes only: (i) objects that we can observe, such as the heavens, the earth, and all that is in them; (ii) objects that we can imitate, such as the marvellous order which pervades all things, and which man ought to imitate in his actions; (iii) objects that we can enjoy, such as the grace of God and His manifold blessing here and for eternity. If man is to acquit himself creditably when brought into contact with this order of nature, he must be trained to know the things that are spread out for his observation in this marvellous amphitheatre, to do the things that it is right for him to do, and finally, to enjoy those things of which the most benign Creator, treating him as a guest in His house, has, with liberal hand, given him the fruition.

6. If we consider ourselves, we see clearly that learning, virtue, and piety are of importance to all alike; whether we look at the essential being of the soul, or at the object of our creation and introduction into the world.

7. The soul in its essential elements consists of three potentialities, which recall the uncreated Trinity, and these are the intellect, the will, and the memory. The province of the intellect is to observe the

differences between things, even down to the smallest details. The will concerns itself with choice—that is to say, with the choice of things that are advantageous and the rejection of those which are not. The memory stores up for future use all the things with which the intellect and the will have been busied, and reminds the soul of its dependence on God and of its duty; in which aspect it is also called conscience.

In order, then, that these faculties may rightly fulfil their offices, it is necessary that they be furnished with such things as may illumine the intellect, direct the will, and stimulate the conscience, so that the intellect may be acute and penetrating, the will may choose without error, and the conscience may greedily refer all things to God. Therefore, just as these faculties (the intellect, the will, and the conscience) cannot be separated, since they constitute the same soul, so it is impossible to separate those three ornaments of the soul, erudition, virtue, and piety.

8. Now, if we consider why we have been sent into the world, it will be evident from two points of view that the object is threefold, namely, that we may serve God, His creatures and ourselves, and that we may enjoy the pleasure to be derived from God, from His creatures, and from ourselves.

9. If we wish to serve God, our neighbours, and ourselves, it is necessary for us to possess, with respect to God, piety; with respect to our neighbours, virtue; and with respect to ourselves, knowledge. These principles, however, are intimately connected, and a man, for his own advantage, should be not only learned, but also virtuous and pious; for that of his neighbour, not only virtuous, but also learned and pious; and for the glory of God, not only pious, but also learned and virtuous.

10. If we consider the happiness to which God has destined mankind, we find that He showed His intention clearly when creating man, since He introduced him into a world furnished with all good things; prepared for him, in addition, a paradise of delights; and, finally, arranged to make him a partner of His eternal happiness.

11. Now, by the term "happiness" we understand not the pleasures of the body (though these, since they consist of the vigour of good health, and of the enjoyment of food and of sleep, can only arise from the virtue of temperance), but those of the soul, which arise either out of the objects around us, or from ourselves, or, finally, from God.

12. The pleasure which arises out of things themselves, is the pleasure that a wise man experiences in speculation. For, wherever he betakes himself, whatever he observes, and whatever he consideres, he finds everywhere such attractions, that often, as it were, snatched out of himself, he merges his identity in them. It is to this that the book of Wisdom refers: "The conversation of wisdom hath no bitterness; and to live with her hath no sorrow, but mirth and joy" (viii. 16). And a

heathen philosopher says: "There is nothing in life more pleasant than to seek out wisdom."

13. Pleasure in self is that very sweet delight which arises when a man, who is given over to virtue, rejoices in his own honest disposition, since he sees himself prompt to all things which the order of justice requires. This pleasure is far greater than the former one, according to the proverb "A good conscience is a perpetual feast."

14. Delight in God is the highest point to which pleasure can attain in this life, and is found when a man, feeling that God is eternally gracious to him, exults in His fatherly and immutable favour to such a degree that his heart melts with the love of God. He desires to know or to do nothing further, but, overwhelmed by God's mercy, he rests in peace and tastes the joys of eternal life. This is "the peace of God which passeth all understanding" (Phil. iv. 7), than which nothing more sublime can be desired or imagined.

These three principles, therefore, learning, virtue, and piety, are the three founts from which all the streams of the most perfect pleasures flow.

15. Lastly, God Himself, manifest in the flesh (that He might exhibit in Himself the perfection of all things), has taught by His example that these three elements must exist in each individual. For the Evangelist testifies that He advanced not only in stature, but also in wisdom and favour with God and man (Luke ii. 52). Here can be seen the blessed Trinity that adorns us. For what is wisdom but the knowledge of things as they are? What is it that brings us favour with men, if not amiability of character? What procures us the grace of God, if not the fear of the Lord, that is to say, inward, serious, and fervid piety? Let us, therefore, realise in ourselves that which we have seen in Jesus Christ, the absolute ideal of all perfection, the standard set up for us to imitate.

16. For this reason He said, "Learn of me" (Matt. xi. 29). And since this same Christ has been given to the human race as the most learned teacher, as the most holy priest, and as the most powerful king, it is evident that Christians should be formed on His model and should be enlightened through their intellects, sanctified through their consciences, and made powerful through their deeds (each in his own calling). Our schools, therefore, will then at length be Christian schools when they make us as like to Christ as is possible.

17. It is, therefore, an unhallowed separation if these three elements be not bound together as if by an adamantine chain. How wretched is the teaching that does not lead to virtue and to piety! For what is literary skill without virtue? He who makes progress in knowledge but not in morality (says an old proverb), recedes rather than advances. And thus, what Solomon said of the beautiful but foolish woman, holds good of the learned man who possesses not virtue: "As a jewel of gold in

a swine's snout, so is a fair woman which is without discretion" (Prov. xi. 22). For, just as gems are set not in lead but in gold, in which combination both are more beautiful, thus should knowledge be joined not to immorality but to virtue, when each will add adornment to the other. For the fear of the Lord, as it is the beginning and the end of wisdom, is also the coping-stone and crown of knowledge. The fear of the Lord is the beginning of wisdom (Prov. i. and elsewhere).

18. Since, therefore, a man's whole life depends on the instruction that he has received during boyhood, every opportunity is lost unless the minds of all are then prepared for every emergency that may arise in life. Just as in his mother's womb each man receives his full complement of limbs,—hands, feet, tongue, etc.—although all men are not to be artificers, runners, scribes, or orators; so at school all men should be taught whatever concerns man, though in after life some things will be of more use to one man, others to another.

To enable the reader to better appreciate Comenius's employment of sense realism in education as well as his remarkable vision, the following excerpts from the Great Didactic *are offered. Not everything he advocated would be accepted by experts today, but remember that this was written in c. 1632.*

THE PRINCIPLES OF FACILITY IN TEACHING AND IN LEARNING

1. We have already considered the means by which the educationist may attain his goal with certainty, we will now proceed to see how these means can be suited to the minds of the pupils, so that their use may be easy and pleasant.

2. Following in the footsteps of nature we find that the process of education will be easy.

(i)   If it begin early, before the mind is corrupted.
(ii)   If the mind be duly prepared to receive it.
(iii)   If it proceed from the general to the particular.
(iv)   And from what is easy to what is more difficult.
(v)   If the pupil be not overburdened by too many subjects.
(vi)   And if progress be slow in every case.
(vii)   If the intellect be forced to nothing to which its natural bent does not incline it, in accordance with its age and with the right method.
(viii) If everything be taught through the medium of the senses.
(ix)   And if the use of everything taught be continually kept in view.
(x)   If everything be taught according to one and the same method.

These, I say, are the principles to be adopted if education is to be easy and pleasant.

Keatinge, op. cit., pp. 279, 294–95, 328–32.

THE PRINCIPLES OF THOROUGHNESS IN
TEACHING AND IN LEARNING

1. It is a common complaint that there are few who leave school with a thorough education, and that most men retain nothing but a veneer, a mere shadow of true knowledge. This complaint is corroborated by facts.

2. The cause of this phenomenon appears on investigation to be twofold: either that the schools occupy themselves with insignificant and unimportant studies, to the neglect of those that are more weighty, or that the pupils forget what they have learned, since most of it merely goes through their heads and does not stick fast there. This last fault is so common that there are few who do not lament it. For if everything that we have ever read, heard, and mentally appreciated were always ready to hand in our memories, how learned we should appear! We do, it is true, make practical use of much that we have learned, but the amount that we recollect is unsatisfactory, and the fact remains that we are continually trying to pour water into a sieve.

3. But can no cure be found for this? Certainly there can, if once more we go to the school of nature, and investigate the methods that she adopts to give endurance to the beings which she has created.

I maintain that a method can be found by means of which each person will be enabled to bring into his mental consciousness not only what he has learned, but more as well; since he will recall with ease all that he has learned from teachers or from books, and, at the same time, will be able to pass sound judgment on the objective facts to which his information refers.

4. This will be possible:

(i) If only those subjects that are of real use be taken in hand.

(ii) If these be taught without digression or interruption.

(iii) If a thorough grounding precede instruction in detail.

(iv) If this grounding be carefully given.

(v) If all that follows be based on this grounding, and on nothing else.

(vi) If, in every subject that consists of several parts, these parts be linked together as much as possible.

(vii) If all that comes later be based on what has gone before.

(viii) If great stress be laid on the points of resemblance between cognate subjects.

(ix) If all studies be arranged with reference to the intelligence and memory of the pupils, and the nature of language.

(x) If knowledge be fixed in the memory by constant practice.

SIXTH PROBLEM

How is it possible to do two or three things by a single operation?

41. The example of nature shows that several things can be done at

one time and by means of the same operation. It is an undoubted fact
that a tree grows above the ground and beneath it at the same time,
and that its wood, its bark, its leaves, and its fruit, all develope simultaneously. The same observation applies to animals, whose limbs all
develope and grow stronger at the same time. Further, each limb
performs several operations. The feet, for instance, not only support a
man but also move him forwards and backwards in various ways. The
mouth is not only the entrance to the body, but also serves as a masti-
cator and as a trumpet that sounds whenever called upon to do so.
With a single inspiration the lungs cool the heart, purify the brain, and
assist in voice-production.

42. We find the same thing in the arts: (1) In the sun-dial, the single
shadow cast by the gnomon points out the hour of the day, the sign of
the zodiac in which the sun is moving, the length of the day and of the
night, the day of the month, and several other things. (2) One pole
serves to direct, to turn, and to hold back a carriage. (3) A good orator
or writer instructs, excites, and pleases at the same time, even though his
subject may make it difficult to combine these three elements.

43. The instruction of the young should be similarly organised, so
that every activity may produce several results. It may be laid down
as a general rule that each subject should be taught in combination
with those which are correlative to it; that is to say, words should be
studied in combination with the things to which they refer; while
reading and writing, exercises in style and in logical thought, teaching
and learning, amusement and serious study, should be continually
joined together.

44. Words, therefore, should always be taught and learned in combination with things, just as wine is bought and sold together with the
cask that contains it, a dagger with its sheath, a tree with its bark, and
fruit with its skin. For what are words but the husks and coverings of
things? Therefore, when instruction is given in any language, even
in the mother-tongue itself, the words must be explained by reference
to the objects that they denote; and contrariwise, the scholars must be
taught to express in language whatever they see, hear, handle, or taste,
so that their command of language, as it progresses, may ever run
parallel to the growth of the understanding.

The rule shall therefore run as follows:

The scholar should be trained to express everything that he sees in
words, and should be taught the meaning of all the words that he uses.
No one should be allowed to talk about anything that he does not
understand, or to understand anything without at the same time being
able to express his knowledge in words. For he who cannot express the
thoughts of his mind resembles a statue, and he who chatters, without
understanding what he says, resembles a parrot.

But we wish to train up *men*, and to do so as quickly as possible, and this end can only be attained when instruction in language goes hand in hand with instruction in facts.

45. From this it follows that we ought to exclude from our schools all books that merely teach words and do not at the same time lead to a knowledge of useful objects. We must bestow our labour on that which is of real importance, and, therefore (as Seneca says in his 9th Letter), must devote ourselves to the improvement of our understanding rather than to the enlargement of our vocabulary. Any reading that is necessary can be got through quickly out of school-hours without tedious explanations or attempts at imitation; since the time thus spent could be better employed in the study of nature.

46. Exercises in reading and writing should always be combined. Even when scholars are learning their alphabet, they should be made to master the letters by writing them; since it is impossible to find a more agreeable method or one that will give them a greater incentive to work. For, since all children have a natural desire to draw, this exercise will give them pleasure, and the imagination will be excited by the twofold action of the senses. Later on, when they can read with ease, they should be made to exercise their powers on subject-matter that would in any case have to be learned, that is to say, something calculated to give them practical information or to instil morality or piety. The same plan may be adopted when they learn to read Latin, Greek, or Hebrew. It will be of great advantage to read and copy the declensions and conjugations over and over again, until, by this means, reading, writing, the meaning of the words, and the formation of the case-endings, have been thoroughly learned. In this case we have a fourfold result from a single exercise. A system of concentration that is of such vital importance should be applied to all branches of study, in order that, as Seneca says, what is learned by reading may be given form by writing, or that, as St. Augustine says of himself, we may write while we make progress and make progress while we write.

47. As a rule, no care is shown in the choice of the subjects that are given as exercises in style, and there is no connection between the successive subjects. The result is that they are exercises in style and nothing else, and have very little influence on the reasoning powers; indeed it frequently happens that, after much time and study have been devoted to them, they prove absolutely worthless and of no use for the business of life. Literary taste should therefore be taught by means of the subject-matter of the science or art on which the reasoning powers of the class are being exercised. The teacher should tell his pupils stories about the originators of the subject and the times in which they lived, or should give them exercises in imitation based on the subject matter, so that, by a single effort, notions of style may be imbibed, the

reasoning powers may be improved, and, since either the teacher or the pupils are continually talking, the faculty of speech also may be exercised.

48. Towards the end of the 18th chapter I have shown that it is possible for the scholars to give instruction in the subject that they have just learned, and, since this process not only makes them thorough but also enables them to make progress more rapidly, it should not be overlooked in this connection.

49. Finally, it will be of immense use, if the amusements that are provided to relax the strain on the minds of the scholars be of such a kind as to lay stress on the more serious side of life, in order that a definite impression may be made on them even in their hours of recreation. For instance, they may be given tools, and allowed to imitate the different handicrafts, by playing at farming, at politics, at being soldiers or architects, etc. In spring they may be taken into the garden or into the country, and may be taught the various species of plants, vying with one another to see who can recognise the greater number. In this way they will be introduced to the rudiments of medicine, and not only will it be evident which of them has a natural bent towards that science, but in many the inclination will be created. Further, in order to encourage them, the mock titles of doctor, licentiate, or student of medicine may be given to those who make the greatest progress. The same plan may be adopted in other kinds of recreation. In the game of war the scholars may become field-marshals, generals, captains, or standard-bearers. In that of politics they may be kings, ministers, chancellors, secretaries, ambassadors, etc., and, on the same principle, consuls, senators, lawyers, or officials; since such pleasantries often lead to serious things. Thus would be fulfilled Luther's wish that the studies of the young at school could be so organised that the scholars might take as much pleasure in them as in playing at ball all day, and thus for the first time would schools be a real prelude to practical life.

Though Comenius had little influence on the school practices of his day, his writing did inspire other contemporaries to advocate reform along the lines he proposed. His advice was sought in several lands, even as far away as colonial Massachusetts where there was talk of offering him the presidency of Harvard College. In England, Richard Mulcaster, John Brinsley, Charles Hoole, and others propagated many of the ideas and ideals introduced by Comenius. The following reading is taken from a work of Charles Hoole (1610–1667) who, in addition to publishing his own works on educational methods, was responsible for the first English edition of Orbis Pictus. *In this excerpt, one easily perceives the influence of Comenius.*

The greatest trouble at the first entrance of children is to teach them how to know their letters one from another, when they see them in the book altogether; for the greatnesse of their number and variety of shape do puzle young wits to difference them, and the sence can but be intent upon one single object at once, so as to take its impression, and commit it to the imagination and memory. Some have therefore begun but with one single letter, and after they have shewed it to the childe in the Alphabet, have made him to finde the same any where else in the book, till he knew that perfectly; and then they have proceeded to another in like manner and so gone through the rest.

Some have contrived a piece of ivory with twenty four flats or squares, in every one of which was engraven a several letter, and by playing with a childe in throwing this upon a table, and shewing him the letter onely which lay uppermost, have in few dayes taught him the whole Alphabet.

Some have got twenty four pieces of ivory cut in the shape of dice, with a letter engraven upon each of them, and with these they have played at vacant hours with a childe, till he hath known them all distinctly. They begin first with one, then with two, afterwards with more letters at once, as the childe got knowledge of them. To teach him likewise to spell, they would place consonants before or after a vowel, and then joyn more letters together so as to make a word, and sometimes divide it into syllables, to be parted or put together; now this kind of letter sport may be profitably permitted among you beginers in a School & in stead of ivory, they may have white bits of wood, or small shreads of paper or past-board, or parchment with a letter writ upon each to play withall amongst themselves.

Some have made pictures in a little book or upon a scroll of paper wrapt upon two sticks within a box of iceing-glass, and by each picture have made three sorts of that letter, with which its name beginneth; but those being too many at once for a childe to take notice on, have proved not so useful as was intended. Some likewise have had pictures and letters printed in this manner on the back side of a pack of cards, to entice children, that naturally love that sport, to the love of learning their books.

Some have writ a letter in a great character upon a card, or chalked it out upon a trencher, and by telling a child what it was, and letting him strive to make the like, have imprinted it quickly in his memory, and so the rest one after another.

One having a Son of two years and a half old, that could but even go about the house, and utter some few gibberish words in a broken

E. T. *Compagnac (ed.)*, Charles Hoole's A New Discovery of the Old Art of Teaching Schoole, *pp. 6–11 ("The Petty-School"), 8–10 ("The Ushers Duty"). Copyright, 1913, by Liverpool University Press. Reprinted by permission of Liverpool University Press.*

manner; observing him one day above the rest to be busied about shells, and sticks, and such like toys, which himself had laid together in a chair, and to misse any one that was taken from him, he saw not how, and to seek for it about the house; became very desireous to make experiment what that childe might presently attain to in point of learning; Thereupon he devised a little wheel, with all the Capital Romane letters made upon a paper to wrap round about it, and fitted it to turn in a little round box, which had a hole so made in the side of it, that onely one letter might be seen to peep out at once; This he brought to the childe, & showed him onely the letter O, and told him what it was; The childe being overjoyed with his new gamball, catcheth the box out of his Fathers hand, and run's with it to his playfellow a year younger then himself, and in his broken language tell's him there was an O, an O; And when the other asked him where, he said, in a hole, in a hole, and shewed it him; which the lesser childe then took such notice of, as to know it againe ever after from all the other letters. And thus by playing with the box, and enquiring concerning any letter that appeared strange to him, what it was, the childe learnt all the letters of the Alphabet in eleven dayes, being in this Character *A B C*, and would take pleasure to shew them in any book to any of his acquaintance that came next. By this instance you may see what a propensity there is in nature betimes to learning, could but the Teachers apply themselves to their young Scholars tenuity; and how by proceeding in a cleare & facil method, that all may apprehend, every one may benefit more or less by degrees. According to these contrivances to forward children, I have published *a New Primar*; in the first leafe, whereof I have set the Roman Capitalls (because that Character is now most in use, & those letters the most easie to be learn't) and have joyned therewith the pictures or images of some things whose names begins with that letter, by which a childs memory may be helped to remember how to call his letters; as A, for an Ape, B, for a Bear, &c. This Hieroglyphicall devise doth so affect Children (who are generally forward to communicate what they know) that I have observed them to teach others, that could not so readily learn, to know all the letters in a few houres space, by asking them, what stands A. for? and so concerning other letters backwards and forwards, or as they best liked.

Thus when a childe hath got the names of his letters, & their several shapes withall in a playing manner, he may be easily taught to distinguish them in the following leaf, which containeth first the greater, and then the smaller Roman Characters, to be learned by five at once or more, as the childe is able to remember them; other Characters I would have forborn, till one be well acquainted with these, because so much variety at the first doth but amaze young wits, and our English characters, (for the most part) are very obscure, & more hard to be imprinted in the memory. And thus much for the learning to know letters; we shall next (and according to Order in Teaching) proceed to an easie way of distinct spelling.

How to teach Children in the first Forme, the Grounds or Rudiments of Grammar *contained in the* Accidents, *and to prepare them for the Latine tongue with ease and delight.*

Being here to deliver my mind concerning entering little ones, by way of Grammar, to the Latine Tongue, (a matter which I may truly say hath ever since I began to teach) cost me more studie and observation, then any one point of my profession, and the more because I see few able Schoole Masters vouchsafe so far to unman themselves as to minde it) I desire three things may be considered by all that goe about to enter children to Grammar-Learning, *viz.* that

1.   *There is a great difference betwixt a man that teacheth, and a Childe that is to be taught.* For though I do not altogether hold with him that sayeth a man in his Childe-hood is no better then a bruit-beast, and useth no power but anger and concupiscence; nor take upon me here to dispute whether a Childe learneth more by rote then by reason, yet this I dare aver, that *the more condescention is made to a Childes capacity, by proceeding orderly and plainly from what he knoweth already, to what doth naturally and necessarily follow thereupon, the more easily he will learn.* A man therefore that hath the strength and full use of reason, must conduct his young learner, to follow him in a rational way, though he must not expect him to goe *æquis passibus,* as fast as himself. And forasmuch as a childe is tender, a man must abate of his roughnesse; seeing a childe is slow of apprehension, he must not be too quick in his delivery; and seeing a childe is naturally awkward to his work, he must not be too passionate, if he do amisse. . . . And I would advise him that hath to deal with a childe, to imitate the nurse in helping him how to go forward, or the Gardiner in furthering the growth of his young plant. *Est & hæc summi ingenii maxima infirmitas non-posse descendere,* saith a Teacher of eloquence; *Tall wits, like long backs, cannot abide to stoop,* but *whosoever is a Schoole-Master, and would do his duty as he ought, must account it a point of wisdom to condescend to a childes capacitie, be it never so mean.* How have I delighted to see an Artist (I mean a watchmaker or the like) spend an hour or two sometimes in findeing a defect in a piece of work, which he hath afterwards remedied in the turning of a hand; whereas a more hasty workman hath been ready to throw the thing aside, and to neglect it as good for no use. *Let the Master ever mind where a childe sticks, and remove the impediments out of his way, and his Scholar will take pleasure, that he can go on in learning.*

VII

Education and the Enlightenment

*T*HE *eighteenth century has been christened by historians "The Age of Enlightenment" and "The Age of Reason." During this period men of ideas and men of action rose up in great numbers to challenge authoritarianism and absolutism in all their varied forms: religious, political, economic, philosophical, social, and educational. Taking their cue from the emerging sciences, reformers rejected the age-old explanations of the status of man and his institutions and turned toward an examination of nature to provide rational new answers. Men like Locke, Montesquieu, Adam Smith, and Rousseau found much that was unnatural in the established order. Absolute rule by virtue of divine right was deemed unnatural as were the concept of man's innate depravity, the mercantile system, the rigidity and impracticality of educational content and methods.*

In England John Locke was a leader in the successful move to strengthen the governing powers of the merchant-class Parliament at the expense of the king. He put forth a political philosophy that displaced rule by divine right with rule resulting from a "social contract" between propertied citizens and a government responsible for the protection of those "natural rights" of all citizens—life, liberty, and property. The influence of Locke's thinking on political liberals of Europe and America was considerable. His impact on modern educational thought was no less significant. His conclusions regarding political institutions were closely related to his convictions concerning human nature. He rejected the concept of a human nature preformed at birth. Although he recognized that the soul and mind had certain independent qualities, he concluded that man's nature was shaped largely by forces of the environment. The mind, he believed, was at birth a blank tablet (tabula rasa), which received impressions from without, i.e., from the individual's surroundings and experiences. Locke's views provided nourishment for those who had faith in the power of man and his institutions to reform society. Here was fresh ammunition to attack an educational system based heavily on the Platonic concept of innate ideas. Locke himself in his writings on education insisted upon content that was relevant to the future duties and responsibilities of children and stressed the value of learning through experience, the empirical approach to knowledge. (1)

In no other country was the Enlightenment's protest against the state of society carried forth with more vigor than France. As in England, intellectuals were in the forefront of the movement for change—Montesquieu, Voltaire, Diderot, Turgot, Condorcet, to mention a few. But perhaps most revolutionary of all was Jean Jacques Rousseau. Through essays, autobiography, poems, plays, operas, and novels, Rousseau denounced a society that was miserable because it was unnatural. His view of the "social contract" included all people, propertied or not. His conception of the proper sphere of government went beyond Locke's protection of "life, liberty and property" to include the promotion of happiness and the general well-being. Among the voluminous writings of Rousseau is one that stands out among the most influential in the history of education, the Émile. In his own day and to a greater extent in the nineteenth and twentieth centuries this work proved to be an inspiration to educational reformers. The theme of the Émile permeates all Rousseau's writings—unnatural conditions have created unhappy results. Education has failed because it has treated children as adults in miniature and stuffed their minds with material that is beyond their comprehension, of little interest and often of little value. The education of Rousseau's Émile is one in which content and method are related to the child's natural growth, attuned to his physical, emotional, social, and intellectual development. The setting of this instruction was, of course, in nature; the materials were largely the products of nature. Rousseau founded no school, never put his theories to the test, and much of the Émile has been labeled as antisocial, anticultural, and pure romantic nonsense. Yet, in focusing attention on the changing needs, interests, and abilities of children as they develop and the necessity for education responsive to these needs, he performed a great service. (2)

During the eighteenth century European education was tied as closely to political and social events as to philosophical thought. In Western Europe absolutism was being put to the test, and the schools mirrored the wider struggle. It was in France that the effort proved most violent and radical. Mutterings against the system began years before the storming of the Bastille in 1789. One such prelude had occurred in 1764 when the schools of the Jesuits, so closely identified with the intrigues of the monarchical regime, were ordered closed. Reformers had long demanded an end to clerical control of education and the establishment of a national system of universal, free schooling. Once the Revolution was set in motion, several proposals for a national system embracing the primary grades through higher education were placed before the various legislative bodies that arose and fell during those turbulent years. These proposals generally favored schooling that would inculcate French nationalism and democratic ideals and that would offer curricula reflecting the practical needs of the people. However, *the chaos of the period and the tide of events turned against the liberal reformers. National education in France was to be established not by the forces of eighteenth-century enlightened liberalism but by those of nineteenth-century reaction. (3)*

In England, beginning with the "Glorious Revolution" of 1688 and continuing through the eighteenth century, political absolutism was successfully challenged without the accompanying disorder and bloodshed that had characterized events in France. In the island kingdom change had been initiated by and remained securely in the hands of the rising commerical class. This class, greatly influenced by the laissez-faire doctrines of Adam Smith, demonstrated no strong sentiment for so radical a step as government control and sponsorship of education, though there were a few, including Smith himself, who proposed government schools as a force for inculcating loyalty to the system, thus protecting the nation from the spread of revolutionary fever across the Channel. Though education remained a private affair, it nevertheless reflected the tone of moderate reform inherent in the English Enlightenment. To supplement the apprentice system, private endowments and religious and charitable organizations increased their efforts to provide schools and workhouses where children of the lower classes could learn the 3 R's, receive religious training, and be introduced to a trade or the household arts. The private grammar schools of England, known by the nineteenth century as the great "public" schools, in the spirit of Locke began to soften the rigors of their classical regimen to attend to the preparation of their students for the life of a gentleman. There was even some limited progress in introducing the new sciences and mathematics into the universities. However, the most notable advancement in offering practical subjects took place in the academies established by the dissenting religious sects. In these schools the classics were supplemented by modern languages, mathematics, natural sciences, and what we today call the social sciences. These Dissenter Academies served as models for nineteenth-century reform of secondary education both in England and America. (4)

Ironically it was in the German states and particularly Prussia that the most striking advances were made in educational reform. Although remaining indifferent to the demands for political liberalization that were sweeping Western Europe, the Prussian Fredericks of the eighteenth century actually strengthened and expanded their kingdom and their personal power. Through internal improvements, social welfare programs, and an efficient civil service, they improved the lives of their subjects and checked latent revolutionary sentiment. The activities of Frederick William I, Frederick II, and Frederick William II in the educational area are typical of this approach to governance. Fully appreciative of the fact that expanded and improved schooling could serve the interests of the state, as they defined them, as well as the welfare of the people, the kings encouraged the activities and welcomed the advice of such educators as August Francke, Johann Hecker, and Johann Basedow. These reformers had established schools in which they utilized the methods of sense realism and instituted programs to extend primary education to the masses and provide practical as well as classical secondary education. King Frederick William I was so impressed by Francke's work that he

*founded several schools based on the reformer's methods and issued laws com-
pelling parents to send their children to school (1713, 1717). Frederick II's
Prussian School Code of 1763, which increased the role of the central government
in education, was formulated by Johann Hecker, and the efforts of Johann
Basedow were significant in the decision of the Prussian government, under
Frederick William II in 1787, to take control of the schools out of the hands of
the various religious sects and place them under the jurisdiction of a state ministry
of education. By the end of the eighteenth century authoritarian Prussia had
progressed furthest in establishing the revolutionary goal of a state system of public
education. It was in German universities that the new subjects—the natural
sciences, modern languages, mathematics, and modern literature—had their
widest acceptance and in German primary and secondary schools that the new
methods of the sense realists, though by no means victorious, had been given their
most thorough test. (5)*

回 1. John Locke on Education

The selections that follow are from Locke's Some Thoughts
Concerning Education *(1693), a treatise on the education proper for sons of
gentlemen. Locke insisted on an education that was relevant to the life the young
man of means and position was to lead. Such training demanded development of the
body as well as the mind and emphasized useful knowledge along with the traditional classical curriculum: English as well as foreign languages, French before
Latin and such studies as shorthand, chronology, mathematics, anatomy, science,
and ethics. Equally important, Locke damned the traditional methods of the
teacher: the stress on memorization and rote repetition of moral precepts and constant resort to the rod. In their place he urged affection, attention to the child's
interests, learning gained through experiences and employment of the senses, and
self-control acquired through practices leading to the development of good habits.
Locke's concern for education for life and advocacy of the empirical approach
were not restricted to the gentlemanly class. In other writings he advocated
removing poor children from their parents and placing them into workhouse
schools and later into apprenticeship.*

§ 1. A sound mind in a sound body, is a short but full description of a
happy state in this world: he that has these two, has little more to wish
for; and he that wants either of them, will be but little the better for any
thing else. Men's happiness or misery is most part of their own making.

John Locke, Works *(London: Printed for Thomas Tegg, et al., 1823), IX, 6–7, 12–13,
14–15, 26–27, 37, 46–48, 69–70, 78, 84–86, 142–43, 152, 194–95, 204–05.*

He whose mind directs not wisely, will never take the right way; and he whose body is crazy and feeble, will never be able to advance in it. I confess, there are some men's constitutions of body and mind so vigorous, and well framed by nature, that they need not much assistance from others; but, by the strength of their natural genius, they are, from their cradles, carried towards what is excellent; and, by the privilege of their happy constitutions, are able to do wonders. But examples of this kind are but few; and I think I may say, that, of all the men we meet with, nine parts of ten are what they are, good or evil, useful or not, by their education. It is that which makes the great difference in mankind. The little, or almost insensible, impressions on our tender infancies, have very important and lasting consequences: and there it is, as in the fountains of some rivers, where a gentle application of the hand turns the flexible waters into channels, that make them take quite contrary courses; and by this little direction, given them at first, in the source, they receive different tendencies, and arrive at last at very remote and distant places.

§ 2. I imagine the minds of children as easily turned, this or that way, as water itself; and though this be the principal part, and our main care should be about the inside, yet the clay cottage is not to be neglected. I shall therefore begin with the case, and consider first the health of the body, as that which perhaps you may rather expect, from that study I have been thought more peculiarly to have applied myself to; and that also which will be soonest despatched, as lying, if I guess not amiss, in a very little compass.

§ 3. How necessary health is to our business and happiness, and how requisite a strong constitution, able to endure hardships and fatigue, is to one that will make any figure in the world, is too obvious to need any proof. . . .

§ 10. Playing in the open air has but this one danger in it, that I know: and that is, that when he is hot with running up and down, he should sit or lie down on the cold or moist earth. This, I grant, and drinking cold drink, when they are hot with labour or exercise, brings more people to the grave, or to the brink of it, by fevers, and other diseases, than any thing I know. These mischiefs are easily enough prevented, whilst he is little, being then seldom out of sight. And if during his childhood he be constantly and rigorously kept from sitting on the ground, or drinking any cold liquor, whilst he is hot, the custom of forbearing, grown into a habit, will help much to preserve him, when he is no longer under his maid's or tutor's eye. This is all I think can be done in the case. For, as years increase, liberty must come with them; and, in a great many things, he must be trusted to his own conduct, since there cannot always be a guard upon him; except what you put into his own mind, by good principles and established habits, which is the best and surest, and therefore most to be taken care of. For, from repeated cautions and rules, ever so often inculcated, you are not to expect any thing, either in this or any other case, farther than practice has established them into habit. . . .

§ 13. As for his diet, it ought to be very plain and simple; and, if I might advise, flesh should be forborn as long as he is in coats, or at least, till he is two or three years old. But whatever advantage this may be, to his present and future health and strength, I fear it will hardly be consented to, by parents, misled by the custom of eating too much flesh themselves; who will be apt to think their children, as they do themselves, in danger to be starved, if they have not flesh, at least twice a day. This I am sure, children would breed their teeth with much less danger, be freer from diseases, whilst they were little, and lay the foundations of an healthy and strong constitution much surer, if they were not crammed so much as they are, by fond mothers and foolish servants, and were kept wholly from flesh, the first three or four years of their lives.

But if my young master must needs have flesh, let it be but once a day, and of one sort, at a meal. Plain beef, mutton, veal, &c. without other sauce than hunger, is best: and great care should be used, that he eat bread plentifully both alone and with every thing else. And whatever he eats, that is solid, make him chew it well. We English are often negligent herein; from whence follows indigestion, and other great inconveniencies. . . .

§ 30. And thus I have done with what concerns the body and health, which reduces itself to these few and easily observable rules. Plenty of open air, exercise, and sleep; plain diet, no wine or strong drink, and very little or no physic; not too warm and strait clothing; especially the head and feet kept cold, and the feet often used to cold water and exposed to wet.

§ 31. Due care being had to keep the body in strength and vigour, so that it may be able to obey and execute the orders of the mind; the next and principal business is, to set the mind right, that on all occasions it may be disposed to consent to nothing but what may be suitable to the dignity and excellency of a rational creature.

§ 32. If what I have said in the beginning of this discourse be true, as I do not doubt but it is, viz. that the difference to be found in the manners and abilities of men is owing more to their education than to any thing else; we have reason to conclude, that great care is to be had of the forming children's minds, and giving them that seasoning early, which shall influence their lives always after. For when they do well or ill, the praise or blame will be laid there: and when any thing is done awkwardly, the common saying will pass upon them, that it is suitable to their breeding.

§ 33. As the strength of the body lies chiefly in being able to endure hardships, so also does that of the mind. And the great principle and foundation of all virtue and worth is placed in this, that a man is able to deny himself his own desires, cross his own inclinations, and purely follow what reason directs as best, though the appetite lean the other way.

§ 34. The great mistake I have observed in people's breeding their children has been, that this has not been taken care enough of in its due season; that the mind has not been made obedient to discipline, and pliant to reason, when at first it was most tender, most easy to be bowed. . . .

§ 47. The usual lazy and short way by chastisement, and the rod, which is the only instrument of government that tutors generally know, or ever think of, is the most unfit of any to be used in education; because it tends to both those mischiefs; which, as we have shown, are the Scylla and Charybdis, which, on the one hand or the other, ruin all that miscarry.

§ 48. 1. This kind of punishment contributes not at all to the mastery of our natural propensity to indulge corporal and present pleasure, and to avoid pain at any rate; but rather encourages it; and thereby strengthens that in us, which is the root, from whence spring all vicious actions and the irregularities of life. From what other motive, but of sensual pleasure, and pain, does a child act, who drudges at his book against his inclination, or abstains from eating unwholesome fruit, that he takes pleasure in, only out of fear of whipping? He in this only prefers the greater corporal pleasure, or avoids the greater corporal pain. And what is it to govern his actions, and direct his conduct, by such motives as these? what it is, I say, but to cherish that principle in him, which it is our business to root out and destroy? And therefore I cannot think any correction useful to a child, where the shame of suffering for having done amiss does not work more upon him than the pain.

§ 49. 2. This sort of correction naturally breeds an aversion to that which it is the tutor's business to create a liking to. . . .

§ 66. But pray remember, children are not to be taught by rules, which will be always slipping out of their memories. What you think necessary for them to do, settle in them by an indispensable practice, as often as the occasion returns; and, if it it be possible, make occasions. This will beget habits in them, which, being once established, operate of themselves easily and naturally, without the assistance of the memory. But here let me give two cautions: 1. The one is, that you keep them to the practice of what you would have grow into a habit in them, by kind words and gentle admonitions, rather as minding them of what they forget, than by harsh rebukes and chiding, as if they were wilfully guilty. 2dly, Another thing you are to take care of, is, not to endeavour to settle too many habits at once, lest by a variety you confound them, and so perfect none. When constant custom has made any one thing easy and natural to them, and they practise it without reflection, you may then go on to another.

This method of teaching children by a repeated practice, and the same action done over and over again, under the eye and direction of the tutor, till they have got the habit of doing it well, and not by relying on rules trusted to their memories; has so many advantages, which way soever we consider it, that I cannot but wonder (if ill customs could be wondered at in any thing) how it could possibly be so much neglected. I shall name one more that comes now in my way. By this method we shall see, whether what is required of him be adapted to his capacity, and any way suited to the child's natural genius and constitution: for that too must be considered in a right education. We must not hope wholly to change their original tempers, nor make the gay pensive and grave, nor the melancholy sportive, without spoiling them. God has stamped certain characters upon men's minds, which, like their shapes, may perhaps be a little mended; but can hardly be totally altered and transformed into the contrary.

He therefore, that is about children, should well study their natures and aptitudes, and see, by often trials, what turn they easily take, and what becomes them; observe what their native stock is, how it may be improved, and what it is fit for: he should consider what they want, whether they be capable of having it wrought into them by industry, and incorporated there by practice; and whether it be worth while to endeavour it. For, in many cases, all that we can do, or should aim at, is, to make the best of what nature has given, to prevent the vices and faults to which such a constitution is most inclined, and give it all the advantages it is capable of. Every one's natural genius should be carried as far as it could; but to attempt the putting another upon him, will be but labour in vain; and what is so plaistered on will at best sit but untowardly, and have always hanging to it the ungracefulness of constraint and affectation. . . .

§ 81. It will perhaps be wondered, that I mention reasoning with children: and yet I cannot but think that the true way of dealing with them. They understand it as early as they do language; and, if I misobserve not, they love to be treated as rational creatures sooner than is imagined. It is a pride should be cherished in them, and, as much as can be, made the greatest instrument to turn them by.

But when I talk of reasoning, I do not intend any other but such as is suited to the child's capacity and apprehension. Nobody can think a boy of three or seven years old should be argued with as a grown man. Long discourses, and philosophical reasonings, at best amaze and confound, but do not instruct, children. When I say, therefore, that they must be treated as rational creatures, I mean, that you should make them sensible, by the mildness of your carriage, and the composure, even in your correction of them, that what you do is reasonable in you, and useful and necessary for them; and that it is not out of caprice, passion, or fancy, that you command or forbid them any thing. This they are capable of understanding; and there is no virtue they should be excited to, nor fault they should be kept from, which I do not think they may be convinced of: but it must be by such reasons as their age and understanding are capable of, and those proposed always in very few and plain words. The foundations on which several duties are built, and the fountains of right and wrong, from which they spring, are not, perhaps, easily to be let into the minds of grown men, not used to abstract their thoughts from common received opinions. Much less are children capable of reasonings from remote principles. They cannot conceive the force of long deductions: the reasons that move them must be obvious, and level to their thoughts, and such as may (if I may so say) be felt and touched. But yet, if their age, temper, and inclinations, be considered, they will never want such motives as may be sufficient to convince them. If there be no other more particular, yet these will always be intelligible, and of force, to deter them from any fault fit to be taken notice of in them, viz. that it will be a discredit and disgrace to them, and displease you.

§ 82. But, of all the ways whereby children are to be instructed, and their manners formed, the plainest, easiest, and most efficacious, is to set before their eyes the examples of those things you would have them do or avoid. Which, when they are pointed out to them, in the practice of persons within their knowledge, with some reflections on their beauty or unbecomingness, are of more force to draw or deter their imitation than any discourses which can be made to them. Virtues and vices can by no words be so plainly set before their understandings as the actions of other men will show them, when you direct their observation, and bid them view this or that good or bad quality in their practice. And the beauty or uncomeliness of many things, in good and ill breeding, will be better learnt, and make deeper impressions on them, in the examples of others, than from any rules or instructions can be given about them. . . .

§ 93. The character of a sober man, and a scholar, is, as I have above observed, what every one expects in a tutor. This generally is thought enough, and is all that parents commonly look for. But when such an one has emptied out, into his pupil, all the Latin and logic he has brought from the university, will that furniture make him a fine gentleman? Or can it be expected, that he should be better bred, better skilled in the world, better principled in the grounds and foundations of true virtue and generosity, than his young tutor is?

To form a young gentleman, as he should be, it is fit his governor should himself be well-bred, understand the ways of carriage, and measures of civility, in all the variety of persons, times, and places; and keep his pupil, as much as his age requires, constantly to the observation of them. This is an art not to be learnt, nor taught by books: nothing can give it but good company and observation joined together. The tailor may make his clothes modish, and the dancing-master give fashion to his motions; yet neither of these, though they set off well, make a well-bred gentleman: no, though he have learning to boot; which, if not well managed, makes him more impertinent and intolerable in conversation. Breeding is that which sets a gloss upon all his other good qualities, and renders them useful to him, in procuring him the esteem and good will of all that he comes near. Without good breeding, his other accomplishments make him pass but for proud, conceited, vain, or foolish.

A great part of the learning now in fashion in the schools of Europe, and that goes ordinarily into the round of education, a gentleman may, in a good measure, be unfurnished with, without any great disparagement to himself, or prejudice to his affairs. But prudence and good breeding are, in all the stations and occurrences of life, necessary; and most young men suffer in the want of them, and come rawer, and more awkward, into the world than they should, for this very reason; because these qualities, which are, of all other, the most necessary to be taught, and stand most in need of the assistance and help of a teacher, are generally neglected, and thought but a slight, or no part of a tutor's business. Latin and learning make all the noise: and the main stress is laid upon his proficiency in things, a great part whereof belongs not to a gentleman's calling; which is to have the knowledge of a man of business, a carriage suitable to his rank, and to be eminent and useful in his country, according to his station. Whenever either spare hours from that, or an inclination to perfect himself in some parts of knowledge, which his tutor did but just enter him in, set him upon any study; the first rudiments of it, which he learned before, will open the way enough for his own industry to carry him as far as his fancy will prompt, or his parts enable him to go: or, if he thinks it may save his time and pains, to be helped over some difficulties by the hands of a master, he may then take a man that is perfectly well skilled in it, or choose such an one as he thinks fittest for his purpose. But to initiate his pupil in any part of learning, as far as is necessary for a young man in the ordinary course of his studies, an ordinary skill in the governor is enough. Nor is it requisite that he should be a thorough scholar, or possess in perfection all those sciences, which it is convenient a young gentleman should have a taste of, in some general view, or short system. A gentleman that would penetrate deeper, must do it by his own genius and industry afterwards:

for nobody ever went far in knowledge, or became eminent in any of the sciences, by the discipline and constraint of a master.

The great work of a governor is to fashion the carriage, and form the mind; to settle in his pupil good habits, and the principles of virtue and wisdom; to give him, by little and little, a view of mankind; and work him into a love and imitation of what is excellent and praiseworthy; and, in the prosecution of it, to give him vigour, activity, and industry. The studies which he sets him upon are but, as it were, the exercises of his faculties, and employment of his time, to keep him from sauntering and idleness, to teach him application, and accustom him to take pains, and to give him some little taste of what his own industry must perfect. For who expects, that under a tutor a young gentleman should be an accomplished critic, orator, or logician; go to the bottom of metaphysics, natural philosophy, or mathematics; or be a master in history or chronology? though something of each of these is to be taught him: but it is only to open the door, that he may look in, and, as it were, begin an acquaintance, but not to dwell there: and a governor would be much blamed, that should keep his pupil too long, and lead him too far in most of them. But of good breeding, knowledge of the world, virtue, industry, and a love of reputation, he cannot have too much: and, if he have these, he will not long want what he needs or desires of the other.

And, since it cannot be hoped he should have time and strength to learn all things, most pains should be taken about that which is most necessary; and that principally looked after which will be of most and frequentest use to him in the world. . . .

§ 147. You will wonder, perhaps, that I put learning last, especially if I tell you I think it the least part. This may seem strange in the mouth of a bookish man: and this making usually the chief, if not only bustle and stir about children, this being almost that alone which is thought on, when people talk of education, makes it the greater paradox. When I consider what ado is made about a little Latin and Greek, how many years are spent in it, and what a noise and business it makes to no purpose, I can hardly forbear thinking, that the parents of children still live in fear of the schoolmaster's rod, which they look on as the only instrument of education; as if a language or two were its whole business. How else is it possible, that a child should be chained to the oar seven, eight, or ten of the best years of his life, to get a language or two, which I think might be had at a great deal cheaper rate of pains and time, and be learned almost in playing?

Forgive me, therefore, if I say, I cannot with patience think, that a young gentleman should be put into the herd, and be driven with a whip and scourge, as if he were to run the gauntlet through the several classes, "ad capiendum ingenii cultum." "What then, say you, would you not have him write and read? Shall he be more ignorant than the clerk of our parish, who takes Hopkins and Sternhold for the best poets in the world, whom yet he makes worse than they are, by his ill reading?" Not so, not so fast, I beseech you. Reading, and writing, and learning. I allow to be necessary, but yet not the chief business. I imagine you would think him a very foolish fellow, that should not value a virtuous, or a wise man, infinitely before a great scholar. Not but that I think learning a great help to both, in well disposed minds; but yet it must be confessed also, that in others not so disposed, it helps them only to be the more foolish, or worse men. I say this, that, when you consider of the breeding of your son, and are looking out for a schoolmaster, or a tutor, you would not have (as is usual) Latin and logic only in your thoughts. Learning must be had, but in the second place, as subservient only to greater qualities. Seek out somebody, that may know how discreetly to frame his manners: place him in hands, where you may, as much as possible, secure his innocence, cherish and nurse up the good, and gently correct and weed out any bad inclinations, and settle in him good habits. This is the main point; and this being provided for, learning may be had into the bargain; and that, as I think, at a very easy rate, by methods that may be thought on. . . .

§ 162. As soon as he can speak English, it is time for him to learn some other language: this nobody doubts of, when French is proposed. And the reason is, because people are accustomed to the right way of teaching that language, which is by talking it into children in constant conversation, and not by grammatical rules. The Latin tongue would easily be taught the same way, if his tutor, being constantly with him, would talk nothing else to him, and make him answer still in the same language. But because French is a living language, and to be used more in speaking, that should be first learned, that the yet pliant organs of speech might be accustomed to a due formation of those sounds, and he get the habit of pronouncing French well, which is the harder to be done the longer it is delayed.

§ 163. When he can speak and read French well, which in this method is usually in a year or two, he should proceed to Latin, which it is a wonder parents, when they have had the experiment in French, should not think ought to be learned the same way, by talking and reading. Only care is to be taken, whilst he is learning these foreign languages, by speaking and reading nothing else with his tutor, that he do not forget to read English, which may be preserved by his mother, or somebody else, hearing him read some chosen parts of the scripture or other English book, every day. . . .

§ 201. I have one thing more to add, which as soon as I mention, I shall run the danger of being suspected to have forgot what I am about, and what I have above written concerning education, all tending towards a gentleman's calling, with which a trade seems wholly to be inconsistent. And yet, I cannot forbear to say, I would have him learn a trade, a manual trade; nay, two or three, but one more particularly.

§ 202. The busy inclination of children being always to be directed to something that may be useful to them, the advantages proposed from what they are set about may be considered of two kinds; 1. Where the skill itself, that is got by exercise, is worth the having. Thus skill not only in languages, and learned sciences, but in painting, turning, gardening, tempering and working in iron, and all other useful arts, is worth the having. 2. Where the exercise itself, without any consideration, is necessary or useful for health. Knowledge in some things is so necessary to be got by children, whilst they are young, that some part of their time is to be allotted to their improvement in them, though those employments contribute nothing at all to their health: such are reading, and writing, and all other sedentary studies, for the cultivating of the mind, which unavoidably take up a great part of gentlemen's time, quite from their cradles. Other manual arts, which are both got and exercised by labour, do many of them, by that exercise, not only increase our dexterity and skill, but contribute to our health too; especially such as employ us in the open air. In these, then, health and improvement may be joined together; and of these should some fit ones be chosen, to be made the recreations of one, whose chief business is with books and study. In this choice, the age and inclination of the person is to be considered, and constraint always to be avoided in bringing him to it. For command and force may often create, but can never cure an aversion; and whatever any one is brought to by compulsion, he will leave as soon as he can, and be little profited and less recreated by, whilst he is at it.

§ 203. That which of all others would please me best would be a painter, were there not an argument or two against it, not easy to be answered. First, ill painting is one of the worst things in the world; and to attain a tolerable degree of skill in it requires too much of a man's time. If he has a natural inclination to it, it will endanger the neglect of all other more useful studies, to give way to that; and if he have no inclination to it, all the time, pains, and money shall be employed in it will be thrown away to no purpose. Another reason why I am not for painting in a gentleman, is, because it is a sedentary recreation, which more employs the mind than the body. A gentleman's more serious employment, I look on to be study; and when that demands relaxation and refreshment, it should be in some exercise of the body, which unbends the thought, and confirms the health and strength. For these two reasons I am not for painting.

§ 204. In the next place, for a country gentleman, I should propose one, or rather both these; viz. gardening or husbandry in general, and working in wood, as a carpenter, joiner, or turner; these being fit and

healthy recreations for a man of study or business. For since the mind
endures not to be constantly employed in the same thing or way; and
sedentary or studious men should have some exercise, that at the same
time might divert their minds, and employ their bodies; I know none
that could do it better for a country gentleman than these two, the one
of them affording him exercise, when the weather or season keeps him
from the other. . . .

CONCLUSION

§ 216. Though I am now come to a conclusion of what obvious
remarks have suggested to me concerning education, I would not have
it thought, that I look on it as a just treatise on this subject. There are a
thousand other things that may need consideration; especially if one
should take in the various tempers, different inclinations, and particular
defaults, that are to be found in children; and prescribe proper remedies.
The variety is so great, that it would require a volume; nor would that
reach it. Each man's mind has some peculiarity, as well as his face, that
distinguishes him from all others; and there are possibly scarce two
children, who can be conducted by exactly the same method. Besides
that, I think a prince, a nobleman, and an ordinary gentleman's son,
should have different ways of breeding. But having had here only some
general views, in reference to the main end and aims in education, and
those designed for a gentleman's son, whom, being then very little, I
considered only as white paper, or wax, to be moulded and fashioned
as one pleases; I have touched little more than those heads, which I
judged necessary for the breeding of a young gentleman of his condition
in general; and have now published these my occasional thoughts, with
this hope, that, though this be far from being a complete treatise on this
subject, or such as that every one may find what will just fit his child in
it; yet it may give some small light to those, whose concern for their
dear little ones makes them so irregularly bold, that they dare venture
to consult their own reason, in the education of their children, rather
than wholly to rely upon old custom.

回 2. The *Émile* of Jean Jacques Rousseau

In the Émile *Rousseau applied his philosophy of naturalism to a
boy's education. The work is divided into four books, each representing a stage in
the child's development: infancy (from birth to five), childhood (from five to*

twelve), early adolescence (from twelve to fifteen), and later adolescence (from fifteen to twenty). During the first two stages the child's needs are considered largely physical. Rousseau stressed the importance of allowing the boy to develop his body and senses and of enabling him to satisfy his natural inclination toward play and manual activities. What Émile must know, nature will teach him.

Unlike Locke, Rousseau disdained as unnatural the idea of developing habits, introducing scholarly subjects, or employing reason in the early stages of Émile's education. Even in the third stage, when the age of reason begins, Rousseau insisted that the motivating factors in learning be Émile's curiosity and the usefulness of knowledge. During this stage Émile, being a child of nature, is interested in nature's subjects: geography, astronomy, natural sciences, agriculture, and the crafts. He is led by his tutor to find the answers to his questions by examining nature. When finally he is introduced to his first book, it is one attuned to his own experiences and interests, Robinson Crusoe.

It is not until the final stage, the social stage, that Émile goes into the world of men to familiarize himself with the conditions of society. He continues to observe and begins to read extensively in literature, history, philosophy, and religion. At this age, when the sex urge is strong, Émile's powers of reason will be developed to the extent that his energies will be directed toward socially useful activities and, finally, the selection of an ideal mate.

SELECTIONS FROM THE *ÉMILE*

Plants are improved by cultivation, and men by education. If man were born large and strong, his size and strength would be useless to him until he had learned to use them. They would be prejudicial to him, by preventing others from thinking of assisting him; and left to himself he would die of wretchedness before he had known his own necessities. We pity the state of infancy; we do not perceive that the human race would have perished if man had not begun by being a child.

We are born weak, we need strength; we are born destitute of all things, we need assistance; we are born stupid, we need judgment. All that we have not at our birth, and that we need when grown up, is given us by education.

This education comes to us from nature itself, or from other men, or from circumstances. The internal development of our faculties and of our organs is the education nature gives us; the use we are taught to make of this development is the education we get from other men; and what we learn, by our own experience, about things that interest us, is the education of circumstances.

Eleanor Worthington (trans.), Émile: Or, Concerning Education, by Jean Jacques Rousseau: Extracts *(Boston: D. C. Heath and Co., Publishers, 1904), pp. 12–15, 15–16, 24–25, 26–27, 43, 52, 57–58, 66–67, 87–88, 124–27, 147–48, 155–57.*

Each of us is therefore formed by three kinds of teachers. The pupil in whom their different lessons contradict one another is badly educated, and will never be in harmony with himself; the one in whom they all touch upon the same points and tend toward the same object advances toward that goal only, and lives accordingly. He alone is well educated.

Now of these three different educations, that of nature does not depend upon us; that of circumstances depends upon us only in certain respects; that of men is the only one of which we are really masters, and that solely because we think we are. For who can hope to direct entirely the speech and conduct of all who surround a child?

As soon, therefore, as education becomes an art, its success is almost impossible, since the agreement of circumstances necessary to this success is independent of personal effort. All that the utmost care can do is to approach more or less nearly our object; but, for attaining it, special good fortune is needed.

What is this object? That of nature itself, as has just been proved. Since the agreement of the three educations is necessary to their perfection, it is toward the one for which we ourselves can do nothing that we must direct both the others. But perhaps this word "nature" has too vague a meaning; we must here try to define it.

In the natural order of things, all men being equal, the vocation common to all is the state of manhood; and whoever is well trained for that, cannot fulfil badly any vocation which depends upon it. Whether my pupil be destined for the army, the church, or the bar, matters little to me. Before he can think of adopting the vocation of his parents, nature calls upon him to be a man. How to live is the business I wish to teach him. On leaving my hands he will not, I admit, be a magistrate, a soldier, or a priest; first of all he will be a man. All that a man ought to be he can be, at need, as well as any one else can. Fortune will in vain alter his position, for he will always occupy his own.

Our real study is that of the state of man. He among us who best knows how to bear the good and evil fortunes of this life is, in my opinion, the best educated; whence it follows that true education consists less in precept than in practice. We begin to instruct ourselves when we begin to live; our education commences with the commencement of our life; our first teacher is our nurse. For this reason the word "education" had among the ancients another meaning which we no longer attach to it; it signified nutriment.

We must then take a broader view of things, and consider in our pupil man in the abstract, man exposed to all the accidents of human life. If man were born attached to the soil of a country, if the same season continued throughout the year, if every one held his fortune by such a tenure that he could never change it, the established customs of to-day would be in certain respects good. The child educated for his position, and never leaving it, could not be exposed to the inconveniences of another.

But seeing that human affairs are changeable, seeing the restless and disturbing spirit of this century, which overturns everything once in a generation, can a more senseless method be imagined than to educate a child as if he were never to leave his room, as if he were obliged to be constantly surrounded by his servants? If the poor creature takes but one step on the earth, if he comes down so much as one stair, he is ruined. This is not teaching him to endure pain; it is training him to feel it more keenly.

We think only of preserving the child: this is not enough. We ought to teach him to preserve himself when he is a man; to bear the blows of fate; to brave both wealth and wretchedness; to live, if need be, among the snows of Iceland or upon the burning rock of Malta. In vain you take precautions against his dying,—he must die after all; and if his death be not indeed the result of those very precautions, they are none the less mistaken. It is less important to keep him from dying than it is to teach him how to live. To live is not merely to breathe, it is to act. It is to make use of our organs, of our senses, of our faculties, of all the powers which bear witness to us of our own existence. He who has lived most is not he who has numbered the most years, but he who has been most truly conscious of what life is. A man may have himself buried at the age of a hundred years, who died from the hour of his birth. He would have gained something by going to his grave in youth, if up to that time he had only lived.

*   *   *   *   *

The new-born child needs to stretch and to move his limbs so as to draw them out of the torpor in which, rolled into a ball, they have so long remained. We do stretch his limbs, it is true, but we prevent him from moving them. We even constrain his head into a baby's cap. It seems as if we were afraid he might appear to be alive. The inaction, the constraint in which we keep his limbs, cannot fail to interfere with the circulation of the blood and of the secretions, to prevent the child from growing strong and sturdy, and to change his constitution. In regions where these extravagant precautions are not taken, the men are all large, strong, and well proportioned. Countries in which children are swaddled swarm with hunchbacks, with cripples, with persons crook-kneed, stunted, rickety, deformed in all kinds of ways. For fear that the bodies of children may be deformed by free movements, we hasten to deform them by putting them into a press. Of our own accord we cripple them to prevent their laming themselves.

Must not such a cruel constraint have an influence upon their temper as well as upon their constitution? Their first feeling is a feeling

of constraint and of suffering. To all their necessary movements they
find only obstacles. More unfortunate than chained criminals, they
make fruitless efforts, they fret themselves, they cry. Do you tell me that
the first sounds they make are cries? I can well believe it; you thwart
them from the time they are born. The first gifts they receive from you
are chains, the first treatment they undergo is torment. Having nothing
free but the voice, why should they not use it in complaints? They cry
on account of the suffering you cause them; if you were pinioned in the
same way, your own cries would be louder.

*   *   *   *   *

The only habit a child should be allowed to form is to contract no
habits whatever. Let him not be carried upon one arm more than
upon another; let him not be accustomed to put forth one hand
rather than the other, or to use if oftener; nor to desire to eat, to sleep,
to act in any way, at regular hours; nor to be unable to stay alone
either by night or by day. Prepare long beforehand for the time when
he shall freely use all his strength. Do this by leaving his body under the
control of its natural bent, by fitting him to be always master of himself, and to carry out his own will in everything as soon as he has a
will of his own.

Since the only kinds of objects presented to him are likely to make
him either timid or courageous, why should not his education begin
before he speaks or understands? I would habituate him to seeing
new objects, though they be ugly, repulsive, or singular. But let this
be by degrees, and from a distance, until he has become accustomed to
them, and, from seeing them handled by others, shall at last handle
them himself. If during his infancy he has seen without fear frogs,
serpents, crawfishes, he will, when grown up, see without shrinking
any animal that may be shown him. For one who daily sees frightful
objects, there are none such.

*   *   *   *   *

In this outset of life, while memory and imagination are still inactive,
the child pays attention only to what actually affects his senses. The
first materials of his knowledge are his sensations. If, therefore, these are
presented to him in suitable order, his memory can hereafter present
them to his understanding in the same order. But as he attends to his
sensations only, it will at first suffice to show him very clearly the connection between these sensations, and the objects which give rise to
them. He is eager to touch everything, to handle everything. Do not
thwart this restless desire; it suggests to him a very necessary apprenticeship. It is thus he learns to feel the heat and coldness, hardness and softness, heaviness and lightness of bodies; to judge of their size, their shape,

and all their sensible qualities, by looking, by touching, by listening; above all, by comparing the results of sight with those of touch, estimating with the eye the sensation a thing produces upon the fingers.

By movement alone we learn the existence of things which are not ourselves; and it is by our own movements alone that we gain the idea of extension.

*   *   *   *   *

O men, be humane! it is your highest duty; be humane to all conditions of men, to every age, to everything not alien to mankind. What higher wisdom is there for you than humanity? Love childhood; encourage its sports, its pleasures, its lovable instincts. Who among us has not at times looked back with regret to the age when a smile was continually on our lips, when the soul was always at peace? Why should we rob these little innocent creatures of the enjoyment of a time so brief, so transient, of a boon so precious, which they cannot misuse? Why will you fill with bitterness and sorrow these fleeting years which can no more return to them than to you? Do you know, you fathers, the moment when death awaits your children? Do not store up for yourselves remorse, by taking from them the brief moments nature has given them. As soon as they can appreciate the delights of existence, let them enjoy it. At whatever hour God may call them, let them not die without having tasted life at all.

*   *   *   *   *

Locke's great maxim was that we ought to reason with children, and just now this maxim is much in fashion. I think, however, that its success does not warrant its reputation, and I find nothing more stupid than children who have been so much reasoned with. Reason, apparently a compound of all other faculties, the one latest developed, and with most difficulty, is the one proposed as agent in unfolding the faculties earliest used! The noblest work of education is to make a reasoning man, and we expect to train a young child by making him reason! This is beginning at the end; this is making an instrument of a result. If children understood how to reason they would not need to be educated. But by addressing them from their tenderest years in a language they cannot understand, you accustom them to be satisfied with words, to find fault with whatever is said to them, to think themselves as wise as their teachers, to wrangle and rebel. And what we mean they shall do from reasonable motives we are forced to obtain from them by adding the motive of avarice, or of fear, or of vanity.

Nature intends that children shall be children before they are men. If we insist on reversing this order we shall have fruit early indeed, but unripe and tasteless, and liable to early decay; we shall have young savants and old children. Childhood has its own methods of seeing, thinking, and feeling. Nothing shows less sense than to try to substitute our own methods for these. I would rather require a child ten years old to be five feet tall than to be judicious. Indeed, what use would he have at that age for the power to reason? It is a check upon physical strength, and the child needs none.

*   *   *   *   *

The earliest education ought, then, to be purely negative. It consists not in teaching truth or virtue, but in shielding the heart from vice and the mind from error. If you could do nothing at all, and allow nothing to be done; if you could bring up your pupil sound and robust to the age of twelve years, without his knowing how to distinguish his right hand from his left, the eyes of his understanding would from the very first open to reason. Without a prejudice or a habit, there would be in him nothing to counteract the effect of your care. Before long he would become in your hands the wisest of men; and beginning by doing nothing, you would have accomplished a marvel in education.

Reverse the common practice, and you will nearly always do well. Parents and teachers desiring to make of a child not a child, but a learned man, have never begun early enough to chide, to correct, to reprimand, to flatter, to promise, to instruct, to discourse reason to him. Do better than this: be reasonable yourself, and do not argue with your pupil, least of all, to make him approve what he dislikes. For if you persist in reasoning about disagreeable things, you make reasoning disagreeable to him, and weaken its influence beforehand in a mind as yet unfitted to understand it. Keep his organs, his senses, his physical strength, busy; but, as long as possible, keep his mind inactive. Guard against all sensations arising in advance of judgment, which estimates their true value. Keep back and check unfamiliar impressions, and be in no haste to do good for the sake of preventing evil. For the good is not real unless enlightened by reason. Regard every delay as an advantage; for much is gained if the critical period be approached without losing anything. Let childhood have its full growth. If indeed a lesson must be given, avoid it to-day, if you can without danger delay it until to-morrow.

*   *   *   *   *

Your little meddler spoils everything he touches; do not be vexed, but put out of his reach whatever he can spoil. He breaks the furniture he uses. Be in no hurry to give him any more; let him feel the disadvantages of doing without it. He breaks the windows in his room; let the wind blow on him night and day. Have no fear of his taking cold; he had better take cold than be a fool.

Do not fret at the inconvenience he causes you, but make him feel it first of all. Finally, without saying anything about it, have the panes of glass mended. He breaks them again. Change your method: say to him coolly and without anger, "Those windows are mine; I took pains to have them put there, and I am going to make sure that they shall not be broken again." Then shut him up in some dark place where there are no windows. At this novel proceeding, he begins to cry and storm: but nobody listens to him. He soon grows tired of this, and changes his tone; he complains and groans. A servant is sent, whom the rebel entreats to set him free. Without trying to find any excuse for utter refusal, the servant answers, "I have windows to take care of, too," and goes away. At last, after the child has been in durance for several hours, long enough to tire him and to make him remember it, some one suggests an arrangement by which you shall agree to release him, and he to break no more windows. He sends to beseech you to come and see him; you come; he makes his proposal. You accept it immediately saying, "Well thought of; that will be a good thing for both of us. Why didn't you think of this capital plan before?" Then, without requiring any protestations, or confirmation of his promise, you gladly caress him and take him to his room at once, regarding this compact as sacred and inviolable as if ratified by an oath. What an idea of the obligation, and the usefulness, of an engagement will he not gain from this transaction! I am greatly mistaken if there is an unspoiled child on earth who would be proof against it, or who would ever after think of breaking a window purposely.

*   *   *   *   *

My pupil, or rather nature's pupil, trained from the first to depend as much as possible on himself, is not continually running to others for advice. Still less does he make a display of his knowledge. On the other hand, he judges, he foresees, he reasons, upon everything that immediately concerns him; he does not prate, but acts. He is little informed as to what is going on in the world, but knows very well what he ought to do, and how to do it. Incessantly in motion, he cannot avoid observing many things, and knowing many effects. He early gains a wide experience, and takes his lessons from nature, not from men. He instructs himself all the better for discovering nowhere any intention of instructing him. Thus, at the same time, body and mind are exercised. Always carrying out his own ideas, and not another person's, two processes are simultaneously going on within him. As he grows robust and strong, he becomes intelligent and judicious.

In this way he will one day have those two excellences,—thought incompatible indeed, but characteristic of nearly all great men,—

strength of body and strength of mind, the reason of a sage and the vigor of an athlete.

I am recommending a difficult art to you, young teacher,—the art of governing without rules, and of doing everything by doing nothing at all. I grant, that at your age, this art is not to be expected of you. It will not enable you, at the outset, to exhibit your shining talents, or to make yourself prized by parents; but it is the only one that will succeed. To be a sensible man, your pupil must first have been a little scapegrace. The Spartans were educated in this way; not tied down to books, but obliged to steal their dinners; and did this produce men inferior in understanding? Who does not remember their forcible, pithy sayings? Trained to conquer, they worsted their enemies in every kind of encounter; and the babbling Athenians dreaded their sharp speeches quite as much as their valor.

*   *   *   *   *

The same instinct animates all the different faculties of man. To the activity of the body, striving to develop itself, succeeds the activity of the mind, endeavoring to instruct itself. Children are at first only restless; afterwards they are inquisitive. Their curiosity, rightly trained, is the incentive of the age we are now considering. We must always distinguish natural inclinations from those that have their source in opinion.

There is a thirst for knowledge which is founded only upon a desire to be thought learned, and another, springing from our natural curiosity concerning anything which nearly or remotely interests us. Our desire for happiness is inborn; and as it can never be fully satisfied, we are always seeking ways to increase what we have. This first principle of curiosity is natural to the heart of man, but is developed only in proportion to our passions and to our advance in knowledge. Call your pupil's attention to the phenomena of nature, and you will soon render him inquisitive. But if you would keep this curiosity alive, do not be in haste to satisfy it. Ask him questions that he can comprehend, and let him solve them. Let him know a thing because he has found it out for himself, and not because you have told him of it. Let him not learn science, but discover it for himself. If once you substitute authority for reason, he will not reason any more; he will only be the sport of other people's opinions.

When you are ready to teach this child geography, you get together your globes and your maps; and what machines they are! Why, instead of using all these representations, do you not begin by showing him the object itself, so as to let him know what you are talking of?

On some beautiful evening take the child to walk with you, in a place suitable for your purpose, where in the unobstructed horizon the setting sun can be plainly seen. Take a careful observation of all the objects marking the spot at which it goes down. When you go for an airing next day, return to this same place before the sun rises. You can see it announce itself by arrows of fire. The brightness increases; the east seems all aflame; from its glow you anticipate long beforehand the coming of day. Every moment you imagine you see it. At last it really does appear, a brilliant point which rises like a flash of lightning, and instantly fills all space. The veil of shadows is cast down and disappears. We know our dwelling-place once more, and find it more beautiful than ever. The verdure has taken on fresh vigor during the night; it is revealed with its brilliant net-work of dew-drops, reflecting light and color to the eye, in the first golden rays of the new-born day. The full choir of birds, none silent, salute in concert the Father of life. Their warbling, still faint with the languor of a peaceful awakening, is now more lingering and sweet than at other hours of the day. All this fills the senses with a charm and freshness which seems to touch our inmost soul. No one can resist this enchanting hour, or behold with indifference a spectacle so grand, so beautiful, so full of all delight.

Carried away by such a sight, the teacher is eager to impart to the child his own enthusiasm, and thinks to arouse it by calling attention to what he himself feels. What folly! The drama of nature lives only in the heart; to see it, one must feel it. The child sees the objects, but not the relations that bind them together; he can make nothing of their harmony. The complex and momentary impression of all these sensations requires an experience he has never gained, and feelings he has never known. If he has never crossed the desert and felt its burning sands scorch his feet, the stifling reflection of the sun from its rocks oppress him, how can he fully enjoy the coolness of a beautiful morning? How can the perfume of flowers, the cooling vapor of the dew, the sinking of his footstep in the soft and pleasant turf, enchant his senses? How can the singing of birds delight him, while the accents of love and pleasure are yet unknown? How can he see with transport the rise of so beautiful a day, unless imagination can paint all the transports with which it may be filled? And lastly, how can he be moved by the beautiful panorama of nature, if he does not know by whose tender care it has been adorned?

Do not talk to the child about things he cannot understand. Let him hear from you no descriptions, no eloquence, no figurative language, no poetry. Sentiment and taste are just now out of the question. Continue to be clear, unaffected, and dispassionate; the time for using another language will come only too soon.

Educated in the spirit of our principles, accustomed to look for resources within himself, and to have recourse to others only when he finds himself really helpless, he will examine every new object for a long time without saying a word. He is thoughtful, and not disposed to ask questions. Be satisfied, therefore, with presenting objects at appropriate times and in appropriate ways. When you see his curiosity fairly at work, ask him some laconic question which will suggest its own answer.

On this occasion, having watched the sunrise from beginning to end with him, having made him notice the mountains and other neighboring objects on the same side, and allowed him to talk about them just as he pleases, be silent for a few minutes, as if in deep thought, and then say to him, "I think the sun set over there, and now it has risen over here. How can that be so?" Say no more; if he asks questions, do not answer them: speak of something else. Leave him to himself, and he will be certain to think the matter over.

To give the child the habit of attention and to impress him deeply with any truth affecting the senses, let him pass several restless days before he discovers that truth. If the one in question does not thus impress him, you may make him see it more clearly by reversing the problem. If he does not know how the sun passes from its setting to its rising, he at least does know how it travels from its rising to its setting; his eyes alone teach him this. Explain your first question by the second. If your pupil be not absolutely stupid, the analogy is so plain that he cannot escape it. This is his first lesson in cosmography.

*   *   *   *   *

Since we must have books, there is one which, to my mind, furnishes the finest of treatises on education according to nature. My Émile shall read this book before any other; it shall for a long time be his entire library, and shall always hold an honorable place. It shall be the text on which all our discussions of natural science shall be only commentaries. It shall be a test for all we meet during our progress toward a ripened judgment, and so long as our taste is unspoiled, we shall enjoy reading it. What wonderful book is this? Aristotle? Pliny? Buffon? No; it is "Robinson Crusoe."

The story of this man, alone on his island, unaided by his fellow-men, without any art or its implements, and yet providing for his own preservation and subsistence, even contriving to live in what might be called comfort, is interesting to persons of all ages. It may be made delightful to children in a thousand ways. Thus we make the desert island, which I used at the outset for a comparison, a reality.

This condition is not, I grant, that of man in society; and to all appearance Émile will never occupy it; but from it he ought to judge of all others. The surest way to rise above prejudice, and to judge of things in their true relations, is to put ourselves in the place of an isolated man, and decide as he must concerning their real utility.

Disencumbered of its less profitable portions, this romance from its beginning, the shipwreck of Crusoe on the island, to its end, the arrival of the vessel which takes him away, will yield amusement and instruction to Émile during the period now in question. I would have him completely carried away by it, continually thinking of Crusoe's fort, his goats, and his plantations. I would have him learn, not from books, but from real things, all he would need to know under the same circumstances. He should be encouraged to play Robinson Crusoe; to imagine himself clad in skins, wearing a great cap and sword, and all the array of that grotesque figure, down to the umbrella, of which he would have no need. If he happens to be in want of anything, I hope he will contrive something to supply its place. Let him look carefully into all that his hero did, and decide whether any of it was unnecessary, or might have been done in a better way. Let him notice Crusoe's mistakes and avoid them under like circumstances. He will very likely plan for himself surroundings like Crusoe's,—a real castle in the air, natural at his happy age when we think ourselves rich if we are free and have the necessaries of life. How useful this hobby might be made if some man of sense would only suggest it and turn it to good account! The child, eager to build a storehouse for his island, would be more desirous to learn than his master would be to teach him. He would be anxious to know everything he could make use of, and nothing besides. You would not need to guide, but to restrain him.

*   *   *   *   *

I think these explanations will suffice to mark distinctly the advance my pupil's mind has hitherto made, and the route by which he has advanced. You are probably alarmed at the number of subjects I have brought to his notice. You are afraid I will overwhelm his mind with all this knowledge. But I teach him rather not to know them than to know them. I am showing him a path to knowledge not indeed difficult, but without limit, slowly measured, long, or rather endless, and tedious to follow. I am showing him how to take the first steps, so that he may know its beginning, but allow him to go no farther.

Obliged to learn by his own effort, he employs his own reason, not that of another. Most of our mistakes arise less within ourselves than from others; so that if he is not to be ruled by opinion, he must receive nothing upon authority. Such continual exercise must invigorate the mind as labor and fatigue strengthen the body.

The mind as well as the body can bear only what its strength will allow. When the understanding fully masters a thing before intrusting it to the memory, what it afterward draws therefrom is in reality its own. But if instead we load the memory with matters the understanding has not mastered, we run the risk of never finding there anything that belongs to it.

Émile has little knowledge, but it is really his own; he knows nothing by halves; and the most important fact is that he does not now know things he will one day know; that many things known to other people he never will know; and that there is an infinity of things which neither he nor any one else ever will know. He is prepared for knowledge of every kind; not because he has so much, but because he knows how to acquire it; his mind is open to it, and, as Montaigne says, if not taught, he is as least teachable. I shall be satisfied if he knows how to find out the "wherefore" of everything he knows and the "why" of everything he believes. I repeat that my object is not to give him knowledge, but to teach him how to acquire it at need; to estimate it at its true value, and above all things, to love the truth. By this method we advance slowly, but take no useless steps, and are not obliged to retrace a single one.

Émile understands only the natural and purely physical sciences. He does not even know the name of history, or the meaning of metaphysics and ethics. He knows the essential relations between men and things, but nothing of the moral relations between man and man. He does not readily generalize or conceive of abstractions. He observes the qualities common to certain bodies without reasoning about the qualities themselves. With the aid of geometric figures and algebraic signs, he knows something of extension and quantity. Upon these figures and signs his senses rest their knowledge of the abstractions just named. He makes no attempt to learn the nature of things, but only such of their relations as concern himself. He estimates external things only by their relation to him; but this estimate is exact and positive, and in it fancies and conventionalities have no share. He values most those things that are most useful to him; and never deviating from this standard, is not influenced by general opinion.

Émile is industrious, temperate, patient, steadfast, and full of courage. His imagination, never aroused, does not exaggerate dangers. He feels few discomforts, and can bear pain with fortitude, because he has never learned to contend with fate. He does not yet know exactly what death is, but accustomed to yield to the law of necessity, he will die when he must, without a groan or a struggle. Nature can do no more at that moment abhorred by all. To live free and to have little to do with human affairs is the best way of learning how to die.

In a word, Émile has every virtue which affects himself. To have the social virtues as well, he only needs to know the relations which make them necessary; and this knowledge his mind is ready to receive. He considers himself independently of others, and is satisfied when others do not think of him at all. He exacts nothing from others, and never thinks of owing anything to them. He is alone in human society, and depends solely upon himself. He has the best right of all to be independent, for he is all that any one can be at his age. He has no errors but such as a human being must have; no vices but those from which no one can warrant himself exempt. He has a sound constitution, active limbs, a fair and unprejudiced mind, a heart free and without passions. Self-love, the first and most natural of all, has scarcely manifested itself at all. Without disturbing any one's peace of mind he has led a happy, contented life, as free as nature will allow. Do you think a youth who has thus attained his fifteenth year has lost the years that have gone before?

回 3. Education in Revolutionary France

The expulsion of the Jesuits from their French schools in 1762 provided one of the first breaches in the walls of the educational establishment, and reformers quickly attempted to take advantage of the situation. In 1768, Rolland d'Erceville proposed a plan to revamp the curriculum of the French secondary schools, the colléges. At first glance it appears to be a continuation of the standard grammar school program dating back to the Renaissance. However, there were significant innovations: history, including modern and national, divorced from grammar and taught by special teachers; a more regular and extensive study of French literature, including its use with Latin and Greek as a source from which to draw illustrations for the principles of rhetoric. Rolland was also among the early proponents of the centralization of educational control.

CURRICULUM OF THE UNIVERSITY
COLLEGES ACCORDING TO ROLLAND

SIXTH FORM. The *Maxims of Tobias,* and the moral books of the Old Testament; the gospels for Sundays and holidays; the catechism of the diocese; Old Testament history; an abridged French grammar; principles of the Latin language; Furgault's Greek grammar; selected stories from the Old Testament; sacred colloquies; Cicero's letters; the fables of Æsop, Phaedrus, and La Fontaine; Aurelius Victor.

Frederick Ernest Farrington, French Secondary Schools *(New York: Longmans, Green and Co., 1910). pp. 399–400.*

FIFTH FORM. The *Maxims of Tobias,* and the moral books of the Old Testament; the gospels for Sundays and holidays; the catechism of the diocese; an abridged French grammar; principles of the Latin language; Furgault's Greek grammar; Nepos; Justin; selections from profane history; selected precepts of Cicero; the fables of Æsop, Phaedrus, and La Fontaine; simple letters chosen from different authors; a knowledge of mythology, the questions and answers being given in French.

FOURTH FORM. Maxims from the Scriptures; the epistles and gospels; the catechism of Paris; principles of the Latin language, second part; Furgault's Greek grammar; an abridged French grammar; Æsop's fables; the gospel according to Luke (in Greek); Cicero's *De senectute* and *De amicitia,* his letter to Quintus, the paradoxes, and moral precepts chosen from him; Cæsar; Ovid; Virgil's *Bucolics* and *Georgics;* an abridged Roman history.

THIRD FORM. Sentences and verses from the Scriptures, the epistles and the gospels.
Before Easter: Cicero: *De officiis, De natura deorum,* and the *Tusculans; Letters to Atticus;* rules of Latin prosody; Quintus Curtius; Paterculus; some books of the *Metamorphoses.*
After Easter: Some of Cicero's orations, such, for example, as the *Catalines,* or the *Manilian law;* Sallust (distributed over two years). The *Georgics* and the first two books of the *Æneid* in alternate years. GREEK: Some of Lucian's dialogues; selected passages from Herodotus; the orations of Isocrates; Plutarch; Greek roots.
FRENCH: *Morning*—Restaut's grammar, together with selections from the best authors; at the end of the year, Vertot's *Roman revolution. Afternoon*—An abridged history of Greece with geographical and chronological commentaries upon that history.

SECOND FORM. Sentences and verses from the Scriptures, the epistles and the gospels.
Before Easter: Cicero: *De oratore,* or oratorical selections.
After Easter: Some of Cicero's orations (other than those read in the third form); selected passages from the *Cyropædia,* or some of Plutarch's *Lives;* the *Æneid,* the first six books alternating yearly with the last six.
Throughout the year: Horace, *Odes* or *Satires;* alternately the satires of Boileau or the finest odes of Rousseau; the finest passages from the *Iliad* or the *Odyssey;* Restaut's French grammar. Several other books in addition, some of which shall be chosen for reading aloud. *Morning*—Bossuet, *Universal History;* Vertot, *Revolution in Portugal;* Abbé Saint-Real, *The Venetian confederation;* Pellisson, *History of the French Academy;* Fontenelles, *Éloges académiques;* Montesquieu, *Grandeur des Romains;* etc. *Evening*—An abridged history of France.

RHETORIC FORM. Ancients: Desmosthenes, Isocrates, Sallust,
Livy, Tacitus, Horace (especially the *Ars poetica*), Virgil, Perseus,
Juvenal.
Moderns: St. Cyprian, St. Jerome, Salvian, Lactantia, St. Basil, St.
Gregory, St. Chrysostom, Bossuet, Fléchier, Mascaron, Fénelon,
d'Aguesseau, Bourdaloue, Massillon, Boileau (especially his *Art
poetique*), the sacred tragedies and *les Cantiques sacrés* of Racine, *le
Poéme de la religion* of Racine the younger, the *Odes* and the *Psalms* of
Rousseau.

In the excerpt that follows from Henry Barnard's American Journal of
Education *the principal proposals regarding elementary schooling put forth
during the Revolutionary period are summarized. In them are reflected many of
the basic ideas advocated by the reformers of the Enlightenment: extension of
educational opportunity, practical and patriotic as well as intellectual training, a
national system of schools with provisions for a degree of local control, and the
teaching methods of the sense realists and naturalists.*

Public elementary instruction, as at present organized, with its
budget, schools, teachers, and officials, can hardly be said to have
existed in France prior to the law of June 28, 1833; although the
germs of the system will be found in the aspirations of her statesmen,
and the earlier laws, decrees, and regulations of the government on
this subject.

(1.) The grand ideas, recognized by Turgot, in his plan of a uniform
system of national education superintended by a royal council, in 1775;
by the Third Estate of the States General of 1787, in its demands "that
public education should be adapted to the wants of all orders in the
state, and designed to form good and useful men in all classes of
society, and that the municipal and lay authorities should share with
the clergy the appointment and supervision of public teachers;" by the
Constituent Assembly, in its fundamental constitution, of September 3,
1792, "to create and organize a public instruction, common to all
citizens, and gratuitous in respect of those branches of tuition which
are indispensable for all men;" by Talleyrand, Condorcet, and Daunau,
in their several reports, in which they advocate plans, diverse, and even
antagonistic, in some of their details, and extravagant in their demands,
—have by degrees been tested and sifted by more practical men, and
are slowly passing into the organization and practice of elementary
instruction, not only in France but in other countries.

(2.) The National Convention, by decrees, dated December 12, 1792,

Henry Barnard (ed.), The American Journal of Education *(Hartford: Office of the
American Journal of Education, 1870), XX, 227–29.*

May 30, 1793, and October 21, 1793, ordered and provided for the establishment of primary schools. Every neighborhood, with 400 inhabitants, "must have a public school, in which children of all classes could
receive that first education, physical, moral, and intellectual, the best
adapted to develope in them republican manners, patriotism, and the
love of labor, and to render them worthy of liberty and equality."
"Pupils must be taught to speak, read, and write correctly the French
language; the geography of France; the rights and duties of men and
citizens; the first notions of natural and familiar objects; the use of
numbers, the compass, the level, the system of weights and measures,
the mechanical powers, and measurement of time. They were to
be taken often into the fields and the workshops where they might
see agricultural and mechanical operations going on, and take part in
the same so far as their age would allow."

By a subsequent decree, (October 29, 1793,) a local commission of
intelligent, public-spirited, and moral persons was to be appointed, to
locate the school, and hold a public examination of all candidates for
the position of teachers, as to their acquirements, aptitude for instruction, and moral character. From a list of the successful candidates, the
parents and guardians of the district in which a school was to be
opened, and any vacancy existed, might in public meeting choose a
teacher. For the teacher thus examined, approved, and selected, the
law fixed a minimum salary of 1,200 francs, to be paid out of the public
treasury. This salary could be increased by the liberality of the district
and of the parents. By a decree of December 19th of the same year
(1793), "liberty of instruction is proclaimed,—citizens and citizenesses,
who can produce a certificate of civism and good morals, can inform the
municipal authorities of their intention to teach, and of the subjects
which they propose to teach, and open a school where they please."
This liberty was abridged by a law passed November 17, 1794, so far
as to subject the teacher and his school to the approbation of a "jury
of instruction to be chosen by the district administration from among
the fathers of families." This law, which was repealed August 31, 1797,
provides that the residence of the clergyman, if not already sold for the
benefit of the republic under the decree of March 8, 1793, should be
assigned to the school-master for a dwelling and a school. The same
law added to the penalty (in the law of 1793,) of a fine on parents
who failed to send their children to school, a requirement "that those
young citizens who have not attended school shall be examined, in the
presence of the people, at the Feast of the Young, and if they shall be
found not to have the requirements necessary for French citizens,
shall be excluded from all public functions until they have attained
them." To the course of instruction laid down in the decree of 1793,
the law of 1794 added "gymnastics, military exercises, and swimming."

There is much that is extravagant in these requirements of a public school to be set up in every neighborhood of 400 inhabitants, poor as the entire rural population of France had been made by exactations of the privileged few, and ignorant as the great majority of parents had been left by all the previous agencies and facilities of education. And yet in these enactments we find expressed the highest aspirations of the most advanced educators of this age, and much that is now realized in the best public schools of Germany and the United States. Just because the law required more than could be performed, or than the existing instrumentalities of administration could educate the public mind to appreciate and sustain, it remained a dead letter, or gave way to enactments less exacting and less salutary.

The only permanent contribution of this period of French legislation to the system of elementary schools was a chapter of eleven articles in the *Decree concerning the Organization of Public Instruction*, October 25th, 1795, (3 *Brumaire, year IV,*) founded on a remarkable report of Daunau, in which the whole subject of public instruction is ably discussed. The following are the provisions respecting primary schools:

ART. 1.   There shall be established in every canton of the republic, one or more primary schools, whose territorial limits shall be determined by the departmental authorities.

2.   There shall be established in every department several juries or committees of instruction, the members not to exceed six, and each to be composed of three members appointed by the departmental authorities.

3.   The teachers of the primary schools shall be examined by one of the juries of instruction, and upon the presentation of the municipal authorities, shall be appointed by the departmental administration.

4.   They shall be dismissed only on the concurrence of the same authorities, at the proposal of a jury of instruction, and after having had a hearing.

5.   In every primary school shall be taught reading, writing, cyphering, and the elements of republican morals.

6.   Every primary teacher shall be furnished by the republic with a residence, (with school-room for his pupils,) and garden. Instead of a residence and garden, the teacher may be paid an equivalent in money.

7.   They, as well as the professors of the central and special schools, may perform other duties, not incompatible with teaching, and receive pay.

8.   They shall receive from each pupil an annual fee, to be fixed by the departmental administration.

9.   The school fee may be remitted to one-fourth of the pupils of each school, on account of poverty.

10.   The regulations of the primary schools shall be decided by the departmental administration, subject to the approbation of the Executive Directory.

11.   The municipal authorities shall exercise direct supervision over the

primary schools, and shall see to the execution of the laws and decrees of the higher administrations relating to the same.

This decree was the sole legacy of the conventions of the people which legislated for France in the matter of primary instruction.

The Directory attempted nothing in respect to primary or public schools, beyond a feeble administration of the law of 1795, and a further development of the central schools, and particularly of the school of public works,—the great Polytechnic School of Paris.

▣ 4. English Education for the Masses

The three brief documents that follow illustrate the middle-class, laissez-faire character of the Enlightenment in England. There was concern for the education of the masses of poor, but it was expressed through private, religious, and charitable channels rather than by political and governmental agencies. The nature of the education deemed appropriate reflects the far-from-democratic views of middle-class England. The children of the poor were to be literate, religious, industrious, and obedient. Above all, they were to know their place and be satisfied in it. Ideally, these aims were to be achieved throgh a primary education followed by a period of apprenticeship in a worthwhile trade.

A FORM OF A SUBSCRIPTION FOR A CHARITY SCHOOL

Whereas Prophaness and Debauchery are greatly owing to a gross Ignorance of the Christian Religion, especially among the poorer sort; And whereas nothing is more likely to promote the practice of Christianity and Virtue, than an early and pious Education of Youth; And whereas many Poor People are desirous of having their Children Taught, but are not able to afford them a Christian and Useful Education; We whose Names are underwritten, do agree to pay Yearly, at Four equal Payments, (during Pleasure) the several and respective Sums of Money over against our Names respectively subscribed, for the setting up of a Charity-School in the Parish of   in the City of
          or in the County of   for Teaching [Poor Boys, or Poor Girls, or] Poor children to Read and Instructing them in

Arthur Leach (ed.), Educational Charters and Documents, 598–1909 *(Cambridge: The University Press, 1911), pp.* 539–41. *By permission of Cambridge University Press.*

the Knowledge and Practice of the Christian Religion, as profess'd and taught in the Church of England; and for Learning them such other Things as are suitable to their Condition and Capacity. That is to say

£ *s.* *d.*

I A. B. do subscribe

In many Schools the Orders are to the effects following:

I. The master to be elected for this SCHOOL, shall be,

1. A member of the Church of England of a sober life and conversation, not under the Age of 25 years.

2. One that frequents the Holy Communion.

3. One that hath a good Government of himself and his Passions.

4. One of a Meek Temper and Humble Behaviour.

5. One of a good Genius for Teaching.

6. One who understands well the Grounds and Principles of the Christian Religion and is able to give a good account thereof to the Minister of the Parish or Ordinary on Examination.

7. One who can Write a good Hand, and who understands the Grounds of Arithmetick.

8. One who keeps good order in his Family.

9. One who is approved by the Minister of the Parish (being a Subscriber) before he is presented to be Licensed by the Ordinary.

II. The following Orders shall be observed by the Master and Scholars.

1. The Master shall constantly attend his proper Business in the School during the Hours appointed for Teaching viz. from 7 to 11 in the Morning and from 1 to 5 in the Evening the Summer half year: And from 8 to 11 in the Morning and from 1 to 4 in the Evening the Winter half year; that he may improve the Children in good Learning to the utmost of his Power and prevent the Disorders that frequently happen for want of the Master's Presence and Care.

2. To the End the chief design of this School, which is for the Education of Poor Children in the Rules and Principles of the Christian Religion as professed and taught in the Church of England, may be the better promoted; The Master shall make it his chief Business to instruct the Children in the Principles thereof, as they are laid down in the Church catechism; which he shall first teach them to pronounce distinctly, and plainly; and then, in order to practice, shall explain it to the meanest capacity, by the help of *The whole Duty of Man*, or some good Exposition approved of by the Minister.

And this shall be done constantly twice a week; that everything in the Catechism may be the more perfectly repeated and understood. And the Master shall take particular care of the Manners and Behaviour of the Poor Children.

And by all proper methods shall discourage and correct the beginnings of Vice, and particularly, Lying, Swearing, Cursing, taking God's name in vain, and the Prophanation of the Lord's Day etc. . . .

3. The Master shall teach them the true spelling of Words, and Distinction of Syllables, with the Points and Stops, which is necessary to true and good Reading, and serves to make the Children more mindful of what they Read.

4. As soon as the Boys can read competently well, the Master shall teach them to write a fair legible Hand, with the Grounds of Arithmetick, to fit them for Services or Apprentices.

NOTE. The Girls learn to read etc. and generally to knit their Stockings and Gloves, to Mark, Sew, make and mend their Cloaths, several learn to write, and some to spin their Cloaths.

[5, 6. To provide for Church going on Sundays and Saints' days and twice daily Prayers in School from the Prayer-Book.]

7. [Names-calling at beginning of School] . . . Great Faults as Swearing, Stealing etc. shall be noted down in monthly or weekly bills to be laid before the Subscribers or Trustees every time they meet, in order to their correction or expulsion.

8. [Holidays.]

9. [Provides that the School is to be free, no charge whatever being made.]

10. [The children are to be sent to school clean.]

11. The Children shall wear their Caps, Bands, Cloaths, and other marks of Distinction every Day, whereby their Trustees and Benefactors may know them, and see what their Behaviour is abroad.

The ordinary charge of a School in London for Fifty Boys Cloath's comes to about £75 per annum, for which a School-Room, Books and Firing is provided, a Master paid, and to each Boy is given yearly Three Bands, one Cap, one Coat, one Pair of Stockings, and one Pair of Shoes.

[The cost for a school of 50 Girls is put at £60 a year to include]

Two Coifs, Two Bands, One Gown and Petticoat, one pair of knit Gloves, One Pair of Stockings, and Two Pair of Shoes.

*   *   *   *   *

BOOKS *Proper to be Used in* CHARITY-SCHOOLS

A Bible, Testament, and Common-Prayer Book.
The Church-Catechism.
The Church-Catechism broke into short Questions.

W. O. B. Allen and Edmund McClure, Two Hundred Years: The History of the Society for Promoting Christian Knowledge, 1698–1898 *(London: SPCK, 1898), p. 187.*

Lewis's Exposition of the Church-Catechism.
Worthington's Scripture-Catechism.
The first Principles of practical Christianity.
Dr. *Woodward's* Short Catechism, with an Explanation of divers hard
    Words.
New Method of Catechizing.
Prayers for the Charity-Schools.
The Christian Scholar.
An Exercise for Charity-Schools upon Confirmation.
Pastoral Advice before, and after Confirmation.
The Whole Duty of Man by Way of Question and Answer.
Abridgment of the History of the Bible, which may be well bound up at
    the Beginning of the Bible, or at the End.
The Anatomy of Orthography: Or, a practical Introduction to the Art
of Spelling and Reading *English.*
The Duty of Public Worship proved, &c.
Lessons for Children, Historical and Practical, &c.
Hymns for the Charity-Schools.

* * * * *

TRANSCRIPT OF MANUSCRIPT INDENTURE
PRESERVED AT CORSHAM, WILTS, DATED
JAN. 16, 1708

    This Indenture made the sixteenth day of January in the Seaventh
yeare of the Reigne of our Sovraigne Lady Anne of Greate Brittaine
ffrance and Ireland Queene Defender of the ffaith ex Anno q° Dom
1708 Betweene William Selman of the pish of Corsham in the County
of Wiltes Husbandman And Richard Selman son of the sd William
Selman of the one pte And Thomas Stokes holder of the pish of Corsham
aforesaid Broadweaver of the other pte Witnesseth that the said
Richard Selman of his owne voluntarie will and with the consent of
his sd ffather William Selman Hath put himselfe an Apprntice unto the
said Thomas Stokes and with him hath convenanted to dwell as his
Appntice from the day of the date hereof untill the full end and terme
of Seaven Yeares fully to be compleate and ended during all which
tyme the said Richard Selman shall well and faithfully serve him the
said Thomas Stokes his master his secrets lawfully to be kept shall keep
his Commandm^ts lawfull and honest shall doe and execute hurt unto his
said Master hee shall not doe nor consent to be done Tavernes or
Alehouses hee shall not haunt Dice Cardes or any other unlawfull games

    O. *Jocelyn Dunlop*, English Apprenticeship and Child Labour, A History *(London:*
T. Fisher Unwin, 1912), pp. 352–53. By permission of Ernest Benn Limited.

hee shall not use ffornication with any woman hee shall not committ during such tyme as he shall stay in his Masters service Matrymony with any woman hee shall not Contract or espouse himselfe during the said Terme of Seven yeares The goods of his said Masters inordinately hee shall not wast nor to any man lend without his Masters Lycence from his Masters house or business hee shall not absent himselfe or plong himselfe by Night or by day without his Masters leave, but as a true and faithfull servant shall honestly behave himselfe towards his sd Master and all his both in words and deedes And the said Thomas Stokes doth for himselfe his Executors and Administrators promise and Covenant to and with the sd William Selman and Richard Selman his Appntice to teach or cause the said Richard Selman to be taught and instructed in the trade Art science or occupacon of a Broadweaver after the best manner that he can or may with moderate Correction finding and allowing unto his sd Servant meate drinke Apparrell Washing Lodging and all other things whatsoev fitting for an appntice of that trade during the said term of Seaven yeares And to give unto his sd Appntice at the end of the sd terme double Apparell (to witt) one suite for holy dayes and one for worken dayes, In witness whereof the said pties to these psent Indentures interchangeably have sett their hands and seales the day and yeare first above written Sealed and Delived in the psence of

his

Thomas ⌒ Stokes

marke

▣ 5. Reform and Nationalism in German Education

One of the most notable sense realist schools of the eighteenth century was the Philanthropinum of Johann Bernhard Basedow, established under the patronage of Prince Leopold of Anhalt-Dessau in 1774, for boys of the upper classes. The article that follows was written in support of the Philanthropinum by Immanuel Kant and published in 1777, in the Konigsberg Gazette. *Though ultimately defeated in their own day by the classical Humanists, the sense realists gained support among intellectuals who found their ideals and methods a refreshing improvement over traditional practices.*

FOR THE COMMON GOOD

There is no want, in the civilized countries of Europe, of educational institutions, or of teachers, ambitious to be useful in their calling; and it is equally clear, that they are all, taken together, spoilt, by the fact that every thing in them operates against nature, and thus they are of very much less benefit to man than nature has made the latter capable of; and it is clear that, inasmuch as by education we become men, from brutish creatures, we should in a short time see around us men of an entirely different character, if a method of education wisely derived from nature herself should come into universal use, instead of one slavishly imitated from the custom of a rude and ignorant antiquity. It is however in vain to expect this benefit to the human race from a gradual improvement of the schools. They must be revolutionized, if any thing good is to be derived from them; for they are bad in their fundamental organization; and even their teachers themselves must receive a new training. It is not a slow reform, but a quick revolution, which can accomplish this. To this end nothing is wanting, except one single school, organized anew from the very beginning, strictly upon the right method, conducted by intelligent men, not from pecuniary but from honorable motives, watched over during its progress to completion by the attentive eyes of men of experience in all countries, and sustained until its maturity by the united contributions of all the benevolent. Such a school would not be merely for those whom it would instruct, but— which is infinitely more important—for those to whom it would give an opportunity to train themselves, in gradually increasing numbers, for teaching upon the true system of education. It would be a seed, from the careful protection of which, in a short time, a multitude of well-trained teachers would spring up, who would supply the whole land with good scholars. Interest for the common good of all countries should first be directed to this end; to get assistance from every place to such a model school, that it may quickly attain that entire completeness, the sources of which are already within it. For to imitate its organization in other countries immediately, and to keep imperfect and hindered in its progress toward completion, what should be the first perfect example and seed-bed of good instruction, would be to sow unripe seed, in order to reap weeds. Such an educational institution is no longer a mere idea; but the actual and visible demonstration of its practicability, which has been so long needed, is given. Such a phenomenon, in our times, though overlooked by common eyes, must have more importance to observers of intelligence, who are interested in the good of humanity, than the

Karl von Raumer, *"Johann Bernhard Basedow and the Philanthropinum,"* in Henry Barnard (ed.), American Journal of Education *(Hartford: F. C. Brownell, 1858),* V, 504–05.

glittering nothingness which appears on the rapidly changing stage of the great world; by which the good of the human race, if not absolutely impeded, is not one hair's breadth promoted. The public designation, and especially the united voice of upright and intelligent men of experience in all countries, have already taught the readers of this paper to recognize the educational institution of Dessau (the Philanthropinum,) as the only one which bears these marks of excellence; of which it is not one of the least that, by the plan of its organization, it must of itself naturally throw off all the faults which belong to its beginning. The incessant attacks and libels which have appeared here and there, are such general marks of censoriousness, and of the old custom of defending one's self with one's tongue, that the indifference of this sort of people, who always look with evil eyes at whatever shows itself good and noble, would raise a suspicion of the mediocrity of the new claimant of excellence. An opportunity is now given to afford to this institution, which is devoted to the good of humanity, and that deserves the sympathy of all men, assistance, which will be insignificant to each person, but important from the large number. If the invention should be tasked to contrive the means by which a small gift should do the greatest, most lasting, and most universal good, it would be found to be that means by which the seeds of good are planted and maintained, so that they may grow and strengthen themselves with time. According to this idea, and to the high opinion which we have of the number of benevolent persons in this country, we refer to the 21st part of this literary and political gazette, with the appendix; where we find a numerous subscription, from men of standing in the church and in schools, and especially from parents to whom nothing can be indifferent which will serve for the better education of their children; and even from those who, although they have no children themselves, have heretofore, as children, received education, and who therefore feel the obligation to contribute, if not to the increase of mankind, at least to the improvement of their education. The subscription to the monthly journal issued by the Dessau educational institution, entitled *"Pedagogical Conversations,"* is two reichsthalers ten groschen of our money. But as it is impracticable exactly to determine the number of issues, and as thus there might be a further payment necessary at the end of the year, it would perhaps be best (though this is left to the good feelings of each man,) to send a ducat for his subscription; the overplus of which, if he demands it, shall be punctually returned to him. The institution indulges in the hope that there are many liberal persons in all countries, who will gladly seize this opportunity to make the small freewill offering of this surplus over the subscription, as a contribution to its support, while it is yet near being completed, but has not received in time the help which it expected. For since, as Herr O. C. R. Büsching says, the governments of the present day do not seem to have any money for the improvement of schools, it must, unless they are to be entirely broken up, be left to wealthy private persons, to sustain, by generous contributions, these so universally-important institutions.

KANT.

The description of the Philanthropinum that follows is contained in an article by Karl von Raumer, translated for Barnard's American Journal of Education. *Note the reference to Rousseau's influence on his own times.*

Like Kant, F. H. Jacobi, Euler, and others, conceived at first great hopes from the institution, and that gained great reputation and received assistance, in and from all parts of Europe. The unnaturalness of much that was usual was so strongly felt, and there was so strong a desire after freedom, after what may be called natural in the best sense of the word, that, as Kant says, there was a powerful wish not only for a reformation, but for a revolution, for the freedom of youth.

Rousseau's oratorical exhortations had caused much attention to be paid to the more intelligent management of little children; mothers nursed them themselves, and many effeminate habits were avoided.

In the Philanthropinum, the same principles were followed in educating boys; and bodily education was attended to in a manner which had never been any where seen before.

The preposterous and painful clothes of boys, embroidered coats, breeches, curling, and hair-bags, were all done away with. It may be imagined how delightful it must have been to the boys, to be let out of their tormenting dress—coats, breeches, and cravats—permitted to wear the most convenient sailor's jackets and pantaloons of striped blue and white tick, to have their necks free and their collars turned down, to be quite rid of the smear of powder and pomade in their hair, and of their hair-bags. A report of the institution for 1779 says, "If parents insist upon it that the hair of their children shall be daily dressed and powdered by the usual barbers, the institution can not answer for the purity of their characters; for, by means of the barbers, they can easily establish a connection with immoral persons, &c." This appeal was efficient.

Care was taken that the body should be disciplined and hardened. The boys learned carpentering and turning, wrestled in the open air, ran foot-races, &c. As the instruction proceeded as much as possible from actual seeing, the training of the eyes was not neglected.

Here also should be mentioned the fact that the Philanthropinum,

von Raumer, op. cit., pp. 510–11, 519–20.

and the teachers who adhered to its principles, made special efforts for the prevention of certain frightful secret practices.

As to instruction, the teachers of the Philanthropinum did many great services to it.

It was one of their favorite principles, that the scholars should learn with love and not with repugnance. In this they were certainly right, although they made many mistakes in their method of inspiring this love of learning. They severely blamed the unloving indifference of so many teachers toward their pupils, and toward their pleasure or displeasure in learning. That teacher will accomplish most, whose work is adapted at once to the growing natural gifts of his scholars, and to their weak conscientiousness. To have regard only to the natural gifts of the children leads to a servile following of them; to make demands upon their conscientiousness only, and to overlook and neglect their individual endowments, leads to the tyrannical practice of requiring every thing from all alike. In the first of these cases, the wills of the children are left to themselves, and they are treated only as personified powers, vegetating and developing themselves; which the teacher must follow only, and to which he must subject himself entirely. In the second case, on the other hand, they are regarded as personified wills, and they are required to will and to do all things, even the impossible; as if one should require a blind man to become a painter by the power of his will. In the Philanthropinum, the ethical element was comparatively neglected; the pleasure and wishes of the children was too much consulted, and their conscience and wills too little called into activity; even a wrong vanity was put in requisition. This may well have happened in opposition to the already mentioned caricaturized character of the ancient pedagogy, and its extreme severity, which commanded and set lessons recklessly, in reliance upon punishment, had reference neither to the pleasure nor the consciences of the children, and would carry all things through by fear.

INTERIOR ARRANGEMENTS IN THE PHILANTHROPINUM

At five o'clock, a house-servant awoke a "famulant," and the latter a teacher, and the other famulants. The teacher then inspected their rooms, to see if every thing was in good order, and their business properly arranged. At a quarter before six, the reveille was sounded, by a servant or famulant, when all the teachers and Philanthropinists arose. Then the teacher and inspector of the day visited all the pupils in their rooms, and called the attention of each to any thing in regard to which he was to blame. After having passed inspection, and washed, and dressed, the pupils met in the fourth auditorium for morning devotions.

After this all went to breakfast, and then, in winter at eight o'clock, in summer at seven, to the school-rooms. The order of exercises there was as follows:—

FOR THE FIRST CLASS OF OLDER BOARDERS

From 8 to 9. Instruction in taste, and in German style, by Prof. Trapp, from Ramler's *"Batteux,"* Schützen's *"Manual for Training the Understanding and the Taste,"* and Sulzer's *"First Exercises,"* (*Vorübungen.*) This for the first three days of the week. In the other three, Prof. Trapp instructed in natural religion and morals, from Basedow's *"Natural Wisdom for those in private stations."*

From 9 to 10. Dancing, with a master, riding, with riding-master Schrödter, under the inspection of Feder and Hauber, alternately, every day, except Wednesday and Saturday. Dancing was taught in the fourth auditorium, riding in the prince's riding-school.

10 to 12. Instruction by Basedow, at his house, in Latin; either in ancient history, (with accompanying studies,) or in practical philosophy, from Cicero *"De Officiis."*

12 to 1. Dinner.

1—2. Moderate exercise; as, turning, planing, and carpentry, in the rooms of Prince Dietrich's palace, granted for that purpose by the prince.

2—3. Monday and Tuesday, Geography, by Hauber, from Pfennig's *"Geography."* Wednesday, knowledge of the human body, and a partial course in Chemistry, by the prince's privy councilor and private physician, Kretzschmar, at his house, where the preparations and instruments were at hand. On the other three days of the week, mathematical drawing, by Prof. Wölke.

3—5. French and universal history, by Prof. Trapp, from Schröckh's *"Universal History,"* and Millot's *"Historie Universelle,"* during five days. Saturday, a news-lecture, by Hauber, to make the elder pupils gradually acquainted with public transactions and remarkable occurrences.

5—6. Mathematics, by Busse, from Ebert's *"Further Introduction to the Philosophical and Mathematical Sciences,"* during the first three days of the week; in the other three, physics, from Erxleben's *"Natural Philosophy."*

6—7. Knowledge of the heavens and the earth, by Wölke, from Schmid's *"Book of the Celestial Bodies,"* twice a week; the other four days, Greek, by Danner, from rector Stroth's *"Chrestomathia Graeca,"* Lucian's *"Timon,"* and Xenophon's *"Memorabilia."*

FOR THE SECOND CLASS OF ELDER SCHOLARS

8—9. Similar to the studies of the first class; by Prof. Trapp.

9—10. Riding and dancing, interchangeably with the first class. Arithmetic for some of them, with Prof. Trapp.

10—11.   Latin, with Hauber; from Basedow's "*Chrestomathia in historia antiqua.*"

11—12.   Latin, with Danner; from Basedow's "*Chrestomathia.*"

1—2.   Turning and planing, in alternation with first class.

2—3.   Drawing, with Doctor Samson. Some were instructed with the first class; and some study arithmetic, with Busse.

3—5.   Same exercises as the first class.

5—6.   Mathematics, with Danner, three days; on the other days, some were taught with the first class, and others received various kinds of private instruction.

6—7.   English, from the "*Vicar of Wakefield,*" with Prof. Trapp.

FOR THE FIRST CLASS OF YOUNGER SCHOLARS

8—9.   Reading German, with Jahn; the books being, Von Rochow's and Weissen's "*Children's Friend,*" Campe's "*Manual of Morals for Children of the Educated Classes,*" Feddersen's "*Examples of Wisdom and Virtue,*" Funk's "*Little Occupations for Children,*" and "*First nourishment for the sound human understanding.*"

9—10.   Writing, with Vogel, alternately with the second class, all the week; and instructive conversation with rector Neuendorf, at his room, or during walks.

10—11.   Latin, with Feder; from "*Phaedrus,*" Büsching's "*Liber Latinus,*" and select parts of Basedow's "*Liber Elementaris,*" and "*Chrestomathia Colloquiorum Erasmi.*"

11—12.   French, with Jasperson.

1—2.   Music, and recreation, under care of Feder.

2—3.   Drawing, with Doctor Samson, under charge, alternately, of Jasperson, Vogel, and Spener.

3—4.   Dancing, with the master, under care of Vogel.

4—5.   French, with Spener; from select portions of Basedow's "*Manual d'education.*"

5—6.   Latin, with Feder; from select portions of the Latin "*Elementary Book.*"

6—7.   For walking, under the care of Neuendorf.

FOR THE SECOND CLASS OF YOUNGER PUPILS

8—9.   Writing, with Vogel.

9—10.   Writing and walking, alternately with first class.

10—12.   Latin, with Wölke.

1—2.   As the first class.

2—3.   Drawing, as in first class.

3—4.   Dancing, as in first class.

4—5.   French, with Jasperson; from select parts of the "*Manual d'education.*"

5—6.   Instructive reading, with Jahn, in his room.

6—7.   Conversation with Neuendorf. On the first and fifteenth of each month, letter-writing was practiced. Walks were taken two afternoons a week.

At the direction of Frederick the Great, the Prussian School Code of 1763 was drawn up by Johann Hecker. Hecker had gained a measure of fame for his efforts in behalf of teacher training and his establishment of the Realschule, a secondary school employing the methods of sense realism in the study of practical, vocationally oriented studies. The Code by no means reflected an attempt on Frederick's part to extend the blessings of education as preparation for democratic participation in government. Rather it was an expression of the near-absolute ruler's "paternal disposition for the best good of all our subjects." The "best good," as he saw it, required a primary education in reading, writing, a good deal of religion, and some arithmetic. The Code's importance lay not in what it immediately accomplished—for there was opposition to it, and Frederick made no great effort to enforce its provisions—but rather in its service as the basis for the program of national elementary education which was to arise in Prussia during the nineteenth century. One cannot fail to be impressed with the extent to which the Code touched on every aspect of schooling. In later years educators from many nations were to travel to Prussia and express their admiration at the thoroughness and efficiency of her educational system.

GENERAL REGULATIONS OF ELEMENTARY SCHOOLS AND TEACHERS

August 12, 1763.

We Frederic, *by the grace of God, King, etc.*:

Whereas, to our great displeasure we have perceived that schools and the instruction of youth in the country have come to be greatly neglected, and that by the inexperience of many sacristans and schoolmasters, the young people grow up in stupidity and ignorance, it is our well considered and serious pleasure, that instruction in the country, throughout all our provinces, should be placed on a better footing, and be better organized than heretofore. For, as we earnestly strive for the true welfare of our country, and of all classes of people; now that quiet and general peace have been restored, we find it necessary and wholesome to have a good foundation laid in the schools by a rational and Christian education of the young for the fear of God and other useful ends. Therefore, by the power of our own highest motive, of our care

Henry Barnard (ed.), The American Journal of Education *(Hartford: Henry Barnard, 1871), XXII, 861–68.*

and paternal disposition for the best good of all our subjects, we command hereby, all governors, consistories and other collegiates of our country; that they shall, on their part, contribute all they can, with affection and zeal, to maintain the following GENERAL SCHOOL REGULATIONS, and in future to arrange all things in accordance with the law to the end that ignorance, so injurious and unbecoming to Christianity, may be prevented and lessened, and the coming time may train and educate in the schools more enlightened and virtuous subjects.

SECTION 1. First, it is our pleasure that all our subjects, parents, guardians or masters, whose duty it is to educate the young, shall send their children to school, and those confided to their care, boys and girls, if not sooner, certainly when they reach the age of five years; and shall continue regularly to do so, and require them to go to school until they are thirteen or fourteen years old, and know not only what is necessary of Christianity, fluent reading and writing, but can give answer in everything which they learn from the school books, prescribed and approved by our consistory.

§ 2. Masters to whom children in Prussia, by custom are bound to render work for certain years, are seriously advised not to withdraw such children from school until they can read well, and have laid a good foundation in Christian knowledge; also made a beginning in writing, and can present a certificate from the minister and school master to this effect to the school-visitors. Parents and guardians ought much more to consider it their bounden duty that their children and wards receive sufficient instruction in the necessary branches.

§ 3. If children, by their own aptitude or by the care of the teacher are sufficiently advanced in the common studies before they attain their thirteenth or fourteenth year, even then the parents or guardians are not at liberty to retain them at home, but can do so only when the superintendents or inspectors, after a notice from the minister and a testimonial of the schoolmaster, that the pupil has acquired a sufficient knowledge, have issued a regular dismissal based on the above testimonial. Still such children must attend the Repetition School, not only on Sundays, at the minister's, but also on week-days at the schoolmaster's.

§ 4. As in many towns, parents do not send their children to school in summer, on the plea that they have to guard the cattle; our magistrates and judges in the districts containing towns and communes, shall see that a special shepherd is engaged, rather than allow the children to be kept from school. Whereas, as in our Westphalia counties, in the Wisher-land, in the old Margraviate and other parts, the houses are scattered far apart, and the cattle cannot be driven into one place to be guarded, one child after the other, if there are several in a family or neighborhood, shall alternately, every day, attend to the herds; or the innkeepers and inhabitants of such towns shall make other arrangements by which each child can go to school at least three days of the week, that it may not forget in summer what it learned in winter. In many cases it could be organized that the children form two divisions, one of which could be in school during the three first days of a week, and the other during the three last days.

§ 5. In order to regulate definitely the summer and winter schools, we decree that winter schools must be held on all the six days of the week, from 8 to 11 o'clock in the forenoon, and from 1 to 4 o'clock in the afternoon, except Wednesday and Saturday afternoons. The winter school must be continued from Michaelmas to the Easter-days. But the summer schools shall be open only in the forenoon or, if necessary by the location of the place, during three hours every week-day, when the ministers can best decide at what hour to commence. No vacations are to be given, not even during harvest time; the schools shall be kept in the prescribed manner, with this distinction, that in summer each lesson is to be of half an hour's duration, and in winter of a full hour.

And since it has not remained unknown to us, that in many places the magistrates and patrons of nobility have taken great pains that schools might be kept winter and summer in the fore and afternoons, we will, by this decree, not at all abolish an arrangement so praiseworthy, but allow the example of Christian care for the interests of the children, to serve as an example to others.

§ 6. On Sundays, beside the lesson of the catechism or repetition school by the minister given in the Church, the schoolmaster shall give in the school a recapitulary lesson to the unmarried people of the township. They shall there practise reading and writing. Reading should be from the New Testament or some other edifying book, and as an exercise in writing, the young people should write some passages, or the epistle, or Gospel of the day. In towns where the school-master is not likewise sexton, and not obliged to travel through the parish with the clergyman, he shall be bound to sing with the children in Church, either morning or afternoons, to hear them recite the catechism and address to them easy questions on the order of salvation. If a sacristan or schoolmaster has no experience in catechising, the minister should write down for him the questions he must ask, that in this manner, together with their children, the people may be edified and improved in scriptural knowledge.

§ 7. In regard to tuition fee, every child, until it can read, shall pay in winter six pennies, after it can read, nine pennies, and when it can write and read, one groschen a week. For the months of summer, however, they shall pay only two-thirds of this fee, so that those who paid six pennies in winter, after his proportion shall pay four; those who paid nine pennies shall pay six, and those who paid one groschen will pay eight pennies. If, in any place the schoolmaster has been paid better, he must continue to receive the customary fees.

§ 8. Parents too poor to pay the tuition fee for their children, and orphan children who cannot pay, must petition the magistrate, patron, minister or church-council for an allowance from any funds of the church or town at their disposal, that the schoolmaster may get his income, and teach the children of the poor and rich with equal diligence and fidelity.

§ 9. In furtherance of this object, there shall be delivered in every town of the country and in the cities, on St. Michael's Sunday of every year, a school discourse, in which a topic, chosen with discretion, from the subjects of christian education and edification of youth, in harmony with the Gospel of the day, or based on another suitable text from the Old or New Testament, shall be expounded to the people. After this discourse, and an earnest exhortation from the minister, a collection will be taken in aid of country schools, and especially for the purchase of school-books for the poor children in village schools; and in the manner customary to the place; they shall also collect voluntary contributions, which together with the regular quarterly collections, shall be forwarded to the consistory of the province to be applied to the purchase of books.

§ 10. Having made good and sufficient provision for the instruction of the young, all parents, guardians, and others, having children to educate, who act contrary to this ordinance, by withholding them from school, shall still be obliged to pay the common school-fee for the term; and guardians shall not be permitted to charge the money thus paid to the account of their wards. And if, after earnest exhortation of the minister, they do not send their children regularly to school, then the magistrate of the town, in the last resort, shall direct execution against them. It is made the duty of the school-visitors to impose on such parents as have not made their children attend school regularly, a fine of sixteen groschen, to be paid into the school-treasury.

We therefore command all officers and magistrates to ascertain without delay, after receiving notice from the schoolmaster, of the non-attendance of any child, from the parent or guardian of the same the cause of such absence, and if it is for other reason than sickness, they shall employ proper legal means to secure that child's attendance.

§ 11. To this end, and to enable him the better to control the matter, the schoolmaster shall receive, from the register of the church or the town in which they are engaged, a list of all children of school age, that they may know who are due to the school; and the teacher shall also keep a monthly register, in which the children are enrolled as follows: (1) By their name and surname; (2) their age; (3) the names of their parents; (4) their residence; (5) the date when they enter school; (6) the lessons they study; (7) the degree of their diligence or negligence;

(8) their abilities of mind; (9) their morals and conduct; (10) the day when they leave school.

This register, which no child should be suffered to read, is sent to the school-visitor before his annual inspection, and inspected by the minister during his weekly visits that he may know the delinquent children, and exhort them to greater diligence, and speak with their parents in this regard.

This register is ruled with lines for every day of the month, on which the teacher can enter his remarks, and check those who are absent with or without permission or excuse. This will incite children to diligence, and remind parents, who send their children irregularly and say, "our children have gone so many years to school, and yet learned nothing," that the fault is not with the school or the teacher, but with themselves.

§ 12. Since the chief requisite in a good school is a competent and faithful teacher, it is our gracious and earnest will, that one and all, who have the right of appointment, shall take heed to bring only well quali-fied persons into office as teachers and sacristans. A schoolmaster should not only possess the necessary attainments and skill in instruction, but should be an example to the children, and not tear down by his daily life what he builds up by his teaching. He should therefore strive after godliness, and guard against everything which might give offence or temptation to parents or children. Above all things, he should endeavor to obtain a correct knowledge of God and Christ, thereby laying a foundation to honest life and true christianity, and feeling that they are entrusted with their office from God, as followers of the Saviour, and in it have an opportunity, by diligence and good example, not only to render the children happy in the present life, but also to prepare them for eternal blessedness.

§ 13. Though we intend to leave undiminished the privileges of the nobility and other patrons to select and appoint their sacristans and teachers, yet our superintendents, inspectors and the clergy must see that no incompetent, unsuitable, nor reckless and wicked person is employed or continued in office. Especially should those be removed who are addicted to drink or theft, who excite dissensions in the commune, or give scandal. If they are addicted to such vices before their engagement they are unfit for the office; and the patrons should be required to present another person, of good repute, to the examiners. But if these vices crop out after they are in office, it must not only be noted on the annual report of conduct, but be directly communicated to our con-sistory, that they may be saved further vexation, and the incumbent be suspended without delay and brought to trial before the proper tribunal. All teachers are forbidden to keep tavern, to sell beer or wine, to engage in any other occupations by which their labor may be hin-dered or the children lured by their example into habits of idleness and dissipation, such as the hanging round taverns or making music at dinners and balls, which is prohibited under high fine and punishment.

§ 14. No sacristan or teacher can be installed into office before his qualifications, ascertained by actual examination, are certified by the Inspector. No clergyman can admit any person to such position in church or school who does not produce said certificate of a successful examination.

With regard to our country schools in towns and villages on our own domains, we repeat our former directions, that no person shall be engaged as school teacher unless he has been a member of the Teachers' Seminary at Berlin and understands the cultivation of silk, as well as the excellent methods of instruction pursued in the German schools of Trinity Church. And those teachers who have received from Chief Counsellor and Pastor Hecker a certificate of qualification, may be elected to a vacancy after giving a trial lesson in singing in the church and in teaching the children in school in presence of the inspector, or of the clergyman and some citizens of the town. Whenever a vacancy occurs, the clergyman must give notice to the inspector, mentioning the specific salary and circumstances of the position, who reports to the chief consistory, waiting for the presentation of a candidate from the Teachers' Seminary; if none such is presented, then, with the assistance of the clergyman, he must find a proper person and send him to Berlin for examination and trial lessons. Should he not be found qualified, he may be permitted to attend the seminary at his own expense until he has obtained the certificate of qualification; and failing that, another candidate must be proposed.

§ 15. No person shall assume to teach in any school of the country, village, or town, who has not regularly obtained a license to teach; and all schools, whether kept by man or woman, not duly authorized, are entirely prohibited. But parents of wealth may, as heretofore, engage private teachers for their children, provided that the children of others who cannot yet be taught the higher branches are not induced to withdraw from the regular school in order to share the private elementary instruction.

§ 16. As a schoolmaster is not permitted to employ his pupils for his own work during school hours, neither shall he attend to his trade or other business during such hours, or entrust his wife with the duties of the school-room: though he may employ her or another person to assist when the school is too large for his personal instruction. If for any cause he neglects to teach the prescribed hours, the clergyman shall remind him of his duty; and, in case of persistent neglect, notice must be sent to the inspector that such irregularities may be corrected or punished.

§ 17. The daily work of the school should begin with prayer to the Giver of all good gifts, that He will send His divine blessing on their work, and give them a heart full of tenderness and sincerity towards the children entrusted to their care, that they may do willingly and without passion all that is incumbent upon them as teachers; being always reminded that they can have no influence over children, nor win their hearts without the divine assistance of Jesus, the friend of children, and of His holy spirit. During the instructions they should devoutly pray that they may not only keep their minds composed, but that God will bless their work, and to planting and watering graciously give His increase.

Teachers should also devise various means to win the confidence of young pupils, especially of the bashful and slow, and to render their task easy. To this end, they should make themselves familiar with the third part of the *"Berlin Schoolbook,"* by which all the elementary branches are successfully taught.

§ 18. As much depends on a good plan of organization, it is ordered that three hours in the forenoon (from 8 to 11) and three in the afternoon (from 1 to 4 o'clock) shall be the school time, unless the minister and town council find it more suitable to begin earlier or to close later in the day, provided six hours each day in summer and winter are devoted to instruction.

§ 19. The order of school shall be thus:

In the first hour of the morning they will—

First. Sing a hymn, the words being slowly pronounced by the schoolmaster, and sung by the children after him. Every month, but one hymn, designated by the clergyman, and not too long or unfamiliar, shall be learned and sung, in order that the old and young may remember the words and tune by frequent repetition. While singing, the teacher must see that all participate, and no child should be permitted to hold open the hymnbook and sing from it, but all should be required to follow him.

Second. After the hymn, a prayer shall be offered, either by the master, or one of the pupils may be allowed to read slowly and distinctly a prescribed prayer, while the rest join in silence. Then all should directly offer up a common prayer, learned by heart; and after the reading of the psalm for the month by one of the pupils, the devotional exercise should close with the Lord's prayer. Any tardy children must wait at the door until prayer is ended, in order not to disturb the others.

Third. After prayer such a portion of the catechism is explained that in every six weeks the book is gone through. In this exercise the following method should be adopted: The portion to be interpreted must be read by the children until it is familiar to most of them. Then the words and their meaning are explained, by questions and answers, and verified by passages from the Scriptures; and finally the children should be told how to apply the truth of what they hear to practical life. For little children Luther's smaller catechism should be used; for the more advanced the clergyman and schoolmaster should use the larger catechism with interpretations.

During the remaining hours of the morning, exercises in reading, spelling, and the A B C should follow according to the proficiency of the pupils.

(1.) In the first half hour the advanced pupils read a chapter from the Old or New Testament, sometimes together, sometimes a certain portion of the class, alternating with a single pupil, as the teacher may designate to keep the order and attention of all alive.

(2.) The next half hour is devoted to spelling, either by the entire class in concert or each child alone. Sometimes a word is written on the "tafel," (*blackboard,*) which all are required to spell and pronounce. During this lesson with the younger pupils the older are practiced in finding passages of Scripture or hymns in the hymnbook; or they commit to memory verses and the names of Biblical books in their succession, that they may become ready in consulting the Scriptures.

(3.) The next hour is devoted to the A B C classes, with copying on their tablets one or two letters from the larger tablet, the teacher often calling them to name the letters, or show them on their slates, while he is hearing an advanced class spell, or attending to their writing, which last is in this wise:

(1.) The larger children write during the first half of the third hour, when their work is inspected and corrected in the next half hour. That no child may be neglected, the teacher keeps a list of the scholars, who present their copy-books in succession, and continues the next day where he left off. In this manner every child will have his book returned and corrected several times each week.

Here it should be remarked, that the left side of the copy-book should be written and corrected first, and the scholar should re-write the same exercise on the right-hand page, free of the errors pointed out by the teacher.

(2.) While the larger pupils are writing, the spelling class is to be exercised and made familiar with the rules of reading, and the power of letters. While the larger scholars have their copies corrected, the spelling class may now and then recite their Bible-verse for the week. Towards the end of the third morning-hour, the whole school is called to prayer, after which the teacher reads the psalm or part of the hymn designated for the season, and then the pupils are quietly dismissed. The master looks to their behavior in going home, that carelessness and wickedness may not dissipate the instructions of the morning.

During the first hour of the afternoon the whole school is occupied with the teacher, and after singing some verses and reading a psalm, they are taught biblical history and the "Manual for the instruction of children in country-schools."

The second hour of the afternoon, the classes alternately learn portions of the catechism. This may be done after the method shown in the third part of the Berlin Reader, by writing down the first letters, or in the following manner:

(1.) The teacher reads repeatedly, slowly and distinctly, the portion which the children are to commit, while the pupils follow in the open book mentally. Then the children read the exercises in concert, while the middle and spelling class listen.

(2.) After this is done, the teacher reads aloud from comma to comma, while the children repeat until they know it by heart; then he proceeds with the next paragraph in the same manner, explaining the Bible phraseology of the catechism, which the children learn together. As regards the interpretation of Luther's catechism, the larger children will learn that by frequent repetition; the middle class, and the small pupils meanwhile listening attentively. After the first class has in concert repeated the lesson a few times, the teacher indicates the individuals to recite the lesson from memory, and thus he satisfies himself as to their mastery of it.

(3.) Finally each class recites its weekly Bible-verse, varying length according to the age of the pupils. In this manner children generally learn the portions of the catechism and Christian Doctrine in their proper connection, together with their Bible-verses, a psalm and a hymn every month.

The next half hour, the larger children attend to reading, the middle class to spelling, and lower class to their letters as in the morning.

During the third and last hour of the afternoon, the first class shall write and cypher; while the middle class continue their spelling, and the little children their A, B, C.

On Saturday, instead of the catechism in the first hour of the morning, the children will repeat the Bible-verses, psalms and hymns they have learned, of which the teacher keeps a memorandum. Then, from week to week, he relates to them a history from the Old or New Testament, explains the same and shows its application to life and conduct. For the older children he may use the Biblical chart, to aid them in more perfectly understanding the Holy Scriptures. After this they shall read the gospel or the epistle for the next Sunday. Next they write on their slate, of which the teacher corrects the orthography. At the conclusion of the school, the children shall be earnestly exhorted to behave well on Sunday; to be quiet and devotional at church; to listen and treasure up the word of God for their salvation.

The schoolmaster, during all the hours above designated, must be constantly with the children, and never be absent from school one hour, much less one day, without the knowledge of the pastor and the permission of his superiors, in which case he must in time provide another person to teach the school, that the young may not be neglected.

In large cities, and villages, where there is more than one class-room, it shall be reported by the inspectors and clergymen to our provincial consistory, which will regulate the order of lessons and method of instruction according to the conditions of the place.

§ 20. As the country has hitherto been deluged with all sorts of school-books, especially with interpretations of the catechism, and so-called "orders of salvation," because every preacher selects the books after his own pleasure, or writes some himself and has them printed, by which children, especially if the parents change their residence, are much confused, it is our will, that henceforth no other books, than such as have been approved by our consistory, shall be used in any country-schools over which we have the right of patron. These books include, according to the wants of the country, the New Testament, the book called "Exercise in Prayer," in which not only are the contents of each book in the Bible, but the main subject of each chapter is framed into a prayer, to assist the young in expressing their invocations in the words of divine truths. Also the Halle or Berlin Bible, both of which agree in their divisions into paragraphs and pages; next the small and large Catechism of Luther; the Index of the books of the Bible; the Christian Doctrines in their connection; the Berlin Spelling-book and Reader; the General Attributes of God, of the world and man; and the Little Book for children in the country, on all sorts of necessary and useful things.

§ 21. Each class must not only have the same books, but the clergyman and teacher must see that every child has his own book, so that two pupils need not look over the same book. Children, whose books are furnished from the funds of the church or the commune, are not allowed to take them home, but will deliver them to the master, who will take charge of them as the property of the school.

§ 22. Discipline should be administered with discretion, and the sin and vices of selfishness, obstinacy, lying, calling bad names, disobedience, wrath, the habit of quarrelling and fighting must be rebuked, corrected and punished, yet always with discretion and after previous inquiry into the circumstances of each act. In punishing the young the teacher must abstain from all unbecoming passion, harsh language, and exhibit a paternal calmness and moderation, so that children may not be spoiled by excessive tenderness, or made timid by excessive severity. When, from the enormity of the offence, or for example, it becomes necessary to punish severely, the teacher shall first consult the clergyman, who shall thoroughly investigate the case, advise impartially, so that parents shall not interfere in the affairs of the school.

§ 23. Before church service on Sundays and holidays, the parents shall be required to send their children to the schoolmaster, that they may walk to church in proper order and be under good supervision while there. He must take them quietly and orderly out of church, after the service; and while in church must occupy a special seat, near the children, that he may note down the absent, and have an eye on those present, that they behave modestly, and join in singing with becoming devotion, without whispering or playing during the sermon, respecting which they should be interrogated on the following day. It is also the duty of the schoolmaster to watch the conduct of the boys who assist at funerals, that they walk reverently two and two, while those who can, join in singing the funeral hymns; and on all public occasions, they should behave modestly, and be courteous in their manners, words and actions.

§24. In all other affairs of the school, the teacher must avail himself of the advice and suggestions of the clergyman, as his superior officer, and by his school-regulation the teachers are so directed. Of all that regards their office they must, on demand, give an account, and accept directions in reference to the prescribed method and discipline, because we have confidence in our ministers and bind it on their consciences that in their towns they will earnestly endeavor to abolish all abuses and defects, and improve the condition of the schools. In case however one or the other of the schoolmasters should neglect the duties of his office, after he is engaged, and be found unreliable, the pastor's duty will be, earnestly to remind him of his duty, with kindness once or twice, and if he still continues in his negligence, to apply for a remedy to the nearest justice: at the same time to inform the Superintendent or Inspector, and if their warning is not heeded, make a report to the consistory, that, according to the circumstances, they may decree a suspension or removal.

§25. Especially is it our pleasure, that clergymen in villages and towns shall visit the schools of their place, generally twice a week, sometimes in the morning and sometimes in the afternoon, and shall not only take the information of the sacristans or schoolmaster, but themselves examine the children in the catechism and question them after other schoolbooks. They shall hold a monthly conference with the schoolteachers *in matre,* and designate to them the portion of the catechism, the hymn, the psalm and Bible-verses which the children shall learn during the next month. Then he instructs them how to observe the principal divisions of the sermon and how to examine the children; he also points out the defects in their instruction in school, their method, discipline, and gives them other information, that the schoolteachers may fulfil their duties. If a clergyman, against our expectation, should be careless in his visits to the schools, or in the performance of the other duties enjoined upon him in these regulations, and not labor earnestly to effect an exact observance of this law on the part of teachers, he shall if convicted of the non-fulfilment of these instructions, be suspended *cum effectu*, for a time, or, as the case may be, removed from office: because the care for the instruction of the young and the supervision thereof, belong to the most important duties of the ministry, as we always desire them to be considered.

§26. The Superintendents and Inspectors of every district are hereby commanded, in the most expressive manner, annually to inspect every country-school in their jurisdiction, and with due attention to inquire into the condition of the schools, and examine whether parents and school authorities have held their children to regular attendance at school or have been negligent; whether the clergymen have done their duty in the observance of these regulations, by visiting the schools and superintending the teacher; especially whether the schoolmaster has the ability required or is not competent, and whatever else is in need of improvement. About all this the said Superintendents and Inspectors shall remit a dutiful report, every year, to our High Consistory in this city, for further examination and disposition. We command that this be done without fail, not only in regard to public schools in the country, in villages or cities, but also where the nobility have the *Jus Patronatus*, that incompetent schoolmasters may be known to the consistory and they take measures to diminish ignorance and immorality among the young. At the same time those children, who have made good progress in school, shall be introduced to the school-visitors at the examination, and afterwards be admitted to the weekly instruction in the catechism at the house of the pastor, where they shall be made thoroughly acquainted with Christianity.

In general we here confirm and renew all wholesome laws, published in former times, especially, that no clergyman shall admit to confirmation and the sacrament any children not of his commune, nor those unable to read, or who are ignorant of the fundamental principles of evangelical religion.

VIII

The Establishment of Education in America, 17th and 18th Centuries

THE United States has never experienced a period during which her development took place in isolation from events in other parts of the world. This is as true of her social and intellectual history as it is of political history. During the first two centuries of settlement the land was occupied by Europeans and Africans. The latter, forcibly removed from their native lands, were brought to America to be slaves or, for a few, at best to endure a limited kind of free status. The conditions of their lives and the active hostility of the white majority discouraged any attempt to transfer intact their native culture and institutions. For the Europeans, however, no matter what the inspiration for leaving home or what their image of a life in the New World, there was the desire, the opportunity, and at times official encouragement to establish in America an approximation of the patterns of life they had known or had striven to attain before they undertook their dangerous voyage. They came as Englishmen, Germans, Swedes, Dutch, and the like, and the culture they established reflected their roots. The European world of the seventeenth and eighteenth centuries combined with the American environment and experience to shape the character of the new land.

Among the European beliefs, practices, and institutions established in colonial America were those concerned with education. To all the colonies eventually came the traditions of apprenticeship, of primary education in the 3 R's for the sake of strengthening religious orthodoxy, and of grammar and collegiate education in the liberal arts, the classics, Aristotelian philosophies, and theological studies. The extent to which the colonists were able to implant this educational tradition and the patterns of schooling which eventually arose in the different colonies were conditioned by such factors as geography, patterns of settlement, wealth, and religious and national makeup of the population.

In New England the town pattern of settlement was conducive to the establishment of formal schooling. The homogeneous religious character of these colonies, excepting Rhode Island, made possible a single system of schools. Finally, close ties between the Puritan ministry and the colonial governments encouraged legislative action in support of a system of publicly maintained and controlled education, which had as a major objective the inculcation of the doctrines of the dominant religion. In a period of less than two decades after the founding of Boston in 1630, the legislature of the Massachusetts Bay Colony had enacted laws establishing Harvard College, calling on parents and masters of apprentices to educate their charges, and, in 1647, requiring towns to provide elementary and Latin-grammar schooling. Though the institutions established under the 1647 law might best be described as providing publicly sponsored parochial schooling, precedents were planted in the new soil of America, which would later provide an important base upon which a system of universal public education would be established. (1)

The multiplicity of national and religious groups that populated the Middle Colonies made a system of public schooling impossible. In an era when a prime purpose of education was to promote religious orthodoxy, Presbyterians, Anglicans, Lutherans, Quakers, Mennonites, and the other sects bore the major responsibility for founding schools and colleges for their own congregants. Their success in these ventures was as varied as the intensity of their respective commitments to the role of education in the salvation of souls. For the wealthier classes in the Middle Colonies, particularly in the urban centers, private schools were established and tutors were available. As in all areas of the Colonies, the apprentice system flourished. (2)

The South, with its scattered population, lack of urban centers, and dominance of the Anglican Church, established an educational structure closely resembling that of England. Private tutors and private schools at home or abroad were the rule for the children of the moneyed. For the poor, educational opportunity was sparse. Though the colonial legislatures made various pronouncements requiring parents and masters of apprentices to provide the rudiments of learning, no steps were taken by the civil authorities to provide schools. What education was available was offered by dedicated ministers, free schools established by charitable endowments and, after 1701, by the Anglicans' Society for the Propagation of the Gospel in Foreign Parts. By the middle of the eighteenth century a distinctly aristocratic pattern of separate education for the masses and the classes had appeared in the Southern Colonies. (3)

The thousands of miles of open sea and the adverse conditions of the seaboard frontier proved to be formidable yet not insurmountable barriers against the establishment of the European cultural tradition in America. Nor was the Atlantic wide enough to prevent the fatal quarrel between England and her colonies or block out the ideas of the eighteenth-century Enlightenment. In fact, the currents of the Enlightenment moved in both directions across the Atlantic, the words and deeds of its leaders both emanating from and affecting the Old World and the New.

In America as in Europe the Enlightenment made an impact on educational thought and practice. The writings of the sense realists and naturalists were known and admired in America. In a land where commerce and industry were beginning to flourish and where the self-made man of practical skill and "know-how" was emerging as an idealized type, the rigidity of the classical curriculum appeared an absurdity to many. It is not surprising that America's most famous self-made man, Benjamin Franklin, became its most outstanding spokesman for the establishment of a more humane and utilitarian secondary education. (4)

Thomas Jefferson, like Franklin, recognized the need for a more utilitarian education, particularly at the collegiate level. As the author of the Declaration of Independence, he was also keenly aware of the need to establish a system of public schools in Virginia. Like his counterparts in France, he sought to abolish a sectarian and aristocratic educational system and provide in its place the means to train an enlightened citizenry and a dedicated, responsible leadership appropriate for a democratic republic. (5)

With the successful culmination of the Revolutionary War, the United States of America emerged as a member of the world community of nations. However, despite the peace treaty and all the trappings of a national government, the concept of nationhood was not quickly and easily grasped in the minds and hearts of its citizens. A history of over one hundred fifty years of colonial existence, during which loyalty to colony and king was the mark of patriotism, could not be readily exchanged in a few years for devotion to the new nation. Yet some recognized that such devotion was essential if the union were to be maintained. It was quite natural that, like the European nationalists, American leaders looked toward the educational establishment as a prime agency for inculcating a spirit of national patriotism. George Washington called upon Congress to consider the establishment of a national university; and new textbooks appeared, which, like Jedidiah Morse's Geography, *included patriotic descriptions of the American scene and American history. Perhaps the most vigorous proponent of nationalistic education was Noah Webster. Reflected in his famous "blue-backed speller," his grammar, and his reader and affirmed in numerous essays was a fervent belief in the importance to the maintenance of the republic of a public school system that would instill the proper moral and patriotic virtues. (6)*

In its call for a more democratic, utilitarian, and nationalistic education, the American Enlightenment echoed that of Europe. However, the similarity did not stop there. As in Europe, the climate and conditions in the United States at the end of the eighteenth century were not yet conducive to the acceptance of many of the liberal proposals. Democratic education would remain an ideal as long as the franchise continued to be restricted on the basis of property and wealth and as long as aristocratic notions of government and society still found numerous advocates. Public sponsorship of nonsectarian education could not be accomplished while many states continued to maintain their official ties with one or more religious sects. Education for national patriotism would have limited support as long as men remained loyal to state above nation. And many a battle would be waged before modern and practical subjects would be granted anything approaching equal status with the classics in the curricula of secondary schools and colleges. The eighteenth century witnessed the attainment of political independence for the American Colonies, but another generation was to pass before many of the social, political, and cultural goals defined by the early national leaders began to be realized.

▣ 1. Education in the Massachusetts Bay Colony: Governmental Initiative

The establishment of Harvard College in 1636, so soon after the founding of the Colony, was a remarkable achievement. With the opening the same year of the Boston Latin Grammar School, the Puritans had taken the necessary first steps to ensure that future generations of leaders would receive the Western tradition of learning. In "The Laws, Liberties and Orders of Harvard College" the direct ties to the English university of the Reformation, specifically Cambridge, are clearly observable. The Greco-Roman tradition of the liberal arts, classical literature, the Aristotelian philosophies, theological studies, and the concern for the moral as well as intellectual well-being of the students are all present in this document.

The Laws, Liberties, and Orders of Harvard College, confirmed by the Overseers and President of the College in the years 1642, 1643, 1644, 1645, and 1646, and published to the Scholars for the perpetual preservation of their welfare and government.

1. When any scholar is able to read Tully, or such like classical Latin author *extempore*, and make and speak true Latin in verse and prose *suo (ut aiunt) Marte*, and decline perfectly the paradigms of nouns and verbs

Henry Barnard (ed.), The American Journal of Education (Hartford: Office of the American Journal of Education, 1877), XXVII, 140–41.

in the Greek tongue, then may he be admitted into the College, nor shall any claim admission before such qualifications.

2. Every one shall consider the main end of his life and studies, to know God and Jesus Christ, which is eternal life. John xvii. 3.

3. Seeing the Lord giveth wisdom, every one shall seriously, by prayer in secret, seek wisdom of Him. Proverbs ii. 2, 3, &c.

4. Every one shall so exercise himself in reading the Scriptures twice a day, that they be ready to give an account of their proficiency therein, both in theoretical observations of language and logic, and in practical and spiritual truths, as their Tutor shall require, according to their several abilities respectively, seeing the entrance of the word giveth light, &c. Psalm cxix. 130.

5. In the public church assembly, they shall carefully shun all gestures that show any contempt or neglect of God's ordinances, and be ready to give an account to their Tutors of their profiting, and to use the helps of storing themselves with knowledge, as their Tutors shall direct them. And all Sophisters and Bachelors (until themselves make common place) shall publicly repeat sermons in the Hall, whenever they are called forth.

6. They shall eschew all profanation of God's holy name, attributes, word, ordinances, and times of worship; and study, with reverence and love, carefully to retain God and his truth in their minds.

7. They shall honor as their parents, magistrates, elders, tutors, and aged persons, by being silent in their presence (except they be called on to answer), not gainsaying; showing all those laudable expressions of honor and reverence in their presence that are in use, as bowing before them, standing uncovered, or the like.

8. They shall be slow to speak, and eschew not only oaths, lies, and uncertain rumors, but likewise all idle, foolish, bitter scoffing, frothy, wanton words, and offensive gestures.

9. None shall pragmatically intrude or intermeddle in other men's affairs.

10. During their residence they shall studiously redeem their time, observe the generally appointed hours for all the scholars, and the special hour for their own lecture, and then diligently attend the lectures, without any disturbances by word or gesture; and, if of any thing they doubt, they shall inquire of their fellows, or in case of non-resolution, modestly of their Tutors.

11. None shall, under any pretence whatsoever, frequent the company and society of such men as lead an ungirt and dissolute life. Neither shall any, without the license of the Overseers of the College, be of the artillery or trainband. Nor shall any, without the license of the Overseers of the College, his Tutor's leave, or, in his absence, the call of parents or guardians, go out to another town.

12. No scholar shall buy, sell, or exchange any thing, to the value of sixpence, without the allowance of his parents, guardians, or Tutor's; and whosoever is found to have sold or bought any such things without acquainting their tutors or parents, shall forfeit the value of the commodity, or the restoring of it, according to the discretion of the President.

13. The scholars shall never use their mother tongue, except that in public exercises of oratory, or such like, they be called to make them in English.

14. If any scholar, being in health, shall be absent from prayers or lectures, except in case of urgent necessity, or by the leave of his Tutor, he shall be liable to admonition (or such punishment as the President shall think meet), if he offended above once a week.

15. Every scholar shall be called by his surname only, till he be invested with his first degree, except he be a fellow commoner, or knight's eldest son, or of superior nobility.

16. No scholar shall, under any pretence of recreation or other cause whatever (unless foreshowed and allowed by the President or his Tutor), be absent from his studies or appointed exercises, above an hour at morning bever, half an hour at afternoon bever, an hour and a half at dinner, and so long at supper.

17. If any scholar shall transgress any of the laws of God, or the House, out of perverseness, or apparent negligence, after twice admonition, he shall be liable, if not *adultus*, to correction; if *adultus*, his name shall be given up to the Overseers of the College, that he may be publicly dealt with after the desert of his fault; but in greater offences such gradual proceeding shall not be exercised.

18. Every scholar, that in proof is found able to read the original of the Old and New Testament into the Latin tongue, and to resolve them logically, withal being of honest life and conversation, and at any public act hath the approbation of the Overseers and Master of the College, may be invested with his first degree.

19. Every scholar, that giveth up in writing a synopsis or summary of Logic, Natural and Moral Philosophy, Arithmetic, Geometry, and Astronomy, and is ready to defend his theses or positions, withal skilled in the originals as aforesaid, and still continues honest and studious, at any public act after trial he shall be capable of the second degree, of Master of Arts.

Sect. 1. Forasmuch as the good education of children is of singular

Grammar school and college in the seventeenth century were meant for the few. It was initially expected that the vast majority of children would receive the rudiments of Christian education in the home. However, the apparent failure of many parents and masters of apprentices to carry out their educational responsibilities led to legislative action in 1642.

behoof and benefit to any commonwealth, and whereas many parents and masters are too indulgent and negligent of their duty in that kind:

It is ordered, that the selectmen of every town, in the several precincts and quarters where they dwell, shall have a vigilant eye over their brethren and neighbours, to see, first that none of them shall suffer so much barbarism in any of their families, as not to endeavour to teach, by themselves or others, their children and apprentices, so much learning, as may enable them perfectly to read the English tongue, and knowledge of the capital laws: upon penalty of twenty shillings for each neglect therein.

Also that all masters of families do once a week (at the least) catechise their children and servants in the grounds and principles of religion; and if any be unable to do so much, that then at the least they procure such children and apprentices to learn some short orthodox catechism without book, that they may be able to answer unto the questions that shall be propounded to them out of such catechism, by their parents or masters, or any of the selectmen when they shall call them to a trial, of what they have learned in that kind.

And farther that all parents and masters do breed and bring up their children and apprentices in some honest lawful calling, labour or employment, either in husbandry or some other trade, profitable for themselves and the commonwealth, if they will not or cannot train them up in learning, to fit them for higher employments.

And if any of the selectmen, after admonition by them given to such masters of families, shall find them still negligent of their duty in the particulars aforementioned, whereby children and servants become rude, stubborn, and unruly: the said selectmen with the help of two magistrates, or the next county court for that shire, shall take such children or apprentices from them, and place them with some masters for years, (boys till they come to twenty-one, and girls eighteen years of age complete) which will more strictly look unto, and force them to submit unto government, according to the rules of this order, if by fair means and former instructions they will not be drawn unto it. [May, 1642.]

Despite powers granted to local authorities to enforce the law of 1642, parents and masters continued to neglect the education of their children. Threats and fines could not compensate for the lack of time and facilities necessary to carry out the law's requirements. Both were at a premium in the frontier

The Charter and General Laws of the Colony and Province of Massachusetts Bay (Boston: T. B. Waite and Co., 1814), pp. 73–74.

environment. Clearly there was a need for institutionalized education, for schools. In 1647, the Massachusetts legislature responded with the historic "Deluder Satan Act." Within its provisions were principles that would serve two centuries later as a foundation for the establishment of a system of nonsectarian public education: the state could require the education of children; local governments could be required to establish, supervise, and maintain schools; public funds could be used to support public schools.

SECT. 1. It being one chief project of [the old deluder] Satan to keep men from the knowledge of the scripture, as in former times keeping them in unknown tongues, so in these latter times by persuading from the use of tongues, that so at least the true sense and meaning of the original might be clouded and corrupted with false glosses of deceivers; to the end that learning may not be buried in the graves of our forefathers, in church and commonwealth, the Lord assisting our endeavours:

It is therefore ordered by this court and authority thereof; that every township within this jurisdiction, after the Lord hath increased them to the number of fifty householders, shall then forthwith appoint one within their towns to teach all such children as shall resort to him to write and read, whose wages shall be paid either by the parents or masters of such children, or by the inhabitants in general, by way of supply, as the major part of those that order the prudentials of the town shall appoint: provided that those who send their children be not oppressed by paying much more than they can have them taught for in other towns.

SECT. 2. And it is further ordered, that where any town shall increase to the number of one hundred families or householders, they shall set up a grammar school, the master thereof being able to instruct youth so far as they may be fitted for the university: and if any town neglect the performance hereof above one year, then every such town shall pay five pounds per annum to the next such school, till they shall perform this order. [May, 1647.]

A primary function of seventeenth-century education, whether primary or collegiate, was to strengthen the ties of children to the faith of their fathers. In all colonies school laws, methods, and materials were designed to accomplish this task. In 1671, the following was enacted in Massachusetts:

Forasmuch as it greatly concerns the welfare of this country, that the youth thereof be educated, not only in good literature, but in sound doctrine:

The Charter and General Laws, op. cit., *p. 186.*

This court doth therefore commend it to the serious consideration and special care of our overseers of the college, and the selectmen in the several towns, not to admit or suffer any such to be continued in the office or place of teaching, educating, or instructing youth or children in the college or schools, that have manifested themselves unsound in the faith, or scandalous in their lives, and have not given satisfaction according to the rules of Christ.

Further testimony of the religious character of the Massachusetts "public" schools is found in Clifton Johnson's, Old Time Schools and School-books.

We get suggestive glimpses of the routine of the early schools in the Dorchester school rules of 1645, which provided that for seven months in the warmer part of the year the master should every day begin to teach at seven o'clock in the morning and dismiss the scholars at five in the afternoon, while in the colder and darker months of the remainder of the year he was to begin at eight and close at four. There was to be a midday intermission from eleven to one, except on Monday, when the master

shall call his scholars together between twelve and one of the clock to examine them what they have learned, at which time also he shall take notice of any misdemeanor or outrage that any of his scholars shall have committed on the sabbath, to the end that at some convenient time due admonition and correction may be administered.

He shall diligently instruct both in humane and good literature, and likewise in point of good manners and dutiful behavior towards all, especially their superiors. Every day of the week at two of the clock in the afternoon, he shall catechise his scholars in the principles of the Christian religion.

He shall faithfully do his best to benefit his scholars, and not remain away from school unless necessary. He shall equally and impartially teach such as are placed in his care, no matter whether their parents be poor or rich. (A necessary warning, for the well-to-do and influential were given a preference in most affairs of the times.)

It is to be a chief part of the schoolmaster's religious care to commend his scholars and his labors amongst them unto God by prayer morning and evening taking care that his scholars do reverently attend during the same.

The rod of correction is a rule of God necessary sometimes to be used upon children. The schoolmaster shall have full power to punish all or any of his scholars, no matter who they are. No parent or other person living in the place shall go about to hinder the master in this. But if any parent or others shall think there is just cause for complaint against the master for too much severity, they shall have liberty to tell him so in friendly and loving way.

The emphasis laid on religious instruction in these rules was very

Clifton Johnson, Old Time Schools and School-books *(New York: The Macmillan Co., 1904), pp. 10–13.*

characteristic of the colonial period. The children were perpetually enveloped, week-days and Sundays, in an atmosphere saturated with religious forms, services, ideas, and language. To illustrate how omnipresent this religious atmosphere was, I cannot do better than to cite the occasion when Judge Sewell found that the spout which conducted the rain water from his roof did not perform its office. After patient searching, a ball belonging to the Sewell children was discovered lodged in the spout. Thereupon the father sent for the minister and had a season of prayer with his boys, that their mischief or carelessness might be set in its proper aspect and that the event might be sanctified to their spiritual good. Powers of darkness and of light were struggling for the possession of every youthful soul, and it was the duty of parents, ministers, and teachers to lose no opportunity to pluck the children as brands from the burning.

The efforts to make the children religious were not by any means uniformly successful. No doubt the insistence of the elders on the solemnities often deadened their charges' sensibilities. At any rate, character and conduct among the young people were far from perfect. A committee appointed to see if the instruction at Harvard remained true to its early adopted motto, *For Christ and the Church*, reported that the Greek Catechism was recited regularly by the freshmen, and that Wollebius's *System of Divinity* was diligently pursued by the other classes, while on Saturday evening, in the presence of the president, the students repeated the sermon of the foregoing Sabbath. "Yet the committee are compelled to lament the continued prevalence of several immoralities, particularly stealing, lying, swearing, idleness, picking of locks, and too frequent use of strong drink."

Boys began to attend the grammar schools when they were seven or eight years of age, and now and then a youngster entered the Boston Latin School no older than six and one-half. Not infrequently the boys had by that time made considerable progress in Latin, and sometimes the merest infants were taught by doting parents to read this learned language as soon as they were taught to read English. Precocity was encouraged, not alone by intelligent parents, but by leading writers and thinkers. A good example of what was expected of the little ones is furnished by Isaac Watts's *The Young Childs' Catechism*. The first half of it was designed for learners of "Three or Four Years Old," and the questions for these beginners included such as

> Have you learnt to know who God is?
> What muft you do to efcape God's Anger, which your Sins have deferved?
> What muft become of you if you are wicked?

The answer to the last is, "If I am wicked, I fhall be fent down to everlafting Fire in Hell among wicked and miferable creatures."

回 2. Education in the Middle Colonies: Sponsorship by Religious and Cultural Groups

Among the several religious and national groups to settle in the Middle Colonies were German Mennonites. The following excerpt from the almanac of Christopher Saur relates the solicitude of a "new-comer" to Pennsylvania for the education of his children and reveals the good fortune of the Mennonites in having in their midst two exceptionally fine teachers. The teachers to whom he referred were Ludwig Hoecker and Christopher Dock.

"*New-Comer.* A matter that is of very great importance to me is, that, in Germany, one is able to send his children to school to have them instructed in reading and writing. Here it is well nigh impossible to get such instruction; especially, where people live so far apart. O, how fortunate are they who have access to a good teacher by whom the children are well taught and trained!

"*Inhabitant.* It is true. On that account many children living on our frontiers grow up like trees. But since the conditions are such that few people live in cities and villages as they do in Germany, it is natural that one meets with certain inconveniences. Where is there a place in this world where one does not meet with some objectionable features during his natural life?

"*New-Comer.* But this is an exceptional want, for if children are thus brought up in ignorance it is an injury to their soul's welfare,—an eternal injury.

"*Inhabitant.* That is true, but, alas, how few good schoolmasters there are! I myself have had many and known many, but few good ones have I seen. Yet, I remember two, in my life-time, who had many good qualities. The one spent most of his time in secret prayer and heartfelt sighing that God might direct and keep the hearts and minds of his pupils. He taught them their letters faithfully. He observed also their natural dispositions. If he found the child ambitious, he would praise it so that it learned its lessons fairly well. He would promise that it should yet lead the class, but he asked God to take the Devil's haughtiness out of the child's heart, to convert it and give it the lowly

Martin G. Brunbaugh (ed.), The Life and Works of Christopher Dock *(Philadelphia: J. P. Lippincott Co., 1908), pp. 18–20.*

spirit of Jesus. After it had reached the head of the class he would tell it alone and in private that haughtiness came from the Devil, but humility was a quality of Christ's spirit for which the child should frequently and heartily join him in prayer to God. Thus he kept such children in his love. To those who were miserly he frequently gave a penny when they studied diligently and if they admired their gift he would tell them that money was the root of all evil, pointing out examples to them. He described for them deceptive riches and the subsequent disappointment if man is not rich in godly things. To the voluptuous and "Lecker-Maüler"[1] he sometimes gave a sugar pretzel, when they learned well. But he also told them that luxuriousness was a sin, that those who belonged to Christ crucified the flesh with its lusts and evil desires. He impressed them so earnestly with these maxims that almost all the pupils loved him. If any failed in the performance of duty, he would say: 'I no longer love you,' (Ich habe dich nicht mehr Lieb). Then they wept until he comforted them. The ill-intentioned, who were not affected by the promise of a penny or a cooky, he threatened with whipping. These then studied out of fear. With some he had to use the rod, but in each case he endeavored, first of all, to win their favor and thus secure obedience through love that they might not only learn their letters, but that they might be able to seek, find and know Jesus Himself.

"I remember still another one who, out of the love of God, loved his pupils as if they all were his own children. They, in turn, loved him dearly. Whenever he was obliged to reprove the children for ill-behavior, he did so with grievous words coming from his wounded heart, so that he frequently softened their hearts; and when they were about to cry, tears crept into his eyes. He studied out many plans so that he might not need to resort to the rod. On going to and from school the children went quietly and orderly without stopping to play, loiter and quarrel. The children of the poor he taught as willingly without pay as he taught others for pay. Those who learned to write, he induced to correspond with one another. The pupils were required to show him the letters and he pointed out for them the places where improvements should be made. He also told them that this was no ordinary matter. For those who could not compose a letter, he set copies so that they might apply their minds to good thoughts for the improvement of their souls. He regarded it indifferently whether he received the tuition fees or not and did not treasure up for himself anything but a good name and a clear conscience.

"*New-Comer.* Such Schoolmasters are few in number, and here in the woods one must be satisfied if only they teach the children to read and

---

[1] *Sweet-toothed, dainty-mouthed.*

write; and it is very deplorable that, during the winter in severe weather, young and tender children cannot well be sent to schools a great distance from home. In the summer time one needs the children at home to work, and here in the woods the schools are closed during the summer. I have often thought that this was a great need in this land and I know of no remedy to suggest."

Christopher Dock came to Pennsylvania sometime between 1710 and 1714. Though he originally intended to establish himself as a farmer, most of his years in the colony were devoted to teaching in German Mennonite schools. In his book Schul-Ordnung [*School Management*] *Dock described his school, its curriculum and methods. As in all elementary education of the period the content was heavily religious. However, the methods of discipline he advocated were far from typical.*

FROM THE *SCHUL-ORDNUNG*

This is the information asked for regarding the way I keep the children quiet, but it is by no means my intention to force this method upon any one else. Each must arrange his affairs in the best way that he can. But if my management written here by request and not from choice, should be in any way objected to, because it differs from that of Germany and other places, I will say in defense, that conditions here are different. Among the free inhabitants of Pennsylvania schools are differently constituted from those in Germany. For a schoolmaster there is definitely installed by the government, and the common man cannot readily remove him, hence he is in no great danger if he is too hard with children. Although I freely confess, even if I were thus installed by high authorities, I should still feel that the power to be hard with children was given me for their good. Now experience teaches that a timid child is harmed rather than benefited by harsh words or much application of the rod, and to improve it, other means must be employed. Likewise a stupid child is only harmed. A child that is treated to too much flogging at home is not benefited by it at school, but it is made still worse. If such children are to be helped, it must happen through other means.

A stubborn child that does not fear to do wrong needs to be sharply punished with the rod, and also earnestly reminded of God's word, in the hope of reaching the heart. But the timid and stupid must be reached by other means that make them more free in spirit and more desirous to learn. When the children are brought thus far it is no longer difficult for teacher or pupil, and my colleagues will agree with me that the souls put in our keeping are very precious. We will be called

Brumbaugh, op. cit., *pp. 122–23.*

to account for them by our God, and though we have the power to punish they would, I think, agree with me in saying that it is preferable to bring the children to do things from a love of doing than to force them by the rod. The words "Thou shalt and must" and the words "I obey gladly" are very different in sound. For the latter the master needs no rod, and it sounds sweeter and is easier to account for. In Psalm cx, 3, it is written: "Thy people shall be willing in the day of thy power, in the beauties of holiness." Now what is done willingly in body or soul is not in need of a rod. Again in Psalm xxxii, 8, 9, we read: "I will instruct thee and teach thee in the way which thou shalt go: I will guide thee with mine eye. Be ye not as the horse or as the mule, which have no understanding; whose mouth must be held in with bit and bridle, lest they come near unto thee." Here again we see that they who allow themselves to be taught and led with the eye have no need of a bit and a bridle. . . .

回   3. Education Among the Virginia Aristocracy

In the late seventeenth and eighteenth centuries the plantation aristocracy of the South emerged with all the accoutrements that have since been associated with it. Not the least of these was the family tutor, for included as part of the grand image of a gentlemanly society was the proper education of its children. Philip Vickers Fithian was a young man from New Jersey who, shortly after graduating from Princeton, was employed by Robert Carter of Nominy Hall as a tutor for his children. Fithian's letters and journal reveal much about the education of a Virginian planter's children and the position of learning and teachers in plantation society.

LETTER TO THE REVEREND ENOCH GREEN, DECEMBER 1, 1773

Rev'd Sir.

As you desired I may not omit to inform you; so far as I can by a letter, of the business in which I am now engaged, it would indeed be vastly agreeable to me if it was in my power to give you particular intelligence concerning the state and plan of my employment here.

John Rogers Williams (ed.), Philip Vickers Fithian, Journal and Letters, 1767–1774 *(Princeton, N.J.: The University Library, 1900), pp. 278–80.*

I set out from home the 20th of Oct[r] and arrived at the Hon: Robert Carters, of Nominy, in Westmorland County, the 28th. I began to teach his children the first of November. He has two sons, and one Nephew; the oldest Son is turned of seventeen, and is reading Salust and the greek grammer; the others are about fourteen, and in english grammer, and Arithmetic. He has besides five daughters which I am to teach english, the eldest is turned of fifteen, and is reading the spectator; she is employed two days in every week in learning to play the Forte-Piana, and Harpsichord——The others are smaller, and learning to read and spell. M[r] Carter is one of the Councellors in the general court at Williamsburg, and posesst of as great, perhaps the clearest fortune according to the estimation of people here, of any man in Virginia. He seems to be a good scholar, even in classical learning, and is remarkable one in english grammar; and notwithstanding his rank, which in general seems to countenance indulgence to children, both himself and M[rs] Carter have a manner of instructing and dealing with children far superior, I may say it with confidence, to any I have ever seen, in any place, or in any family. They keep them in perfect subjection to themselves, and never pass over an occasion of reproof; and I blush for many of my acquaintances when I say that the children are more kind and complaisant to the servants who constantly attend them than we are to our superiors in age and condition. M[r] Carter has an overgrown library of Books of which he allows me the free use. It consists of a general collection of law books, all the Latin and Greek Classicks, vast number of books on Divinity chiefly by writers who are of the established Religion; he has the works of almost all the late famous writers, as Locke, Addison, Young, Pope, Swift, Dryden, &c. in Short, Sir, to speak moderately, he has more than eight times your number—— His eldest Son,[1] who seems to be a Boy of genius and application is to be sent to Cambridge University, but I believe will go through a course either in Philadelphia or Princeton College first. As to what is commonly said concerning Virginia that it is difficult to avoid being corrupted with the manners of the people, I believe it is founded wholly in a mistaken notion that persons must, when here frequent all promiscuous assemblies; but this is so far from truth that any one who does practise it, tho' he is accused of no crime, loses at once his character; so that either the manners have been lately changed, or the report is false, for he seems now to be best esteemed and most applauded who attends to his business, whatever it be, with the greatest diligence. I believe the virginians have of late altered their manner very much, for they begin to find that their estates by even small

[1] *Ben Carter did not take a course at Princeton; he is said to have died in youth, probably before entering any college, as it is shown by letters of Fithian that he was in very delicate health in 1775.*

extravagance, decline, and grow involved with debt, this seems to be the spring which induces the People of fortune who are pattern of all behaviour here, to be frugal, and moderate. You may expect me at home by the permission of Providence the latter end of april next, or the beginning of may; and as I proposed I shall present my exercises for the examination of the presbytery; and if they think proper I shall gladly accept of a license in the fall: I must beg your favour to mention me to such of my acquaintances in Deerfield as you think proper, but especially to M˚ Green, Miss *Betsy*, your family, and M˚ Pecks ———I must also beg you to transmit so much of this intelligence to M˚ Hunter as that my relations in Greenwich may know that I am through the mercy of heaven in good health. I beg, Sir, you will not fail to write, and let it be known to M˚ Hunter, that a Letter will come as secure by the Post as from Cohansie to Philadelphia; the Letters are to be directed to me thus, To M˚ Philip V. Fithian at M˚ *Carters* of Nominy, to be left at Hobes Hole.

I am, Sir, yours

PHILIP V. FITHIAN.

FROM THE JOURNAL

Sunday 31.

Rode to Church six miles———Heard Mr. Gibbern preach on Felixes trembling at Pauls Sermon.

Monday Novem˚ 1st.

We began School———The School consists of eight——— Two of M˚ Carters Sons———One Nephew———And five Daughters——— The eldest Son is reading Salust: Gramatical Exercises, and latin Grammer———The second Son is reading english Grammar & Reading English: Writing and Cyphering in Subtraction——— The Nephew is Reading and Writing as above; and Ciphering in Reduction——— The eldest daughter is Reading the Spectator; Writing; & beginning to Cypher——— The second is reading next out of the Spelling-Book, and beginning to write——— The next is reading in the Spelling-Book ———the fourth is Spelling in the beginning of the Spelling-Book ——— And the last is beginning her letters.

Teusday 1.

Busy in School——— begun to read Pictete [Benedict Pictet, *Theologia Christiana*, 1696].

Williams, op. cit., *pp. 50–52.*

Wednesday 3.

   Busy in School.

Thursday 4.

   Busy in School——To day the two eldest daughters, and second Son attended the Dancing School.

Fryday 5.

   Busy in School.

Saturday 6.

   Catechised in School til twelve——the Children. And dismissed them. Afternoon rode with Ben Carter to the Bank of Potowmack—8 miles——Returned in the evening——Expence Ferriage *1/.*

Sunday 7.

   Rode to Ucomico Church——8 miles——Heard Parson Smith. He shewed to us the uncertainty of Riches, and their Insufficiency to make us happy——Dined at Captain Walkers; With Parson Smith; his wife; her Sister, a young Lady; &c——Returned in the Evening.

Monday 8.

   Busy in School——Finished reading the first, and begun to read the Second Book of Pictetes Theology. Expence to Boy */4.*

Teusday 9.

   Busy in School.

Wednesday 10.

   Busy in School——The eldest Daughter taken off by her teacher in Music: M.ʳ Stadley who is learning her to play the *Forte-piano.*

Thursday 11.

   Rose by seven——Busy in School——Miss Carter still absent.

Fryday 12.

   Rose by Seven——Ben begun his Greek Grammar——Three in the afternoon M.ʳ Carter returned from *Williamsburg.* He seems to be agreeable, discreet, and sensible——He informed me more particularly concerning his desire as to the Instruction of his Children.

Saturday 13.

Catechised the Children and dismissed them about Eleven————
Read in Pictete————and proceeded in writing my Sermon for the
Presbytery————Expence for my Horse *1/3.*

Sunday 14.

Rode to Nominy Church about six Miles————the day cold————
Parson Smith preached————"What shall a man be profited" &c.
Rode home after Sermon————Dined at M.ͬ Carters to day M.ͬˢ
Turbuville, Miss Jenny Corbin, and M.ͬ Cunningham a young
Merchant.

*The following is an excerpt from a letter written by Fithian on August 12,
1774, to John Peck, who was about to succeed him as tutor at Nominy Hall.*

The very Slaves in some families here, could not be bought under
30000£. Such amazing property, no matter how deep it is involved,
blows up the owners to an imagination, which is visible in all, but in
various degrees according to their respective virtue, that they are
exalted as much above other Men in worth & precedency, as blind
stupid fortune has made a difference in their property; excepting
always the value they put upon posts of honour, & mental acquirements
————For example, if you should travel through this Colony, with a
well-confirmed testimonial of your having finished with Credit a Course
of studies at Nassau-Hall; you would be rated, without any more
questions asked, either about your family, your Estate, your business,
or your intention, at 10,000£; and you might come, & go, & converse,
& keep company, according to this value; and you would be despised
and slighted if you rated yourself a farthing cheaper. But when I am
giving directions to you from an expectation that you will be shortly a
resident here, altho you have gone through a College Course, & for
anything I know, have never written a Libel, nor stolen a Turkey, yet I
think myself in duty bound to advise you, lest some powdered Coxcomb
should reproach your education, to cheapen your price about 5000£;
because any young Gentleman travelling through the Colony, as I said
before, is presumed to be acquianted with Dancing, Boxing, playing
the Fiddle, & Small-Sword, & Cards. Several of which you was only
entering upon, when I left New-Jersey; towards the Close of last year;
and if you stay here any time your Barrenness in these must be detected. I
will, however, allow, that in the Family where you act as tutor you place
yourself, according to your most acute Calculation, at a perfect

Williams, op. cit., *pp. 286–89.*

equidistance between the father & the eldest Son. Or let the same distance be observed in every article of behaviour between you & the eldest Son, as there ought to be, by the latest & most approved precepts of Moral-Philosophy, between the eldest Son & his next youngest Brother. But whenever you go from Home, where you are to act on your own footing, either to a Ball; or to a *Horse-Race,* or to a *Cock-Fight,* or to a *Fish-Feast,* I advise that you rate yourself very low & if you bett at all, remember that 10,000£ in Reputation & learning does not amount to a handfull of Shillings in ready Cash!————One considerable advantage which you promise yourself by coming to this Colony is to extend the Limits of your acquaintance; this is laudable, & if you have enough of prudence & firmness, it will be a singular advantage————Yet attempt slowly & with the most Jealous Circumspection————If you fix your familiarity wrong in a single instance, you are in danger of total, if not immediate ruin————You come here, it is true, with an intention to teach, but you ought likewise to have an inclination to learn. At any rate I solemnly injoin it upon you, that you never suffer the Spirit of a Pedagogue to attend you without the walls of your little Seminary. In all promiscuous Company be as silent & attentive as Decency will allow you, for you have nothing to communicate, which such company, will hear with pleasure, but you may learn many things which, in after life, will do you singular service. ————In regard to Company in general, if you think it worth your while to attend to my example, I can easily instruct you in the manner of my Conduct in this respect. I commonly attend Church; and often, at the request of Gentlemen, after Service according to the custom, dine abroad on Sunday————I seldom fail, when invited by Mr & Mrs *Carter,* of going out with them; but I make it a point, however strongly solicited to the contrary, to return with them too———— Except in one of these cases, I seldom go out, but with a valuable variety of books I live according to Horace's direction. & love "Secretum Iter et fallentis Semita Vitæ." Close retirement and a life by Stealth. The last direction I shall venture to mention on this head, is, that you abstain totally from Women. What I would have you understand from this, is, that by a train of faultless conduct in the whole course of your tutorship, you make every Lady within the Sphere of your acquaintance, who is between twelve & forty years of age, so much pleased with your person, & so satisfied as to your ability in the capacity of a Teacher; & in short, fully convinced, that, from a principle of Duty you have, both by night and by day endeavoured to acquit yourself honourably, in the Character of a Tutor; & that on this account, you have their free and hearty consent, without making any manner of demand upon you, either to stay longer in the County with them, which they would choose, or whenever your business calls you away, that they may not have it in their Power either by charms or Justice to detain you, & when you must leave them, have their sincere wishes & constant prayers for Length of days & much prosperity, I therefore beg that you will attend literally to this advice, & abstain totally from Women. . . .

Peck clearly did not follow the last bit of advice. He married Carter's daughter.

回 4. Benjamin Franklin: Education for Utility

In his own day Benjamin Franklin came to represent the pinnacle of what could be achieved in the untamed New World by a man willing to exercise his wits and work tirelessly. His arrival at the French court during the Revolution, dressed in homespun, hair hanging down to his shoulders, attests to his shrewd recognition of his image as rustic America's finest product. Though Franklin exploited this romantic view to endear himself and the American cause to the French, he was by no means perpetrating a fraud. Franklin had in fact gained success without benefit of extensive formal education. In his Autobiography *he told of his early education.*

My elder brothers were all put apprentices to different trades. I was put to the grammar-school at eight years of age, my father intending to devote me, as the tithe of his sons, to the service of the Church. My early readiness in learning to read (which must have been very early, as I do not remember when I could not read), and the opinion of all his friends, that I should certainly make a good scholar, encouraged him in this purpose of his. My Uncle Benjamin, too, approved of it, and proposed to give me all his short-hand volumes of sermons, I suppose as a stock to set up with, if I would learn his character. I continued, however, at the grammar-school not quite one year, though in that time I had risen gradually from the middle of the class of that year to be the head of it, and farther, was removed into the next class above it, in order to go with that into the third at the end of the year. But my father, in the meantime, from a view of the expense of a college education, which having so large a family he could not well afford, and the mean living many so educated were afterwards able to obtain—reasons that he gave to his friends in my hearing—altered his first intention, took me from the grammar-school, and sent me to a school for writing and

Barnard, op. cit., *XXVII, 402–03, 406–07.*

arithmetic, kept by a then famous man, Mr. George Brownell, very successful in his profession generally, and that by mild, encouraging methods. Under him I acquired fair writing pretty soon, but I failed in the arithmetic, and made no progress in it. At ten years old I was taken home to assist my father in his business, which was that of a tallow-chandler and soap-boiler; a business he was not bred to, but had assumed on his arrival in New England, and on finding his dying trade would not maintain his family, being in little request. Accordingly, I was employed in cutting wick for the candles, filling the dipping mold and the molds for cast candles, attending the shop, going of errands, etc.

I disliked the trade, and had a strong inclination for the sea, but my father declared against it; however, living near the water, I was much in and about it, learnt early to swim well, and to manage boats; and when in a boat or canoe with other boys, I was commonly allowed to govern, especially in any case of difficulty; and upon other occasions I was generally a leader among the boys, and sometimes led them into scrapes, of which I will mention one instance, as it shows an early projecting public spirit, though not then justly conducted.

There was a salt-marsh that bounded part of the mill-pond, on the edge of which, at high water, we used to stand to fish for minnows. By much tramping, we had made it a mere quagmire. My proposal was to build a wharf there fit for us to stand upon, and I showed my comrades a large heap of stones, which were intended for a new house near the marsh, and which would very well suit our purpose. Accordingly, in the evening, when the workmen were gone, I assembled a number of my playfellows, and working with them diligently like so many emmets, sometimes two or three to a stone, we brought them all away and built our little wharf. The next morning the workmen were surprised at missing the stones, which were found in our wharf. Inquiry was made after the removers; we were discovered and complained of; several of us were corrected by our fathers; and, though I pleaded the usefulness of the work, mine convinced me that nothing was useful which was not honest.

*   *   *   *   *

. . . My father's little library consisted chiefly of books in polemic divinity, most of which I read, and have since often regretted that, at a time when I had such a thirst for knowledge, more proper books had not fallen in my way, since it was now resolved I should not be a clergyman. Plutarch's Lives there was in which I read abundantly, and I still think that time spent to great advantage. There was also a book of De Foe's, called an Essay on Projects, and another of Dr. Mather's, called Essays to do Good, which perhaps gave me a turn of thinking that had an influence on some of the principal future events of my life.

This bookish inclination at length determined my father to make me a printer, though he had already one son (James) of that profession. In 1717 my brother James returned from England with a press and letters to set up his business in Boston. I liked it much better than that of my father, but still had a hankering for the sea. To prevent the apprehended effect of such an inclination, my father was impatient to have me bound to my brother. I stood out some time, but at last was persuaded, and signed the indentures when I was yet but twelve years old. I was to serve as an apprentice till I was twenty-one years of age, only I was to be allowed journeyman's wages during the last year. In a little time I made great proficiency in the business, and became a useful hand to my brother. I now had access to better books. An acquaintance with the apprentices of booksellers enabled me sometimes to borrow a small one, which I was careful to return soon and clean. Often I sat up in my room reading the greatest part of the night, when the book was borrowed in the evening to be returned early in the morning, lest it should be missed or wanted.

About this time I met with an old volume of the *Spectator*. It was the third. I had never before seen any of them. I bought it, read it over and over, and was much delighted with it. I thought the writing excellent, and wished, if possible, to imitate it. With this view I took some of the papers, and, making short hints of the sentiment in each sentence, laid them by a few days, and then, without looking at the book, tried to complete the papers again, by expressing each hinted sentiment at length, and as fully as it had been expressed before, in any suitable words that should come to hand. Then I compared my *Spectator* with the original, discovered some of my faults, and corrected them. But I found I wanted a stock of words, or a readiness in recollecting and using them, which I thought I should have acquired before that time if I had gone on making verses; since the continual occasion for words of the same import, but of different length, to suit the measure, or of different sound for the rhyme, would have laid me under a constant necessity of searching for variety, and also have tended to fix that variety in my mind, and make me master of it. Therefore I took some of the tales and turned them into verse; and, after a time, when I had pretty well forgotten the prose, turned them back again.

And now it was that, being on some occasion made ashamed of my ignorance in figures, which I had twice failed in learning when at school, I took Cocker's book of Arithmetic, and went through the whole by myself with great ease. I also read Seller's and Shermy's books of Navigation, and became acquainted with the little geometry they contain; but never proceeded far in that science. And I read about this time, Locke *on Human Understanding*, and the *Art of Thinking*, by Messrs. du Port Royal.

While I was intent on improving my language, I met with an English grammar (I think it was Greenwood's), at the end of which there were two little sketches of the arts of rhetoric and logic, the latter finishing with a specimen of a dispute in the Socratic method; and soon after I procured Xenophon's Memorable Things of Socrates, wherein there are many instances of the same method. I was charmed with it, adopted it, dropt my abrupt contradiction and positive argumentation, and put on the humble inquirer and doubter.

Franklin's own experiences led him to value practical knowledge above the classics as most beneficial to the young man who hoped to make his way in the world of business and commerce. His personal success in self-education encouraged him to espouse the method for others. In Poor Richard's Almanacs *and essays Franklin preached the doctrine of frugality and hard work. He established a self-improvement club called the "Junto" under whose auspices he and his friends exchanged books and explored such subjects as science, politics, and morals. He was instrumental in founding a subscription library of books printed exclusively in English and was a charter member of the American Philosophical Society, in many respects a prestigious "Junto". Perhaps his most ambitious project in the area of utilitarian education was to encourage the founding of an academy in which middle-class boys could receive an education appropriate to the lives they were to lead. In 1749, Franklin published and distributed with his newspaper,* The Pennsylvania Gazette, *an essay entitled "Proposals Relating to the Education of Youth in Pennsylvania."*

ADVERTISEMENT TO THE READER

It has long been regretted as a misfortune to the youth of this province that we have no Academy in which they might receive the accomplishments of a regular education. The following paper of *Hints* towards forming a plan for that purpose, is so far approved by some public-spirited gentlemen, to whom it has been privately communicated, that they have directed a number of copies to be made by the press, and properly distributed, in order to obtain the sentiments and advice of men of learning, understanding, and experience in these matters; and have determined to use their interest and best endeavors to have the scheme, when completed, carried gradually into execution; in which they have reason to believe they shall have the hearty concurrence and assistance of many, who are well-wishers to their country. Those who incline to favor the design with their advice, either as to the parts of learning to be taught, the order of study, the method of teaching, the economy of the school, or any other matter of importance to the success of the undertaking, are desired to communicate their sentiments as soon as may be by letter, directed to B. Franklin, Printer, in Philadelphia.

Barnard, op. cit., pp. 441–44.

PROPOSED HINTS FOR AN ACADEMY

The good education of youth has been esteemed by wise men in all ages, as the surest foundation of the happiness both of private families and of commonwealths. Almost all governments have therefore made it a principal object of their attention to establish and endow with proper revenues such seminaries of learning, as might supply the succeeding age with men qualified to serve the public with honor to themselves and to their country.

Many of the first settlers of these provinces were men who had received a good education in Europe; and to their wisdom and good management we owe much of our present prosperity. But their hands were full, and they could not do all things. The present race are not thought to be generally of equal ability; for, though the American youth are allowed not to want capacity, yet the best capacities require cultivation; it being truly with them, as with the best ground, which, unless well tilled and sowed with profitable seed, produces only ranker weeds.

That we may obtain the advantages arising from an increase of knowledge, and prevent, as much as may be, the mischievous consequences that would attend a general ignorance among us, the following *hints* are offered towards forming a plan for the education of the youth of Pennsylvania, viz.:

A Charter

That some persons of leisure and public spirit apply for a charter, by which they may be incorporated, with power to erect an Academy for the education of youth, to govern the same, provide masters, make rules, receive donations, purchase lands, and to add to their number, from time to time, such other persons as they shall judge suitable.

Voluntary Action of Trustees

That the members of the corporation make it their pleasure, and in some degree their business, to visit the Academy often, encourage and countenance the youth, countenance and assist the masters, and by all means in their power advance the usefulness and reputation of the design; that they look on the students as in some sort their children, treat them with familiarity and affection, and, when they have behaved well, and gone through their studies, and are to enter the world, zealously unite, and make all the interest that can be made to establish them, whether in business, offices, marriages, of any other thing for their advantage, preferably to all other persons even of equal merit.

Building—Location—Equipment

That a house be provided for the Academy, if not in the town, not many miles from it; the situation high and dry, and, if it may be, not far from a river, having a garden, orchard, meadow, and a field or two.

That the house be furnished with a library if in the country (if in the town, the town libraries may serve), with maps of all countries, globes, some mathematical instruments, an apparatus for experiments in natural philosophy, and for mechanics; prints of all kinds, prospects, buildings, and machines.

Rector—Physical Training of Pupils

That the Rector be a man of good understanding, good morals, diligent and patient, learned in the languages and sciences, and a correct, pure speaker and writer of the English tongue; to have such tutors under him as shall be necessary.

That the boarding scholars diet together, plainly, temperately, and frugally.

That to keep them in health, and to strengthen and render active their bodies, they be frequently exercised in running, leaping, wrestling, and swimming.

That they have peculiar habits to distinguish them from other youth, if the Academy be in or near the town; for this, among other reasons, that their behavior may be the better observed.

Studies to be selected and Adapted

As to their studies, it would be well if they could be taught *everything* that is useful, and *everything* that is ornamental. But art is long, and their time is short. It is therefore proposed that they learn those things that are likely to be *most useful* and *most ornamental;* regard being had to the several professions for which they are intended.

Writing, Drawing, and Arithmetic

All should be taught to write a fair hand, and swift, as that is useful to all. And with it may be learned something of drawing, by imitation of prints, and some of the first principles of perspective. Arithmetic, accounts, and some of the first principles of geometry and astronomy.

English Language—Composition and Pronunciation

The English language might be taught by grammar, and reading some of our best authors (Tillotson, Addison, Pope, Algenon Sidney), having reference to clearness and conciseness of style, and distinct and emphatic pronunciation.

To form their style, they should be put on writing letters to each other, making abstracts of what they read, or writing the same things in their own words; telling or writing stories lately read, in their own expressions —all to be revised and corrected by the tutor, who should give his reasons, and explain the force and import of words.

To form their pronunciation, they may be put on making declamations, repeating speeches, and delivering orations; the tutor assisting at the rehearsals, teaching, advising, and correcting their accent.

Reading made Serviceable to all Useful Knowledge

If History (with Universal and National) be made a constant part of their reading, may not almost all kinds of useful knowledge be that way introduced to advantage, and with pleasure to the student? As

Chronology, by the help of charts and tables, fixing the dates of important events, and the epochs of famous men.

Ancient Customs, civil and religious, their origin and distinctive features by prints of medals and monuments.

Morality, by timely observations on the causes of the rise and fall of individuals and States—the advantages of temperance, order, frugality, industry, and perseverance.

Religion, the necessity of its principles to the public, and advantages to individuals, and the superiority of the Christian above all others, ancient or modern.

Politics, or the advantages of civil order and constitutions; the encouragement of industry, the protection of property, the encouragement of inventions, the necessity of good laws, and due execution of justice.

The power of oratory and logic on great historical occasions—governing, turning, and leading great bodies of mankind, armies, cities, and nations.

Discussions—Oral and Written

On historical occasions, questions of right and wrong, justice and injustice, will naturally arise, and may be put to youth, which they may debate in conversation and in writing. When they ardently desire victory, for the sake of the praise attending it, they will begin to feel the want, and be sensible of the use of *logic*, or the art of reasoning to *discover* truth, and of arguing to *defend* it, and *convince* adversaries. This would be the time to acquaint them with the principles of that art. Grotius, Puffendorff, and some other writers of the same kind, may be used to decide their disputes. Public disputes warm the imagination, whet the industry, and strengthen the natural abilities.

Foreign Languages—Ancient and Modern

When youth are told that the great men whose lives and actions they read in history spoke two of the best languages that ever were, the most expressive, copious, beautiful; and that the finest writings, the most correct compositions, the most perfect productions of human wit and wisdom, are in those languages which have endured for ages, and will endure while there are men; that no translation can do them justice, or give the pleasure found in reading the originals; that those languages contain all science; that one of them is become almost universal, being the language of learned men in all countries; and that to understand them is a distinguishing ornament; they may be thereby made desirous of learning those languages, and their industry sharpened in the acquisition of them. All intended for divinity should be taught the Latin and Greek; for physic, the Latin, Greek, and French; for law, the Latin and French; merchants, the French, German, and Spanish; and, though all should not be compelled to learn Latin, Greek, or the modern foreign languages, yet none that have an ardent desire to learn them should be refused; their English, arithmetic, and other studies absolutely necessary, not being neglected.

If the new *Universal History* were also read, it would give a connected idea of human affairs, so far as it goes, which should be followed by the best modern histories, particularly of our mother country; then of these colonies, which should be accompanied with observations on their rise, increase, use to Great Britain, encouragements and discouragements, the means to make them flourish, and secure their liberties.

Sciences of Observation and Experiment

With the history of men, times, and nations, should be read at proper hours or days, some of the best *histories of nature*, which would not only be delightful to youth, and furnish them with matter for their letters, as well as other history, but would afterwards be of great use to them, whether they are merchants, handicrafts, or divines; enabling the first the better to understand many commodities and drugs, the second to improve his trade or handicraft by new mixtures and materials, and the last to adorn his discourses by beautiful comparisons, and strengthen them by new proofs of divine providence. The conversation of all will be improved by it, as occasions frequently occur of making natural observations, which are instructive, agreeable, and entertaining in almost all companies. Natural history will also afford opportunities of introducing many observations, relating to the preservation of health, which may be afterwards of great use. Arbuthnot on Air and Ailment, Sanctorius on Perspiration, Lemery on Foods, and some others, may now be read, and a very little explanation will make them sufficiently intelligible to youth.

Gardening and Agriculture—Commerce—Mechanic Arts

While they are reading natural history, might not a little gardening, planting, grafting, and inoculating, be taught and practised; and now and then excursions made to the neighboring plantations of the best farmers, their methods observed and reasoned upon for the information of youth, the improvement of agriculture being useful to all, and skill in it no disparagement to any?

The *history of commerce,* of the invention of arts, rise of manufacturers, progress of trade, change of its seats, with the reasons and causes, may also be made entertaining to youth, and will be useful to all. And this with the accounts in other history of the prodigious force and effect of engines and machines used in war, will naturally introduce a desire to be instructed in mechanics, and to be informed of the principles of that art by which weak men perform such wonders, labor is saved, and manufactures expedited. This will be the time to show them prints of ancient and modern machines; to explain them, to be copied, and for lectures in mechanical philosophy.

Good Breeding and Doing Good

With the whole should be constantly inculcated and cultivated that *benignity of mind* which shows itself in searching for and seizing every opportunity to serve and to oblige; and is the foundation of what is called *good breeding;* highly useful to the possessor, and most agreeable to all.

The idea of what is *true merit* should also be often presented to youth, explained and impressed on their minds, as consisting in an *inclination,* joined with an *ability,* to serve mankind, one's country, friends, and family; which ability is, with the blessing of God, to be acquired or greatly increased by *true learning;* and should, indeed, be the great *aim* and *end* of all learning.

The influence of the sense realists and naturalists on Franklin is evident in this essay. To strengthen his argument he included numerous supportive notes citing such figures as Locke, Milton, and Charles Rollin. The following provides an example:

Mr. Locke, speaking of *Grammar,* (p. 252) says, that "To those, the greatest part of whose business in this world is to be done with their tongue, and with their pens, it is convenient, if not necessary, that they should speak properly and correctly, whereby they may let their thoughts into other men's minds the more easily, and with the greater impression. Upon this account it is, that any sort of speaking, so as will make him be understoood, is not thought enough for a gentleman. He ought to study *grammar,* among the other helps of speaking well; but it *must be* the grammar of his own tongue, of the language he uses, that he may understand his own country speech nicely, and speak it properly,

Jared Sparks (ed.), The Works of Benjamin Franklin *(Boston: Hilliard, Gray and Co., 1836), II, 134–35.*

without shocking the ears of those it is addressed to with solecisms and offensive irregularities. And to this purpose *grammar is necessary*; but it is the grammar *only of their own proper tongues*, and to those who would take pains in cultivating their language, and perfecting their styles. Whether all gentlemen should not do this, I leave to be considered; since the want of propriety and grammatical exactness is thought very misbecoming one of that rank, and usually draws on one, guilty of such faults, the imputation of having had a lower breeding and worse company than suit with his quality. If this be so, (as I suppose it is,) it will be matter of wonder, why young gentlemen are forced to learn the grammars of foreign and dead languages, and are never once told of the grammar of their own tongues. They do not so much as know there is any such thing, much less is it made their business to be instructed in it. Nor is their own language ever proposed to them as worthy their care and cultivating, though they have *daily use* of it, and are not seldom in the future course of their lives judged of by their handsome or awkward way of expressing themselves in it. Whereas the languages, whose grammars they have been so much employed in, are such as probably they shall scarce ever speak or write; or, if upon occasion this should happen, they should be excused for the mistakes and faults they make in it. Would not a Chinese, who took notice of this way of breeding, be apt to imagine, that all our young gentlemen were designed to be teachers and professors of the dead languages of foreign countries, and not to be men of business in their own?"

The same author adds, (p. 255,) "That if grammar ought to be taught at any time, it must be to one that can speak the language already; how else can he be taught the grammar of it? This at least is evident from the practice of the wise and learned nations among the ancients. They made it a *part of education*, to cultivate *their own*, not foreign tongues. The Greeks counted all other nations barbarous, and had a contempt for their languages. And though the Greek learning grew in credit among the Romans towards the end of their commonwealth, yet it was the Roman tongue that was made the study of their youth. *Their own* language they were to make use of, and therefore it was *their own* language they were *instructed* and *exercised* in." And, (p. 281,) "There can scarce be a greater defect," says he, "in a gentleman, than not to express himself well either in writing or speaking. But yet I think I may ask the reader, whether he doth not know a great many, who live upon their estates, and so, with the name, should have the qualities of gentlemen, who cannot so much as tell a story as they should, much less speak clearly and persuasively in any business. This I think not to be so much their fault as the *fault of their education*." Thus far Locke.

Monsieur Rollin reckons the neglect of teaching their own tongue a great fault in the French universities. He spends great part of his first volume of *Belles Lettres* on that subject; and lays down some excellent rules or methods of teaching French to Frenchmen grammatically, and making them masters therein, which are very applicable to our language but too long to be inserted here. He practised them on the youth under his care with great success.

The academy was established with a traditional Latin School and an English School designed along lines proposed by Franklin in 1749 and elaborated upon in his 1751 "Sketch of an English School." Unfortunately, utilitarian and classical education did not prove compatible housemates. In the struggles that ensued for funds, teachers, and facilities, the English School suffered and eventually went under. Franklin's scheme of education was too novel for his own times and the forces of traditionalism too well entrenched. In 1789, Franklin revealed his disappointment at the course of events.

OBSERVATIONS RELATIVE TO THE INTENTIONS OF THE ORIGINAL FOUNDERS OF THE ACADEMY IN PHILADELPHIA. JUNE, 1789.

As the English school in the Academy has been, and still continues to be, a subject of dispute and discussion among the trustees since the restitution of the charter, and it has been proposed that we should have some regard to the original intention of the founders in establishing that school, I beg leave, for your information, to lay before you what I know of that matter originally, and what I find on the minutes relating to it, by which it will appear how far the design of that school has been adhered to or neglected.

Having acquired some little reputation among my fellow-citizens, by projecting the public library in 1732, and obtaining the subscriptions by which it was established; and by proposing and promoting, with success, sundry other schemes of utility in 1749; I was encouraged to hazard another project, that of a public education for our youth. As in the scheme of the library I had provided only for English books, so in this new scheme my ideas went no further than to procure the means of a good English education. A number of my friends, to whom I communicated the proposal, concurred with me in these ideas; but Mr. Allen, Mr. Francis, Mr. Peters, and some other persons of wealth and learning, whose subscriptions and countenance we should need, being of opinion that it ought to include the learned languages, I submitted my judgement to theirs, retaining however a strong pre-possession in favor of my first plan, and resolving to preserve as much of it as I could, and to nourish the English school by every means in my power.

*   *   *   *   *

Sparks, op. cit., *pp. 133–34, 158–59.*

But there is in mankind an unaccountable prejudice in favor of ancient customs and habitudes, which inclines to a continuance of them after the circumstances, which formerly made them useful, cease to exist. A multitude of instances might be given, but it may suffice to mention one. Hats were once thought an useful part of dress; they kept the head warm and screened it from the violent impression of the sun's rays, and from the rain, snow, hail, etc. Though, by the way, this was not the more ancient opinion or practice; for among all the remains of antiquity, the bustos, statues, basso-rilievos, medals, etc., which are infinite, there is no representation of a human figure with a cap or hat on, nor any covering for the head, unless it be the head of a soldier, who has a helmet; but that is evidently not a part of dress for health, but as a protection from the strokes of a weapon.

At what time hats were first introduced we know not, but in the last century they were universally worn throughout Europe. Gradually, however, as the wearing of wigs, and hair nicely dressed prevailed, the puting on of hats was disused by genteel people, lest the curious arrangements of the curls and powdering should be disordered; and umbrellas began to supply their place; yet still our considering the hat as a part of dress continues so far to prevail, that a man of fashion is not thought dressed without having one, or something like one, about him, which he carries under his arm. So that there are a multitude of the politer people in all the courts and capital cities of Europe, who have never, nor their fathers before them, worn a hat otherwise than as a *chapeau bras*, though the utility of such a mode of wearing it is by no means apparent, and it is attended not only with some expense, but with a degree of constant trouble.

The still prevailing custom of having schools for teaching generally our children, in these days, the Latin and Greek languages, I consider therefore, in no other light than as the *chapeau bras* of modern literature.

Thus the time spent in that study might, it seems, be much better employed in the education for such a country as ours; and this was indeed the opinion of most of the original trustees.

5. Thomas Jefferson: Education for a Democratic Republic

As chairman of the Committee of Revisors of the Virginia Assembly, Thomas Jefferson was the leading spokesman for liberal reform in the state during the Revolutionary War years. The bills Jefferson and his colleagues introduced represented an attempt to bring the laws of Virginia into line with the changing conditions and the professed ideals of the emerging nation. Jefferson's "A Bill for the More General Diffusion of Knowledge," introduced in 1779, called for sweeping changes in the state's aristocratic pattern of education. He proposed a system of public elementary and grammar schools that would guarantee a primary education for all white children at public expense and afford an opportunity for the very brightest male students to proceed through the grammar schools and college under government scholarship. In his attempt not only to broaden educational opportunity but also to secularize the curriculum Jefferson once more proved himself a champion of the Enlightenment.

A BILL FOR THE MORE GENERAL DIFFUSION OF KNOWLEDGE

(CHAPTER LXXIX.)

SECTION I. Whereas it appeareth that however certain forms of government are better calculated than others to protect individuals in the free exercise of their natural rights, and are at the same time themselves better guarded against degeneracy, yet experience hath shewn, that even under the best forms, those entrusted with power have, in time, and by slow operations, perverted it into tyranny; and it is believed that the most effectual means of preventing this would be, to illuminate, as far as practicable, the minds of the people at large, and more especially to give them knowledge of those facts, which history exhibiteth, that, possessed thereby of the experience of other ages and countries, they may be enabled to know ambition under all its shapes, and prompt to exert their natural powers to defeat its purposes; And whereas it is generally true that that people will be happiest whose laws are best, and are best administered, and that laws will be wisely formed, and honestly administered, in proportion as those who form and administer them are wise and honest; whence it becomes expedient for promoting the publick happiness that those persons, whom nature hath endowed with genius and virtue, should be rendered by liberal education worthy to receive, and able to guard the sacred deposit of the rights and liberties of their fellow citizens, and that they should be called to that charge without regard to wealth, birth or other accidental condition or circumstance; but the indigence of the greater number disabling them from so educating, at their own expence, those of their children whom nature hath fitly formed and disposed to become useful instruments for the public, it is better that such should be sought for and educated at the

Paul Leicester Ford (ed.), The Works of Thomas Jefferson *(New York: G. P. Putnam's Sons, 1892–1899), II, 220–29.*

common expence of all, than that the happiness of all should be confined to the weak or wicked:

Sect. II. Be it therefore enacted by the General Assembly, that in every country within this commonwealth, there shall be chosen annually, by the electors qualified to vote for Delegates, three of the most honest and able men of their county, to be called the Aldermen of the county; and that the election of the said Aldermen shall be held at the same time and place, before the same persons, and notified and conducted in the same manner as by law is directed, for the annual election of Delegates for the county.

Sect. III. The person before whom such election is holden shall certify to the court of the said county the names of the Aldermen chosen, in order that the same may be entered of record, and shall give notice of their election to the said Aldermen within a fortnight after such election.

Sect. IV. The said Aldermen on the first Monday in October, if it be fair, and if not, then on the next fair day, excluding Sunday, shall meet at the court-house of their county, and proceed to divide their said county into hundreds, bounding the same by water courses, mountains, or limits, to be run and marked, if they think necessary, by the county surveyor, and at the county expence, regulating the size of the said hundreds, according to the best of their discretion, so as that they may contain a convenient number of children to make up a school, and be of such convenient size that all the children within each hundred may daily attend the school to be established therein, and distinguishing each hundred by a particular name; which division, with the names of the several hundreds, shall be returned to the court of the county and be entered of record, and shall remain unaltered until the increase or decrease of inhabitants shall render an alteration necessary, in the opinion of any succeeding Alderman, and also in the opinion of the court of the county. . . .

Sect. V. The electors aforesaid residing within every hundred shall meet on the third Monday in October after the first election of Aldermen at such place, within their hundred, as the said Aldermen shall direct, notice thereof being previously given to them by such person residing within the hundred as the said Aldermen shall require who is hereby enjoined to obey such requisition, on pain of being punished by amercement and imprisonment. The electors being so assembled shall choose the most convenient place within their hundred for building a school-house. If two or more places, having a greater number of votes than any others, shall yet be equal between themselves, the Aldermen, or such of them as are not of the same hundred, on information thereof, shall decide between them. The said Aldermen shall forthwith proceed to have a school-house built at the said place, and shall see that the same shall be kept in repair, and, when necessary, that it be rebuilt; but whenever they shall think necessary that it be rebuilt, they shall give notice as before directed, to the electors of the hundred to meet at the said school-house, on such a day as they shall appoint, to determine by vote, in the manner before directed, whether it shall be rebuilt at the same, or what other place in the hundred.

Sect. VI. At every of those schools shall be taught reading, writing, and common arithmetick, and the books which shall be used therein for instructing the children to read shall be such as will at the same time make them acquainted with Græcian, Roman, English, and American history. At these schools all the free children, male and female, resident within the respective hundred, shall be intitled to receive tuition gratis, for the term of three years, and as much longer, at their private expence, as their parents, guardians, or friends shall think proper.

Sect. VII. Over every ten of these schools (or such other number nearest thereto, as the number of hundreds in the county will admit, without fractional divisions) an overseer shall be appointed annually by the aldermen at their first meeting, eminent for his learning, integrity, and fidelity to the commonwealth, whose business and duty it shall be, from time to time, to appoint a teacher to each school, who shall give assurance of fidelity to the commonwealth, and to remove him as he shall see cause; to visit every school once in every half year at the least; to examine the scholars; see that any general plan of reading and instruction recommended by the visiters of William and Mary College shall be observed; and to superintend the conduct of the teacher in everything relative to his school.

Sect. VIII. Every teacher shall receive a salary of——— by the year, which, with the expences of building and repairing the school-houses, shall be provided in such manner as other county expences are by law directed to be provided and shall also have his diet, lodging, and washing found him, to be levied in like manner, save only that such levy shall be on the inhabitants of each hundred for the board of their own teacher only.

Sect. IX. And in order that grammer schools may be rendered convenient to the youth in every part of the commonwealth, be it therefore enacted, that on the first Monday in November, after the first appointment of overseers for the hundred schools, if fair, and if not, then on the next fair day, excluding Sunday, after the hour of one in the afternoon, the said overseer appointed for the schools in the counties of Princess Ann, Norfolk, Nansemond and Isle-of-Wight shall meet at Nansemond court-house; those for the counties of Southampton, Sussex, Surry and Prince George, shall meet at Sussex court-house; those for the counties of Brunswick, Mecklenburg and Lunenburg, shall meet at Lunenburg court-house; those for the counties of Dinwiddie,

Amelia and Chesterfield, shall meet at Chesterfield court-house; those for the counties of Powhatan, Cumberland, Goochland, Henrico and Hanover, shall meet at Henrico court-house; those for the counties of Prince Edward, Charlotte and Halifax shall meet at Charlotte court-house; those for the counties of Henry, Pittsylvania and Bedford, shall meet at Pittsylvania court-house; those for the counties of Buckingham, Amherst, Albemarle and Fluvanna, shall meet at Albemarle court-house; those for the counties of Botetourt, Rockbridge, Montgomery, Washington and Kentucky, shall meet at Botetourt court-house; those for the counties of Augusta, Rockingham and Greenbriar, shall meet at Augusta court-house; those for the counties of Accomack and North-ampton, shall meet at Accomack court-house; those for the counties of Elizabeth City, Warwick, York, Gloucester, James City, Charles City and New-Kent, shall meet at James City court-house; those for the counties of Middlesex, Essex, King and Queen, King William and Caroline, shall meet at King and Queen court-house; those for the counties of Lancaster, Northumberland, Richmond and Westmoreland, shall meet at Richmond court-house; those for the counties of King George, Stafford, Spotsylvania, Prince William and Fairfax, shall meet at Spotsylvania court-house; those for the counties of Loudoun and Fauquier, shall meet at Loudoun court-house; those for the counties of Culpeper, Orange and Louisa, shall meet at Orange court-house; those for the county of Shenandoah and Frederick, shall meet at Frederick court-house; those for the counties of Hampshire and Berkeley, shall meet at Berkeley court-house; and those for the counties of Yohogania, Monongalia, and Ohio, shall meet at the Monongalia court-house; and shall fix on such place in some one of the counties in their district as shall be most proper for situating a grammer school-house, endeavoring that the situation be as central as may be to the inhabitants of the said counties, that it be furnished with good water, convenient to plentiful supplies of provision and fuel, and more than all things that it be healthy. And if a majority of the overseers present should not concur in their choice of any one place proposed, the method of determining shall be as follows; If two places only were proposed, and the votes be divided, they shall decide between them by fair and equal lot; if more than two places were proposed, the question shall be put on those two which on the first division had the greater number of votes; or if no two places had a greater number of votes than the others then it shall be decided by fair and equal lot (unless it can be agreed by a majority of votes) which of the places having equal numbers shall be thrown out of the competition, so that the question shall be put on the remaining two, and if on this ultimate question the votes shall be equally divided, it shall then be decided finally by lot.

SECT. X. The said overseers having determined the place at which the grammer school for their district shall be built, shall forthwith (unless they can otherwise agree with the proprietors of the circumjacent lands as to location and price) make application to the clerk of the county in which the said house is to be situated, who shall thereupon issue a writ in the nature of a writ of ad quod damnum, directed to the sheriff of the said county commanding him to summon and impannel twelve fit persons to meet at the place, so destined for the grammer school-house, on a certain day, to be named in the said writ, not less than five, nor more than ten, days from the date thereof; and also to give notice of the same to the proprietors and tenants of the lands to be viewed if they be found within the county, and if not, then to their agents therein if any they have. Which freeholders shall be charged by the said sheriff impartially, and to the best of their skill and judgment to view the lands round about the said place, and to locate and circumscribe, by certain meets and bounds, one hundred acres thereof, having regard therein principally to the benefit and convenience of the said school, but respecting in some measure also the convenience of the said proprietors, and to value and appraise the same in so many several and distinct parcels as shall be owned or held by several and distinct owners or tenants, and according to their respective interests and estates therein. And after such location and appraisement so made, the said sheriff shall forthwith return the same under the hands and seals of the said jurors, together with the writ, to the clerk's office of the said county and the right and property of the said proprietors and tenants in the said lands so circumscribed shall be immediately devested and be transferred to the commonwealth for the use of the said grammer school, in full and absolute dominion, any want of consent or disability to consent in the said owners or tenants notwithstanding. But it shall not be lawful for the said overseers so to situate the grammer school-house, nor to the said jurors so to locate the said lands, as to include the mansion-house of the proprietor of the lands, nor the offices, curtilage, or garden, thereunto immediately belonging.

Sect. XI. The said overseers shall forthwith proceed to have a house of brick or stone, for the said grammer school, with necessary offices, built on the said lands, which grammer school-house shall contain a room for the school, a hall to dine in, four rooms for a master and usher, and ten or twelve lodging rooms for the scholars.

Sect. XII. To each of the said grammer schools shall be allowed out of the public treasury, the sum of   pounds, out of which shall be paid by the Treasurer, on warrant from the Auditors, to the proprietors or tenants of the lands located, the value of their several interests as fixed by the jury, and the balance thereof shall be delivered to the said overseers to defray the expense of the said buildings.

Sect. XIII. In either of these grammer schools shall be taught the

Latin and Greek languages, English Grammer, geography, and the higher part of numerical arithmetick, to wit, vulgar and decimal fractions, and the extrication of the square and cube roots.

SECT. XIV. A visiter from each county constituting the district shall be appointed, by the overseers, for the county, in the month of October annually, either from their own body or from their county at large, which visiters, or the greater part of them, meeting together at the said grammer school on the first Monday in November, if fair, and if not, then on the next fair day, excluding Sunday, shall have power to choose their own Rector, who shall call and preside at future meetings, to employ from time to time a master, and if necessary, an usher, for the said school, to remove them at their will, and to settle the price of tuition to be paid by the scholars. They shall also visit the school twice in every year at the least, either together or separately at their discretion, examine the scholars, and see that any general plan of instruction recommended by the visiters, of William and Mary College shall be observed. The said masters and ushers, before they enter on the execution of their office, shall give assurance of fidelity to the commonwealth.

SECT. XV. A steward shall be employed, and removed at will by the master, on such wages as the visiters shall direct; which steward shall see to the procuring provisions, fuel, servants for cooking, waiting, house cleaning, washing, mending, and gardening on the most reasonable terms; the expence of which, together with the steward's wages, shall be divided equally among all the scholars boarding either on the public or private expence. And the part of those who are on private expence, and also the price of their tuitions due to the master or usher, shall be paid quarterly by the respective scholars, their parents, or guardians, and shall be recoverable, if withheld, together with costs, on motion in any Court of Record, ten days notice thereof being previously given to the party, and a jury impannelled to try the issue joined, or enquire of the damages. The said steward shall also, under the direction of the visiters, see that the houses be kept in repair, and necessary enclosures be made and repaired, the accounts for which, shall from time to time, be submitted to the Auditors, and on their warrant paid by the Treasurer.

SECT. XVI. Every overseer of the hundred schools shall, in the month of September annually, after the most diligent and impartial examination and inquiry, appoint from among the boys who shall have been two years at the least at some one of the schools under his superintendance, and whose parents are too poor to give them farther education, some one of the best and most promising genius and disposition, to proceed to the grammer school of his district; which appointment shall be made in the court-house of the county, and on the court day for that month if fair, and if not, then on the next fair day, excluding Sunday, in the presence of the Aldermen, or two of them at the least, assembled on the bench for that purpose, the said overseer being previously sworn by them to make such appointment, without favor or affection, according to the best of his skill and judgment, and being interrogated by the said Aldermen, either on their own motion, or on suggestions from the parents, guardians, friends, or teachers of the children, competitors for such appointment; which teachers the parents shall attend for the information of the Aldermen. On which interrogatories the said Aldermen, if they be not satisfied with the appointment proposed, shall have right to negative it; whereupon the said visiter may proceed to make a new appointment, and the said Aldermen again to interrogate and negative, and so toties quoties until an appointment be approved.

SECT. XVII. Every boy so appointed shall be authorized to proceed to the grammer school of his district, there to be educated and boarded during such time as is hereafter limited; and his quota of the expences of the house together with a compensation to the master or usher for his tuition, at the rate of twenty dollars by the year, shall be paid by the Treasurer quarterly on warrant from the Auditors.

SECT. XVIII. A visitation shall be held, for the purpose of probation, annually at the said grammer school on the last Monday in September, if fair, and if not, then on the next fair day, excluding Sunday, at which one third of the boys sent thither by appointment of the said overseers, and who shall have been there one year only, shall be discontinued as public foundationers, being those who, on the most diligent examination and enquiry, shall be thought to be the least promising genius and disposition; and of those who shall have been there two years, all shall be discontinued save one only the best in genius and disposition, who shall be at liberty to continue there four years longer on the public foundation, and shall thence forward be deemed a senior.

SECT. XIX. The visiters for the districts which, or any part of which, be southward and westward of James river, as known by that name, or by the names of Fluvanna and Jackson's river, in every other year, to wit, at the probation meetings held in the years, distinguished in the Christian computation by odd numbers, and the visiters for all other districts at their said meetings to be held in those years, distinguished by even numbers, after diligent examination and enquiry as before directed shall chuse one among the said seniors, of the best learning and most hopeful genius and disposition, who shall be authorized by them to proceed to William and Mary College; there to be educated, boarded, and clothed, three years; the expense of which annually shall be paid by the Treasurer on warrant from the Auditors.

To complete his planned reform of education, Jefferson accompanied the above legislation with "A Bill for Ammending the Constitution of the College of William and Mary." In the segment of the bill that follows, Jefferson described the existing curriculum and the circumstances that he believed necessitated changes in the college.

. . . And the said trustees, in pursuance of the trust reposed in them, proceeded to erect the said College, and established one school of sacred theology, with two professorships therein, to wit, one for teaching the Hebrew tongue, and expounding the holy scriptures; and the other for explaining the common places of divinity, and controversies with heretics; one other school for philosophy, with two professorships therein, to wit, one for the study of rhetoric, logic, and ethics, and the other of physics, metaphysics, and mathematics; one other school for teaching the Latin and Greek tongues; and one other for teaching Indian boys reading, writing, vulgar arithmetic, the catechism and the principles of the Christian religion; which last school was founded on the private donation of the honorable Robert Boyle, of the kingdom of England, and by authority from his executors, submitted to the direction of the Earl of Burlington, one of the said executors, of the bishop of London, for the time being, and in default thereof, to the said trustees, and over the whole they appointed one president as supervisor.

Sect. II. And whereas the experience of near an hundred years hath proved, that the said College, thus amply endowed by the public, hath not answered their expectations, and there is reason to hope, that it would become more useful, if certain articles in its constitution were altered and amended, which being fixed, as before recited, by the original charters, cannot be reformed by the said trustees whose powers are created and circumscribed by the said charters, and the said College being erected and constituted on the requisition of the General Assembly by the Chief Magistrate of the state, their legal fiduciary for such purposes, being founded and endowed with the lands and revenues of the public, and intended for the sole use and improvement, and no wise in nature of a private grant, the same is of right subject to the public direction, and may by them be altered and amended, until such form be devised as will render the institution publicly advantageous, in proportion as it is publicly expensive; and the late change in the form of our government, as well as the contest of arms in which we are at present engaged, calling for extraordinary abilities both in council and field, it becomes the peculiar duty of the Legislature, at this time, to aid and improve that seminary, in which those who are to be the future

Ford, op. cit., *pp. 232–33.*

guardians of the rights and liberties of their country may be endowed with science and virtue, to watch and preserve the sacred deposit; . . .

Jefferson's curriculum proposals reflected his desire to make the offerings more practical as well as more secular in character.

Instead of the President and six Professors, licensed by the said charter, and established by the former visiters, there shall be eight Professors, one of whom, shall also be appointed President, with an additional salary of one hundred pounds a year, before they enter on the execution of their office, they shall give assurance of fidelity to the commonwealth, before some justice of the Peace. These shall be deemed the lawful successors of the President and Professors appointed under the said charter, and shall have all their rights, powers and capabilities, not otherwise disposed of by this act; to them shall belong the ordinary government of the College, and administration of its revenues, taking the advice of the visiters on all matters of great concern. There shall, in like manner, be eight Professorships, to wit, one of moral philosophy, and the laws of nature and of nations, and of the fine arts; one of law and police; one of history, civil and ecclesiastical; one of mathematics; one of anatomy and medicine; one of natural philosophy and natural history; one of the ancient languages, oriental and northern; and one of modern languages. The said Professors shall likewise appoint, from time to time, a missionary, of approved veracity, to the several tribes of Indians, whose business shall be to investigate their laws, customs, religions, traditions, and more particularly their languages, constructing grammars thereof, as well as may be, and copious vocabularies, and, on oath to communicate, from time to time, to the said President and Professors the materials he collects, to be by them laid up and preserved in their library. . . . And that this commonwealth may not be without so great an ornament, nor its youth such an help towards attaining astronomical science, as the mechanical representation, or model of the solar system, conceived and executed by that greatest of astronomers, David Ryttenhouse; Be it further enacted, that the visiters, first appointed under this act, and their successors, shall be authorized to engage the said David Ryttenhouse, on the part of this commonwealth, to make and erect in the said College of William and Mary, and for its use, one of the said models, to be called by the name of the Ryttenhouse, the cost and expence of making, transporting and erecting whereof shall, according to the agreement or allowance of the said visiters, be paid by the Treasurer of this commonwealth, on warrant from the Auditors.

Ford, op. cit., pp. 234–35.

For the conservative segment of the planter aristocracy and the Anglican Church leadership Jefferson's educational plans were far too radical. In 1779, they still possessed enough power to prevent passage of either bill.

回 6. George Washington and Noah Webster: Education and Nationalism

George Washington was the first of a long line of presidents to advocate a national university, which would promote learning, strengthen the ties of union, and check the tendencies of young Americans to seek an education abroad. The following is from his "Eighth Annual Address," December 7, 1796.

I have heretofore proposed to the consideration of Congress the expediency of establishing a national university and also a military academy. The desirableness of both these institutions has so constantly increased with every new view I have taken of the subject that I can not omit the opportunity of once for all recalling your attention to them.

The assembly to which I address myself is too enlightened not to be fully sensible how much a flourishing state of the arts and sciences contributes to national prosperity and reputation.

True it is that our country, much to its honor, contains many seminaries of learning highly respectable and useful; but the funds upon which they rest are too narrow to command the ablest professors in the different departments of liberal knowledge for the institution contemplated, though they would be excellent auxiliaries.

Amongst the motives to such an institution, the assimilation of the principles, opinions, and manners of our countrymen by the common education of a portion of our youth from every quarter well deserves attention. The more homogeneous our citizens can be made in these particulars the greater will be our prospect of permanent union; and a primary object of such a national institution should be the education of our youth in the science of *government*. In a republic what species of knowledge can be equally important and what duty more pressing on its legislature than to patronize a plan for communicating it to those who are to be the future guardians of the liberties of the country?

James D. Richardson (ed.), The Messages and Papers of the Presidents, 1789–1897 *(Washington: Government Printing Office, 1896), I, 202–03.*

The institution of a military academy is also recommended by cogent reason. However pacific the general policy of a nation may be, it ought never to be without an adequate stock of military knowledge for emergencies. The first would impair the energy of its character, and both would hazard its safety or expose it to greater evils when war could not be avoided; besides that, war might often not depend upon its own choice. In proportion as the observance of pacific maxims might exempt a nation from the necessity of practicing the rules of the military art ought to be its care in preserving and transmitting, by proper establishments, the knowledge of that art. Whatever argument may be drawn from particular examples superficially viewed, a thorough examination of the subject will evince that the art of war is at once comprehensive and complicated, that it demands much previous study, and that the possession of it in its most improved and perfect state is always of great moment to the security of a nation. This, therefore, ought to be a serious care of every government, and for this purpose an academy where a regular course of instruction is given is an obvious expedient which different nations have successfully employed.

Noah Webster was an enthusiastic proponent of American nationalism. As an essayist, newspaperman, lexicographer, and author of textbooks, he employed his talents to foster patriotism and morality and to develop and promote a standardized, distinctively American usage of the English language. The following selection is from two essays written by Webster in 1788 and 1790 and reprinted in Barnard's American Journal of Education. *Webster presented an analysis of what he considered the faults of the schools of his day and offered his concept of an education appropriate for the new republic.*

The first error that I would mention is a too general attention to the dead languages, with a neglect of our own . . . . This neglect is so general that there is scarcely an institution to be found in the country where the English tongue is taught regularly from its elements to its pure and regular construction in prose and verse. Perhaps in most schools boys are taught the definition of the parts of speech, and a few hard names which they do not understand, and which the teacher seldom attempts to explain: this called learning grammar. . . . The principles of any science afford pleasure to the student who comprehends them. In order to render the study of language agreeable, the distinctions between words should be illustrated by the difference in visible objects. Examples should be presented to the senses which are the inlets of all our knowledge.

Another error which is frequent in America, is that a master undertakes to teach many different branches in the same school. In new

Barnard, op. cit. *(1876)*, *XXVI, 196–200.*

settlements, where the people are poor, and live in scattered situations, the practice is often unavoidable. But in populous towns it must be considered as a defective plan of education. For suppose the teacher to be equally master of all the branches which he attempts to teach, which seldom happens, yet his attention must be distracted with a multiplicity of objects, and consequently painful to himself, and not useful to his pupils. Add to this the continual interruptions which the students of one branch suffer from those of another, which must retard the progress of the whole school. It is a much more eligible plan to appropriate an apartment to each branch of education, with a teacher who makes that branch his sole employment. . . . Indeed what is now called a liberal education disqualifies a man for business. Habits are formed in youth and by practice; and as business is in some measure mechanical, every person should be exercised in his employment in an early period of life, that his habits may be formed by the time his apprenticeship expires. An education in a university interferes with the forming of these habits, and perhaps forms opposite habits; the mind may contract a fondness for ease, for pleasure, or for books, which no efforts can overcome. An academic education, which should furnish the youth with some ideas of men and things, and leave time for an apprenticeship before the age of twenty-one years, would be the most eligible for young men who are designed for active employments.

* * * * *

But the principal defect in our plan of education in America is the want of good teachers in the academies and common schools. By good teachers I mean men of unblemished reputation, and possessed of abilities competent to their station. That a man should be master of what he undertakes to teach is a point that will not be disputed; and yet it is certain that abilities are often dispensed with, either through inattention or fear of expense. To those who employ ignorant men to instruct their children, let me say, it is better for youth to have no education than to have a bad one; for it is more difficult to eradicate habits than to impress new ideas. The tender shrub is easily bent to any figure; but the tree which has acquired its full growth resists all impressions. Yet abilities are not the sole requisites. The instructors of youth ought, of all men, to be the most prudent, accomplished, agreeable, and respectable. What avail a man's parts, if, while he is "the wisest and brightest," he is the "meanest of mankind?" The pernicious effects of bad example on the minds of youth will probably be acknowledged; but, with a view to improvement, it is indispensably necessary that the teachers should possess good breeding and agreeable manners. In order to give full effect to instructions it is requisite that they should proceed from a man who is loved and respected. But a low-bred clown or

morose tyrant can command neither love nor respect; and that pupil
who has no motive for application to books but the fear of the rod, will
not make a scholar.

From a strange inversion of the order of nature, the cause of which it
is not necessary to unfold, the most important business in civil society,
is, in many parts of America, committed to the most worthless characters.
The education of youth, an employment of more consequence than
making laws and preaching the gospel, because it lays the foundation on
which both law and gospel rest for success; this education is sunk to a
level with the most menial services. In most instances we find the higher
seminaries of learning intrusted to men of good characters, and possessed
of the moral virtues and social affections. But many of our inferior
schools, which, so far as the heart is concerned, are as important as
colleges, are kept by men of no breeding, and many of them, by men
infamous for the most detestable vices. Will this be denied? will it be
denied, that before the war, it was a frequent practice for gentlemen to
purchase convicts, who had been transported for their crimes, and
employ them as private tutors in their families?

Gracious Heavens! Must the wretches, who have forfeited their lives,
and been pronounced unworthy to be inhabitants of a *foreign* country,
be intrusted with the education, the morals, the character of *American*
youth?

Will it be denied that many of the instructors of youth, whose
examples and precepts should form their minds for good men and
useful citizens, are often found to sleep away, in schools, the fumes of a
debauch, and to stun the ears of their pupils with frequent blasphemy?
It is idle to suppress such truths; nay, more, it is wicked. The practice of
employing low and vicious characters to direct the studies of youth, is, in
a high degree, criminal; it is destructive of the order and peace of
society; it is treason against morals, and of course, against government;
it ought to be arraigned before the tribunal of reason, and condemned
by all intelligent beings. The practice is so exceedingly absurd, that it is
surprising it could have ever prevailed among rational people. Parents
wish their children to be *well bred,* yet place them under the care of
clowns. They wish to secure their hearts from *vicious principles* and *habits,*
yet commit them to the care of men of the most *profligate lives.* They wish
to have their children taught *obedience* and *respect* for superiors, yet give
them a master that both parents and children *despise.* A practice so
glaringly absurd and irrational has no name in any language! Parents
themselves will not associate with the men whose company they *oblige*
their children to keep, even in that most important period, when habits
are forming for life.

Our legislators frame laws for the suppression of vice and immorality;
our divines thunder from the pulpit the terrors of infinite wrath against

the vices that stain the characters of men. And do laws and preaching effect a reformation of manners? Experience would not give a very favorable answer to this inquiry. The reason is obvious; the attempts are directed to the wrong objects. Laws can only check the public effects of vicious principles; but can never reach the principles themselves; and preaching is not very intelligible to people till they arrive at an age when their principles are rooted, or their habits firmly established. An attempt to eradicate old habits, is as absurd, as to lop off the branches of a huge oak, in order to root it out of a rich soil. The most that such clipping will effect, is to prevent a further growth.

The only practicable method to reform mankind, is to begin with children; to banish, if possible, from their company, every low bred, drunken, immoral character. Virtue and vice will not grow together in a great degree, but they will grow where they are planted, and when one has taken root, it is not easily supplanted by the other. The great art of correcting mankind, therefore, consists in prepossessing the mind with good principles.

For this reason society requires that the education of youth should be watched with the most scrupulous attention. Education, in a great measure, forms the moral characters of men, and morals are the basis of government. Education should therefore be the first care of a legislature; not merely the institution of schools, but the furnishing of them with the best men for teachers. A good system of education should be the first article in the code of political regulations; for it is much easier to introduce and establish an effectual system for preserving morals, than to correct, by penal statutes, the ill effects of a bad system. I am so fully persuaded of this, that I shall almost adore that great man, who shall change our practice and opinions, and make it respectable for the first and best men to superintend the education of youth.

Another defect in our schools, which, since the revolution, is become inexcusable, is the want of proper books.[1] The collections which are now used consist of essays that respect foreign and ancient nations. The minds of youth are perpetually led to the history of Greece and Rome or to Great Britain; boys are constantly repeating the declamations of Demosthenes and Cicero, or debates upon some political question in the British Parliament. These are excellent specimens of good sense, polished style, and perfect oratory; but they are not interesting to children. They can not be very useful, except to young men who want them as models of reasoning and eloquence, in the pulpit or at the bar.

But every child in America should be acquainted with his own

---

[1] *This want the author very judiciously for himself, and wisely for the country, set himself to the work of supplying.*

country. He should read books that furnish him with ideas that will be useful to him in life and practice. As soon as he opens his lips, he should rehearse the history of his own country; he should lisp the praise of liberty, and of those illustrious heroes and statesmen who have wrought a revolution in her favor.

A selection of essays, respecting the settlement and geography of America; the history of the late revolution, and of the most remarkable characters and events that distinguished it, and a compendium of the principles of the federal and provincial governments, should be the principal school book in the United States. These are interesting objects to every man; they call home the minds of youth and fix them upon the interests of their own country, and they assist in forming attachments to it, as well as in enlarging the understanding.

In several States we find laws passed, establishing provision for colleges and academies, where people of property may educate their sons; but no provision is made for instructing the poorer rank of people, even in reading and writing. Yet in these same States, every citizen who is worth a few shillings annually, is entitled to vote for legislators. This appears to me a most glaring solecism in government. The constitutions are *republican*, and the laws of education are *monarchial*. The *former* extend civil rights to every honest industrious man; the *latter* deprive a large proportion of the citizens of a most valuable privilege.

In our American republics, where governments are in the hands of the people, knowledge should be universally diffused by means of public schools. Of such consequence is it to society, that the people who make laws should be well informed, that I conceive no legislature can be justified in neglecting proper establishments for this purpose.

When I speak of a diffusion of knowledge, I do not mean merely a knowledge of spelling-books and the New Testament. An acquaintance with ethics, and with the general principles of law, commerce, money, and government, is necessary for the yeomanry of a republican state. This acquaintance they might obtain by means of books calculated for schools, and read by the children, during the winter months, and by the circulation of public papers.

In Rome it was the common exercise of boys at school to learn the laws of the twelve tables by heart, as they did their poets and classic authors. What an excellent practice this in a free government!

How superficial must be that learning which is acquired in four years! Severe experience has taught me the errors and defects of what is called a liberal education. I could not read the best Greek and Roman authors while in college, without neglecting the established classical studies; and after I left college, I found time only to dip into books that every scholar should be master of; a circumstance that fills me with the deepest regret.

In a letter to Henry Barnard, Webster recalled with apparent satisfaction his and Jedidiah Morse's contributions to American education. In the letter Webster referred to a grammar written by the Englishman Thomas Dilworth. This work was first published in London in 1740, and reprinted in Philadelphia by Benjamin Franklin in 1747.

NEW HAVEN, MARCH 10th, 1840.

MR. BARNARD: *Dear Sir*—You desire me to give you some information as to the mode of instruction in common schools when I was young, or before the Revolution. I believe you to be better acquainted with the methods of managing common schools, at the present time, than I am; and I am not able to institute a very exact comparison between the old modes and the present. From what I know of the present schools in the country, I believe the principal difference between the schools of former times and at present consists in the books and instruments used in the modern schools.

When I was young, the books used were chiefly or wholly Dilworth's Spelling Books, the Psalter, Testament, and Bible. No geography was studied before the publication of Dr. Morse's small books on that subject, about the year 1786 or 1787. No history was read, as far as my knowledge extends, for there was no abridged history of the United States. Except the books above mentioned, no book for reading was used before the publication of the Third Part of my Institute, in 1785. In some of the early editions of that book, I introduced short notices of the geography and history of the United States, and these led to more enlarged descriptions of the country. In 1788, at the request of Dr. Morse, I wrote an account of the transactions in the United States, after the Revolution; which account fills nearly twenty pages in the first volume of his octavo editions.

Before the Revolution, and for some years after, no slates were used in common schools: all writing and the operations in arithmetic were on paper. The teacher wrote the copies and gave the sums in arithmetic; few or none of the pupils having any books as a guide. Such was the condition of the schools in which I received my early education.

The introduction of my Spelling Book, first published in 1783, produced a great change in the department of spelling; and, from the information I can gain, spelling was taught with more care and accuracy for twenty years or more after that period, than it has been since the introduction of multiplied books and studies.[1]

Barnard, op. cit., *pp. 195–96.*

[1] *The general use of my Spelling Book in the United States has had a most extensive effect in correcting the pronunciation of words, and giving uniformity to the language. Of this change, the present generation can have a very imperfect idea.*

No English grammar was generally taught in common schools when I was young, except that in Dilworth, and that to no good purpose. In short, the instruction in schools was very imperfect, in every branch; and if I am not misinformed, it is so to this day, in many branches. Indeed there is danger of running from one extreme to another, and instead of having too few books in our schools, we shall have too many.

I am, sir, with much respect, your friend and obedient servant,

N. WEBSTER.

IX

Education and the Birth of the Modern Era, 1800–1860

*D*URING *the first six decades of the nineteenth century, the breezes of change stirred up by the Enlightenment finally attained gale intensity. So great was the force of the storm that some of the oldest traditions and institutions of the Western world were uprooted, blown away, and replaced by patterns of thought and action that appear strikingly familiar to the modern observer. During these years our contemporary world was being born, and revolutionary change appeared in every sphere of life.*

To enumerate all these changes would require volumes. It is enough to remind the reader of Malthus, Mill, Marx, and the development of industrial capitalism with all its familiar accoutrements: cities, great poverty in the midst of vast wealth, technological miracles, etc. It is sufficient to mention Jacksonian Democracy, the Congress of Vienna, the revolutions of 1848, and the continuing, if painfully slow, progress of liberalism and democracy in the face of conservative intransigence. It is enough to recall the name Charles Darwin and the impact his theories were to have on man's conception of himself and the universe in which he dwells. Finally, we must speak of Napoleon, who in his efforts to realize an empire unleashed the spirit of nationalism from Moscow to New Orleans.

Science, industry, liberalism, nationalism—in the minds of men these were and continue to be terms associated with progress. And for many of those who advocate progress, the schools were and continue to be considered prime instruments of change. The dynamic spirit of the early years of the nineteenth century is evident to the student of educational history. Focusing attention on three men of this period—Johann Heinrich Pestalozzi, Friedrich Froebel, and Johann

297

Friedrich Herbart—one can observe the formulation of educational theories and practices whose origins were in the Enlightenment and whose destinies were to provide a major part of the foundations of modern education.

Clearly reflecting the humanitarian spirit stemming from the Enlightenment, Pestalozzi sought to enlist education as a tool for the social and moral improvement of the common people. Inspired by the naturalism and sense realism of the Émile, he went beyond Rousseau in studying children, in devising practical methods of teaching, and in testing these methods in the several schools with which he was associated. His success both in teaching children and in training teachers attracted to his schools observers and prospective disciples from throughout Europe and America. As a prototype for future liberal educational theorists and the inspirer of numerous schools founded largely upon his principles, Pestalozzi rightfully deserves his title, "Father of Modern Elementary Education." (1)

One of those upon whom Pestalozzi's ideas had a most profound influence was Friedrich Froebel. As a teacher in Pestalozzi's school at Yverdon, Froebel had first hand contact with the Swiss master and his methods. However, other factors were influential in the development of Froebel's thought. A keen student of science, he applied its techniques and findings to the study of children. He was also greatly affected by the spirit of democracy and the romantic idealism of the post-Kantian movement in philosophy. In his own philosophical conclusions he envisioned a major role for education in helping to realize a world in harmony with God's will. The grand product of these influences was the institution he founded, the kindergarten. Though long since stripped of most of the romantic symbolism attached to it by Froebel, the kindergarten remains today an important first rung on the ladder of Western education. (2)

Third, Johann Friedrich Herbart considered education's primary responsibility to be the development of sound moral character, of citizens who would be capable of freely making intelligent decisions for their own betterment and that of their society. In contrast to these highly idealistic aims, Herbart advocated a methodological approach to teaching which was primarily intellectual and scientific. Effective learning, he believed, resulted from the association of ideas in the mind. He stressed the importance of developing student interest in the subject to be studied and of relating new knowledge to previously acquired information and ideas. To accomplish this, Herbart and his followers devised a step-by-step "scientific" approach to teaching, which gained popularity in teacher training institutions in Europe and, later in the century, in America. With the developing significance of science in shaping the modern era, the Herbartian methods helped add a measure of prestige to the teaching profession. Herbart's ideas eventually fell out of favor when later philosophers and psychologists found fault with his neglect of the role of feeling and impulse in the educative process. Nevertheless, he retains an important place in the history of education for his pioneering work in employing the methods of science in the study of education. (3)

In the political arena education continued in many lands to reflect the blossoming nationalism that had its roots in the seventeenth and eighteenth centuries. Napoleon, both directly and indirectly, played a fascinating role in the educational developments of several countries. In Switzerland the frightful thoroughness of his troops in ravaging the town of Stanz created the orphans who in turn afforded the first significant groups on which Pestalozzi could test his educational ideas. In his own country Napoleon established a system of public education under national control which substantially remains to this day. (4)

In Prussia, where the foundation for a state educational system had been laid during the previous century, the defeat at the hands of Napoleon in 1807 led Frederick William III to depend more than ever on the power of the schools to promote patriotism. As part of a general attempt to rise out of the ashes on the back of a liberal social and political program, Prussian educators embraced Pestalozzianism, and their elementary schools along with their liberalized universities soon became models of enlightened education. The trend, however, was short-lived. The reactionary spirit of the Congress of Vienna left a heavy imprint on Prussia. In education as in politics, Prussia began to move away from freedom, returning to its more traditional, conservative allegiance to the discipline of family, church, state, and army. A system of class-oriented schools run in partnership by state and religious authorities remained virtually unchanged through World War I. (5)

In the United States Napoleon's machinations helped bring on the War of 1812, which contributed to a spirit of national patriotism. Convinced by a bit of self-delusion that they had whipped the British, Americans engaged in three decades of national muscle-flexing, typified by the concept of "Manifest Destiny." For the advocates of public education this boded well. The educational arguments of eighteenth-century nationalists had largely fallen on deaf ears. Now, however, time and events had created a climate conducive to acceptance of the concept of public schools to foster national patriotism. Of course, the American public school was constructed on a base far broader than nationalism. The egalitarian spirit of Jacksonian Democracy contributed to a call for a school common to all classes, a radical departure from the European pattern. The separation of church and state, which had been finally achieved by 1833, paved the way for public schools that were nonsectarian in character. The beginnings of industry provided taxable wealth necessary for the maintenance of public schools and led to the creation of a socially conscious workingmen's movement, which viewed education as the best guarantee of their children's rise and the best protection against the growth of monopoly. The dislocations brought about by rapid urban growth prompted reformers to support the public school as an agency for social and moral uplift. Leaders of the common school movement, realizing that the time was opportune, appealed to all classes and interests to endorse their cause. The letters, lectures, articles, and reports of Horace Mann make it apparent that the success of the movement was due in large measure to the political acumen of its advocates. (6)

The supporters of national education in England had far less success than their late American colonies and their neighbors across the Channel. The tradition of church, charitable, and private sponsorship of schooling was not easily shaken. Radical reformers had for a number of years stressed the need for state support of education for the masses, and after the Whigs came to power in 1830, they were successful in pushing through an appropriation for that purpose. The break with tradition was hardly complete, however. The limited funds made available by Parliament were distributed to religious schools "for the Education of the Children of the Poorer Classes in Great Britain." Nothing approaching true national sponsorship of education was to appear in England prior to 1870. (7)

▣ 1. Johann Heinrich Pestalozzi

In 1818, an American, John Griscom, visited Pestalozzi at his school at Yverdon. His observations provide an excellent picture of much of Pestalozzi's philosophy and method. He took particular note of Pestalozzi's emphasis on the child's natural interests and abilities, his distaste for memorized learning, his resort to a "thinking love" rather than the rod, and his concern for the education of the whole child through the development of the intellectual, physical, and moral faculties. Griscom also revealed the international flavor of the school where teachers, students, and visitors gathered from throughout the Western world.

VISIT TO YVERDON IN OCTOBER, 1818

Breakfast finished, our first and chief concern was to visit the celebrated institute of Pestalozzi. This establishment occupies a large castle, the use of which was granted to Pestalozzi by the canton of Berne, when the town of Yverdon was included in that canton, and the government of Pays de Vaud, to which it now belongs, continues the grant. On entering the castle, we were invited into a private room. I gave my letters to the person in attendance, who took them immediately to the chief. The good old man soon came in, seized me warmly by the hand, and, seeing my hat on my head, he pointed to it in a sort of ecstasy, with his eyes almost filled with tears. I hardly knew how to interpret this emotion, and I asked him if he wished me to take it off. He answered very earnestly, "No, no, no, keep it on, you are right." He seemed very glad to see us, and as he speaks French very imperfectly, and with an indistinct accent, he said he would call Monsieur Greaves to talk with us. This gentleman came and entered immediately into a detail of the institution, its principles, its spirit, its arrangement, etc. He is an Englishman, and, as I found upon inquiry, brother to the lady whom I had seen at Lausanne. He has been some weeks with Pestalozzi, for the purpose of understanding his system thoroughly, in order to aid a

Henry Barnard (ed.), The American Journal of Education *(Hartford: Office of the American Journal of Education, 1888), XXX, 569–72.*

sister in England in the education of her children. He enters warmly
into its concerns, and will be useful in making it better known. He
explained to us very clearly the leading ideas and views of human
nature, which induced Pestalozzi to become an instructor of youth. The
two great instruments with which he works are faith and love. He
discards the motives of ambition and emulation as unnecessary, and
as tending to counteract the sentiment of good-will toward others. He
thinks there is enough in the intuitive understanding of every child to
accomplish the complete growth and maturity of its faculties, if its
reason be properly trained and nourished, and not warped by in-
judicious treatment. The common plans of education he regards as too
artificial, too wide a departure from nature. Too much stress is laid
upon the memory, while the imagination is too much neglected. If the
native feelings of the heart are allowed to operate, under the dominion
of the native powers of the mind, drawn out and expanded by faith and
love, the child is competent of itself to arrive gradually at the most
correct and important conclusions in religion and science. There is a
native and inherent life, which only requires to be cherished by genial
treatment, to bring it into the full attainment of truth, and to the
utmost perfection of its being. He therefore insists upon the greatest
pains being taken to draw out this native life and to preserve it in full
vigor. There is constant danger of urging the child wardfor beyond its
natural strength, of anticipating its conclusions and thus weakening its
confidence in its own powers. In the plans he adopts nothing is to be got
by heart. The understanding is to be thoroughly reached, and then the
memory will take care of itself.

His school consists at present of about ninety boys, German, Prussian,
French, Swiss, Italian, Spanish, and English. It is divided into four
principal classes, according to the attainments of the pupils. These
classes are subdivided into others. There are seven school-rooms in
the castle, and twelve teachers or professors. His head professor, Joseph
Schmidt, has been brought up in the institution, and is a very efficient
and worthy man. He is a native of one of the German cantons, and
speaks and writes perfectly the German and French. He is a man of
modest demeanor and entirely devoted to the institution. He has
written treatises on several of the subjects taught in the school, and
adapted to its methods.

We spent most of the day in the different school-rooms, witnessing
the exercises of the scholars. Very few books are used, as it is expected
the children can read well before they come there. But to describe the
modes of teaching, so as to render them clearly intelligible, would
require much more time and space than I can possibly allot to it, were
I ever so competent to make it known. We saw the exercises of arithmetic, writing, drawing, mathematics, lessons in music and gymnastics,

something of geography, French, Latin, and German. To teach a school in the way practiced here, without book, and almost entirely by verbal instruction, is extremely laborious. The teacher must be constantly with the child, always talking, questioning, explaining, and repeating. The pupils, however, by this process, are brought into very close intimacy with the instructor. Their capacities, all their faculties and propensities, become laid open to his observation. This gives him an advantage which cannot possibly be gained in the ordinary way in which schools are generally taught. The children look well, appear very contented, and apparently, live in great harmony one with another; which, considering the diversity of national character and temper here collected, can be attributed only to the spirit of love and affection which sways the breast of the principal of the institution, and extends its benign influence throughout all the departments. In the afternoon we went with Pestalozzi, Greaves, and Bucholz, a German clergyman (who is here on a visit to the institution), and one or two others, to visit a free school of twelve or fourteen children which Pestalozzi has established in the village of Clendy, at a short distance from the castle. These are children taken from the families of poor people, selected on account of their character and talents, in order to be educated as teachers, with a view to extend and perpetuate the principles and operation of the system. One-half of them are boys and the other half girls. Their principal instructor is a sister of Schmidt, the chief master, an exceedingly clever and interesting young woman. She has another sister also with her, younger than herself, who will soon become qualified to act as an instructor. These pupils were exercised before us, in drawing, in arithmetic, and in music. The girls, seated round a table, and busy with their needles, had questions in arithmetic given them by the mistress, which they were to solve by their heads. They are thus led on from the most simple beginnings to comprehend the principles of arithmetic, and to work questions with great expertness, solely by a mental process. A male teacher is provided for the boys, though the mistress often asists in the instruction. This little school promises to be well cared for, and of service to the Pestalozzian cause. We were much pleased with its appearance, and with the assurance it affords, that whatever there is of value and importance in the system will not be lost.

The success of this mode of instruction, greatly depends on the personal qualifications of those who undertake to conduct it. There is nothing of mechanism in it, as in the Lancasterian plan; no laying down of precise rules for managing classes, etc. It is all mind and feeling. Its arrangements must always depend on the ages, talents, and tempers of the scholars, and require, on the part of the teachers the most diligent and faithful attention. Above all, it requires that the teacher should consider himself as the father and bosom friend of his pupils, and to be animated with the most affectionate desires for their good. Pestalozzi himself is all this. His heart glows with such a spirit that the good old man can hardly refrain from bestowing kisses on all with whom he is concerned. He holds out his hands to his pupils on every occasion, and they love him as a child loves its mother. His plan of teaching is just fit for the domestic fireside, with a father or mother in the center, and a circle of happy children around them. He is aware of this, and wished to extend the knowledge of his plan to every parent. Pestalozzi is seventy-two years of age. It has been quite unfortunate for the progress of his system on the continent, that he pays so little attention to exteriors, regarding dress, furniture, etc., as of no moment, provided the mind and heart be right.

The weather continuing wet, we resolved to wait till the morrow, and take the diligence to Lausanne and Geneva. Much of the day was spent at the castle, in the school-rooms, and in conversation with Greaves. I omitted to mention that we attended, last evening, to the religious exercise which terminates the business of the day. The scholars assembled in a room called the chapel, but very simply furnished with benches and a table. When all were collected, Pestalozzi, directing his face chiefly to the boys, began to speak in German, moving about, from side to side, directing his attention for some time to the boys on his right and then advancing toward those on his left. This motion, backward and forward, continued about twenty minutes; he was constantly speaking, and sometimes with considerable earnestness. It was altogether unintelligible to me, but I afterward learned that it consisted of a recapitulation of the occurrences of the day, noticing particularly everything of moment, and intermingling the whole with short prayers, adapted to the circumstances mentioned in the discourse. If, for example, any of the boys had quarreled or behaved unseemly to each other, or to their teacher, he would speak to the case, and accompany his remarks with a pious ejaculation. It is probable that he sometimes engages more formally in this exercise. As it was, it appeared to gain the whole attention of his audience. It was concluded by reading from a small book what appeared to be a hymn or psalm.

A company of English visitors attended at the castle to-day, consisting of men and women. The boys performed some of their gymnastic exercises before them, consisting chiefly of simple but simultaneous movements of the arms, legs, feet, head, etc., stepping, marching, turning, and jumping, all intended to exercise the various muscles which give motion to the limbs and head, and to make the boys acquainted with the elements of all those movements. This exercise took place in one of the large bedrooms. We attended, by invitation, last evening, a lecture given by Schmidt, the head teacher, to a number of young men, among whom were four Russians, sent by the Emperor, to gain information in England and other countries relative to the best modes of teaching. They had been in England, and spoke our language tolerably well. The lectures are to illustrate more fully the principles and processes adopted in the Pestalozzian institution.

We have the company, this evening, at our lodgings, of Frederick Bucholz, who was lately a chaplain to the king's German legion in England. He had been some time with Pestalozzi, and was able to give us more information with respect to some parts of the system than we could obtain by a short visit to the school itself.

We had had at our table d'hote, during the last two days, ten or twelve boys, with their preceptors, constituting a boarding-school at Geneva. They are on an excursion round the lake of Geneva, taking Yverdon in the way. They came to this place on foot, through the rain, and intended to perform the whole journey on foot: but the weather continuing very wet, they went off this morning in carriages. One of them is a young prince of Wirtemburg, about twelve years of age, of plain juvenile manners, no extraordinary talent, but apparently of an amiable temper.

We left Yverdon in the diligence, after going again to the castle, and taking leave of some of the professors. Pestalozzi was not in; he had been to see us at the inn, but missed of us. Before we set off, however, the good old man came down again, and parted with us very affectionately. In the course of two days which we have spent at the castle he several times pressed my hand to his lips, and seemed to possess all the love and fervency of a true disciple in the cause in which he is engaged. If his personal talents, address, and management were equal to his genius or his zeal, his influence would have been much greater even than it has been. Nevertheless, the period of his life and labors will, I fully believe, be hereafter regarded as a most important epoch in the history of education. When his principles come to be more generally understood, they will be found to contain much that is extremely valuable. It is to be feared, however, that many years will still elapse before the world is put in possession of a complete explanatory view of his whole system. He does not himself possess the faculty (as Bucholz informed me) of explaining in familiar and intelligible terms his own principles. He conceives with wonderful acuteness, and expresses himself in language of extraordinary force and energy; but it requires a deep and steady attention to be able to embrace his whole meaning. He has published largely in explanation and in support of his plans of instruction; but there is so much of vernacular pith—of idiomatic force and peculiarity in his style and manner, as to render it rather difficult to read him, and still more so to translate his writings. He is now, however, anxious to have all his works translated into English, fully believing that the merit of his plans will be better understood, and his principles more industriously supported, by the English nation than by his own people. His career has been marked with perplexities. He has had to struggle intensely against poverty, neglect, prejudice, and gross misrepresentation; but his patience, his meekness, his perseverance, his ardent love of his fellow creatures, have borne him through all his trials, and notwithstanding his advanced age the reputation of his school is now as high, if not higher, than it ever has been. Toward those who have generously contributed to aid him in his pecuniary difficulties his heart glows with the liveliest gratitude. Of two of my acquaintances, one of London, and the other of Philadelphia, who had thus befriended him, he could not speak without emotion.

Like Locke, Pestalozzi believed that it is primarily through the senses that the child receives knowledge. Accordingly, he designed his famous "object lessons," which enabled the child to use his senses in acquiring the fundamentals of knowledge—form, language, and number. (The object method of teaching had great vogue in America in the 1860's and 1870's.) Pestalozzi urged that learning must proceed from the concrete to the abstract, from the known to the unknown. The following is from Pestalozzi's, An Account of the Method.

All instruction of man is then only the Art of helping Nature to develop in her own way; and this Art rests essentially on the relation and harmony between the impressions received by the child and the exact degree of his developed powers. It is also necessary in the impressions that are brought to the child by instruction that there should be a sequence, so that beginning and progress should keep pace with the beginning and progress of the powers to be developed in the child. I soon saw that an inquiry into this sequence throughout the whole range of human knowledge, particularly those fundamental points from which the development of the human mind originates, must be the simple and only way ever to attain and to keep satisfactory school and instruction books, of every grade, suitable for our nature and our wants. I saw just as soon that in making these books the constituents of instruction must be separated according to the degree of the growing power of the child; and that in all matters of instruction, it is necessary to determine with the greatest accuracy which of these constituents is fit for each age of the child, in order on the one hand not to hold him back if he is ready; and on the other, not to load him and confuse him with anything for which he is not quite ready.

This was clear to me. The child must be brought to a high degree of

Johann Heinrich Pestalozzi, How Gertrude Teaches Her Children and An Account of the Method, *trans. Lucy E. Holland and Frances C. Turner, ed. Ebenezer Cooke (Syracuse, N.Y.: C. W. Bardeen, Publisher, 1898), pp. 57–61.*

knowledge both of things seen and of words before it is reasonable to teach him to spell or read. I was quite convinced that at their earliest age children need psychological training in gaining intelligent sense-impressions of all things. But since such training, without the help of art, is not to be thought of or expected of men as they are, the need of picturebooks struck me perforce. These should precede the A B C books, in order to make those ideas that men express by words clear to the children [by means of well-chosen real objects, that either in reality, or in the form of well-made models and drawings, can be brought before their minds.]

A happy experiment confirmed my then unripe opinion in a striking way, [in spite of all the limitations of my means, and the error and one-sidedness in my experiments]. An anxious mother entrusted her hardly three-year-old child to my private teaching. I saw him for a time every day for an hour; and for a time felt the pulse of a method with him. I tried to teach him by letters, figures, and anything handy; that is, I aimed at giving him clear ideas and expressions by these means. I made him name correctly what he knew of anything—color, limbs, place, form, and number. I was obliged to put aside that first plague of youth, the miserable letters; he would have nothing but pictures and things.

He soon expressed himself clearly about the objects that lay within the limits of his knowledge. He found common illustrations in the street, the garden, and the room; and soon learned to pronounce the hardest names of plants and animals, and to compare objects quite unknown to him with those known, and to produce a clear sense-impression of them in himself. Although this experiment led to byeways, and worked for the strange and distant to the disadvantage of the present, it threw many-sided light on the means of quickening the child to his surroundings, and showing him the charm of self-activity in the extension of his powers.

But yet the experiment was not satisfactory for that which I was particularly seeking, because the boy had already three unused years behind him. I am convinced that nature brings the children even at this age to a definite consciousness of innumerable objects. It only needs that we should with psychological art unite speech with this knowledge in order to bring it to a high degree of clearness; and so enable us to connect the foundations of many-sided arts and truths with that which nature herself teaches, and also to use what nature teaches as a means of explaining all the fundamentals of art and truth that can be connected with them. Their power and their experience both are great at this age; but our unpsychological schools are essentially only artificial stifling-machines for destroying all the results of the power and experience that nature herself brings to life in them.

You know it, my friend. But for a moment picture to yourself the horror of this murder. We leave children up to their fifth year in the full enjoyment of nature; we let every impression of nature work upon them; they feel their power; they already know full well the joy of unrestrained liberty and all its charms. The free natural bent which the sensuous happy wild thing takes in his development, has in them already taken its most decided direction. And after they have enjoyed this happiness of sensuous life for five whole years, we make all nature round them vanish from before their eyes; tyrannically stop the delightful course of their unrestrained freedom; pen them up like sheep, whole flocks huddled together, in stinking rooms; pitilessly chain them for hours, days, weeks, months, years, to the contemplation of unattractive and monotonous letters (and, contrasted with their former condition), to a maddening course of life.

I cease describing; else I shall come to the picture of the greater number of schoolmasters, thousands of whom in our days merely on account of their unfitness for any means of finding a respectable livelihood have subjected themselves to the toilsomeness of this position, which they in accordance with their unfitness for anything better look upon as a way that leads little further than to keep them from starvation. How infinitely must the children suffer under these circumstances, or, at least, be spoiled!

▣ 2. Friedrich Froebel

Froebel's writings and the institution he founded, the kindergarten, reveal both his realistic understanding of the needs of early childhood and his idealism, which deemed education a means to attain the realization of universal unity. Froebel's theory of unity regarded each object in nature not only as a whole unto itself but also a part of a greater unity stemming from the presence of the guiding spirit of God in all things. Through education the individual could gain a clear perception of himself and his unity with God and God's universe.

An eternal law pervades and governs all things. The basis of this all-controlling law is an all-pervading, living, self-conscious and therefore eternal Unity. This Unity is God. God is the source of all things. Each thing exists only because the divine spirit lives in it and this divine spirit is its essence. The destiny of every thing is to reveal its essence, that is, the divine spirit dwelling in it. It is the special function of man

S. S. F. Fletcher and J. Welton (trans.), Froebel's Chief Writings on Education, *pp. 31–33. Copyright, 1912, by Edward Arnold and Co. Reprinted by permission of Edward Arnold (Publishers) Ltd.*

as an intelligent and rational being to realize his essence fully and clearly, to exercise, practise, and reveal the divine spirit in him, freely and consciously in his own life.

The Theory of Education is the body of doctrine derived by thoughtful men from insight into this law, as a guidance in the apprehension and attainment of man's true calling.

The Art of Education is the free application of this knowledge and insight to the development of rational beings and their training towards the fulfilment of their destiny.

The Purpose of Education is the realization of a faithful, pure, inviolate, and therefore holy, life.

Education, then, must develop the divine spirit in man and make him conscious of it, so that his life may become a free expression of that spirit. Education, in other words, should lead man to a clear knowledge of himself, to peace with nature, to unity with God.

The divine essence of things is recognized by its manifestations. But although all education, all instruction, all teaching, all free life, attaches itself to these manifestations of men and things, and through them acts upon the inner spirit, yet education must not draw conclusions concerning the spirit directly from the manifestations. The nature of things is such that in some ways inferences should be drawn negatively.

Failure in applying this truth—that is drawing conclusions concerning the essence directly from its manifestations—is the chief reason for the many mistakes of life and education. Hence it is of the utmost importance that parents and teachers should familiarize themselves with the application of it in its smallest details. This would secure a clearness, certainty, and serenity, in the relations between parents and children, pupils and teachers, which are now sought in vain. For the child who outwardly appears to be good is often not good inwardly; that is, he does not desire the good deliberately, nor from love, esteem, and recognition, of it. On the other hand, the churlish, stubborn, self-willed, child, who outwardly appears to be naughty, has frequently within himself the most active, eager and vigorous desire for the good; while the absent-minded boy is often following a fixed thought which makes him disregard everything around him.

Hence the fundamental principles of education, instruction, and teaching, should be passive and protective, not directive and interfering.

We give room and time to young plants and animals, well knowing that then they will develop and grow according to the laws inherent in them. We do not interfere, because we know that this would disturb their healthy development. But the young child is treated as wax or clay which can be moulded into any form. Why does man, wandering through gardens and fields, meadows and groves, fail to open his mind, and refuse to listen to the lesson which nature silently teaches? See how the weed, growing amid obstacles and restraints, scarcely gives a hint that it obeys an inner law. Then look at its growing in the open field, and see what conformity to law it shows, what harmonious life in all its parts. So children who appear sickly and constrained because their parents have forced upon them in their tender years a form and calling opposed to their nature, might under natural conditions develop with beauty, uniformity, and harmony.

In dealing with objects of nature we often follow the right road, but go astray when we deal with men. And yet, forces are at work in both which have sprung from one source, and which obey the same law. Hence it is important that man should consider nature also from this point of view. . . .

The role of education in Froebel's theory of unity is illustrated in his children's garden.

The great importance for the development both of the individual and of the race of an intimate familiarity with nature has already been several times emphasized. It is really the one sure foundation of all true culture, for to know nature well means to see in it the first and most immediate revelation of the divine energy. But we have not as yet worked out the thought in detail. This importance is especially related to growth and development in nature observed and compared with growth and development in mankind, and so in the individual himself. But important as this is for all men, it is yet more so for the human being who is still growing and developing, that is, for the child and the youth. Hence, a full and sufficient education must give opportunity for such comparative observation. This is the complete and perfect idea of a *kindergarten,* which implies in its very name that it is a *garden of children.* So the root-idea of a kindergarten demands that it should have gardens for the children who attend it.

This association of gardens with a kindergarten is also demanded by social and civic life. For the child, as part of humanity, must not only be recognized by others as at once an individual and a part of the larger whole of life, but he must so regard himself, and must order his life on that principle. This interchange of activity between the individual and the community is nowhere more strikingly and beautifully seen than in the tending of plants in common when each child has his own little plot in the family garden. But in the kindergarten, where there are many children and their gardens are the most important thing, a somewhat different arrangement is required. Here the little garden-beds of the children must be surrounded by the common garden, as always the

Fletcher and Welton, op. cit., pp. 237–38.

particular rests amid the general by which it is surrounded and protected.

Besides showing this relation of the particular to the general, of the
part to the whole, and so symbolizing the child in the family, the citizen
in the community, the garden should furnish instruction about things,
and particularly about shrubs and plants. This is secured by asking the
child to compare the plants and shrubs standing near each other.

*To the various objects and games he employed in his kindergarten, Froebel
usually attached both symbolic and "useful" values.*

The ball, as the type of the self-contained, represents everything
which can be thought and treated as a whole. Other objects doubtless
can give the ideas of being, disappearing, returning, seeking, finding,
fetching, grasping, holding, rolling, and so on, but none gives so great
variety of movements as the ball. It is this which makes it so excellent a
plaything. But what has been done with the ball may be attempted with
other things, such as an apple, a ball of thread, a key, a nut, a flower.
So will these objects be brought before the child in different actions and
relations, and thus his development will be broadened. But amid all
such variety the ball remains the unifying and explanatory plaything
through which comes understanding.

When the child begins to crawl the ball is given him to play with as
he will. He is placed on a rug on the floor, and a ball somewhat larger
than those with which he has hitherto played may be suspended above
him from the ceiling, and thus incite him to learn to stand, and so
strengthen the muscles of hip and thigh. In this play the father may well
take part.

The ball shows the child unity amid variety and the vital connexion
between them. It presents content, mass, matter, space, form, magni-
tude; it has elasticity and consequently is capable of rest and of motion,
and is both independent and self-active. It partakes of the general
characteristics of all bodies, for it has colour, weight, and gravitation,
and is capable of producing sound. Through quicker movement on a
shorter string and slower movement on a longer string, it opens the way
to the most important phenomena and laws of nature. So the ball as a
plaything connecting parent and child places man in the centre of the
universe. And it is never too early so to place him, that he may rest
consciously in unity with himself and in harmony with nature and with
life. But the ball does more. It also early gives a central core to the
child's own life.

It has been seen that games with the ball are valuable to the child in

Fletcher and Welton, op. cit., *pp. 178–80.*

his three-fold aspect as a creating, feeling, and thinking, being. It may now be noted that another whole set of games may in a way be called *useful*, because they are obviously related to actual working life. Yet another may be styled *beautiful*, as having no reference to anything outside themselves, and satisfying by their own harmonious variety and completeness. A third set attracts the child by their *truth*, because through them certain relations, qualities, and connexions, are made explicit, each of which was already implicitly felt in his soul.

So we see that this first plaything of the child leads him in harmonious development towards the useful, the beautiful, and the true. Parents have thus an early opportunity of noticing towards which of these their child predominantly inclines and so of avoiding a one-sided development, even as life, art, and science are not mutually exclusive.

The games with the ball further develop the child's mental power. They practise him in perceiving and remembering; they awaken the capacity to compare, infer, judge, think; they foster the feelings; in them speech is cultivated. So man, even when a child, by games with the ball is placed in the centre of his own life and of all life.

The two brief paragraphs that follow help reveal a lasting contribution of Froebel to the development of modern educational practice.

Play, then, is the highest expression of human development in childhood, for it alone is the free expression of what is in the child's soul. It is the purest and most spiritual product of the child, and at the same time it is a type and copy of human life at all stages and in all relations. So it induces joy, freedom, contentment, inner and outer repose, peace with all the world. From it flows all good. A child who plays vigorously, freely, and quietly, and who persists till he is thoroughly tired, will of a certainty grow into a capable and quietly persistent man, ready to sacrifice his own present ease when a higher good for himself or for others demands it. Can childhood ever show more beautiful than in a child so absorbed in play that sleep has overcome him unawares?

Childhood's play is not mere sport; it is full of meaning and of serious import. Cherish and encourage it, then, O parents! For to one who has insight into human nature, the trend of the whole future life of the child is revealed in his freely chosen play.

The following is a description by a French visitor to the Froebelian Institute of Berlin in 1880. This kindergarten was established by Madame Henrietta Schrader, niece and pupil of Friedrich Froebel, specifically to put into practice the Froebelian system. The kindergarten was separated into divisions according

Fletcher and Welton, op. cit., *pp. 50–51.*

to the age of the pupils: Third Division, ages 2½ to 4; Second Division, ages 4 to 5; First Division, ages 5 to 6.

A VISIT TO MADAME SCHRADER'S ESTABLISHMENT

On my arrival the children all gathered in room No. 2. They are singing a morning hymn. After a few kind affectionate words from the principal, they separate, and the work of the day begins.

THIRD, OR YOUNGEST DIVISION

Follow a part of these divisions to the play-room, where the children set about enjoying themselves as they please. Some join in a round game, others play quite alone. They have at their disposal very plain and simple toys, such as dolls, little chairs, tables, tea services, etc. A teacher overlooks them without taking an active part in their game, unless they desire it particularly.

From two to four years of age, play is the principal occupation of the child; it is for him the power of giving a form to his ideas by the help of surrounding objects, and at the same time the means of giving vent to the full play of his activity. Pestalozzi says: "that no force can be developed unless by the play of its own power of action." We must then conclude that if we wish to see in the child the development of his most essential faculties, he is to be allowed the full play of his energies and faculties, and no restraint whatever to be put on the first working of his individuality in his relation with the outer world. At this period of his development the result of his efforts is less interesting to the child than the activity itself; for this reason the influence of elders must here be principally indirect.

As the child draws the materials for his ideas out of the things about him, we must try to surround him with such an atmosphere as may create in him good, sound, healthy ideas; to attain this end, we must give him room and space enough to permit him to enjoy himself fully and freely, toys and things appropriate to his physical strength, which he may easily handle and transform without breaking or destroying them. But above all, he must be surrounded with sympathy and love; he must feel that we are always ready to enter into his ideas, to be the partakers of his joy, taking at the same time due care that he should not feel any restraint nor any special direction forced upon him. This full liberty, of such an absolute necessity to the child, is also the best means offered to the educator of becoming acquainted with his true nature, as it shows itself through his tastes and inclinations freely manifested.

Henry Barnard (ed.), The American Journal of Education *(Hartford: Henry Barnard, 1881), XXXI, 456–58.*

The home is generally the best place for the education of the child, but when the necessary conditions for his development are not to be found in the family, the Kindergartner must fill his void and create for the child what is wanting to him.

I leave this room and enter one where the other children of the third division are assembled. They are gathered round the teacher; she is showing to them a picture out of Froebel's book *Mutter und Koselieder*, the basket of flowers. She gives no explanations, her object not being to teach, but merely to create joyful impressions. The children look and make remarks, the teacher answers so as to encourage them, to draw them out, and awaken their attention more and more. The picture represents a garden, where a mother and a little girl are plucking flowers to take up to the father. They examine the picture, express their feelings about it, and when they have done it long enough, some pretty flowers are shown to them. The teacher asks whether they would not like to take some home with them? But for this, they must have baskets; baskets can be made out of the children's own fingers. She makes them all join their hands in the form of a basket, making them, at the same time, sing "Little child, let us make baskets" *(Mutter und Koselieder)*. When the song is finished they receive little paper baskets, to carry home to their parents.

The talk is at an end; the children seat themselves round the table; little wooden sticks are distributed among them, out of which they make different things—vases, baskets, etc.

Froebel's book, *Mutter und Koselieder*, is the starting point for all the occupations of this division. These occupations are already a kind of work, for the child is no longer left to the full play of his imagination, but he is limited by a given space and materials, and he must bring himself to execute an idea which has not spontaneously come into his mind, but has been suggested by others. Work, as well as play, has activity for its basis; but if, with the latter, activity in itself is the principal end, with work, on the contrary, the result has its importance; therefore the child cannot be left entirely free, he must be guided so as to employ his forces in a useful way. Activity in itself is so charming for the child that he does not, at first, make a great difference between play and work; it is only when the latter presents too great difficulties and puts too great a restraint upon his liberty that it becomes irksome and painful to him.

By proportioning the work to the child's powers and strength, by awakening in him a desire of being useful, by taking care not to fatigue him, one may succeed in making him feel as much pleasure in work as in play.

There are in the child, as in the man, two personalities: the individual, and the social being. Man lives not isolated, but moves in a society to which he owes his own share of profit and usefulness. Education must take this into account, and try to develop simultaneously in the child, the individual and the social being by giving a full play to the spontaneous action of the child's powers, but at the same time giving such a direction to their powers that they may be productive of general good. Play and work are both necessary, and it is to their united and combined action that the child owes sound and normal development.

SECOND DIVISION

The children follow their teacher to the kitchen, where they are entrusted with flower-pots, earth, plants, little rounds of paper, each of them carrying something.

They return to the class-room, and gather round the table, where they place the things they have brought with them. A spoon in the hand; they, one after the other, half fill the flower-pots with earth; they then put the plants in and cover them with earth. They then water the plants and set them before the window, when the weather is too cold to set them out in the open air. And thus the children are, from the beginning, placed directly in contact with nature; they are brought to understand the relation in which men and nature stand to each other, and the necessity of reciprocal action. In order that the flower may please our eyes and rejoice us with its perfume, we must, after having planted, water it; we must take every care of it, to give and to receive; everything goes on in this world by the law of reciprocation.

Another day this same plant, the violet, furnishes the material for a new work. It is stitched on a piece of paper, marked, and afterwards drawn; it appears in different aspects, but it is always the violet that is presented to the child, in order that all the experiments he is making may leave deep and lasting impressions upon his mind. Almost all the occupations of this division relate to work, and the reality is the starting point, thus, always proceeding by gradual steps; passing from the image to the reality. First, the picture, then the flower, and last the plant; the semblance of work, then the work itself.

FIRST DIVISION

The same occupations are continued. The teacher tells a little story, in which the violet plays the first part; the children listen with pleased attention, and ask that it should again be told to them. The tale finished, they are shown a pretty picture by Ludwig Rickbe, representing a family, enjoying the beauty of the spring. The mother has the child in her arms; she points out to him, over the wall, the green fields, the houses; she seems to say: "See, my child, the world which is offering itself to you." Then slates are distributed among them; they are allowed to draw whatever they please, but they endeavor, generally, to represent an episode of the story they have just heard.

The children learn, also, by heart, a little poem on the violet, and this poem, expressing only feelings and ideas created by the thing itself, no explanations are required. The child follows unconsciously the same path taken by the poet, he goes through the same impressions that have created his poem, which becomes for him as a revelation, the half-veiled expression of feelings to which he is himself as yet unable to give a form.

Berlin, Oct. 15, 1880.

回 3. Johann Friedrich Herbart

The selections that follow are from Herbart's Outlines of Educational Doctrine *with annotations by Charles De Garmo. Included are references to Herbart's concept of the double basis of pedagogics, his emphasis upon the social sciences and literary studies, his stress on many-sidedness of interest, and finally his systematic method of teaching, which in the hands of his disciples became the "Five Formal Steps of Instruction."*

Pedagogics as a science is based on ethics and psychology. The former points out the goal of education; the latter the way, the means, and the obstacles.

This relationship involves the dependence of pedagogics on experience, inasmuch as ethics includes application to experience, while psychology has its starting-point, not in metaphysics alone, but in experience correctly interpreted by metaphysics. But an exclusively empirical knowledge of man will not suffice for pedagogics. It is the less adequate in any age the greater the instability of morals, customs, and opinions; for, as the new gains on the old, generalizations from former observations cease to hold true.

* * * * *

In order that instruction may act on the pupil's ideas and disposition, every avenue of approach should be thrown open. The mere fact that we can never know with certainty, beforehand, what will influence the pupil most, warns us against one-sidedness of instruction.

John Frederick Herbart, Outlines of Educational Doctrine, *trans. Alexis F. Lange (New York: The Macmillan Company, 1901), pp. 2, 24–25, 44, 52–54, 57–59.*

Ideas spring from two main sources,—experience and social intercourse. Knowledge of nature—incomplete and crude—is derived from the former; the later furnishes the sentiments entertained toward our fellowmen, which, far from being praiseworthy, are on the contrary often very reprehensible. To improve these is the more urgent task; but neither ought we to neglect the knowledge of nature. If we do, we may expect error, fantastical notions, and eccentricities of every description.

Hence, we have two main branches of instruction,—the historical and the scientific. The former embraces not only history proper, but language study as well; the latter includes, besides natural science, mathematics.

"Historical" must be interpreted to include all human sciences, such as history, literature, languages, æsthetics, and political, economic, and social science. "Scientific" may include applied as well as pure science, and then we add all forms of industrial training to the curriculum. Other divisions of the subject-matter of instruction are often helpful. Thus one may speak of the human sciences, the natural sciences, and the economic sciences. The economic sciences include those activities where man and nature interact. Dr. Wm. T. Harris speaks of five coordinate groups of subjects, corresponding to what he calls the "five windows of the soul."

*   *   *   *   *

The ultimate purpose of instruction is contained in the notion, virtue. But in order to realize the final aim, another and nearer one must be set up. We may term it, *many-sidedness of interest*. The word *interest* stands in general for that kind of mental activity which it is the business of instruction to incite. Mere information does not suffice; for this we think of as a supply or store of facts, which a person might possess or lack, and still remain the same being. But he who lays hold of his information and reaches out for more, takes an interest in it. Since, however, this mental activity is varied, we need to add the further determination supplied by the term *many-sidedness*.

*   *   *   *   *

Some teachers lay great stress on the explication, step by step, of the smaller and smallest components of the subject, and insist on a similar reproduction on the part of the pupils. Others prefer to teach by conversation, and allow themselves and their pupils great freedom of expression. Others, again, call especially for the leading thoughts, but demand that these be given with accuracy and precision, and in the prescribed order. Others, finally, are not satisfied until their pupils are self-actively exercising their minds in systematic thinking.

Various methods of teaching may thus arise; it is not necessary, however, that one should be habitually employed to the exclusion of the rest.

We may ask rather whether each does not contribute its share to a many-sided culture. In order that a multitude of facts may be apprehended, explications or analyses are needed to prevent confusion; but since a synthesis is equally essential, the latter process may be started by conversation, continued by lifting into prominence the cardinal thoughts, and completed by the methodical independent thinking of the pupil: *clearness, association, system, method.*

In teaching we need to have (1) *clearness* in the presentation of specific facts, or the elements of what is to be mastered; (2) *association* of these facts with one another, and with other related facts formerly acquired, in order that assimilation, or apperception, may be adequately complete; (3) when sufficient facts have been clearly presented and sufficiently assimilated, they must be *systematically* ordered, so that our knowledge will be more perfectly unified than it could be did we stop short of thorough classification, as in the study of botany, or of the perception of rules and principles, as in mathematics and grammar; (4) finally the facts, rules, principles, and classifications thus far assumed must be secured for all time by their efficient *methodical* application in exercises that call forth the vigorous self-activity of the pupil. These four stages of teaching may be considered fundamental, though varying greatly according to the nature of the subject and the ability of the pupil. It is good exercise for a pupil to take long, rapid steps when able to do so; it is hopeless confusion to undertake them when they are too great or too rapid for his capacity. These four stages in methods of teaching conceived to be essential, form the nucleus of an interesting development in the Herbartian school, under the title of "The Formal [*i.e.* Essential] Steps of Instruction."

* * * * *

Herbart found his basis for the four steps of method, viz. *clearness, association, system, method,* in the ideas of absorption and reflection, the alternate pulsation of consciousness in absorbing and assimilating knowledge. Others, adopting this classification as essentially correct, have related these steps to customary psychological analysis. Thus Dörpfeld and Wiget point out that the mind goes through three well-marked processes when it performs the complete act of learning, namely, *perception* of new facts; *thought,* or the bringing of ideas into logical relations; and *application,* or the exercise of the motor activities of the mind in putting knowledge into use. Perception gives the *percept,* thought gives the *conception* (or rule, principle, generalization), and application gives *power.* In other words, the receptive and reflective capacities of the mind come to their full fruition when they result in adequate motor activities. With respect to perception a good method will first *prepare* the mind for facts and will then *present* them so that they may be apperceived. The first two steps are therefore *preparation* and *presentation.* The first step, as Ziller pointed out, is essentially *analytic* in character, since it analyzes the present store of consciousness in order to bring facts to the front that are closely related to those of the present lesson; the second step, *i.e.,* presentation, is essentially *synthetic*, since its function is to add the matter of the new lesson to related knowledge already in possession. Both together constitute the initial stages of apperception.

Thought consists of two processes that may also be termed steps, and that are more or less observable in all good teaching; they are (1) the *association* of newly apperceived facts with one another and with older and more firmly established ideas in order that rational connection may be established in what one knows, and especially in order that what is general and essential in given facts may be grasped by the mind; and (2) the condensation of knowledge into a *system*, such for instance as we see in the classifications of botany and zoölogy, or in the interdependence of principles as in arithmetic. Thought, in brief, involves the association of ideas and the derivation of generalizations such as are appropriate to the matter in hand and to the thought power of the pupils.

The third stage, that of *application*, is not subdivided. Most other followers of Herbart, both German and American, though varying in methods of approach, conform essentially to the results of this analysis, distinguishing *five* steps, as follows:—

1. Preparation—Analysis ⎱
2. Presentation—Synthesis ⎰ Apperception of percepts.
3. Association   ⎱ Thought. The derivation and arrangement of rule,
4. Systemization   ⎰   principle, or class.
5. Application. From knowing to doing: use of motor powers.

🔲 4. National Control of French Education

One of Napoleon's chief interests was the establishment of a national system of education controlled ultimately by the central government in Paris. The law of 1802 provided the first step. Interested primarily in secondary and higher education, Napoleon gave the Church general control over elementary schooling while making provisions for state secondary schools and national control of the higher professional, scientific, and artistic faculties. In 1806, Napoleon took the giant step, establishing the Imperial University (later known as the University of France) as the supreme administrator of all French secondary and higher education. The following discussion of the law of 1806 was written by the French historian of education, Gabriel Compayré.

FOUNDATION OF THE UNIVERSITY (1806).—The law of May 11, 1806, completed by the decrees of March 17, 1808, and of

Gabriel Compayré, The History of Pedagogy *(Boston: D. C. Heath and Company, Publishers, 1885), pp. 510–13.*

1811, established the University, that is, a teaching corporation, unique and entirely dependent on the State:—

"There shall be constituted a body charged exclusively with instruction and public education throughout the whole extent of the Empire."

Instruction thus became a function of the State, on the same basis as the administration of justice or the organization of the army.

At the same time that it lost all autonomy, all independence, the University gained the formidable privilege of being alone charged with the national instruction.

"No one can open a school or teach publicly, without being a member of the Imperial University and without having been graduated from one of its Faculties." "No school can be established outside of the University, and without the authorization of its head."

We know what protestations were excited, even on the start, by the establishment of this University monopoly. "It was not enough to enchain parents; it was still necessary to dispose of the children. Mothers have been seen hastening from the extremities of the Empire, coming to reclaim, in an agony of tears, the sons whom the government had carried off from them." Thus spoke Chateaubriand, before lavishing his adulations on the restorer of altars, and he added, with an extravagance of imagination which recoils on itself, "Children were placed in schools where they were taught at the sound of the drum, irreligion, debauchery, and contempt for the domestic virtues!" Joseph de Maistre was more just: "Fontanes,"[1] he said, "has large views and excellent intentions. The plan of his University is grand and comprehensive. It is a Noble body. The soul will come to it when it can. Celibacy, subordination, devotion of the whole life without religious motive, are required. Will they be obtained?"[2]

ORGANIZATION OF THE IMPERIAL UNIVERSITY.—The Imperial University comprised, like the present University, Colleges, Lycées, and Faculties. The Colleges furnished secondary instruction, like the Lycées, but less complete. There were a Faculty of Letters and a Faculty of Sciences for each academic centre; but these Faculties were very poorly equipped, with their endowment of from five to ten thousand francs at most, and with their few professors. The professors at the neighboring Lycée (professors of rhetoric and mathematics) formed a part of the establishment, and each Faculty included at most but two or three other chairs.

Latin and mathematics formed the basis of the instruction in the Lycées. The Revolution had not come in vain, since that which it had vigorously demanded was now realized; the sciences and the classical languages were put on a footing of equality.

[1] *Fontanes (1757–1821), first Grand Master of the University.*
[2] Memoire politique *of Joseph de Maistre, Paris, 1858, p. 30.*

DYNASTIC PREPOSSESSIONS.—That which absorbed the attention of the founder of the Imperial University was less the schemes of study than the general principles on which the rising generations were to be nourished. In this respect the thought of the Emperor is not obscure. He does not dissemble it. God and the Emperor are the two words which must be graven into the depths of the soul.

"All the schools of the Imperial University will make as the basis of their instruction: 1. the precepts of the Catholic religion; 2. fidelity to the Emperor, to the imperial monarchy, the depository of the happiness of the people, and to the Napoleonic dynasty, the *conservator of the unity of France*, and of all the ideas proclaimed by the Constitution."

"Napoleon," as Guizot says, "attempted to convert into an instrument of despotism an institution which tended to be only a centre of light."

PRIMARY INSTRUCTION NEGLECTED.—Primary instruction never occupied the attention of Napoleon I. The decree of 1805 contented itself with promising measures intended to assure the recruitment of teachers, especially the creation of one or more normal classes within the colleges and lycées. Moreover, the Grand Master was to encourage and to license the Brethren of the Christian Schools, while supervising their establishments. Finally, the right to establish schools was left to families or to religious corporations, the budget of the Empire containing no item of appropriation for the cause of popular instruction.

The restoration was scarcely more generous towards the instruction of the people. By the ordinance of February 29, 1815, it granted *fifty thousand francs* as encouragement to the primary schools. Was this derisive liberality any better than complete silence and neglect? A more important measure was the establishment of cantonal committees charged with the supervision of primary schools. These committees were placed, sometimes under the direction of the rector, and at others under the authority of the bishop, at the pleasure of the vicissitudes of politics. Certificates of qualification were delivered to the members of the authorized congregations, on the simple presentation of their letters of permission. We can imagine what a body of teachers could be assured by such a mode of recruitment.

In anticipation of the monarchy of July, which in its liberal dispositions was to appear more regardful of popular education, private initiative signalized itself under the Restoration by the foundation of the *Society for Elementary Instruction*, and also by the encouragement it gave to the first attempts at mutual instruction.

Under the July monarchy of Louis Philippe primary education was finally incorporated into the national system. Prodded by the reform-minded Minister of

Public Education Guizot and by Victor Cousin, whose laudatory report on the organization of Prussia's educational system was extremely influential, Parliament took the necessary steps in 1833. The following discussion of the law of 1833 provides a vivid picture of France's nationwide pattern of primary education with its organization, standards and curriculum established in large measure by act of Parliament and its administration the responsibility ultimately of the Minister of Public Instruction.

The central government, the departmental authorities, the municipal authorities, the religious authorities, the heads of families, have each their sphere of action, and their influence in the administration of primary schools.

The local management of a primary school is intrusted to a committee of the commune, consisting of the mayor, the president of the council, the curé, or pastor, and one person appointed by the committee of the arrondissement in which the commune is situated.

The general supervision of the schools of each arrondissement is assigned to a committee of the arrondissement, which consists of the mayor of the chief town, of the *juge de paix*, a pastor of each of the recognized religious sects, a professor of a college or school of secondary instruction, a primary schoolmaster, three members of the council of the arrondissement, and the members of the council-general of the department who reside in the arrondissement.

These committees meet once a month. The communal committees inspect and report the condition of the schools in the commune to the committee of the arrondissement. Some member of the committee of the arrondissement is present at each local inspection, and a report of the whole committee on the state of education in the arrondissement is made annually to the Minister of Public Instruction.

In each department there is a commission of primary education, composed of at least seven members, among which there must be a minister of each of the religious denominations recognized by law, and at least three persons who are at the time, or have been, engaged in teaching public schools of secondary instruction. This committee is charged with the examination of all candidates for the certificate of qualification to teach primary schools, or to enter the Normal School of the department. These examinations must be public, at a time fixed, and notified by the minister, and in the chief town of the department. The examination is varied according to the grade of school for which the candidate applies. With a certificate of capacity from this commission, the candidate can teach in any commune in the department, without any local examination.

Henry Barnard (ed.), The American Journal of Education *(Hartford: Office of the American Journal of Education, 1870), XX, 244–46.*

Besides these local committees the minister of public instruction appoints an inspector for every department, with assistant inspectors, when required by the exigences of the public service. The duty of the inspector is to visit every school in the department, at least once a year, and to inquire into the state of the school-house, the classification, moral character, and methods of discipline and instruction of each school. He must leave a written memorandum of all deficiencies noted in his visit, for the use of the local committee, and report annually to the prefect of the department, and through him to the minister. This stimulates and encourages teachers, as well as communes, and informs the minister of the true wants of different localities, as well as the deficiencies of the law. The inspectors are required to pay particular attention to the Normal Schools in their several departments. The inspector has a salary of two thousand francs, and an allowance of three francs a day for traveling expenses, and one franc for every school visited. In 1843 there were eighty-seven inspectors, and one hundred and fourteen sub-inspectors; and the number of communes visited by them in that year, was 30,081, making 50,986 visits to schools.

The resources of the state, the departments, the communes, and the contributions paid by parents, combine to insure the creation and maintenance of the school. Every commune must provide a school-house and residence for the school-master, and to the first expense of this outfit, the state contributes one third. Every teacher must have a lodging, or its equivalent in money, and a fixed salary of 200 francs, or 400 francs, (from $40 to $80), according to the grade of school, in addition to the monthly fees paid by parents, and collected by the commune. If the commune refuses, or neglects to provide by tax on the property of the commune, the government imposes and collects the same. If the commune, on account of poverty or disaster to crops or depression in business, can not raise its necessary sum, the department to which it belongs must provide it, and if the revenues of the department are not sufficient to supply the deficiencies of all the communes, the deficit must be supplied by the state. In every department, the prefect and general-council, annually draw up in concert a special estimate in which the expense of primary instruction is fixed, and necessary revenue provided. In each commune, the Mayor and municipal council make a special estimate of the same kind; and at the same time fix the monthly tuition fee to be paid by each parent.

Every department must by itself, or in concert with adjoining departments, support a Normal School, to supply the annual demand for teachers of primary schools. The sum to be expended on a Normal School, for the salaries of teachers, apparatus, and bursaries, or scholarships in aid of poor pupils, is not left with the department to fix, but is regulated by the council of public instruction. The salary of the Director is borne by the state and department combined; that of the assistant teachers by the department. The expense of the normal pupils for board is borne by themselves, unless they enjoy an exhibition or scholarship, founded by the state, department, university, commune, or by individual benevolence. The scholarships are sometimes divided so as to meet, in part, the expense of two or three pupils. In 1846, there were ninety-two Normal Schools, seventy-six of which were for the education of schoolmasters, and sixteen for the education of schoolmistresses. To fifty-two of these schools enough land is attached to teach agriculture and horticulture.

The course of instruction in these elementary schools, embraces Moral and Religious Instruction, Reading, Writing, the elements of Arithmetic, elements of the French Language, legal system of Weights and Measures, Geography, (particularly of France,) History, (particularly of France,) Linear Drawing, and Singing. In the superior primary schools, or High School, the above course is extended so as to embrace Modern Languages, Book-keeping, Perspective Drawing, Chemistry, and the Mathematics, in their application to the arts. There is a special course of instruction open in evening schools, to those children and youth who can not attend the day school; and in evening classes for adults, whose early education was neglected, or who may wish to pursue particular studies connected with their pursuits as artizans, manufacturers, and master-workmen.

Provision is made to encourage teachers to form associations, and to hold frequent conferences for improvement in their professional knowledge and skill, and to found libraries of books on education.

In each department a fund is accumulating for the relief of aged teachers, and of the widows and children of teachers, who die in the exercise of their important functions. Each master must subscribe one twentieth part of the salary he receives from the commune; and the sum-total which he subscribes, together with the interest upon it, is returned to him when he retires, or to his widow and children, when he dies.

The government awards medals of silver and bronze to those masters who distinguish themselves in the management of their schools. This encourages and stimulates them to continued efforts, and connects them in an honorable way, with the government and the nation.

▣ 5. Prussian Education, A Model for the World

Although the liberal spirit of Prussian education was rather short-lived, educational reformers from England, France, and the United States flocked to examine the system and found much to praise. True, by 1830 the schools were established on a two-track (mass and class) basis, and education was dedicated to maintaining rather than liberalizing the social system. Yet, the Prussian educational system was remarkably efficient and Pestalozzian influences were still evident in the 1840's. One of those visitors who found in Prussian education much to recommend to his countrymen was the American advocate of public education, Horace Mann. In his "Seventh Annual Report" to the Massachusetts Board of Education in 1843, Mann acknowledged that the Prussian system was sustained by and dedicated to the maintenance of an "arbitrary power." However, he did not allow this to detract his attention from its positive accomplishments. Selections from that report follow.

Among the nations of Europe, Prussia has long enjoyed the most distinguished reputation for the excellence of its schools. In reviews, in speeches, in tracts, and even in graver works devoted to the cause of education, its schools have been exhibited as models for the imitation of the rest of Christendom. For many years, scarce a suspicion was breathed that the general plan of education in that kingdom was not sound in theory and most beneficial in practice. Recently, however, grave charges have been preferred against it by high authority. The popular traveller, Laing, has devoted several chapters of his large work on Prussia to the disparagement of its school-system. An octavo volume, entitled "The Age of Great Cities," has recently appeared in England, in which that system is strongly condemned; and during the pendency of the famous "Factories' Bill" before the British House of Commons, in 1843, numerous tracts were issued from the English press, not merely calling in question, but strongly denouncing, the whole plan of education in Prussia, as being not only designed to produce, but as actually producing, a spirit of blind acquiescence to arbitrary power, in things spiritual as well as temporal,—as being, in fine, a system of education adapted to enslave, and not to enfranchise, the human mind. And even in some parts of the United States, the very nature and essence of whose institutions consist in the idea that the people are wise enough to distinguish between what is right and what is wrong,—even here some have been illiberal enough to condemn, in advance, every thing that savors of the Prussian system, because that system is sustained by arbitrary power.

My opinion of these strictures will appear in the sequel. But I may here remark, that I do not believe either of the first two authors above referred to had ever visited the schools they presumed to condemn. The

Life and Works of Horace Mann *(Boston: Lee and Shepard, Publishers, 1891),* III, 240–42, 304–5, 352, 356–59.

English tract-writers, too, were induced to disparage the Prussian system from a motive foreign to its merits. The "Factories' Bill," which they so vehemently assailed, proposed the establishment of schools to be placed under the control of the church. Against this measure, the dissenters wished to array the greatest possible opposition. As there was a large party in the kingdom who doubted the expediency of any interference on the part of government in respect to public education, it was seen that an argument derived from the alleged abuses of the Prussian system could be made available to turn this class into opponents of the measure then pending in Parliament. Thus the errors of that system, unfortunately, were brought to bear, not merely against proselytizing education, but against education itself.

But, allowing all these charges against the Prussian system to be true, there were still two reasons why I was not deterred from examining it.

In the first place, the evils imputed to it were easily and naturally separable from the good which it was not denied to possess. If the Prussian schoolmaster has better methods of teaching reading, writing, grammar, geography, arithmetic, &c., so that, in half the time, he produces greater and better results, surely we may copy his modes of teaching these elements, without adopting his notions of passive obedience to government, or of blind adherence to the articles of a church. By the ordinance of Nature, the human faculties are substantially the same all over the world; and hence the best means for their development and growth in one place must be substantially the best for their development and growth everywhere. The spirit which shall control the action of these faculties when matured, which shall train them to self-reliance or to abject submission, which shall lead them to refer all questions to the standard of reason or to that of authority,—this spirit is wholly distinct and distinguishable from the manner in which the faculties themselves should be trained; and we may avail ourselves of all improved methods in the earlier processes, without being contaminated by the abuses which may be made to follow them. The best style of teaching arithmetic or spelling has no necessary or natural connection with the doctrine of hereditary right; and an accomplished lesson in geography or grammar commits the human intellect to no particular dogma in religion.

In the second place, if Prussia can pervert the benign influences of education to the support of arbitrary power, we surely can employ them for the support and perpetuation of republican institutions. A national spirit of liberty can be cultivated more easily than a national spirit of bondage; and, if it may be made one of the great prerogatives of education to perform the unnatural and unholy work of making slaves, then surely it must be one of the noblest instrumentalities for rearing a nation of freemen. If a moral power over the understandings and affections of the people may be turned to evil, may it not also be employed for good?

*   *   *   *   *

About twenty years ago, teachers in Prussia made the important discovery, that children have five senses, together with various muscles and mental faculties, all which, almost by a necessity of their nature, must be kept in a state of activity, and which, if not usefully, are liable to be mischievously employed. Subsequent improvements in the art of teaching have consisted in supplying interesting and useful, instead of mischievous occupation for these senses, muscles, and faculties. Experience has now proved that it is much easier to furnish profitable and delightful employment for all these powers than it is to stand over them with a rod and stifle their workings, or to assume a thousand shapes of fear to guard the thousand avenues through which the salient spirits of the young play outward. Nay, it is much easier to keep the eye and hand and mind at work together than it is to employ either one of them separately from the others. A child is bound to the teacher by so many more cords, the more of his natural capacities the teacher can interest and employ.

In the case I am now to describe, I entered a classroom of sixty children of about six years of age. The children were just taking their seats, all smiles and expectation. They had been at school but a few weeks, but long enough to have contracted a love for it. The teacher took his station before them, and after making a playful remark which excited a light titter around the room, and effectually arrested attention, he gave a signal for silence. After waiting a moment, during which every countenance was composed and every noise hushed, he made a prayer consisting of a single sentence, asking that, as they had come together to learn, they might be good and diligent. He then spoke to them of the beautiful day, asked what they knew about the seasons, referred to the different kinds of fruit-trees then in bearing, and questioned them upon the uses of trees in constructing houses, furniture, &c. Frequently he threw in sportive remarks which enlivened the whole school, but without ever producing the slightest symptom of disorder. During this familiar conversation, which lasted about twenty minutes, there was nothing frivolous or trifling in the manner of the teacher: that manner was dignified, though playful; and the little jets of laughter which he caused the children occasionally to throw out were much more favorable to a receptive state of mind than jets of tears.

Here I must make a preliminary remark in regard to the equipments of the scholars, and the furniture of the schoolroom. Every child had a slate and pencil, and a little reading-book of letters, words, and short sentences. Indeed, I never saw a Prussian or Saxon school, above an infant school, in which any child was unprovided with a slate and pencil. By the teacher's desk, and in front of the school, hung a blackboard. The teacher first drew a house upon the blackboard; and here the value of the art of drawing—a power universally possessed by Prussian teachers—became manifest. By the side of the drawing, and under it, he wrote the word "house" in the German script hand, and printed it in the German letter. With a long pointing-rod—the end being painted white to make it more visible,—he ran over the form of the letters; the children, with their slates before them, and their pencils in their hands, looking at the pointing-rod, and tracing the forms of the letters in the air. In all our good schools, children are first taught to imitate the forms of letters on the slate, before they write them on paper; here they were first imitated on the air, then on slates, and subsequently, in older classes, on paper. . . .

* * * * *

. . . In some of my opinions and inferences, I may have erred; but, of the following facts, there can be no doubt:—

1. During all this time, I never saw a teacher hearing a lesson of any kind (excepting a reading or spelling lesson) *with a book in his hand.*

2. I never saw a teacher *sitting* while hearing a recitation.

3. Though I saw hundreds of schools, and thousands—I think I may say, within bounds, tens of thousands—of pupils, *I never saw one child undergoing punishment, or arraigned for misconduct. I never saw one child in tears from having been punished, or from fear of being punished.*

* * * * *

. . . I can only say, that, during all the time mentioned, I never saw a blow struck, I never heard a sharp rebuke given, I never saw a child in tears, nor arraigned at the teacher's bar for any alleged misconduct. On the contrary, the relation seemed to be one of duty first, and then affection, on the part of the teacher; of affection first, and then duty, on the part of the scholar. The teacher's manner was better than parental; for it had a parent's tenderness and vigilance without the foolish dotings or indulgences to which parental affection is prone. I heard no child ridiculed, sneered at, or scolded, for making a mistake. On the contrary, whenever a mistake was made, or there was a want of promptness in giving a reply, the expression of the teacher was that of grief and disappointment, as though there had been a failure, not merely to answer the question of a master, but to comply with the expectations of a friend. No child was disconcerted, disabled, or bereft of his senses, through fear. Nay, generally, at the ends of the answers, the teacher's practice is to encourage him with the exclamation, "good," "right," "wholly right," &c., or to check him with his slowly and painfully articulated "no;" and this is done with a tone of voice that marks every degree of *plus* and *minus* in the scale of approbation or regret. When a difficult question has been put to a young child which tasks all his energies, the teacher approaches him with a mingled look of concern and encouragement; he stands before him, the light and shade of hope and fear alternately crossing his countenance; he lifts his arms and turns his body, as a bowler who has given a wrong direction to his bowl will writhe his person to bring the ball back upon its track; and finally, if the little wrestler with difficulty triumphs, the teacher felicitates him upon his success, perhaps seizes and shakes him by the hand in token of congratulation; and when the difficulty has been really formidable, and the effort triumphant, I have seen the teacher catch up the child in his arms and embrace him, as though he were not able to contain his joy. At another time, I have seen a teacher actually clap his hands with delight at a bright reply; and all this has been done so naturally and so unaffectedly as to excite no other feeling in the residue of the children than a desire, by the same means, to win the same caresses. What person worthy of being called by the name, or of sustaining the sacred relation of a parent, would not give any thing, bear any thing, sacrifice any thing, to have his children, during eight or ten years of the period of their childhood, surrounded by circumstances, and breathed upon by sweet and humanizing influences, like these?

I mean no disparagement of our own teachers by the remark I am about to make. As a general fact, these teachers are as good as public opinion has demanded; as good as the public sentiment has been disposed to appreciate; as good as public liberality has been ready to reward; as good as the preliminary measures taken to qualify them would authorize us to expect. But it was impossible to put down the questionings of my own mind,—whether a visitor could spend six weeks in our own schools without ever hearing an angry word spoken, or seeing a blow struck, or witnessing the flow of tears?

In the Prussian schools, I observed the fair operation and full result of two practices which I have dwelt upon with great repetition and urgency at home. One is, when hearing a class recite, always to ask the question before naming the scholar who is to give the answer. The question being first asked, all the children are alert; for each one knows that he is liable to be called upon for the reply. On the contrary, if the scholar who is expected to answer is first named, and especially if the scholars are taken in succession, according to local position,—that is, in the order of their seats or stations,—then the attention of all the rest has a reprieve until their turns shall come. In practice, this designation of the answerer before the question is propounded operates as a temporary leave of absence or furlough to all the other members of the class.

The other point referred to is that of adjusting the ease or difficulty of the questions to the capacity of the pupil. A child should never have any excuse or occasion for making a mistake; nay, at first he should be most carefully guarded from the fact, and especially from the consciousness, of making a mistake. The questions should be ever so childishly simple, rather than that the answers should be erroneous. No expense of time can be too great, if it secures the habit and the desire of accuracy. Hence a false answer should be an event of the rarest occurrence,—one to be deprecated, to be looked upon with surprise and regret, and almost as an offence. Few things can have a worse effect upon a child's character than to set down a row of black marks against him at the end of every lesson.

The value of this practice of adjusting questions to the capacities and previous attainments of the pupils cannot be over-estimated. The opposite course *necessitates* mistakes, habituates and hardens the pupils to blundering and uncertainty, disparages the value of correctness in their eyes, and—what is a consequence as much to be lamented as any— gives plausibility to the argument in favor of emulation as a means of bringing children back to the habit of accuracy from which they have been driven. Would the trainer of horses deserve any compensation, or have any custom, if the first draughts which he should impose upon the young animals were beyond their ability to move?

The first of the above-named practices can be adopted by every teacher immediately, and whatever his degree of competency in other respects may be. The last improvement can only be fully effected when the teacher can dispense with all text-books, and can teach and question from a full mind only. The case is hopeless where a conspiracy against the spread of knowledge has been entered into between an author who compiles, and a teacher who uses, a text-book in which the questions to be put are all prepared and printed.

回 6. Horace Mann and the American Common School Movement

Horace Mann was particularly well equipped to be one of the great leaders of the common school movement in the United States. He was a Unitarian, a member of a sect that emerged as part of and contributed to a more tolerant religious climate. He was an advocate of moral and social reform and looked to the public schools as the hub of all reform. He was an astute politician who as Secretary to the Massachusetts Board of Education utilized the meager powers granted him so skillfully and so successfully that he affected education both within and without his state. He was a lecturer whose addresses, written reports, and editorship of the Common School Journal *provided platforms from which emanated proposals for the extension and improvement of the common schools, the establishment of high schools and normal schools (teacher training institutions), and a host of other educational reforms (see readings 5 and 7). One of the most influential of his twelve annual reports was the tenth, issued in 1846. In the selections from this report that follow Mann restates many of his arguments for the support of public schools. But, the brunt of his attack is directed against those who considered the school tax an unjust infringement upon the sanctity of private property.*

In later times, and since the achievement of American independence, the universal and ever-repeated argument in favor of free schools has been, that the general intelligence which they are capable of diffusing, and which can be imparted by no other human instrumentality, is indispensable to the continuance of a republican government. This argument, it is obvious, assumes, as a *postulatum*, the superiority of a republican over all other forms of government; and, as a people, we religiously believe in the soundness both of the assumption and of the argument founded upon it. But if this be all, then a sincere monarchist, or a defender of arbitrary power, or a believer in the divine right of kings, would oppose free schools for the identical reasons we offer in their behalf. A perfect demonstration of our doctrine—that free schools are the only basis of republican institutions—would be the perfection of proof, to his mind, that they should be immediately exterminated.

Admitting, nay, claiming for ourselves, the substantial justness and soundness of the general grounds on which our system was originally established, and has since been maintained, yet it is most obvious, that, unless some broader and more comprehensive principle can be found, the system of free schools will be repudiated by whole nations as impolitic and dangerous; and, even among ourselves, all who deny our premises will, of course, set at nought the conclusions to which they lead.

Again: the expediency of free schools is sometimes advocated on grounds of political economy. An educated people is always a more industrious and productive people. Knowledge and abundance sustain to each other the relation of cause and effect. Intelligence is a primary ingredient in the wealth of nations. Where this does not stand at the head of the inventory, the items in a nation's valuation will be few, and the sum at the foot of the column insignificant.

Mann, op. cit., IV, 113–17, 123–25, 131–32.

The moralist, too, takes up the argument of the economist. He demonstrates that vice and crime are not only prodigals and spend-thrifts of their own, but defrauders and plunderers of the means of others; that they would seize upon all the gains of honest industry, and exhaust the bounties of Heaven itself, without satiating their rapacity for new means of indulgence; and that often, in the history of the world, whole generations might have been trained to industry and virtue by the wealth which one enemy to his race has destroyed.

And yet, notwithstanding these views have been presented a thousand times with irrefutable logic, and with a divine eloquence of truth which it would seem that nothing but combined stolidity and depravity could resist, there is not at the present time, with the exception of the States of New England and a few small communities elsewhere, a country or a state in Christendom which maintains a system of free schools for the education of its children. Even in the State of New York, with all its noble endowments, the schools are not free.[1]

I believe that this amazing dereliction from duty, especially in our own country, originates more in the false notions which men entertain *respecting the nature of their right to property* than in any thing else. In the district-school-meeting, in the town-meeting, in legislative halls, every-where, the advocates for a more generous education could carry their respective audiences with them in behalf of increased privileges for our children, were it not instinctively foreseen that increased privileges must be followed by increased taxation. Against this obstacle, argument falls dead. The rich man who has no children declares that the exaction of a contribution from him to educate the children of his neighbor is an invasion of his rights of property. The man who has reared and educated a family of children denounces it as a double tax when he is called upon to assist in educating the children of others also; or, if he has reared his own children without educating them, he thinks it peculiarly oppressive to be obliged to do for others what he refrained from doing even for himself. Another, having children, but disdaining to educate them with the common mass, withdraws them from the public school, puts them under what he calls "selecter influences," and then thinks it a grievance to be obliged to support a school which he contemns. Or if these different parties so far yield to the force of traditionary sentiment and usage, and to the public opinion around them, as to consent to do something for the cause, they soon reach the limit of expense at which their admitted obligation or their alleged charity terminates.

It seems not irrelevant, therefore, in this connection, and for the

---

[1] *By an act of the New-York legislature, passed at its last session, the question whether free schools shall be established throughout the State is to be submitted to the decision of the people, to be determined by ballot, at their primary meetings, during the current year.*

purpose of strengthening the foundation on which our free-school system reposes, to inquire into the nature of a man's right to the property he possesses; and to satisfy ourselves respecting the question, whether any man has such an indefeasible title to his estates, or such an absolute ownership of them, as renders it unjust in the government to assess upon him his share of the expenses of educating the children of the community up to such a point as the nature of the institutions under which he lives, and the well-being of society, require.

I believe in the existence of a great, immortal, immutable principle of natural law, or natural ethics,—a principle antecedent to all human institutions, and incapable of being abrogated by any ordinance of man,—a principle of divine origin, clearly legible in the ways of Providence as those ways are manifested in the order of Nature and in the history of the race, which proves the *absolute right* to an education of every human being that comes into the world; and which, of course, proves the correlative duty of every government to see that the means of that education are provided for all.

In regard to the application of this principle of natural law,—that is, in regard to the extent of the education to be provided for all at the public expense,—some differences of opinion may fairly exist under different political organizations; but, under our republican government, it seems clear that the minimum of this education can never be less than such as is sufficient to qualify each citizen for the civil and social duties he will be called to discharge,—such an education as teaches the individual the great laws of bodily health, as qualifies for the fulfilment of parental duties, as is indispensable for the civil functions of a witness or a juror, as is necessary for the voter in municipal and in national affairs, and, finally, as is requisite for the faithful and conscientious discharge of all those duties which devolve upon the inheritor of a portion of the sovereignty of this great Republic.

The will of God, as conspicuously manifested in the order of Nature, and in the relations which he has established among men, founds the *right* of every child that is born into the world, to such a degree of education as will enable him, and, as far as possible, will predispose him, to perform all domestic, social, civil, and moral duties, upon the same clear ground of natural law and equity as it founds a child's *right*, upon his first coming into the world, to distend his lungs with a portion of the common air, or to open his eyes to the common light, or to receive that shelter, protection, and nourishment, which are necessary to the continuance of his bodily existence. And so far is it from being a wrong or a hardship to demand of the possessors of property their respective shares for the prosecution of this divinely-ordained work, that they themselves are guilty of the most far-reaching injustice when they seek to resist or to evade the contribution. The complainers are the wrong-doers. The cry, "Stop thief!" comes from the thief himself.

* * * * *

But sometimes the rich farmer, the opulent manufacturer, or the capitalist, when sorely pressed with his natural and moral obligation to contribute a portion of his means for the education of the young, replies, —either in form or in spirit,—"My lands, my machinery, my gold, and my silver, are mine: may I not do what I will with my own?" There is one supposable case, and only one, where this argument would have plausibility. If it were made by an isolated, solitary being,—a being having no relations to a community around him, having no ancestors to whom he had been indebted for ninety-nine parts in every hundred of all he possesses, and expecting to leave no posterity after him,—it might not be easy to answer it. If there were but one family in this Western hemis-phere, and only one in the Eastern hemisphere, and these two families bore no civil and social relations to each other, and were to be the first and last of the whole race, it might be difficult, except on very high and almost transcendental grounds, for either one of them to show good cause why the other should contribute to help educate children not his own. And perhaps the force of the appeal for such an object would be still further diminished if the nearest neighbor of a single family upon our planet were as far from the earth as Uranus or Sirius. In self-defence or in selfishness, one might say to the other, "What are your fortunes to me? You can neither benefit nor molest me. Let each of us keep to his own side of the planetary spaces." But is this the relation which any man amongst us sustains to his fellows? In the midst of a populous community to which he is bound by innumerable ties, having had his own fortune and condition almost predetermined and fore-ordained by his predecessors, and being about to exert upon his successors as com-manding an influence as has been exerted upon himself, the objector can no longer shrink into his individuality, and disclaim connection and relationship with the world at large. He cannot deny that there are thousands around him on whom he acts, and who are continually re-acting upon him. The earth is much too small, or the race is far too numerous, to allow us to be hermits; and therefore we cannot adopt either the philosophy or the morals of hermits. All have derived benefits from their ancestors, and all are bound, as by an oath, to transmit those benefits, even in an improved condition, to posterity. We may as well attempt to escape from our own personal identity as to shake off the threefold relation which we bear to others,—the relation of an associate with our contemporaries; of a beneficiary of our ancestors; of a guardian to those who, in the sublime order of Providence, are to succeed us. Out of these relations, manifest duties are evolved. The society of which we necessarily constitute a part must be preserved; and, in order to preserve, it, we must not look merely to what one individual or one family needs, but to what the whole community needs; not merely to what one generation needs, but to the wants of a succession of generations. To draw conclusions without considering these facts is to leave out the most important part of the premises.

*   *   *   *   *

In obedience to the laws of God and to the laws of all civilized communities, society is bound to protect the natural life of children; and this natural life cannot be protected without the appropriation and use of a portion of the property which society possesses. We prohibit infanticide under penalty of death. We practise a refinement in this particular. The life of an infant is inviolable, even before he is born; and he who feloniously takes it, even before birth, is a subject to the extreme penalty of the law as though he had struck down manhood in its vigor, or taken away a mother by violence from the sanctuary of home where she blesses her offspring. But why preserve the natural life of a child, why preserve unborn embryos of life, if we do not intend to watch over and to protect them, and to expand their subsequent existence into usefulness and happiness? As individuals, or as an organized community, we have no natural right, we can derive no authority or countenance from reason, we can cite no attribute or purpose of the divine nature, for giving birth to any human being, and then inflicting upon that being the curse of ignorance, of poverty, and of vice, with all their attendant calamities. We are brought, then, to this startling but inevitable alternative,—the natural life of an infant should be extinguished as soon as it is born, or the means should be provided to save that life from being a curse to its possessor; and, therefore, every State is morally bound to enact a code of laws legalizing and enforcing infanticide, or a code of laws establishing free schools.

The three following propositions, then, describe the broad and everduring foundation on which the common-school system of Massachusetts reposes:—

The successive generations of men, taken collectively, constitute one great commonwealth.

The property of this commonwealth is pledged for the education of all its youth, up to such a point as will save them from poverty and vice, and prepare them for the adequate performance of their social and civil duties.

The successive holders of this property are trustees, bound to the faithful execution of their trust by the most sacred obligations; and embezzlement and pillage from children and descendants have not less of criminality, and have more of meanness, than the same offences when perpetrated against contemporaries.

回 7. English Education, Stronghold of Tradition

In 1833 English reformers won a precedent-shattering victory. On August 17 of that year Parliament for the first time voted funds for the aid of elementary education. However, the historian De Montmorency's description of the Parliamentary debates over the education bill makes it quite apparent that many years of battle lay ahead before a system of universal public education would be established in that country.

On July 30th, 1833, Mr. Roebuck brought forward, in opposition to the changed views of Lord Brougham, a compulsory scheme of education. He moved "That this House, deeply impressed with the necessity of providing for a due Education of the People at large; and believing that to this end the aid and care of the State are absolutely needed, will, early during the next Session of Parliament, proceed to devise a means for the universal and national Education of the whole People." His lengthy and didactic speech is very interesting as showing the way in which the idea of national education was growing. "Education," said Mr. Roebuck, "means not merely these necessary means or instruments for the acquiring of knowledge, but it means also the so training or fashioning the intellectual and moral qualities of the individual, that he may be able and willing to acquire knowledge, and to turn it to its right use." Mr. Roebuck referred to the compulsory system of education that had in 1833 been introduced into France, and to the compulsory systems at work in Prussia and Saxony, and stated his opinion that it was necessary to introduce a similar system into this country. "In general terms, I would say, that I would oblige, by law, every child in Great Britain and Ireland, from, perhaps, six years of age to twelve years of age to be a regular attendant at school. If the parents be able to give, and actually do give their children elsewhere sufficient education, then they should not be compelled to send them to the national school. If, however, they should be unable or unwilling to give them such instruction, then the State should step in and supply this want, by compelling the parent to send the child to the school of the State." This of course was the exact

J. E. G. De Montmorency, State Intervention in English Education, *pp. 236–40. Copyright, 1902, by Cambridge University Press. Reprinted by permission of Cambridge University Press.*

idea of the Act of 1876. Mr. Roebuck's conception was to set up three classes of State schools—namely, infants' schools, schools of industry, in which would be taught, in addition to reading, writing, and arithmetic, the elements of art, hygiene, natural history, and the proper knowledge of some trade, and normal schools, for the training of teachers, who would receive from such schools the qualifying teaching certificate. Evening schools in towns were also advocated. Mr. Roebuck believed that the country should be divided into school districts, where the voters should elect a school committee. The control of education should, he thought, be placed in the hands of a member of the Cabinet, who would supervise the National School system.

It is probable that Mr. Roebuck's ideas to an appreciable extent affected the ultimate settlement of 1870. An interesting debate followed. Mr. Grote was in favour of a national system. Lord Althorp could not agree that there should be any provision to make it penal in a father not to educate his child. "He was of opinion, that they might give a father the means of educating his children, and put it in the power of a man who could not afford the expense to do so without expense; but the actually punishing a man for not having his child properly educated, would, in his mind, be going further than they ought." Mr. O'Connell thought that a normal school would give great offence to the people. They should go no further than give countenance to religious instruction and assist literary instruction. "Facility of education should be encouraged, but all domination ought to be abolished. Nothing could be more destructive than to imitate the example of France, in respect to her system of national education." Mr. Hume advocated undenominational State education for the very poor. Sir Robert Peel considered "it was not quite correct to assert that education in this empire was so very imperfect." The care of the State towards education was a doubtful question. "A compulsory system of education appeared to him to trench upon religious toleration; for it must, almost of necessity, interfere with religious opinion.....He did not wish to speak with disrespect of the mayors of this country, but would the French system of leaving the education of every town to its mayor do here? Any Bill which made the mayors of the different towns of England comptrollers of education within them, would create a degree of jealousy and resistance which the hon. Member would not be able to overcome." He doubted whether education ought not in a free country to be left free from control. This debate occupies thirty-five columns of Hansard, a fact that shows how great had been the increase of popular interest in the subject.

On August 16th, 1833, the sum of £1,264 was granted by Parliament to defray the expenses of salaries and allowances to certain professors in the Universities of Oxford and Cambridge. There were some objections to the grant on the ground that Dissenters were not admitted to the

Universities, and one Member (Mr. Ewart) said that were they admitted he would have wished to have seen a far larger grant.

On Saturday, August 17th, 1833, in a very empty House of Commons, a vote of £20,000 for the purposes of education was passed after a hot debate by 50 votes to 26 votes. Mr. T. B. Macaulay voted with the majority in favour of the grant. Lord Althorp explained that the object of the grant was to build schools where there already existed the means of carrying on such schools. In the debate Lord John Russell pointed out, in answer to a complaint that no ground for the experiment had been shown that in the Report of the Education Committee in 1818 there were cases referred to of parishes which, if they could have been assisted in the first outlay, would afterwards have supported their own schools. This was still the case in 1833, and justified a vote for building grants. Mr. William Cobbett, the Member for Oldham, opposed the grant on the ground that education was not improving the condition of the country. In the country districts, he said, the father was a better man and a better labourer than his son. Reports on the table of the House proved, he declared, that men became more and more immoral every year. Then what had become of the benefits of education? Education had been more and more spread; but to what did it all tend? "Nothing but to increase the number of schoolmasters and schoolmistresses—that new race of idlers. Crime, too, went on increasing. If so, what reason was there to tax the people for the increase of education? It was nothing but an attempt to force education—it was a French—it was a Doctrinaire—plan, and he should always be opposed to it." It is difficult to realise that Mr. Cobbett—a praiser of times past, a hater of State intervention, a despiser of French philosophy—was the advanced reformer of his day. One does not usually couple such opinions with the conceptions of reform. Mr. Joseph Hume opposed the grant on the somewhat reasonable ground that it was too small to constitute a national system, and without such a system there was no justification for the grant. In the division on the grant he acted as one of the tellers for the Noes. The form of vote was as follows: "That a Sum, not exceeding Twenty thousand pounds, be granted to His Majesty, to be issued in aid of Private Subscriptions for the Erection of School Houses, for the Education of the Children of the Poorer Classes in *Great Britain*, to the 31st day of March 1834; and that the said sum be issued and paid without any fee or other deduction whatsoever." The vote of £20,000 appears in the Revenue Act, 1833, as a grant for the erection of school houses in Great Britain.

Horace Mann's description of education and social conditions in England (Common School Journal, *VI, 1844*) *was obviously intended to provide a moral lesson to his American readers as well as generally to enlighten them. There is more than adequate evidence in literature and historical writing to support the accuracy of his shocking picture.*

Among those European countries which, with any propriety, can be called civilized, England is the only one which has no system for the general education of its people. In proportion to its population it expends more for education than any other country in Europe; but this expenditure is for classes, and not for the whole. The consequence, of course, is, an appalling degree of inequality in the condition of its subjects. The highest educational refinement exists side by side with the most brutish ignorance. The most elegant literary culture shines out among communities who cannot speak their native English tongue in a manner to be understood by Englishmen. Schools, colleges, and universities, where the profoundest acquaintance with classical literature and with all its libraries of annotation and commentary is obtained, contrast with hovels within which a book was never seen, and whose occupants could not read one if they had it.[1] A thirst for knowledge in a few, and a patronage of it by the government, which prompts them to invade the eternal solitudes of either pole, and to break through the phalanx of disease and death that guards the headsprings of the Niger, is applauded, and its objects pursued at immense expense, while there are tens of thousands around who do not know whether the land of their nativity is an island or a continent. There may be seen the loftiest orders of hierarchy,—bishops and archbishops, and the Defender of the Christian Faith,—with such miserable imposters and dupes as Courtenay and his followers. There is a church establishment twenty thousand strong, possessing an annual revenue of eight millions sterling, with thousands of native born subjects, arrived at manhood, who never heard the name of Christ. Such are the headings of only a few chapters in the terrific volume of English inequality. This is the condition of a country, in all whose multitudes of churches that Book is weekly read, which declares that God made of one blood all nations of men. The source, origin, cause, of all this is, the neglect of the masses by the possessors of wealth and of power;—mainly and primarily, the neglect of the education of the masses. That attended to, all else would have been changed. A few noble-souled individuals have attended to it, sought to foster and promote it, given money and time to accomplish it; but not the whole, not even any one *class*. The clergy have neglected it, forgetting that eternal truth, that God is a "God of *intelligence* as well as of love, and that exalted purity requires no less the cultivation of the intellect than the purity and warmth of the affection." The great

Mann, op. cit., V, 82–87.

[1] *The book-shelves of one English library, it is said, are more than ten miles in length.*

landholders, the powerful lords of the soil, have neglected it. They advocate and defend the radical, fundamental, and, in the end, destructive error, that the masses of men are by nature incapable of self-government; and hence, by virtue of their theory, all necessity for inculcating the virtues of self-control, for imparting that interior light of intelligence which can guide and direct every man, is superseded. The great commercial classes of the nation have never been brought, like the clergy and the land-holders, into immediate proximity and contact with the children of the realm, and so they, as a body, have paid no attention to the rising generation around them. In later times, a new department of labor has been opened, a new order in society has arisen,—the manufacturers,—who have not only lived among children, like the land-owners and the ecclesiastical body, but have prosecuted a kind of business in which the services of children could be made available. This was a new epoch. Enterprise, the love of gain of this nation, had before acted upon all the nations of the earth, and upon all the kingdom of nature, and made them all tributary to its wealth. Here the spirit of cupidity was brought to act directly upon human beings, upon children. To gratify his passion, Herod sacrificed only children under two years of age,—helpless, unconscious, too young to suffer through the torments of fear, or the crushings of hope. But the English manufacturers suffers children to reach the age of hope, of fear, of conscious suffering; and then!—Moloch himself was a god of long-suffering, of tenderness, of boundless love, compared with them. They have tortured the body with years of pining, watching and hunger. They have pinched it with cold, and dwarfed and deformed it in all its proportions. The calm, restorative night,—that beautiful season which God has appointed and inwrought as an organic fact into the very structure of the universe, for the rest, refreshment and growth of His children,—they have stricken from the order of nature. Through its long watches they have bound children to their wheels. They have stived them in hot, suffocating rooms; when exhausted nature failed, they have plied the hellish lash. They have cut their pittance of compensation down, and down, and down, to the very minimum point of existence, because they could not work as long as water and steam. More than this, they have deprived them not only of the joys of childhood and the pleasures of knowledge, but of the consolations of religion and the hopes of immortality, that they might coin their souls as well as their bodies into gold. Let any one read the report of the English Factory Commissioners and Factory Inspectors, and he will say that the Fejee Islanders, the Caribs, or the most ferocious tribes of cannibals that prowl in the interior of Africa, thousands of miles from the confines of civilization, ought to send missionaries to England, to raise, if possible, the English manufacturer to their own level of humanity. Under this manufacturing system, forms of privation, of suffering and crime, have grown up, such as have never before been known in any part of Christendom or heathendom. We have ourselves seen some of the abodes in which the victims of this system congregate,—houses, so called, erected on narrow courts,— courts opening at one end only upon a street,—framed back to back, with one story under ground, with no means of ingress or egress but through a front door, through which all the refuse and offal of the house must be daily cast into an unpaved court, to ferment and breed putrescence, and darken the heavens with its exhalations of disease and death. This mode of building is not confined to a solitary block or group, but in some places,—at Manchester, for instance, within and without the town,—squares and acres are covered with such dwellings, and such only. From their pallets of straw in these wretched sties, as we learn from the above-mentioned reports, children of the tenderest age are scourged up to travel three miles on foot to be at their tasks by daylight in the morning. At noon, children still younger are sent to carry them an apology for a meal. We have seen the manner in which some of these victims of avarice and oppression live, less like human beings than like a knot of eels in their slime.

The horrible disclosures recently made in regard to the treatment of children in the mines, almost throughout the mining districts of England, are another record of the same turpitude and enormity. But it is painful to record these atrocities and sufferings. We wish only to draw attention to the consequences of such a systematic neglect of the moral and intellectual culture of children, and to deduce a moral in reference to our own duties. The victims of this neglect have now become so numerous that the paupers are one in twelve of the population of England. The frequency and the enormity of crime have materially reduced the value of life and property. This little island of Great Britain has already planted daughter colonies of convicts and malefactors in the islands of three great oceans,—the Indian, the Pacific, and the Atlantic,—yet her selfish institutions breed them at home faster than she can convict and export them; and when we left England, in October last, portions of each of the three kingdoms were in commotion, and the government was marching large bodies of troops into Ireland, Scotland and Wales to put down insurrections by the sword.

The moral we derive from these facts, in reference to our own country, is, the duty of every class of men, and of every individual man, to do whatever in him lies for the welfare of the rising generation,—not to talk only, but to act; not to preach only, but to practise, lest those terrible retributions, which God, by his eternal laws, has denounced against such offences, come also upon us. Every farmer or mechanic who stints his child of knowledge, because he can *mint* his bones and sinews into money; every manufacturer who beats children as though they were merely *live* instead of *dead* machinery, who does not allow them a full measure of time for rest, a full measure of time for food, a full measure of time for sleep, and, above all, a full measure of time for the cultivation of mind and heart, is traitorous to the institutions of his country; or, what is worse, he is preparing a class of men who will, in the end, perpetrate more treason against the happiness of mankind, than it is possible for any one man, individually, to commit. The common criminal has but two hands; the man who cherishes ignorance lifts many hands against his country.

It would be as repugnant to our own feelings as it would be opposite to truth to include every English manufacturer in this sketch of the class. There are a few,—however painful to use words of limitation, we must say there are only a few,—who prove that they are humane and rational men. A few miles from Liverpool, for instance, there is the large establishment owned by the Messrs. Rollins, who have for years maintained a school for all the children, and kept open a reading-room for all the adults, upon their premises. They give, not money only, but time and personal encouragement; for one of the brothers meets with his operatives in the evening, instructing them, aiding their inquiries and giving countenance to their laudable efforts for self-improvement. Had England such an aristocracy as this, she would then, indeed, be "happy England." At what a bargain might she exchange her lords by the score for one real nobleman like these!

X

Education in a Technological Civilization, 1860–

To *enumerate adequately the countless events that have made the world and life itself during the last hundred years so vastly different from what they had been would require a number of pages equivalent at least to the previous nine chapters. Certainly statements to the effect that the extent of change during these years has surpassed that of the previous two thousand years have been heard time and again. What we can do in this final chapter is reflect briefly on the major forces for change and the general ways in which society and its institutions, specifically the schools, have responded to them.*

Whether one focuses his attention on political events or the social, intellectual, or economic developments of this period, he cannot avoid being impressed by the pervasive influence of science and technology. He cannot fail to recognize that the urban, industrial civilization, which was their product, wrought concurrent dramatic changes in modes of living and systems of religion, philosophy, economics, and politics. It was almost inevitable that education would be affected as demands arose that the schools respond to the new conditions; that they prepare children to enter into the new society. Herbert Spencer, applying Darwin's theories of biological man to man as a social being, was in the forefront of those insisting that education prepare the individual to participate adequately in the struggle for survival. In 1859, launching his attack directly upon the time-honored methods and content of classical education, Spencer proclaimed that it was science that could best prepare the individual not only to survive but also to gain the fullest satisfaction from life and to contribute most to the benefit of society. (1) The immense prestige of Spencer and Spencerian social Darwinism in the United

States during the last half of the nineteenth century contributed notably to the rising position of science and utilitarian subjects in secondary school and college curricula.

The example of the German universities also exerted considerable influence on higher education in the United States. In spite of attempts by the forces of German reaction to snuff out the liberal spirit that had arisen in the universities early in the century, a tradition of freedom to study and teach continued to flourish and, incidentally, to advance the development of Germany as a major industrial power. The growing renown of these universities as centers of advanced research and teaching attracted numerous American graduate students to Berlin, Heidelberg, Freiburg, Göttingen, and other university towns. Upon returning home they not only served as college teachers but as propagandists for the idea of the university as an institute for research and the discovery of knowledge as well as for its conservation and dissemination. (2)

It is true that no nation of the Western world was left untouched by the cataclysmic changes wrought by the impact of science and technology. But, it is also true that no nation underwent a more drastic transformation in the hundred years following 1860 than did the United States. Huge waves of immigrants, the movement from a primarily agrarian and rural society to one predominantly industrial and urban, and its evolving status as the richest, most powerful nation on earth brought to this country a major share of the benefits and dislocations that were the fruits of the industrial revolution. In facing the challenges of change, the nation seemed to reflect the spirit of youth as it exhibited a willingness to innovate. Developments in education illustrate this characteristic. Depite conservative opposition, not only the ideas of Spencer but also those of Pestalozzi, Froebel, and Herbart were widely accepted during the last half of the nineteenth century. When, in the early years of the twentieth century, the Progressive reform movement arose in response to the numerous problems brought on by rapid industrialization and urbanization, educators joined the movement, demanding institutional changes that would foster social, economic, and political democracy. As the leading philosopher of the Progressive movement in education, John Dewey excited and inspired reformers throughout Europe and America. The Progressives' faith that a scientific and democratic orientation to schooling could improve the welfare of the individual and his society continues to this day to hold meaning for people everywhere. (3)

During this period much of the history of Western civilization focuses upon attempts to deal with the problems and prospects created by the technological age. Parties and nations have been bitterly divided over such issues as the role of the individual versus that of the state in the control of the means of production and distribution of goods and the degree of popular participation in political life. The twentieth century has seen two general patterns arise to dominate the scene: one, bearing such labels as Nazism, Communism, and Fascism, in which a totalitarian state places complete economic and political control in the hands of an elite, and the other in which democratic procedures are employed to determine the proper *relationship between the economic freedom of individuals and groups and the restraining hand of the government. Though the multiplicity of "isms" has tended to divide the world into ideological camps, on at least one point there has been general agreement: education is a powerful and essential force for the attainment of desired ends. If the history of education during the past one hundred years has demonstrated anything, it is that the school as an instrument of national policy can be employed to control and restrict as well as to emancipate. (4, 5, 6, 7)* With the tradition of a common, rigid Western curriculum finally broken and educational innovation encouraged in many lands, the schools of the future are more likely than ever to reflect the political and social climate of the nations in which they exist.*

▣ 1. Herbert Spencer, *What Knowledge Is of Most Worth?*

   Herbert Spencer was in the vanguard of the struggle for more realistic curricula, for studies that would prepare English children for "complete living." Thanks to the work of William Graham Sumner of Yale and other American scholars, Spencer's writings and social Darwinian views attained great popularity in this country. It is fair to say that the era of modern curricula reform began with the appearance of Spencer's essay What Knowledge Is of Most Worth? *Excerpts from this essay follow:*

WHAT KNOWLEDGE IS OF MOST WORTH?

It has been truly remarked that, in order of time, decoration precedes dress. Among people who submit to great physical suffering that they may have themselves handsomely tattooed, extremes of temperature are borne with but little attempt at mitigation. Humboldt tells us that an Orinoco Indian, though quite regardless of bodily comfort, will yet labour for a fortnight to purchase pigment wherewith to make himself admired; and that the same woman who would not hesitate to leave her hut without a fragment of clothing on, would not dare to commit such

Herbert Spencer, Education: Intellectual, Moral and Physical *(London: Williams and Norgate, 1888), pp. 1–3, 6–7, 10–13, 53–55.*

**These readings include selections illustrative of the directions in education taken by the United States, Great Britain, Germany, and the Soviet Union during this period. As a group these nations shared experiences of rather sharp breaks with educational traditions. In pairs the United States and Great Britain illustrate the force of education in democratic societies, whereas Germany and the Soviet Union furnish examples of the utilization of education by totalitarian systems.*

a breach of decorum as to go out unpainted. Voyagers find that coloured beads and trinkets are much more prized by wild tribes, than are calicoes or broadcloths. And the anecdotes we have of the ways in which, when shirts and coats are given, savages turn them to some ludicrous display, show how completely the idea of ornament predominates over that of use. Nay, there are still more extreme illustrations: witness the fact narrated by Capt. Speke of his African attendants, who strutted about in their goat-skin mantles when the weather was fine, but when it was wet, took them off, folded them up, and went about naked, shivering in the rain! Indeed, the facts of aboriginal life seem to indicate that dress is developed out of decorations. And when we remember that even among ourselves most think more about the fineness of the fabric than its warmth, and more about the cut than the convenience—when we see that the function is still in great measure subordinated to the appearance—we have further reason for inferring such an origin.

It is curious that the like relations hold with the mind. Among mental as among bodily acquisitions, the ornamental comes before the useful. Not only in times past, but almost as much in our own era, that knowledge which conduces to personal well-being has been postponed to that which brings applause. In the Greek schools, music, poetry, rhetoric, and a philosophy which, until Socrates taught, had but little bearing upon action, were the dominant subjects; while knowledge aiding the arts of life had a very subordinate place. And in our own universities and schools at the present moment, the like antithesis holds. We are guilty of something like a platitude when we say that throughout his after-career, a boy, in nine cases out of ten, applies his Latin and Greek to no practical purposes. The remark is trite that in his shop, or his office, in managing his estate or his family, in playing his part as director of a bank or a railway, he is very little aided by this knowledge he took so many years to acquire—so little, that generally the greater part of it drops out of his memory; and if he occasionally vents a Latin quotation, or alludes to some Greek myth, it is less to throw light on the topic in hand than for the sake of effect. If we inquire what is the real motive for giving boys a classical education, we find it to be simply conformity to public opinion. Men dress their children's minds as they do their bodies, in the prevailing fashion. As the Orinoco Indian puts on paint before leaving his hut, not with a view to any direct benefit, but because he would be ashamed to be seen without it; so, a boy's drilling in Latin and Greek is insisted on, not because of their intrinsic value, but that he may not be disgraced by being found ignorant of them—that he may have "the education of a gentleman"—the badge marking a certain social position, and bringing a consequent respect.

*   *   *   *   *

The question which we contend is of such transcendent moment, is, not whether such or such knowledge is of worth, but what is its *relative* worth? When they have named certain advantages which a given course of study has secured them, persons are apt to assume that they have justified themselves: quite forgetting that the adequateness of the advantages is the point to be judged. There is, perhaps, not a subject to which men devote attention that has not *some* value. A year diligently spent in getting up heraldry, would very possibly give a little further insight into ancient manners and morals. Any one who should learn the distances between all the towns in England, might, in the course of his life, find one or two of the thousand facts he had acquired of some slight service when arranging a journey. Gathering together all the small gossip of a county, profitless occupation as it would be, might yet occasionally help to establish some useful fact—say, a good example of hereditary transmission. But in these cases, every one would admit that there was no proportion between the required labour and the probable benefit. No one would tolerate the proposal to devote some years of a boy's time to getting such information, at the cost of much more valuable information which he might else have got. And if here the test of relative value is appealed to and held conclusive, then should it be appealed to and held conclusive throughout. Had we time to master all subjects we need not be particular. To quote the old song:—

> Could a man be secure
> That his days would endure
> As of old, for a thousand long years,
> What things might he know!
> What deeds might he do!
> And all without hurry or care.

"But we that have but span-long lives" must ever bear in mind our limited time for acquisition. And remembering how narrowly this time is limited, not only by the shortness of life, but also still more by the business of life, we ought to be especially solicitous to employ what time we have to the greatest advantage. Before devoting years to some subject which fashion or fancy suggests, it is surely wise to weigh with great care the worth of the results, as compared with the worth of various alternative results which the same years might bring if otherwise applied.

In education, then, this is the question of questions, which it is high time we discussed in some methodic way. The first in importance, though the last to be considered, is the problem—how to decide among the conflicting claims of various subjects on our attention. Before there can be a rational *curriculum*, we must settle which things it most concerns us to know; or, to use a word of Bacon's, now unfortunately obsolete—we must determine the relative values of knowledges.

*　*　*　*　*

Such then, we repeat, is something like the rational order of subordination:—That education which prepares for direct self-preservation; that which prepares for indirect self-preservation; that which prepares for parenthood; that which prepares for citizenship; that which prepares for the miscellaneous refinements of life. We do not mean to say that these divisions are definitely separable. We do not deny that they are intricately entangled with each other, in such way that there can be no training for any that is not in some measure a training for all. Nor do we question that of each division there are portions more important than certain portions of the preceding divisions: that, for instance, a man of much skill in business but little other faculty, may fall further below the standard of complete living than one of but moderate ability in money-getting but great judgment as a parent; or that exhaustive information bearing on right social action, joined with entire want of general culture in literature and the fine arts, is less desirable than a more moderate share of the one joined with some of the other. But, after making due qualifications, there still remain these broadly-marked divisions; and it still continues substantially true that these divisions subordinate one another in the foregoing order, because the corresponding divisions of life make one another *possible* in that order.

Of course the ideal of education is—complete preparation in all these divisions. But failing this ideal, as in our phase of civilization every one must do more or less, the aim should be to maintain *a due proportion* between the degrees of preparation in each. Not exhaustive cultivation in any one, supremely important though it may be—not even an exclusive attention to the two, three, or four divisions of greatest importance; but an attention to all:—greatest where the value is greatest; less where the value is less; least where the value is least. For the average man (not to forget the cases in which peculiar aptitude for some one department of knowledge, rightly makes pursuit of that one the bread-winning occupation)—for the average man, we say, the desideratum is, a training that approaches nearest to perfection in the things which most subserve complete living, and falls more and more below perfection in the things that have more and more remote bearings on complete living.

In regulating education by this standard, there are some general considerations that should be ever present to us. The worth of any kind of culture, as aiding complete living, may be either necessary or more or less contingent. There is knowledge of intrinsic value; knowledge of quasi-intrinsic value; and knowledge of conventional value. Such facts

as that sensations of numbness and tingling commonly precede paraly-
sis, that the resistance of water to a body moving through it varies as
the square of the velocity, that chlorine is a disinfectant,—these, and
the truths of Science in general, are of intrinsic value: they will bear on
human conduct ten thousand years hence as they do now. The extra
knowledge of our own language, which is given by an acquaintance
with Latin and Greek, may be considered to have a value that is quasi-
intrinsic: it must exist for us and for other races whose languages owe
much to these sources; but will last only as long as our languages last.
While that kind of information which, in our schools, usurps the name
History—the mere tissue of names and dates and dead unmeaning
events—has a conventional value only: it has not the remotest bearing
on any of our actions; and is of use only for the avoidance of those unpleasant criticisms which current opinion passes upon its absence. Of
course, as those facts which concern all mankind throughout all time
must be held of greater moment than those which concern only a portion of them during a limited era, and of far greater moment than those
which concern only a portion of them during the continuance of a
fashion; it follows that in a rational estimate, knowledge of intrinsic
worth must, other things equal, take precedence of knowledge that is of
quasi-intrinsic or conventional worth.

One further preliminary. Acquirement of every kind has two values
—value as *knowledge* and value as *discipline*. Besides its use for guiding
conduct, the acquisition of each order of facts has also its use as mental
exercise; and its effects as a preparative for complete living have to be
considered under both these heads.

These, then, are the general ideas with which we must set out in discussing a *curriculum:*—Life as divided into several kinds of activity of
successively decreasing importance; the worth of each order of facts as
regulating these several kinds of activity, intrinsically, quasi-intrinsi-
cally, and conventionally; and their regulative influences estimated
both as knowledge and discipline.

*   *   *   *   *

We conclude, then, that for discipline, as well as for guidance, science
is of chiefest value. In all its effects, learning the meanings of things, is
better than learning the meanings of words. Whether for intellectual,
moral, or religious training, the study of surrounding phenomena is
immensely superior to the study of grammars and lexicons.

Thus to the question we set out with—What knowledge is of most
worth?—the uniform reply is—Science. This is the verdict on all the
counts. For direct self-preservation, or the maintenance of life and
health, the all-important knowledge is—Science. For that indirect self-
preservation which we call gaining a livelihood, the knowledge of greatest

value is—Science. For the due discharge of parental functions, the proper guidance is to be found only in—Science. For that interpretation of national life, past and present, without which the citizen cannot rightly regulate his conduct, the indispensable key is—Science. Alike for the most perfect production and highest enjoyment of art in all its forms, the needful preparation is still—Science. And for purposes of discipline—intellectual, moral, religious—the most efficient study is, once more—Science. The question which at first seemed so perplexed, has become, in the course of our inquiry, comparatively simple. We have not to estimate the degrees of importance of different orders of human activity, and different studies as severally fitting us for them; since we find that the study of Science, in its most comprehensive meaning, is the best preparation for all these orders of activity. We have not to decide between the claims of knowledge of great though conventional value, and knowledge of less though intrinsic value; seeing that the knowledge which proves to be of most value in all other respects, is intrinsically most valuable: its worth is not dependent upon opinion, but is as fixed as is the relation of man to the surrounding world. Necessary and eternal as are its truths, all Science concerns all mankind for all time. Equally at present and in the remotest future, must it be of incalculable importance for the regulation of their conduct, that men should understand the science of life, physical, mental, and social; and that they should understand all other science as a key to the science of life.

And yet this study, immensely transcending all other in importance, is that which, in an age of boasted education, receives the least attention. While what we call civilization could never have arisen had it not been for science; science forms scarcely an appreciable element in our so-called civilized training. Though to the progress of science we owe it, that millions find support where once there was food only for thousands; yet of these millions but a few thousands pay any respect to that which has made their existence possible. Though increasing knowledge of the properties and relations of things has not only enabled wandering tribes to grow into populous nations, but has given to the countless members of these populous nations, comforts and pleasures which their few naked ancestors never even conceived, or could have believed, yet is this kind of knowledge only now receiving a grudging recognition in our highest educational institutions. To the slowly growing acquaintance with the uniform co-existences and sequences of phenomena—to the establishment of invariable laws, we owe our emancipation from the grossest superstitions. But for science we should be still worshiping fetishes; or, with hecatombs of victims, propitiating diabolical deities. And yet this science, which, in place of the most degrading conceptions of things, has given us some insight into the grandeurs of creation, is written against in our theologies and frowned upon from our pulpits.

Paraphrasing an Eastern fable, we may say that in the family of knowledges, Science is the household drudge, who, in obscurity, hides unrecognized perfections. To her has been committed all the work; by her skill, intelligence, and devotion, have all conveniences and gratifications been obtained; and while ceaselessly ministering to the rest, she has been kept in the background, that her haughty sisters might flaunt their fripperies in the eyes of the world. The parallel holds yet further. For we are fast coming to the *dénouement*, when the positions will be changed; and while these haughty sisters sink into merited neglect, Science, proclaimed as highest alike in worth and beauty, will reign supreme.

回 2. Daniel Coit Gilman, Spokesman for the University

The modern university, with its attention to research and specialization and its acceptance of the more utilitarian studies on an equal footing with the traditional classical curriculum, did not come to the fore without a challenge. Conservatives like Yale's President Noah Porter insisted that the form and content of the traditional college had served the nation well. They saw no reason for major change. Opposing the traditionalists were the presidents of some of America's most prestigious institutions: Eliot of Harvard, Barnard of Columbia, White of Cornell, and Gilman of Johns Hopkins.

Daniel Coit Gilman was perhaps first among the champions of the university movement. He had helped found the Sheffield Scientific School at Yale, served as president of the University of California, was instrumental in establishing Johns Hopkins as the first all-graduate American university, and in 1875 became its first president. In the selections that follow from one of his addresses, Gilman presents his views on the functions of a modern university. Particularly noteworthy is his stress on the relationship between university research and the dramatic advances in science and technology, which had made so significant an impact on nineteenth-century life.

First, it is the business of a university to advance knowledge; every professor must be a student. No history is so remote that it may be neglected; no law of mathematics is so hidden that it may not be sought out; no problem in respect to physics is so difficult that it must be

D. C. *Gilman,* The Benefits Which Society Derives from Universities, An Address *(Baltimore: Publication Agency for the Johns Hopkins University, 1885), pp. 16–19, 32–34, 38–39.*

shunned. No love of ease, no dread of labor, no fear of consequences, no desire for wealth will divert a band of well chosen professors from uniting their forces in the prosecution of study. Rather let me say that there are heroes and martyrs, prophets and apostles of learning as there are of religion. To the claims of duty, to the responsibilities of station, to the voices of enlightened conscience such men respond, and they throw their hearts into their work with as much devotion, and as little selfishness, as it is possible for human nature to exhibit. By their labors, knowledge has been accumulated, intellectual capital has been acquired. In these processes of investigation the leading universities of the world have always been engaged.

This is what laboratories, museums and libraries signify. Nothing is foreign to their purpose, and those who work in them are animated by the firm belief that the advancement of knowledge in any direction contributes to the welfare of man. Nor is research restricted to material things; the scholars of a university are equally interested in all that pertains to the nature of man, the growth of society, the study of language, and the establishment of the principles of intellectual and moral conduct.

2. Universities are conservative. They encourage the study of the history, the philosophy, the poetry, the drama, the politics, the religion, in fine, the experience of antecedent ages. Successors of the ancient monasteries, they keep alive in our day the knowledge of ancient languages and art, enrich the literature of our mother tongue, hold up to us the highest standards of excellence in writing and enable us to share in the thoughts of the noblest of our race. Let me especially remind you that to the universities men turn instinctively for light on the interpretation of the Scriptures. When new manuscripts are discovered, or new versions are proposed, or new monuments are unearthed, it is to the universities, where the knowledge of ancient and remote tongues has been cherished, that the religious world looks for enlightenment and guidance. Their dominant influence is highly spiritualizing; I would even go farther and say that it is truly religious. I am not unmindful that within the academic circles men are found whose spiritual insight is but dim,—so it is in all other circles,—but I assert without fear of contradiction, that the influence of study is, on the whole, favorable to the growth of spiritual life, to the development of uprightness, unselfishness and faith, or, in other words, it is opposed to epicureanism and materialism. In belief, there are tides as there are in the ocean, ebb and flow, ebb and flow; but the great ocean is there, with its deep mysteries, unchanging amid all superficial changes. Faith, with all its fluctuations, is as permanently operative in human thought as Knowledge.

3. Universities are refining. They are constantly, by laborious processes, by intricate systems of coöperation, and by ingenious methods,

engaged in eliminating human errors and in submitting all inherited possessions to those processes which remove the dross and perpetuate the gold. No truth which has once been discovered is allowed to perish, —but the incrustations which cover it are removed. It is the universities which edit, interpret, translate and reiterate the acquisitions of former generations both of literature and science. Their revelation of error is sometimes welcomed but it is generally opposed; nevertheless the process goes on, indifferent alike to plaudits or reproaches. If their lessons are hard to the beginners, they lead the persevering to high enjoyment.

4. Universities distribute knowledge. The scholar does but half his duty who simply acquires knowledge. He must share his possessions with others. This is done in the first place by the instruction of pupils. Experience has certainly demonstrated that with rare exceptions, those men are most learned who produce most. The process of acquiring seems to be promoted by that of imparting. The investigator who is surrounded by a bright circle of friendly inquisitors and critics, finds his best powers developed by this influence. Next to its visible circle of pupils, the university should impart its acquisitions to the world of scholars. Learned publications are therefore to be encouraged. But beyond these formal and well recognized means of communicating knowledge, universities have innumerable less obvious, but not less useful opportunities of conveying their benefits to the outside world.

*   *   *   *   *

In regard to pure mathematics we may most confidently say,

> Yet I doubt not thro' the ages one increasing purpose runs,
> And the thoughts of men are widened with the process of the suns.

Many who hesitate to assent to these views of the relation of pure mathematics to civilization, have no question whatever in lauding applied mathematics, especially astronomy and physics; and no wonder, for within the memory of this generation, the world has gained these five results of physical science, steam locomotion, telegraphy, telephony, photography, and electric lighting. The first three, it may be said, have revolutionized the methods of human intercourse; the fourth has multiplied infinitely the means of communicating knowledge to the brain by what Sir William Thomson, following John Bunyan, has termed the Eye-gate; and the fifth, still in its dawn, includes possibilities of illumination, which we are not likely to exaggerate. But I have no time to eulogize these recent gains of civilization; every word I can spare must be given to emphasize the fact which is most likely to be forgotten, that these wonderful inventions are the direct fruit of university studies. I do not undervalue the work of practical men when I say that the most brilliant inventor who ever lived has been dependent upon an unseen company of scholars, the discoverers and the formulators of laws which he has been able to apply to methods and instruments. Nor do I forget that Faraday, like Shakespeare, was not a university man. But I mean to say that the manifold applications of science, about which everybody is talking, are only possible because of the abstract studies which universities promote. The electro-magnetic inventions which are now so multiform are only possible because scores of the greatest intellects of the century, one after another, have applied their powers of absolute reasoning to the interpretation of phenomena, which could have been elucidated in any part of the world, and at any epoch of the past, if only the right methods had been employed. As long as universities held aloof from experimental sciences, these discoveries were not made, but when laboratories for investigation were established, an alliance was formed by mathematics and physics, and a new type of intellectual workers was produced, men whose hands were as cunning to construct and make use of instruments, as their brains were cunning to develop the formulas of mathematics. Take the splendid list of leaders who have followed Franklin and Rumford. They may be called the School of Sir Isaac Newton, so much of their inspiration is due to him. Not all were trained in academic walls; but not one failed to derive help from the advantages which universities provide and perpetuate.

*　　*　　*　　*　　*

The science which began with the century is going forward more rapidly than ever. Yet, if we examine a recent exposition of the principles of theoretical chemistry, we may discover that here, as in mathematics and in physics, the most expert perceive that the field which is open to investigation is much vaster than that which has been surveyed. Here, as everywhere else, the highet one ascends the greater his horizon. What good is to come to men from these researches it would not be wise to predict; but we may reflect on what has recently occurred. Within the last few months a boon has been conferred on humanity so great that all the cost of all the laboratories of all the lands in Christendom would have been a small price to pay for so precious a pearl. It came into the world never again to leave it, unheralded, unexpected, from the laboratory of science, to deaden for a few moments and then restore to life the organs of the sight, so that operations on the eye, hitherto dreaded, may be performed without the slightest pain. The chemists may modestly say that this discovery was an accident not to be compared in significance with the discovery of Avogadro's law. That may be so, yet this sort of accident does not happen in Africa or the Fiji Islands—it "happens" where there are universities and laboratories, and trained men able and ready to observe, discover and apply.

3. John Dewey, Philosopher of Progressive Education

In John Dewey's philosophy two great movements of his time— science and social democracy—coalesced. He urged that educators utilize the findings of psychology to assist the child in developing to his fullest capacity; and, like Mann before him, he was convinced that the school is the fundamental agency of social progress and reform. In his work The School and Society *(1899), the titles of the first two lectures, "The School and Social Progress" and "The School and the Life of the Child," mirror his belief in the school's dual commitment to the child and to society. The third lecture, "Waste in Education," illustrates the Progressive faith in institutional improvement through more efficient organization and management.*

EXCERPTS FROM "THE SCHOOL AND SOCIAL PROGRESS"

We are apt to look at the school from an individualistic standpoint, as something between teacher and pupil, or between teacher and parent. That which interests us most is naturally the progress made by the individual child of our acquaintance, his normal physical development, his advance in ability to read, write, and figure, his growth in the knowledge of geography and history, improvement in manners, habits of promptness, order, and industry—it is from such standards as these that we judge the work of the school. And rightly so. Yet the range of the outlook needs to be enlarged. What the best and wisest parent wants for his own child, that must the community want for all of its children. Any other ideal for our schools is narrow and unlovely; acted upon, it destroys our democracy. All that society has accomplished for itself is put, through the agency of the school, at the disposal of its future members. All its better thoughts of itself it hopes to realize through the new possibilities thus opened to its future self. Here individualism and socialism are at one. Only by being true to the full growth of all the individuals who make it up, can society by any chance be true to itself. And

John Dewey, The School and Society *(Chicago: The University of Chicago Press; New York: McClure, Phillips and Company, 1900), pp. 19–21, 26–27, 38–39, 43–44, 51–53, 59–60, 71–73, 77–78, 85–86, 89–90.*

in the self-direction thus given, nothing counts as much as the school, for, as Horace Mann said, "Where anything is growing, one former is worth a thousand re-formers."

Whenever we have in mind the discussion of a new movement in education, it is especially necessary to take the broader, or social view. Otherwise, changes in the school institution and tradition will be looked at as the arbitrary inventions of particular teachers; at the worst transitory fads, and at the best merely improvements in certain details—and this is the plane upon which it is to customary to consider school changes. It is as rational to conceive of the locomotive or the telegraph as personal devices. The modification going on in the method and curriculum of education is as much a product of the changed social situation, and as much an effort to meet the needs of the new society that is forming, as are changes in modes of industry and commerce.

It is to this, then, that I especially ask your attention: the effort to conceive what roughly may be termed the "New Education" in the light of larger changes in society. Can we connect this "New Education" with the general march of events? If we can, it will lose its isolated character, and will cease to be an affair which proceeds only from the over-ingenious minds of pedagogues dealing with particular pupils. It will appear as part and parcel of the whole social evolution, and, in its more general features at least, as inevitable. Let us then ask after the main aspects of the social movement; and afterwards turn to the school to find what witness it gives of effort to put itself in line. And since it is quite impossible to cover the whole ground, I shall for the most part confine myself to one typical thing in the modern school movement— that which passes under the name of manual training, hoping if the relation of that to changed social conditions appears, we shall be ready to concede the point as well regarding other educational innovations.

*   *   *   *   *

When we turn to the school, we find that one of the most striking tendencies at present is toward the introduction of so-called manual training, shop-work, and the household arts—sewing and cooking.

This has not been done "on purpose," with a full consciousness that the school must now supply that factor of training formerly taken care of in the home, but rather by instinct, by experimenting and finding that such work takes a vital hold of pupils and gives them something which was not to be got in any other way. Consciousness of its real import is still so weak that the work is often done in a half-hearted, confused, and unrelated way. The reasons assigned to justify it are painfully inadequate or sometimes even positively wrong.

If we were to cross-examine even those who are most favorably disposed to the introduction of this work into our school system, we should,

I imagine, generally find the main reasons to be that such work engages the full spontaneous interest and attention of the children. It keeps them alert and active, instead of passive and receptive; it makes them more useful, more capable, and hence more inclined to be helpful at home; it prepares them to some extent for the practical duties of later life—the girls to be more efficient house managers, if not actually cooks and sempstresses; the boys (were our educational system only adequately rounded out into trade schools) for their future vocations. I do not underestimate the worth of these reasons. Of those indicated by the changed attitude of the children I shall indeed have something to say in my next talk, when speaking directly of the relationship of the school to the child. But the point of view is, upon the whole, unnecessarily narrow. We must conceive of work in wood and metal, of weaving, sewing, and cooking, as methods of life not as distinct studies.

We must conceive of them in their social significance, as types of the processes by which society keeps itself going, as agencies for bringing home to the child some of the primal necessities of community life, and as ways in which these needs have been met by the growing insight and ingenuity of man; in short, as instrumentalities through which the school itself shall be made a genuine form of active community life, instead of a place set apart in which to learn lessons.

*   *   *   *   *

When occupations in the school are conceived in this broad and generous way, I can only stand lost in wonder at the objections so often heard, that such occupations are out of place in the school because they are materialistic, utilitarian, or even menial in their tendency. It sometimes seems to me that those who make these objections must live in quite another world. The world in which most of us live is a world in which everyone has a calling and occupation, something to do. Some are managers and others are subordinates. But the great thing for one as for the other is that each shall have had the education which enables him to see within his daily work all there is in it of large and human significance. How many of the employed are today mere appendages to the machines which they operate! This may be due in part to the machine itself, or to the *régime* which lays so much stress upon the products of the machine; but it is certainly due in large part to the fact that the worker has had no opportunity to develop his imagination and his sympathetic insight as to the social and scientific values found in his work. At present, the impulses which lie at the basis of the industrial system are either practically neglected or positively distorted during the school period. Until the instincts of construction and production are systematically laid hold of in the years of childhood and youth, until they are trained in social directions, enriched by historical interpretation, controlled and illuminated by scientific methods, we certainly are in no position even to locate the source of our economic evils, much less to deal with them effectively.

* * * * *

But why should I make this labored presentation? The obvious fact is that our social life has undergone a thorough and radical change. If our education is to have any meaning for life, it must pass through an equally complete transformation. This transformation is not something to appear suddenly, to be executed in a day by conscious purpose. It is already in progress. Those modifications of our school system which often appear (even to those most actively concerned with them, to say nothing of their spectators) to be mere changes of detail, mere improvement within the school mechanism, are in reality signs and evidences of evolution. The introduction of active occupations, of nature study, of elementary science, of art, of history; the relegation of the merely symbolic and formal to a secondary position; the change in the moral school atmosphere, in the relation of pupils and teachers—of discipline; the introduction of more active, expressive, and self-directing factors—all these are not mere accidents, they are necessities of the larger social evolution. It remains but to organize all these factors, to appreciate them in their fullness of meaning, and to put the ideas and ideals involved into complete, uncompromising possession of our school system. To do this means to make each one of our schools an embryonic community life, active with types of occupations that reflect the life of the larger society, and permeated throughout with the spirit of art, history, and science. When the school introduces and trains each child of society into membership within such a little community, saturating him with the spirit of service, and providing him with the instruments of effective self-direction, we shall have the deepest and best guarantee of a larger society which is worthy, lovely, and harmonious.

* * * * *

EXCERPTS FROM "THE SCHOOL AND THE LIFE OF THE CHILD"

I may have exaggerated somewhat in order to make plain the typical points of the old education: its passivity of attitude, its mechanical massing of children, its uniformity of curriculum and method. It may be summed up by stating that the center of gravity is outside the child. It is in the teacher, the text-book, anywhere and everywhere you please except in the immediate instincts and activities of the child himself. On that basis there is not much to be said about the *life* of the child. A good deal might be said about the studying of the child, but the school is not the place where the child *lives*. Now the change which is coming into our education is the shifting of the center of gravity. It is a change, a revolution, not unlike that introduced by Copernicus when the astronomical center shifted from the earth to the sun. In this case the child becomes the sun about which the appliances of education revolve; he is the center about which they are organized.

If we take an example from an ideal home, where the parent is intelligent enough to recognize what is best for the child, and is able to supply what is needed, we find the child learning through the social converse and constitution of the family. There are certain points of interest and value to him in the conversation carried on: statements are made, inquiries arise, topics are discussed, and the child continually learns. He states his experiences, his misconceptions are corrected. Again the child participates in the household occupations, and thereby gets habits of industry, order, and regard for the rights and ideas of others, and the fundamental habit of subordinating his activities to the general interest of the household. Participation in these household tasks becomes an opportunity for gaining knowledge. The ideal home would naturally have a workshop where the child could work out his constructive instincts. It would have a miniature laboratory in which his inquiries could be directed. The life of the child would extend out of doors to the garden, surrounding fields, and forests. He would have his excursions, his walks and talks, in which the larger world out of doors would open to him.

Now, if we organize and generalize all of this, we have the ideal school. There is no mystery about it, no wonderful discovery of pedagogy or educational theory. It is simply a question of doing systematically and in a large, intelligent, and competent way what for various reasons can be done in most households only in a comparatively meager and haphazard manner. In the first place, the ideal home has to be enlarged. The child must be brought into contact with more grown people and with more children in order that there may be the freest and richest social life. Moreover, the occupations and relationships of the home environment are not specially selected for the growth of the child; the main object is something else, and what the child can get out of them is incidental. Hence the need of a school. In this school the life of the child becomes the all-controlling aim. All the media necessary to further the growth of the child center there. Learning?—certainly, but living primarily, and learning through and in relation to this living. When we take the life of the child centered and organized in this way, we do not find that he is first of all a listening being; quite the contrary.

*   *   *   *   *

If we roughly classify the impulses which are available in the school, we may group them under four heads. There is the social instinct of the children as shown in conversation, personal intercourse, and communication. We all know how self-centered the little child is at the age of four or five. If any new subject is brought up, if he says anything at all, it is: "I have seen that;" or, "My papa or mamma told me about that." His horizon is not large; an experience must come immediately home to him, if he is to be sufficiently interested to relate it to others and seek theirs in return. And yet the egoistic and limited interest of little children is in this manner capable of infinite expansion. The language instinct is the simplest form of the social expression of the child. Hence it is a great, perhaps the greatest of all educational resources.

Then there is the instinct of making—the constructive impulse. The child's impulse to do finds expression first in play, in movement, gesture, and make-believe, becomes more definite, and seeks outlet in shaping materials into tangible forms and permanent embodiment. The child has not much instinct for abstract inquiry. The instinct of investigation seems to grow out of the combination of the constructive impulse with the conversational. There is no distinction between experimental science for little children and the work done in the carpenter shop. Such work as they can do in physics or chemistry is not for the purpose of making technical generalizations or even arriving at abstract truths. Children simply like to do things, and watch to see what will happen. But this can be taken advantage of, can be directed into ways where it gives results of value, as well as be allowed to go on at random.

And so the expressive impulse of the children, the art instinct, grows also out of the communicating and constructive instincts. It is their refinement and full manifestation. Make the construction adequate, make it full, free, and flexible, give it a social motive, something to tell, and you have a work of art. . . .

* * * * *

Speaking of culture reminds me that in a way I have been speaking only of the outside of the child's activity—only of the outward expression of his impulses toward saying, making, finding out, and creating. The real child, it hardly need be said, lives in the world of imaginative values, and ideas which find only imperfect outward embodiment. We hear much nowadays about the cultivation of the child's "imagination." Then we undo much of our own talk and work by a belief that the imagination is some special part of the child, that finds its satisfaction in some one particular direction—generally speaking, that of the unreal and make-believe, of the myth and made-up story. Why are we so hard of heart and so slow to believe? The imagination is the medium in which the child lives. To him there is everywhere and in everything that occupies his mind and activity at all, a surplusage of value and significance. The question of the relation of the school to the child's life is at bottom simply this: shall we ignore this native setting and tendency, dealing not with the living child at all, but with the dead image we have erected, or shall we give it play and satisfaction? If we once believe in life and in the life of the child, then will all the occupations and uses spoken of, then will all history and science, become instruments of appeal and materials of culture to his imagination, and through that to the richness and the orderliness of his life. Where we now see only the outward doing and the outward product, there, behind all visible results, is the re-adjustment of mental attitude, the enlarged and sympathetic vision, the sense of growing power, and the willing ability to identify both insight and capacity with the interests of the world and man. Unless culture be a superficial polish, a veneering of mahogany over common wood, it surely is this—the growth of the imagination in flexibility, in scope, and in sympathy, till the life which the individual lives is informed with the life of nature and of society. When nature and society can live in the schoolroom, when the forms and tools of learning are subordinated to the substance of experience, then shall there be an opportunity for this identification, and culture shall be the democratic password.

*   *   *   *   *

EXCERPTS FROM "WASTE IN EDUCATION"

The subject announced for today was "Waste in Education." I should like first to state briefly its relation to the two preceding lectures. The first dealt with the school in its social aspects, and the necessary re-adjustments that have to be made to render it effective in present social conditions. The second dealt with the school in relation to the growth of individual children. Now the third deals with the school as itself an institution, both in relation to society and to its own members— the children. It deals with the question of organization, because all waste is the result of the lack of it, the motive lying behind organization being promotion of economy and efficiency. This question is not one of the waste of money or the waste of things. These matters count; but the primary waste is that of human life, the life of the children while they are at school, and afterward because of inadequate and perverted preparation.

So, when we speak of organization, we are not to think simply of the externals; of that which goes by the name "school system"—the school board, the superintendent, and the building, the engaging and promotion of teachers, etc. These things enter in, but the fundamental organization is that of the school itself as a community of individuals, in its relations to other forms of social life. All waste is due to isolation. Organization is nothing but getting things into connection with one another, so that they work easily, flexibly, and fully. Therefore in speaking of this question of waste in education, I desire to call your attention to the isolation of the various parts of the school system, to the lack of unity in the aims of education, to the lack of coherence in its studies and methods.

* * * * *

It is interesting to follow out the inter-relation between primary, grammar, and high schools. The elementary school has crowded up and taken many subjects previously studied in the old New England grammar school. The high school has pushed its subjects down. Latin and algebra have been put in the upper grades, so that the seventh and eighth grades are, after all, about all that is left of the old grammar school. They are a sort of amorphous composite, being partly a place where children go on learning what they already have learned (to read, write, and figure), and partly a place of preparation for the high school. The name in some parts of New England for these upper grades was "Intermediate School." The term was a happy one; the work was simply intermediate between something that had been and something that was going to be, having no special meaning on its own account.

Just as the parts are separated, so do the ideals differ—moral development, practical utility, general culture, discipline, and professional training. These aims are each especially represented in some distinct part of the system of education; and with the growing interaction of the parts, each is supposed to afford a certain amount of culture, discipline, and utility. But the lack of fundamental unity is witnessed in the fact that one study is still considered good for discipline, and another for culture; some parts of arithmetic, for example, for discipline and others for use, literature for culture, grammar for discipline, geography partly for utility, partly for culture; and so on. The unity of education is dissipated, and the studies become centrifugal; so much of this study to secure this end, so much of that to secure another, until the whole becomes a sheer compromise and patchwork between contending aims and disparate studies. The great problem in education on the administrative side is to secure the unity of the whole, in the place of a sequence of more or less unrelated and overlapping parts and thus to reduce the waste arising from friction, reduplication and transitions that are not properly bridged.

* * * * *

From the standpoint of the child, the great waste in the school comes from his inability to utilize the experiences he gets outside the school in any complete and free way within the school itself; while, on the other hand, he is unable to apply in daily life what he is learning at school. That is the isolation of the school—its isolation from life. When the child gets into the schoolroom he has to put out of his mind a large part of the ideas, interests, and activities that predominate in his home and neighborhood. So the school, being unable to utilize this everyday experience, sets painfully to work, on another track and by a variety of means, to arouse in the child an interest in school studies. While I was visiting in the city of Moline a few years ago, the superintendent told me that they found many children every year, who were surprised to learn that the Mississippi river in the text-book had anything to do with the stream of water flowing past their homes. The geography being simply a matter of the schoolroom, it is more or less of an awakening to many children to find that the whole thing is nothing but a more formal and definite statement of the facts which they see, feel, and touch every day. When we think that we all live on the earth, that we live in an atmosphere, that our lives are touched at every point by the influences of the soil, flora, and fauna, by considerations of light and heat, and then think of what the school study of geography has been, we have a typical idea of the gap existing between the everyday experiences of the child, and the isolated material supplied in such large measure in the school. This is but an instance, and one upon which most of us may reflect long before we take the present artificiality of the school as other than a matter of course or necessity.

回 4. The Progress of Education in the United States

Looking back over twentieth-century developments in American education one is impressed by the continuing and ever more rapid advance of democratic tendencies. Paralleling the general trend toward greater political, social, and economic opportunity, increasing numbers of children have been attending schools at all levels and engaging in the study of an increasing variety of subjects. The traditions of the aristocratic secondary school and college with their uniform, classical curricula have finally been breached. In 1918 the National Education Association's Commission on the Reorganization of Secondary Schools issued a report entitled "Cardinal Principles of Secondary Education," which clearly illustrates the response of American educators to the significant changes in American society. Excerpts from this report follow.

I. THE NEED FOR REORGANIZATION

Secondary education should be determined by the needs of the society to be served, the character of the individuals to be educated, and the knowledge of educational theory and practice available. These factors are by no means static. Society is always in process of development; the character of the secondary-school population undergoes modification; and the sciences on which educational theory and practice depend constantly furnish new information. Secondary education, however, like any other established agency of society, is conservative and tends to resist modification. Failure to make adjustments when the need arises leads to the necessity for extensive reorganization at irregular intervals. The evidence is strong that such a comprehensive reorganization of secondary education is imperative at the present time.

1. *Changes in society.*—Within the past few decades changes have taken place in American life profoundly affecting the activities of the individual. As a citizen, he must to a greater extent and in a more direct way cope with problems of community life, State and National Governments, and international relationships. As a worker, he must adjust himself to a more complex economic order. As a relatively independent personality, he has more leisure. The problems arising from these three dominant phases of life are closely interrelated and call for a degree of intelligence and efficiency on the part of every citizen that can not be secured through elementary education alone, or even through secondary education unless the scope of that education is broadened.

The responsibility of the secondary school is still further increased because many social agencies other than the school afford less stimulus for education than heretofore. In many vocations there have come such significant changes as the substitution of the factory system for the domestic system of industry; the use of machinery in place of manual labor; the high specialization of processes with a corresponding subdivision of labor; and the breakdown of the apprentice system. In connection with home and family life have frequently come lessened responsibility on the part of the children; the withdrawal of the father and sometimes the mother from home occupations to the factory or store; and increased urbanization, resulting in less unified family life. Similarly, many important changes have taken place in community life, in the church, in the State, and in other institutions. These changes in American life call for extensive modifications in secondary education.

2. *Changes in the secondary school population.*—In the past 25 years there

National Education Association, Commission on the Reorganization of Secondary Schools, Cardinal Principles of Secondary Education, *Bureau of Education, Bulletin 1918, No. 35 (Washington: Government Printing Office, 1918), pp. 7–11.*

have been marked changes in the secondary-school population of the United States. The number of pupils has increased, according to Federal returns, from one for every 210 of the total population in 1889–90, to one for every 121 in 1899–1900, to one for every 89 in 1909–10, and to one for every 73 of the estimated total population in 1914–15. The character of the secondary-school population has been modified by the entrance of large numbers of pupils of widely varying capacities, aptitudes, social heredity, and destinies in life. Further, the broadening of the scope of secondary education has brought to the school many pupils who do not complete the full course but leave at various stages of advancement. The needs of these pupils can not be neglected, nor can we expect in the near future that all pupils will be able to complete the secondary school as full-time students.

At present only about one-third of the pupils who enter the first year of the elementary school reach the four-year high school, and only about one in nine is graduated. Of those who enter the seventh school year, only one-half to two-thirds reach the first year of the four-year high school. Of those who enter the four-year high school about one-third leave before the beginning of the second year, about one-half are gone before the beginning of the third year, and fewer than one-third are graduated. These facts can no longer be safely ignored.

3. *Changes in educational theory.*—The sciences on which educational theory depends have within recent years made significant contributions. In particular, educational psychology emphasizes the following factors:

(a) *Individual differences in capacities and aptitudes among secondary-school pupils.* Already recognized to some extent, this factor merits fuller attention.

(b) *The reexamination and reinterpretation of subject values and the teaching methods with reference to "general discipline."*—While the final verdict of modern psychology has not as yet been rendered, it is clear that former conceptions of "general values" must be thoroughly revised.

(c) *Importance of applying knowledge.*—Subject values and teaching methods must be tested in terms of the laws of learning and the application of knowledge to the activities of life, rather than primarily in terms of the demands of any subject as a logically organized science.

(d) *Continuity in the development of children.*—It has long been held that psychological changes at certain stages are so pronounced as to overshadow the continuity of development. On this basis secondary education has been sharply separated from elementary education. Modern psychology, however, goes to show that the development of the individual is in most respects a continuous process and that, therefore, any sudden or abrupt break between the elementary and the secondary school or between any two successive stages of education is undesirable.

The foregoing changes in society, in the character of the secondary-school population, and in educational theory, together with many other considerations, call for extensive modifications of secondary education. Such modifications have already begun in part. The present need is for the formulation of a comprehensive program of reorganization, and its adoption, with suitable adjustments, in all the secondary schools of the Nation. Hence it is appropriate for a representative body like the National Education Association to outline such a program. This is the task entrusted by that association to the Commission on the Reorganization of Secondary Education.

II. THE GOAL OF EDUCATION IN A DEMOCRACY

Education in the United States should be guided by a clear conception of the meaning of democracy. It is the ideal of democracy that the individual and society may find fulfillment each in the other. Democracy sanctions neither the exploitation of the individual by society, nor the disregard of the interests of society by the individual. More explicitly—

The purpose of democracy is so to organize society that each member may develop his personality primarily through activities designed for the well-being of his fellow members and of society as a whole.

This ideal demands that human activities be placed upon a high level of efficiency; that to this efficiency be added an appreciation of the significance of these activities and loyalty to the best ideals involved; and that the individual choose that vocation and those forms of social service in which his personality may develop and become most effective. For the achievement of these ends democracy must place chief reliance upon education.

Consequently, education in a democracy, both within and without the school, should develop in each individual the knowledge, interests, ideals, habits, and powers whereby he will find his place and use that place to shape both himself and society toward ever nobler ends.

III. THE MAIN OBJECTIVES OF EDUCATION

In order to determine the main objectives that should guide education in a democracy it is necessary to analyze the activities of the individual. Normally he is a member of a family, of a vocational group, and of various civic groups, and by virtue of these relationships he is called upon to engage in activities that enrich the family life, to render important vocational services to his fellows, and to promote the common welfare. It follows, therefore, that worthy home-membership, vocation, and citizenship, demand attention as three of the leading objectives.

Aside from the immediate discharge of these specific duties, every individual should have a margin of time for the cultivation of personal and social interests. This leisure, if worthily used, will recreate his powers and enlarge and enrich life, thereby making him better able to meet his responsibilities. The unworthy use of leisure impairs health, disrupts home life, lessens vocational efficiency, and destroys civic-mindedness. The tendency in industrial life, aided by legislation, is to decrease the working hours of large groups of people. While shortened hours tend to lessen the harmful reactions that arise from prolonged strain, they increase, if possible, the importance of preparation for leisure. In view of these considerations, education for the worthy use of leisure is of increasing importance as an objective.

To discharge the duties of life and to benefit from leisure, one must have good health. The health of the individual is essential also to the vitality of the race and to the defense of the Nation. Health education is, therefore, fundamental.

There are various processes, such as reading, writing, arithmetical computations, and oral and written expression, that are needed as tools in the affairs of life. Consequently, command of these fundamental processes, while not an end in itself, is nevertheless an indispensable objective.

And, finally, the realization of the objectives already named is dependent upon ethical character, that is, upon conduct founded upon right principles, clearly perceived and loyally adhered to. Good citizenship, vocational excellence, and the worthy use of leisure go hand in hand with ethical character; they are at once the fruits of sterling character and the channels through which such character is developed and made manifest. On the one hand, character is meaningless apart from the will to discharge the duties of life, and, on the other hand, there is no guarantee that these duties will be rightly discharged unless principles are substituted for impulses, however well-intentioned such impulses may be. Consequently ethical character is at once involved in all the other objectives and at the same time requires specific consideration in any program of national education.

This commission, therefore, regards the following as the main objectives of education: 1. Health. 2. Command of fundamental processes. 3. Worthy home-membership. 4. Vocation. 5. Citizenship. 6. Worthy use of leisure. 7. Ethical character.

The naming of the above objectives is not intended to imply that the process of education can be divided into separated fields. This can not be, since the pupil is indivisible. Nor is the analysis all-inclusive. Nevertheless, we believe that distinguishing and naming these objectives will aid in directing efforts; and we hold that they should constitute the principal aims in education.

No more significant illustration can be found of the continuing deep faith of Americans in the power of schooling than the long struggle of Negro civil rights forces for equality in education. Not only did the Supreme Court's decision in Brown v. Board of Education of Topeka *strike out at legal and de facto school segregation, but it also marked the beginning of the intensive and far-ranging struggle for racial equality in all areas of life, which has dominated the American scene since 1954.*

BROWN *v.* BOARD OF EDUCATION OF TOPEKA.

Decided May 17, 1954

Mr. Chief Justice Warren delivered the opinion of the Court. These cases come to us from the States of Kansas, South Carolina, Virginia, and Delaware. They are premised on different facts and different local conditions, but a common legal question justifies their consideration together in this consolidated opinion.

In each of the cases, minors of the Negro race, through their legal representatives, seek the aid of the courts in obtaining admission to the public schools of their community on a nonsegregated basis. In each instance, they have been denied admission to schools attended by white children under laws requiring or permitting segregation according to race. This segregation was alleged to deprive the plaintiffs of the equal protection of the laws under the Fourteenth Amendment. In each of the cases other than the Delaware case, a three-judge federal district court denied relief to the plaintiffs on the so-called "separate but equal" doctrine announced by this Court in Plessy v. Ferguson, 163 U.S. 537, 16 S.Ct. 1138, 41 L.Ed. 256. Under that doctrine, equality of treatment is accorded when the races are provided substantially equal facilities, even though these facilities be separate. In the Delaware case, the Supreme Court of Delaware adhered to that doctrine, but ordered that the plaintiffs be admitted to the white schools because of their superiority to the Negro schools.

The plaintiffs contend that segregated public schools are not "equal" and cannot be made "equal," and that hence they are deprived of the equal protection of the laws. Because of the obvious importance of the question presented, the Court took jurisdiction. Argument was heard in the 1952 Term, and reargument was heard this Term on certain questions propounded by the Court.

Reargument was largely devoted to the circumstances surrounding

Brown, et al. *v.* Board of Education of Topeka, et al., *347 U.S. 483 (1954).*

the adoption of the Fourteenth Amendment in 1868. It covered exhaustively consideration of the Amendment in Congress, ratification by the states, then existing practices in racial segregation, and the views of proponents and opponents of the Amendment. This discussion and our own investigation convince us that, although these sources cast some light, it is not enough to resolve the problem with which we are faced. At best, they are inconclusive. The most avid proponents of the post-War Amendments undoubtedly intended them to remove all legal distinctions among "all persons born or naturalized in the United States." Their opponents, just as certainly, were antagonistic to both the letter and the spirit of the Amendments and wished them to have the most limited effect. What others in Congress and the state legislatures had in mind cannot be determined with any degree of certainty.

An additional reason for the inconclusive nature of the Amendment's history, with respect to segregated schools, is the status of public education at that time. In the South, the movement toward free common schools, supported by general taxation, had not yet taken hold. Education of white children was largely in the hands of private groups. Education of Negroes was almost nonexistent, and practically all of the race were illiterate. In fact, any education of Negroes was forbidden by law in some states. Today, in contrast, many Negroes have achieved outstanding success in the arts and sciences as well as in the business and professional world. It is true that public school education at the time of the Amendment had advanced further in the North, but the effect of the Amendment on Northern States was generally ignored in the congressional debates. Even in the North, the conditions of public education did not approximate those existing today. The curriculum was usually rudimentary; ungraded schools were common in rural areas; the school term was but three months a year in many states; and compulsory school attendance was virtually unknown. As a consequence, it is not surprising that there should be so little in the history of the Fourteenth Amendment relating to its intended effect on public education.

In the first cases in this Court construing the Fourteenth Amendment, decided shortly after its adoption, the Court interpreted it as proscribing all state-imposed discriminations against the Negro race. The doctrine of "separate but equal" did not make its appearance in this Court until 1896 in the case of Plessy v. Ferguson, supra, involving not education but transportation. American courts have since labored with the doctrine for over half a century. In this Court, there have been six cases involving the "separate but equal" doctrine in the field of public education. In Cumming v. Board of Education of Richmond County, 175 U.S. 528, 20 S.Ct. 197, 44 L.Ed. 262, and Gong Lum v. Rice, 275 U.S. 78, 48 S.Ct. 91, 72 L.Ed. 172, the validity of the doctrine itself was not challenged. In more recent cases, all on the graduate school level, inequality was found in that specific benefits enjoyed by white students were denied to Negro students of the same educational qualifications. State of Missouri ex rel. Gaines v. Canada, 305 U.S. 337, 59 S.Ct. 232, 83 L.Ed. 208; Sipuel v. Board of Regents of University of Oklahoma, 332 U.S. 631, 68 S.Ct. 299, 92 L.Ed. 247; Sweatt v. Painter, 339 U.S. 629, 70 S.Ct. 848, 94 L.Ed. 1114; McLaurin v. Oklahoma State Regents, 339 U.S. 637, 70 S.Ct. 851, 94 L.Ed. 1149. In none of these cases was it necessary to re-examine the doctrine to grant relief to the Negro plaintiff. And in Sweatt v. Painter, supra, the Court expressly reserved decision on the question whether Plessy v. Ferguson should be held inapplicable to public education.

In the instant cases, that question is directly presented. Here, unlike Sweatt v. Painter, there are findings below that the Negro and white schools involved have been equalized, or are being equalized, with respect to buildings, curricula, qualifications and salaries of teachers, and other "tangible" factors. Our decision, therefore, cannot turn on merely a comparison of these tangible factors in the Negro and white schools involved in each of the cases. We must look instead to the effect of segregation itself on public education.

In approaching this problem, we cannot turn the clock back to 1868 when the Amendment was adopted, or even to 1896 when Plessy v. Ferguson was written. We must consider public education in the light of its full development and its present place in American life throughout the Nation. Only in this way can it be determined if segregation in public schools deprives these plaintiffs of the equal protection of the laws.

Today, education is perhaps the most important function of state and local governments. Compulsory school attendance laws and the great expenditures for education both demonstrate our recognition of the importance of education to our democratic society. It is required in the performance of our most basic public responsibilities, even service in the armed forces. It is the very foundation of good citizenship. Today it is a principal instrument in awakening the child to cultural values, in preparing him for later professional training, and in helping him to adjust normally to his environment. In these days, it is doubtful that any child may reasonably be expected to succeed in life if he is denied the opportunity of an education. Such an opportunity, where the state has undertaken to provide it, is a right which must be made available to all on equal terms.

We come then to the question presented: Does segregation of children in public schools solely on the basis of race, even though the physical facilities and other "tangible" factors may be equal, deprive the children of the minority group of equal educational opportunities? We believe that it does.

In Sweatt v. Painter, supra [339 U.S. 629, 70 S.Ct. 850], in finding that a segregated law school for Negroes could not provide them equal educational opportunities, this Court relied in large part on "those qualities which are incapable of objective measurement but which make for greatness in a law school." In McLaurin v. Oklahoma State Regents, supra [339 U.S. 637, 70 S.Ct. 853], the Court, in requiring that a Negro admitted to a white graduate school be treated like all other students, again resorted to intangible considerations: "* * * his ability to study, to engage in discussions and exchange views with other students, and, in general, to learn his profession." Such considerations apply with added force to children in grade and high schools. To separate them from others of similar age and qualifications solely because of their race generates a feeling of inferiority as to their status in the community that may affect their hearts and minds in a way unlikely ever to be undone. The effect of this separation on their educational opportunities was well stated by a finding in the Kansas case by a court which nevertheless felt compelled to rule against the Negro plaintiffs:

Segregation of white and colored children in public schools has a detrimental effect upon the colored children. The impact is greater when it has the sanction of the law; for the policy of separating the races is usually interpreted as denoting the inferiority of the Negro group. A sense of inferiority affects the motivation of the child to learn. Segregation with the sanction of law, therefore, has a tendency to [retard] the educational and mental development of Negro children and to deprive them of some of the benefits they would receive in a racial[ly] integrated school system.

Whatever may have been the extent of psychological knowledge at the time of Plessy v. Ferguson, this finding is amply supported by modern authority. Any language in Plessy v. Ferguson contrary to this finding is rejected.

We conclude that in the field of public education the doctrine of "separate but equal" has no place. Separate educational facilities are inherently unequal. Therefore, we hold that the plaintiffs and others similarly situated for whom the actions have been brought are, by reason of the segregation complained of, deprived of the equal protection of the laws guaranteed by the Fourteenth Amendment. This disposition makes unnecessary any discussion whether such segregation also violates the Due Process Clause of the Fourteenth Amendment.

Because these are class actions, because of the wide applicability of this decision, and because of the great variety of local conditions, the formulation of decrees in these cases presents problems of considerable complexity. On reargument, the consideration of appropriate relief was necessarily subordinated to the primary question—the constitutionality of segregation in public education. We have now announced that such segregation is a denial of the equal protection of the laws. In order that we may have the full assistance of the parties in formulating decrees, the cases will be restored to the docket, and the parties are requested to present further argument on Questions 4 and 5 previously propounded by the Court for the reargument this Term. The Attorney General of the United States is again invited to participate. The Attorney's General of the states requiring or permitting segregation in public education will also be permitted to appear as *amici curiae* upon request to do so by September 15, 1954, and submission of briefs by October 1, 1954.

It is so ordered.

5. British Education and the March of Democracy

It is often stated that British democracy was born with the Reform Act of 1867. By its provisions a million voters were added to the rolls, nearly doubling the size of the electorate. Though complete manhood suffrage had not yet been attained, the march toward that goal had started well on its way. As in the case of the Reform Act of 1832, the cause of universal education was a benefactor of the liberal course of events in Parliament. With the passage of the Forster Act in 1870, Parliament set the framework for universal, free, compulsory elementary education.

EXCERPTS FROM THE FORSTER ACT, 1870

SUPPLY OF SCHOOLS

5. There shall be provided for every school district a sufficient amount of accommodation in public elementary schools (as herein-after defined) available for all the children resident in such district for whose elementary education efficient and suitable provision is not otherwise made, and where there is an insufficient amount of such accommodation, in this Act referred to as "public school accommodation," the deficiency shall be supplied in manner provided by this Act.

6. Where the Education Department, in the manner provided by this Act, are satisfied and have given public notice that there is an insufficient amount of public school accommodation for any school district, and the deficiency is not supplied as herein-after required, a school board shall be formed for such district, and shall supply such deficiency, and in case of default by the school board the Education

The Education Acts, *1870–1904 (London: Printed for His Majesty's Stationery Office, 1904), pp. 18–19, 22–23, 46–47.*

Department shall cause the duty of such board to be performed in manner provided by this Act.

7.   Every elementary school which is conducted in accordance with the following regulations shall be a public elementary school within the meaning of this Act: and every public elementary school shall be conducted in accordance with the following regulations (a copy of which regulations shall be conspicuously put up in every such school); namely,

(1)   It shall not be required, as a condition of any child being admitted into or continuing in the school, that he shall attend or abstain from attending any Sunday school, or any place of religious worship, or that he shall attend any religious observance or any instruction in religious subjects in the school or elsewhere, from which observance or instruction he may be withdrawn by his parent, or that he shall, if withdrawn by his parent, attend the school on any day exclusively set apart for religious observance by the religious body to which his parent belongs:

(2)   The time or times during which any religious observance is practised or instruction in religious subjects is given at any meeting of the school shall be either at the beginning or at the end or at the beginning and the end of such meeting, and shall be inserted in a time table to be approved by the Education Department, and to be kept permanently and conspicuously affixed in every schoolroom; and any scholar may be withdrawn by his parent from such observance or instruction without forfeiting any of the other benefits of the school:

(3)   The school shall be open at all times to the inspection of any of Her Majesty's inspectors, so, however, that it shall be no part of the duties of such inspector to inquire into any instruction in religious subjects given at such school, or to examine any scholar therein in religious knowledge or in any religious subject or book:

(4)   The school shall be conducted in accordance with the conditions required to be fufilled by an elementary school in order to obtain an annual parliamentary grant.

*   *   *   *   *

MANAGEMENT AND MAINTENANCE OF
SCHOOLS BY SCHOOL BOARD

14.   Every school provided by a school board shall be conducted under the control and management of such board in accordance with the following regulations:

(1) The school shall be a public elementary school within the meaning of this Act:

(2) No religious catechism or religious formulary which is distinctive of any particular denomination shall be taught in the school.

15. *The school board may, if they think fit, from time to time delegate any of their powers under this Act except the power of raising money, and in particular may delegate the control and management of any school provided by them, with or without any conditions or restrictions, to a body of managers appointed by them, consisting of not less than three persons.*

The school board may from time to time remove all or any of such managers, and within the limits allowed by this section add to or diminish the number of or otherwise alter the constitution or powers of any body of managers formed by it under this section.

Any manager appointed under this section may resign on giving written notice to the board. The rules contained in the third schedule to this Act respecting the proceedings of bodies of managers appointed by a school board shall be observed.

16. *If the school board do or permit any act in contravention of or fail to comply with the regulations according to which a school provided by them is required by this Act to be conducted, the Education Department may declare the school board to be and such board shall accordingly be deemed to be a board in default, and the Education Department may proceed accordingly, and every act or omission of any member of the school board, or manager appointed by them, or any person under the control of the board, shall be deemed to be permitted by the board, unless the contrary be proved.*

If any dispute arises as to whether the school board have done or permitted any act in contravention of or have failed to comply with the said regulations, the matter shall be referred to the Education Department, whose decision thereon shall be final.

17. Every child attending a school provided by any school board shall pay such weekly fee as may be prescribed by the school board with the consent of the Education Department but the school board may from time to time, for a renewable period not exceeding six months, remit the whole or any part of such fee in the case of any child when they are of opinion that the parent of such child is unable from poverty to pay the same, but such remission shall not be deemed to be parochial relief given to such parent.

18. The school board shall maintain and keep efficient every school provided by such board, and shall from time to time provide such additional school accommodation as is, *in their opinion,* necessary in order to supply a sufficient amount of public school accommodation for their district.

A school board may discontinue any school provided by them, or change the site of any such school, if they satisfy the Education

Department that the school to be discontinued is unnecessary, or that such change of site is expedient.

If at any time the Education Department are satisfied that a school board have failed to perform their duty, either by not maintaining or keeping efficient every school provided by them, or by not providing such additional school accommodation as in the opinion of the Education Department is necessary in order to supply a sufficient amount of public school accommodation in their district, the Education Department may send them a requisition requiring them to fulfil the duty which they have so failed to perform; and if the school board fail within the time limited by such requisition, not being less than three months, to comply therewith to the satisfaction of the Education Department, such board shall be deemed to be a school board in default, and the Education Department may proceed accordingly.

19.   Every school board for the purpose of providing sufficient public school accommodation for their district *whether in obedience to any requisition or not,* may provide, by building or otherwise, schoolhouses properly fitted up, and improve, enlarge, and fit up any schoolhouse provided by them, and supply school apparatus and everything necessary for the efficiency of the schools provided by them, and purchase and take on lease any land, and any right over land, or may exercise any of such powers.

*   *   *   *   *

ATTENDANCE AT SCHOOL

74.   Every school board may from time to time, with the approval of the Education Department, make byelaws for all or any of the following purposes:

(1)   Requiring the parents of children of such age, not less than five years nor more than *thirteen* years, as may be fixed by the byelaws, to cause such children (unless there is some reasonable excuse) to attend school:

(2)   Determining the time during which children are so to attend school; provided that no such byelaw shall prevent the withdrawal of any child from any religious observance or instruction in religious subjects, or shall require any child to attend school on any day exclusively set apart for religious observance by the religious body to which his parent belongs, or shall be contrary to anything contained in any Act for regulating the education of children employed in labour:

(3)   Providing for the remission *or payment* of the whole or any part of the fees of any child where the parent satisfies the school board that he is unable from poverty to pay the same:

(4)   Imposing penalties for the breach of any byelaws:

(5)   Revoking or altering any byelaw previously made.

Provided that any byelaw under this section requiring a child between *ten* and *thirteen* years of age to attend school shall provide for the total or partial exemption of such child from the obligation to attend school if one of Her Majesty's inspectors certifies that such child has reached a standard of education specified in such byelaw.

Any of the following reasons shall be a reasonable excuse; namely,

(1) That the child is under efficient instruction in some other manner:

(2) That the child has been prevented from attending school by sickness or any unavoidable cause:

(3) That there is no public elementary school open which the child can attend within such distance, not exceeding three miles, measured according to the nearest road from the residence of such child, as the byelaws may prescribe.

As a result of a number of acts passed in the decades following 1870, government support of elementary education was extended. But, it was as part of a general movement of social reform, which came to a head during World War II, that Britain finally made its great commitment to educational opportunity for all from nursery school through the university. In 1943 a white paper entitled "Educational Reconstruction" was presented to Parliament and received wide support throughout the country. The paper not only led to the Education Act of 1944, which incorporated most of its proposals, but also established goals for future educational reform. Excerpts from the document follow.

EDUCATIONAL RECONSTRUCTION

"Upon the education of the people of this country the fate of this country depends."

I. INTRODUCTION

1. The Government's purpose in putting forward the reforms described in this Paper is to secure for children a happier childhood and a better start in life; to ensure a fuller measure of education and opportunity for young people and to provide means for all of developing the various talents with which they are endowed and so enriching the inheritance of the country whose citizens they are. The new educational opportunities must not, therefore, be of a single pattern. It is just as important to achieve diversity as it is to ensure equality of educational opportunity. But such diversity must not impair the social unity within the educational system which will open the way to a more closely knit

Educational Reconstruction *(London: Printed and Published by His Majesty's Stationery Office, 1943), pp. 3, 32–33.*

society and give us strength to face the tasks ahead. The war has revealed afresh the resources and character of the British people—an enduring possession that will survive all the material losses inevitable in the present struggle. In the youth of the nation we have our greatest national asset. Even on a basis of mere expediency, we cannot afford not to develop this asset to the greatest advantage. It is the object of the present proposals to strengthen and inspire the younger generation. For it is as true to-day, as when it was first said, that "the bulwarks of a city are its men".

2. With these ends in view the Government propose to recast the national education service. The new layout is based on a recognition of the principle that education is a continuous process conducted in successive stages. For children below the compulsory school age of 5 there must be a sufficient supply of nursery schools. The period of compulsory school attendance will be extended to 15 without exemptions and with provision for its subsequent extension to 16 as soon as circumstances permit. The period from 5 to the leaving age will be divided into two stages, the first, to be known as primary, covering the years up to about 11. After 11 secondary education, of diversified types but on equal standing, will be provided for all children. At the primary stage the large classes and bad conditions which at present are a reproach to many elementary schools will be systematically eliminated; at the secondary stage the standard of accommodation and amenities will be steadily raised to the level of the best examples. The provision of school meals and milk will be made obligatory.

3. When the period of full-time compulsory schooling ends the young person will continue under educational influences up to 18 years of age either by remaining in full-time attendance at a secondary school, or by part-time day attendance at a young people's college. Throughout all the foregoing stages the benefits of medical inspection and treatment will be available without charge. Opportunities for technical and adult education will be increased.

4. Among other important features of the plan are an effective system of inspection and registration of schools outside the public system; new financial and administrative arrangements for the voluntary schools, and the recognition of the special place of religious instruction in school life.

*   *   *   *   *

XIII. SUMMARY OF PRINCIPAL REFORMS

126. The changes described in this document may be summarised as follows.

A. The legislative changes proposed will include:—

(*a*) the improvement of the facilities for the training of children below compulsory school age by the provision of nursery schools wherever they are needed;

(*b*) the raising of the school leaving age to 15 without exemptions, with provision for a later raising to 16;

(*c*) the completion of the reorganisation of the present public elementary schools, so that well-designed and equipped primary schools are available for all children up to the age of 11 and secondary schools, with varied facilities for advanced work, for all children over that age;

(*d*) an amendment of the existing law so as

   (i) to emphasise the position of religious instruction as an essential element of education; and

   (ii) to enable the schools provided by voluntary bodies to play their part in the proposed developments;

(*e*) the introduction of a system of compulsory part-time education in working hours for young persons up to the age of 18;

(*f*) the provision of adequate and properly co-ordinated facilities for technical and adult education;

(*g*) the extension of the existing facilities for securing the health and physical well-being of children and young persons;

(*h*) the introduction of a system of inspection and registration of all independent schools which cater for children of compulsory school age;

(*i*) the adjustment of the present system of local educational administration to the new educational layout.

B. The changes to be effected by administrative action, include:—

(*a*) a progressive decrease in the size of classes in primary schools;

(*b*) the abolition of the present Special Place examination and the adoption of other arrangements for the classification of the children when they pass from primary to secondary schools;

(*c*) the introduction of a common Code of Regulations applicable to secondary schools of all types, so framed as to secure that standards of accommodation and amenities generally are raised to the level of those of grammar schools;

(*d*) the remodelling of the curriculum of secondary schools;

(*e*) the further expansion of the Youth Service;

(*f*) the improvement of the facilities for enabling poor students to proceed to the universities;

(*g*) the reform of the present methods of recruiting and training teachers.

回 6. Nazi Germany: Education for a Totalitarian State

During the late nineteenth century the schools of Prussia and the other states of the German Empire were generally held in high esteem. German scholars were acknowledged to be pioneers in the development of the scientific approach to education and curriculum innovators in such areas as mathematics, science, and vocational training. However, the German educational system was also recognized as an extremely effective instrument for maintaining a rigid class system and for instilling obedience and loyalty to church and state. Under the Weimar Republic of the 1920's there was some success in extending educational opportunity in a more democratic fashion, in de-emphasizing the role of religion in the public schools, and in introducing a relatively progressive approach to discipline and curriculum reform. Unfortunately, this came to an abrupt halt with the rise of Adolph Hitler. Under complete centralized control of the state, the schools and other educational agencies were exploited ruthlessly as instruments of Hitler's nightmarish plans. Intellectual training was subordinate to the indoctrination of militarism, racism, and abject obedience to the Nazi state, and the old university tradition of freedom of teaching and learning was completely destroyed. The following excerpts from a book published in Nazi Germany for distribution abroad effectively captures the spirit of their education.

Surveying the present age a hundred years hence, the historian will probably point out that, in Germany, National Socialism effected a return to the laws of life, in all spheres, but especially in the sphere of education. By this we do not mean simply Rousseau's "Back to Nature". For, the National Socialist idea of life has nothing to do with romantic dreaming and is free of all sentimentality. We have brought life into its own again. In the past centuries the laws of natural life were broken in three ways:

1) Instead of considering the peoples of the world as representatives of different *stocks* we let ourselves be deceived by the ideal of a humanity which could only exist in the "mind's eye". We imagined men as beings built on a universal pattern, each one endowed with the other's capacities—the same throughout the world.

2) Instead of treating him as a natural member of a natural community, in which he is as deeply rooted as a plant in the soil, we

Theodor Wilheim and Gerhard Graefe, German Education Today *(Berlin: Terramare Office, 1936), pp. 3, 6–7, 17–19.*

separated man from the type of people to which he belongs and, like a chemist analysing a preparation, put him, so to speak, in a test tube.

3) Finally we did violence to this isolated human being by denying him the existence of heart, determination, emotions, and feelings and by judging only his intellect to be of importance and worth. And it was to the exclusion of everything else and only to this intellect that educationists and teachers directed their attention for nearly two centuries.

The entire civilised world was guilty of these three misconceptions. It would serve no useful purpose were we to discover which nations have sacrificed any more or less to the idols of individualism and intellectualism, during the past centuries, than has Germany. For results would show only slight differences. There can be little doubt, however, that the evils resulting from this over-emphasis of the intellect were more marked here than anywhere else in the world. This can be attributed partly to the social structure of Germany, and partly to the important rôle played by the development of philosophical idealism in our country. In Japan and England other forces were at work which counter-acted this belief in the supreme value of the individual and the intellect. The importance attached to the Emperor in the Japanese schools and the co-operation which exists between the army officer and the schoolmaster is sufficient evidence of this. . . .

* * * * *

If we would reduce the manifold ideals of present-day German education to some common factor, we could aptly choose that ancient principle of the trinity of mind, soul, and body. For, in the education of the German of the future there must be three clearly-defined aspects— the training of the mind, of the soul and of the body. The complaint has often been made that *Adolf Hitler* considered the training of the body to be more important than the training of the mental faculties. But this is not, as has been claimed, evidence of the barbarism of modern Germany. It is simply a natural truth. If we wish to serve our nation—and to the the youth of this country this is a matter of course—we must first become *capable* of rendering this service. Having first aquired the *power* to serve then the second task will be to awaken in ourselves the *readiness* to do so. The capacity to serve requires a careful training of the body, which has nothing to do with the craze for record-breaking, but which seeks to give a natural vigour to every part of the body. But the *readiness* to serve one's nation requires that iron training of will, of courage, and of character as a whole, which Hitler has stated to be the ultimate aim of education. It is taken for granted by every German that, in so doing, mental training must not be neglected. No-one need point out *that* to a German. But what must be driven home to him is this—that his mind is useless unless it can bear witness to the living organism that is man, can bear witness, that is to say, not only to his intellect but also to his heart and will.

The German school-child of the future will strive to attain these virtues: Honour, loyalty, a cheerful willingness to bear responsibility, self-sacrifice, courage, determination, self-confidence, modesty, obedience, and a thorough knowledge of all that appertains to his profession. "In our eyes the German youth of the future must be slim and strong, as fast as a greyhound, as tough as leather and as hard as Krupp steel." (Hitler).

Ernft Krieck and *Alfred Baeumler* based their philosophy of education on the idea of the community of the people and the comradeship of groups of men, as being essential to all German education of the future. The formative forces of the community will remain an integral part of education whether it is provided mainly within or apart from the classroom. The school, must realize then, that even though its methods of teaching were fundamentally altered, as a place of instruction, it can make only a small contribution to education as a whole. Labour service, for instance, will perhaps for many years play a far more decisive part than the school in the training of the youth of this country. Nevertheless a fierce struggle will be fought in Germany as to what form the school should take. For, our aim is not to abolish the school but to win for it its rightful place in the hearts of German children. The training of teachers has therefore become a burning question of the day. For it is beyond all shadow of doubt that no essential change can take place in the German school until either school-masters become leaders of youth or leaders of youth become school-masters.

*   *   *   *   *

SCHOOL AND HITLER YOUTH

Since the beginning of the 20th century, repeated efforts have been made to model the training of the young people of Germany upon the most suitable lines possible. Whilst in the schools, the relationship between teacher and pupil was usually determined by the actual process of teaching and learning, outside the school it was the comradeship of youth for youth that gave birth to a relationship such as exists between a leader and those who are led. A teacher acquires his official authority once he has completed the State-controlled training for his profession and has therein proved himself capable, but a youth leader must constantly prove and maintain his authority over his comrades by exerting an unceasing, personal influence upon them. The educational plans evolved by the *Hitler Youth* are not just the haphazard consequences of the work done in school; instead, they are founded on the passionate desire to create which is so strongly in the hearts of the young. Alive to the fact that they themselves will be the Germany of tomorrow, they are ready to carry upon their own shoulders the responsibility for its welfare. Mindful of this, these young Germans, when their romantic experiments with the Pre-war Youth Movement proved fruitless, found new expression for their ideals in one vast, comprehensive organisation of youth under a common leader.

In the National Socialist State, therefore, the school, the Hitler Youth leaders and the parents are all three responsible for the education of youth. The Reich Minister of Education and the Reich Youth Leader have assured the fruitful collaboration of these three agents by issuing a special regulation. According to this, Sunday belongs entirely to the parents and the family, while Saturday, as the State Youth Day (*Staatsjugendtag*), and in addition one evening a week are free from school-work and are devoted to the educational activities of the Hitler Youth. The other week days are reserved unrestrictedly as school-days. In this way, the education of the young generation in Germany has been given a broad uniform basis. To counteract the intellectual training given to the pupil in the school, the State Youth Day makes provision for the physical training and the stimulation of his team-spirit.

Every boy may decide for himself whether to join the Hitler Youth, which is divided into the following sub-organisations:

1) The *Hitler Jugend*, which includes boys aged 14–18;
2) The *Jungvolk*, which includes boys from 10–14;
3) The *Bund Deutscher Mädchen*, composed of girls from 15–21;
4) The *Jungmädel*, consisting of girls from 10–15.

The Reich Youth Leader (*Reichsjugendführer*) is the head of the whole organization. Its many responsibilities include the social and national training of the young, their hygienic well-being, and the administration and extension of the Youth Hostel Movement.

In Co-operation with the German Labour Front, it also runs the Reich Apprentices' Competition (*Reichsberufswettkampf*) open to all workers between the ages of 14 and 21, who are still apprenticed to a trade or training for a profession. By its practical nature, and to an extent unparalleled in any other country, this competition has impressed the youth of Germany with the nobility of achievement. The competitors are divided into groups according to their professions, and the various achievement classes must complete different practical and theoretical tasks. Throughout the competition employers and employees work together and, at a certain fixed time, workshops and offices all over Germany are carefully prepared for it. The underlying motive is neither money nor material reward of any sort, but the distinction and honour accorded to what is judged to be the best personal achievement, in any particular group of professions. On the first of May, the Day of National Labour, the youthful winners of this competition, along with the workers' delegations, are received and congratulated by the Führer himself. In this way, the achievements of the young manual worker are placed on the same level as those of the brain-worker. This recognition, of the dignity and nobility of every honourable achievement proves to young Germany that it is the worker and not the capitalist who guides the destiny of the nation, that the important factor is, not money, but creative achievement.

After World War II the Western allies undertook the task of establishing democratic values and institutions in a land whose traditions had been almost totally autocratic. One of the major efforts at reorientation was directed toward the schools. Could education be successfully employed to help undo all that the Nazis had so efficiently accomplished in the area of thought control? Could the schools help to instill an allegiance to democratic principles? The effort has been made. The results are yet to be fully determined. The remarks that follow are from an address delivered in 1948 by Alonzo G. Grace, Director of Educational and Cultural Relations of the U.S. Office of Military Government for Germany.

Some of the fundamental principles which are concerned with our policy are:

1. The only certain method of establishing a society based on the democratic ideal is to abandon the use of the term and by practice and precept lead the German people to accept this ideal.
2. The true reform of the German people will come from within. It will be spiritual and moral. The types of school organization or structure, for example, are of less importance to the future of Germany and the world than **what is taught, how it is taught and by whom it is taught.** This is not to underestimate structure but

   external reforms are temporary and inevitably lead to the return to previous practices.
3. We will neither enlist the support of the German people in the struggle of the ideologies nor prevent them from arising again superimposing an educational structure or program which ignores the history of this and other European countries. The solution to the so-called German problem will be more readily attained when we recognize that it is a European problem and a part of the moral collapse of civilization.
4. It will not be the purpose of Military Government to superimpose an American system of education on the German people. It is our

Conference on Educational Reconstruction in Germany, Educational Reconstruction in Germany (*Berchtesgaden: Office of Military Government for Germany* [*U.S.*], *1948*), *pp. 6–7.*

purpose to indicate to the German people that the education of children and youth should be so organized and developed

    a. That each individual irrespective of race, class, creed, or economic status shall have equal access to education.

    b. That each individual be allowed to pursue that form or type of educational opportunity for which he is endowed.

    c. That each individual shall, as a result of his schooling, be able to make the maximum contribution toward the maintenance of world peace and international understanding, the maintenance of law and order and the development of social justice.

5. We must observe that schooling does not necessarily guarantee education; that the acquisition of knowledge does not indicate the possession of wisdom; that instruction does not necessarily mean learning; that schooling, instruction and knowledge without moral responsibility, spiritual enlightenment and intellectual integrity will fail to produce the character necessary to resist the effort of those who would destroy the dignity of the individual. The provision for a corps of educated teachers and leaders is of primary necessity.

6. There must be a clear understanding of the meaning of reorientation, the special responsibilities of each division, and the necessity of coordination by all divisions. Who does a particular job is of less importance than how well and how early it is accomplished.

7. Effective and durable education reform will come in Germany as it has in other countries including England, France, Sweden, Norway, Denmark and the United States, when people recognize, and those who speak for the people realize, that free institutions and the natural rights of men can best be perpetuated through an education system which places major emphasis on the development of moral responsibility, education for freedom and education for responsible citizenship.

8. Education for responsible citizenship involves not only the basic knowledge of the history of the past, but also the knowledge of how to act intelligently in the solution of contemporary problems. It involves not only book knowledge but the opportunity to learn how to protect freedom by experiencing freedom in school organization, by the free flow of ideas, and the capacity of individuals to make decisions.

9. We must not be guilty of attempting to develop the ideal, which may not have been accomplished elsewhere, in the midst of an environment which generates realism.

10. The redirection of the goals, programs or policies of social institutions must grow from the people. Wide citizen participation in community planning, in the discussion of community problems and

in aiding in the formulation of public policy is one guarantee that no one individual can dominate their thinking and living. Power with people must supplant power over people.

*　　*　　*　　*　　*

It is important that we be aware of the history of the past. There is little time here to do more than indicate the necessity of possessing a clear understanding of the history, tradition and culture of Germany and Europe as a basis for wise action on the part of the representatatives of Military Government. For example, Germany after 1918 was faced with a tremendous economic and social problem involving a social revolution with disastrous results to the so-called middle class. Hitler and the Nazis, in the absence of vision and intelligent action on the part of the statesmen or groups of statesmen in the intervening period, found a way to solve the social and economic difficulties of the German people. But accompanying this program also was a spiritual program, which is illustrated in at least one area, in the law concerning Hitler Youth, December 1, 1936. In paragraph two, it is stated that "In the Hitler Youth as well as in the home and school, all German youth are to be educated physically, intellectually and morally in the spirit of National Socialism for service to the nation and toward a national community." Again on March 25, 1939, the Second Enforcement Decree to the law concerning Hilter Youth states that "All persons from the 10th to the completed 18th year of age are obliged to do service to the Hitler Youth." This is merely to indicate that along with social and economic reform came an organized program which provided youth with some definite goal.

There is little time to enter into a discussion of the 19th century revolution against materialism or to recall the events following the failure of the liberal revolution and the beginning of the substitution of the idea of violence and strength as the only means for solving problems. Hitler secured the support of the German people because he provided a program of material security. But more than that, the program provided relief from the necessity of personal decision; it created an atmosphere of escape from materialism; it made individual responsibility unimportant. This mission cannot ignore this historical background or the architecture of the village, traditions of the land or the place of Germany in the European structure.

I would state the general aims of reorientation as follows:

1. To instill in the minds and implant in the hearts of the German people the will to recognize, the power to develop, the spirit to **protect a society** based upon natural rights of men and to learn that:

    a. Those who would trade the natural rights of man for material security, in the end lose both.

    b. The state is the creation of man and exists to enhance the dignity of the individual. **A government of the people will make impossible a people of the government.**

    c. When individual responsibility becomes unimportant and personal decision unnecessary, the state becomes master of the will of the individual.

    d. Man can control his destiny, for it is not alone a characteristic of the machine age for men to feel that they are but cogs in a machine; it is rather a twentieth century materialistic phenomenon to feel frustrated by the fact.

    e. Discrimination in education, employment or socio-economic relationships on the basis of sex, creed, race, nationality or economic state violates a primary principle of group living.

    f. Reason, wisdom and tolerance must supplant blood and violence as the road to freedom and the full life.

2. To aid the German people to aid themselves in the readjustment, reorganization or redirection of their social organization.

7. The U.S.S.R.: Commitment to Education

The Russia over which the Communists gained control in 1917 contained one of the world's largest populations with one of the world's higher rates of illiteracy (c. 80 percent). As the following reading makes abundantly clear, the generally narrow, often reactionary policies of the Russian czars, which ultimately led to their downfall, extended to the field of education. Note that the work from which this excerpt is taken was written in 1919, at a time when civil war was raging in Russia and the future of educational reform, initiated by the short-lived provisional government under Lvov and Kerensky, lay in doubt.

The old aristocracy, shattered so easily, left a heavy heritage. As is well known, education in Russia is very imperfectly developed. The policy of the czars was to impart to the people knowledge that would strengthen their own imperialistic aims. Nevertheless, it differed with

Therese Bach, Educational Changes in Russia, *Bureau of Education, Bulletin 1919, No. 37 (Washington: Government Printing Office, 1919), pp. 4–5.*

each monarch. The reign of Czar Alexander I (1801–1825), especially its first half, was marked by an endeavor to build up a national system of education; his successor, Nicholas I (1825–1855) saw in the spread of schools and popular education a dangerous weapon against autocracy. The system by which schools of different grades formed one continuous ascending chain was destroyed and a high barrier was set up between the elementary and secondary grades.

Education was intended for the privileged classes only, and, although the school system was divided into four grades (parish school, district school, gymnasium, and university), leading from the primary school to the highest type of educational institution, no peasant's children, according to the Ukase issued in 1813 and reaffirmed in 1827, were to be admitted beyond the district school. A few years later even this privilege was denied them, and the tiller of the soil had to be content with the parish school only, though in Russia 85 per cent of the total population is rural.

The fourth Minister of Instruction, Shishkov, with the approval of Czar Alexander and in his presence, issued the following statement:

Knowledge is useful only, when, like salt, it is used and offered in small measure according to the people's circumstances and their needs. To teach the mass of people, or even the majority of them, how to read will bring more harm than good.

This attitude was held by the higher authorities for a number of decades, and neither the abolition of serfdom in the sixties nor any subsequent reforms in Russian state affairs had any considerable effect upon educational conditions in that country.

The accession of Alexander II (1855–1881) was marked by an intellectual revival and freedom of speech, but his assassination plunged the country into a state of reaction. A number of schools came under the control of the church and were governed by the Holy Synod, Russia's highest ecclesiastical authority. The church authorities also opened a series of church schools, where the child spent his years in learning how to read church music and church Slavonic characters, the role of which in eastern Europe may be compared to the part played in the west by Latin. The inevitable cleavage between the secular public schools and the parochial church schools became wide and deep and the passing over of a pupil from a school of one type to that of another was attended with great difficulties.

With Nicholas II (1894–1917) came a general revival of interest in educational matters, especially during the years following the Russo-Japanese war. The second part of his reign was marked by an era of many pedagogical congresses, of various schemes for reforming the schools, of incessant attempts toward the improvement of the methods of teaching and the organization of schools of a new type. Thie revival, taken up by the zemstvos (rural councils) and numerous private agencies, did not succeed, however, in bringing about complete reform. The most thoroughly democratic reforms, for which the progressive elements had been striving for decades, became effective in the early months of new Russia, and only the unfortunate internal strife of later days prevented their complete realization.

That the Communist leaders had grand plans for education as part of their scheme to reconstruct Russia into a socialist, industrial state is now common knowledge. Their amazing success in so rapidly transforming a nation of illiterate peasants into a major technological power capable of launching the first man-made satellite has led Western educators to focus increased attention on Soviet education. In 1959 a group of distinguished educators, constituting the first U.S. education mission to the Soviet Union, issued a report of their month-long study. The first chapter of that report follows.

A NATION COMMITTED

The one fact that most impressed us in the U.S.S.R. was the extent to which the Nation is committed to education as a means of national advancement. In the organization of a planned society in the Soviet Union, education is regarded as one of the chief resources and techniques for achieving social, economic, cultural, and scientific objectives in the national interest. Tremendous responsibilities are therefore placed on Soviet schools, and comprehensive support is provided for them by all segments and agencies of Soviet society.

One of the leading Soviet educators told us: "We believe in a planned society, you in individual initiative. Let time tell." They are convinced that time is on their side and that through education and hard work they can win their way to world acceptance of Communist ideology.

Everywhere we went in the U.S.S.R. we were struck by the zeal and enthusiasm which the people have for education. It is a kind of grand passion with them.

Wherever we turned we heard the slogan: "Reach and over-reach America." And everywhere, the people seem to respond in the conviction that education, in addition to hard work and the postponement of many creature comforts, is the best means of winning world supremacy.

Education reaches far beyond school-age children and youth and is eagerly sought by hundreds of thousands of full-time workers who are

Report of the First Official U.S. Educational Mission to the U.S.S.R., Soviet Commitment to Education, *Office of Education, Bulletin 1959, No. 16 (Washington: Government Printing Office, 1959), pp. 1–4.*

also full-time students; hundreds of thousands of others take correspondence courses. Many of these correspondence students also hope to qualify for university entrance. They do this because being well educated is the key to advancement. We are sure that the Soviet people anticipate the day when their present sacrifice for knowledge will bring them many rewards, but right now, as we see it, they regard good schools and universities as the necessities in their race for world supremacy.

And they have been building schools and universities at a rapid pace. Down on the borders of China where only a half-century ago the people were almost 100 percent illiterate, we saw thriving schools, an impressive scientific academy, and other institutions that have reduced illiteracy and advanced knowledge to an astonishing degree. From the shores of the Black Sea to remote Siberia we found the attitude summed up in the expression of a Soviet education official: "A child can be born healthy, but he can't be born educated."

We have the impression that most people in the U.S.S.R. feel that conditions are improving gradually, that they are looking ahead for 5, 10, 15, or 20 years. They appear to be completely confident about achieving a quality of life and a standard of living fully as high as ours but realize that it will take time, sacrifice, and hard work.

There is still a considerable shortage of building resulting in part from tremendous damage during World War II. Very likely few people in the United States are familiar with the extent of the damage to both cities and rural communities in the Soviet Union in World War II—we were shown films of whole cities in ruins. Although whole cities have been rebuilt in less than 15 years, the normal supply of building and housing replacements, always low, has necessarily fallen behind. Housing is scarce, though relatively cheap.

People appear to be well fed and to have ample access to food stores and restaurants. Food is abundant, though not of much variety, and it is expensive. Clothing seemed to us to be very expensive and not readily available. In general, however, people seemed to be neatly, if not stylishly, dressed, by American standards.

There seems to be complete equality between men and women. The relationship between boys and girls in school appears to be characterized by dignity and mutual respect for each other. At each desk there is usually one boy and one girl. A professor at the University of Leningrad said: "With us, boys and girls, men and women, are partners. We are partners in education, partners in love, and partners in work."

A woman is expected to do any job as well as a man. Many women have entered the professions, particularly medicine. We saw women working with electrical crews, repairing telephone equipment, operating streetcars and busses, and working in factories. We noticed that many women specialized in mathematics and physics.

Education has been and is recognized as the source of past accomplishments and as the way to the future. The developments in the organization and practices of education at all levels during the past half century have been impressive both for their speed and for their extent. Wherever we went our hosts described with pride the contrasts between the present conditions and those existing before the revolution. That we returned with our faith renewed in the superiority of the American system for our society does not discount the tremendous efforts the Soviets are exerting to advance their kind of education to strengthen the Communist system. They tell many dramatic stories of the progress of their education, and all credited education with the improvement in their condition. The story summarized below, which we heard at the Ministry of Education in the Uzbek Republic, is one of the more dramatic but perhaps typical.

This is a highly developed agricultural and industrial region now, but before the revolution it was a colony of Czarist Russia and was much retarded. Agriculture was primitive, crops were small, and the country was underdeveloped. Only 2 percent of the population was literate; there were no institutions of higher education, and the 160 schools were attended by 17,300 children of privileged families. There were no engineers, doctors, or teachers with higher education.

Opportunity for education came immediately after the revolution, although schools were developed gradually. On December 2, 1920, Lenin decreed the establishment of the University of the Republics of Asia. In 1919 a decree on the elimination of illiteracy was published, and shortly afterward literate people began to teach the illiterate. Now we have an academy of science, an academy of agricultural sciences, 34 higher education establishments, 100 technicums, 50 special technical schools, 5,800 general or 10-year schools, 12 pedagogical institutes to prepare teachers, and 1,400 kindergartens. We have schools for people of each nationality in their own tongue, and we also have inservice education establishments. Altogether 1,300,000 children of all nationalities have an opportunity for education. More than 50 percent of our 80,000 teachers have higher education.

We have many establishments to develop the interests of children. We work out our own courses of study for schools. Each Republic develops curriculums for itself because of differences in language.

We have enough money to expand our education programs and buildings. Our people are rich; they like to work. All our people want peace. *We are sure we are able to meet the problems we face.*

As is indicated earlier, Uzbekistan is not an isolated example; we heard similar stories in other places—the description of similar accomplishments in the Tatar Republic, for example, was equally impressive. Such progress is dramatized for the people of the U.S.S.R. continuously by the State and the Party. In every possible way—particularly through art, music, and literature—the people are reminded of what has been done. Everywhere, in every school we visited, we saw pictures or statues of Lenin, and less frequently, Marx and Stalin, even in kindergartens. From infancy, children are taught that the highest good is to serve the State; school children through their clubs or circles, in classes, and in games are taught to identify all good things with the State; on class excursions and tours of museums, shrines, factories, they are taught the history of the revolution and to honor its heroes, underplaying the prerevolutionary achievements and emphasizing Soviet progress.

What we observed of Soviet education gave us the impression that the entire operation was being carried out on a systematically planned basis to achieve Communist objectives. To be sure, there were some excellent prerevolutionary foundations, institutions, and traditions of Russian education on which to build the Soviet structure—the academic secondary school of Imperial Russia; the Ballet School in Leningrad, over 200 years old; the great universities, especially in Leningrad and Moscow; the National Academy of Sciences; and the School for the Blind in Moscow that celebrated its 75th anniversary in 1947. These are just a few of the substantial roots from the past, and they should not be overlooked. It was always stressed, however, that education was restricted in prerevolutionary days to a very small proportion of the population of the vast area—one-sixth of the earth's surface—that today is the U.S.S.R.

Today, of course, education is planned, financed, controlled, and administered by the State. Even though education in the U.S.S.R. is controlled by the Government and is therefore standardized and regimented, there is some flexibility of operation. Furthermore decisions on policy, on textbooks, on teacher training, on curriculum, and on similar matters are not always made arbitrarily. We found fairly widespread evidence that before making decisions on education, the Government seeks opinions from specialists at all levels of education, from teachers throughout the country, and information based on research and experience. And it seems to get willing cooperation.

Few nations or people are today more passionately committed to education than the Soviet Union and the Soviet people are. The Soviets see what has already been accomplished and are confident of the future.